The Revolutionary Constitution

The Revolutionary Constitution

David J. Bodenhamer

OXFORD
UNIVERSITY PRESS

OXFORD

UNIVERSITY PRESS

Oxford University Press, Inc., publishes works that further
Oxford University's objective of excellence
in research, scholarship, and education.

Oxford   New York
Auckland   Cape Town   Dar es Salaam   Hong Kong   Karachi
Kuala Lumpur   Madrid   Melbourne   Mexico City   Nairobi
New Delhi   Shanghai   Taipei   Toronto

With offices in
Argentina   Austria   Brazil   Chile   Czech Republic   France   Greece
Guatemala   Hungary   Italy   Japan   Poland   Portugal   Singapore
South Korea   Switzerland   Thailand   Turkey   Ukraine   Vietnam

Copyright © 2012 by David J. Bodenhamer

Published by Oxford University Press, Inc.
198 Madison Avenue, New York, New York 10016

www.oup.com

Library of Congress Cataloging-in-Publication Data
Bodenhamer, David J.
The revolutionary constitution / David J. Bodenhamer.
   p.   cm.
ISBN 978-0-19-537833-7 (hardback)
1. Constitutional history—United States. 2. Constitutional law—United States.
3. United States—Politics and government. I. Title.
   KF4541.B63   2012
   346.7302′3—dc23   2011031493

1 3 5 7 9 8 6 4 2

Printed in the United States of America
on acid-free paper

To Karen, Jeff, and Jace, with love

CONTENTS

ACKNOWLEDGMENTS

The Revolutionary Constitution is a work of synthesis and interpretation. It seeks to guide general readers and students through the vast literature on the United States Constitution and its significance in American history. The book also is an effort to trace the course of important constitutional themes and relate them to developments in the broader society. My focus is on the continuing relevance of the ideas and tensions that led to and flowed from the American Revolution. My aim is to promote an appreciation for their central importance to our conceptions of power, liberty, individual rights, and the role of government, as well as for how they have defined and shaped who we are as a people.

I have anticipated the day when I could thank publicly those individuals who have made this work possible. Only cynics will conclude that my eagerness reflects the knowledge that it ends my creative labor on this book.

My greatest intellectual debt is to all the scholars who have written so well and with such skill and sophistication on the Constitution and its role in American history and culture. I have learned from them, marveled at their insights, embraced the lessons they have taught, and used their works to reach my own interpretations. Any misreading of their scholarship is my fault alone, but without their contributions *The Revolutionary Constitution* would be impoverished and uninspired. The section Further Reading recognizes those individuals whose work I have found most helpful.

I owe special thanks to individuals who have read all or parts of the manuscript and noted the errors that, left uncorrected, would have caused me great embarrassment. Chief among them are the two anonymous reviewers for Oxford University Press. James W. Ely Jr. graciously read the chapter on property and offered many useful suggestions. Nancy Toff has been the consummate editor: she encouraged me, responded quickly to my questions, and read the finished work carefully. She has my deepest appreciation.

The encouragement of colleagues and friends is important in writing a book, but it is the support of family that makes the enterprise worthwhile. The staff of the Polis Center at Indiana University-Purdue University, Indianapolis kept the office environment both stimulating and rewarding, and they perhaps too gleefully accepted my need on occasion to write at home. My wife, Penny, read every draft, caught many mistakes, offered her incomparable gifts of friendship and love, and made sure that the dogs and cats in our domestic zoo provided necessary breaks from the computer. The dedication is to our children, who already have accepted the challenges of extending the revolutionary promise of America to yet another generation.

The Revolutionary Constitution

Introduction

The United States Constitution is a revolutionary document. The text crafted in 1787 and amended within four years by the Bill of Rights is the product of history's first modern revolution. It embodied a fundamental re-scripting of assumptions about government. In this invented nation, the people were both rulers and ruled, sovereigns and subjects. For the first time, citizens were responsible for creating their government and then deciding—election by election—how they would govern themselves.

Revolutions are by definition moments when the past shifts toward an unfamiliar future, one radically different from what was foreseen only a brief time earlier. But the disjuncture between what was and what will be is less noticeable the further we move from the events that give rise to a new order. Over months and years, what was innovative becomes commonplace. We blur the distinction between old and new even more when we write history. The past always contains hints of what is to come, and, as a result, we often see continuity instead of a break with the past. But antecedents are not the revolution, which comes only when people begin to see their world in a fresh and original way.

The American Revolution was a radical experience that reshaped society as much as it restructured government. It freed ideas of sovereignty, liberty, equality, representation, and power from their traditional moorings and gave them rein to recast how men and women related to one another as citizens within and outside government. The signature phrase of the Declaration of Independence—"all men are created equal"—summed up a century-old understanding of the tie between government and citizens, but in its new context led generations of Americans to claim equality as a mandate to redesign social relationships and not just political ones. As its political expression—and constitutions are the highest form of statecraft—the Constitution was the revolutionary answer to the ages-old antagonism in Western culture between power and liberty. James Madison, who shaped the document and our understanding of it more than any other founder, recognized this role when he wrote in 1792, "Every word of the [Constitution] decides a question between power and liberty." What made the American experience unique, he argued, was its answer:

"In Europe, charters of liberty have been granted by power. America has set the example . . . of charters of power decided by liberty."[1]

Too often we misunderstand the nature of our foundational documents because we do not fully appreciate their history. Nowhere is this more apparent than with the Constitution. History reveals nothing approaching the certainty that we often assign to its words. Within two years after ratification, two leaders of the Revolution, Thomas Jefferson and Alexander Hamilton, were quarreling bitterly about what a key clause of the Constitution meant. Jefferson insisted that the text must be read strictly, with its meaning limited to the plain sense of its terms. For him, the Constitution was a restraint on power. Hamilton argued for a flexible interpretation in which any power delegated to the central government should be read expansively unless it was limited elsewhere within the text. The Constitution, to Hamilton, was a grant of power.

This debate was emblematic of what would follow. Time after time, we as a nation have been torn between Hamilton's and Jefferson's views—and the policies that flowed from them—and, as a result, we frequently cast our policy choices as constitutional issues. Yet the constitutional language we claim to understand with such confidence is general and undefined except by history and even then ambiguously: What does due process mean? What is necessary and proper? What powers are encompassed by the role of commander-in-chief? None of these important questions (and countless others) had clear answers in 1787, nor are they certain now. Decade after decade, Americans have had to wrestle anew with how to apply the Constitution to unfamiliar situations.

In seeking answers to questions of constitutional meaning, we often turn to the founders, expecting their debates and writings to serve as talismanic guides, oracles of the truth. But evidence from the framers and the subsequent ratifying debates is scanty and filled with contradictions. A surer standard perhaps is the constellation of circumstances that gave rise to the Constitution, which offers ample clues to the problems the framers were trying to solve as well as to the principles and ideas that influenced their choices.

The delegates to Philadelphia were practical politicians who faced a crisis of republican government. The revolution they had waged and won was in danger of collapse. When the members of the founding generation sought independence in 1776 as the only way to salvage their liberty, they did not have ready-made governments-in-waiting to guarantee their future as a free people. What they had instead was a set of principles—under the rubric of republicanism—to guide them in making colonial institutions into revolutionary governments. Among their beliefs was faith in the emergence of a new citizenry filled with civic virtue. A republican concern for the public good would allow men and women to set aside the selfish interests and impulses so destructive to liberty throughout history. This moral transformation would limit the need for power, always the foe of liberty, and ensure the survival of thirteen fledgling republics.

When this new type of citizen did not emerge, the framers had to devise a government that would work well even in the presence of imperfect people. They did so not by abandoning revolutionary republicanism but by rethinking its basic assumptions and coming to a new understanding of its terms.

What surfaced was something that could not have been predicted in 1776: the idea that power and liberty need not stand in opposition to each other. Power in government, properly structured, could promote and protect liberty. Not everyone agreed with their remedy. For opponents of the Constitution, perhaps half of the population, power in government remained what it had been throughout history—the enemy of liberty. The ratification debates of 1787 and 1788 presaged the clash between Hamilton and Jefferson a few years later. One irony of American history, of course, is that both were right. The Constitution was a synthesis: it restrained power on behalf of liberty, but it also granted power to promote and protect liberty.

The Revolutionary Constitution explores this dynamic of power and liberty by examining seven major themes in American constitutional history—federalism, balance of powers, property, representation, equality, rights, and security. It does so first by recognizing how much the framers relied upon the past even as they sought to break with it. No constitution is a naïve document, one free of history or the ideas that gave it birth. The ideas and forms embodied in the U.S. Constitution had evolved over several centuries by the time of the Philadelphia Convention, and it is this long evolution that often hides the radical nature of what happened from 1776 to 1787. The themes traced in this book are not comprehensive but are sufficient to explore how the Constitution was conceived—and continues to serve—as a revolutionary framework both for legitimating power and advancing liberty. An ancillary thread examines indirectly Alexis de Tocqueville's classic observation that in the United States all political questions ultimately become legal questions, a process that makes the Constitution both revolutionary and conservative at once.

This book does not contain everything that readers might want to know about constitutional history and interpretation. Instead, it examines core concepts historically, ending with their contemporary expression. The goal is to explain the Constitution as an organic, contested, and dynamic frame for government in which our past concerns and experiences influence our present understanding. Major political and legal controversies as captured by cases or events in American history, some landmark and others less well known, illustrate these themes. But our knowledge of the Constitution does not stem from cases alone. Constitutional meaning ultimately reflects a consensus of opinion among the American people more than it does the critical commentaries of lawyers or the decisions of judges. American constitutionalism, in brief, is the product of more forces than the justices on the nation's highest court. The aim here is to understand how it has been shaped and reshaped by American politics and culture.

We do not operate today under the same Constitution ratified in 1788 or the Constitution as completed by the Bill of Rights in 1791. Nor are we the same nation. The United States, then a plural noun and now a singular one, has grown from thirteen states hugging the Atlantic seaboard to fifty states spread across a continent and beyond. We have experienced a civil war that ended one social and political regime and ultimately ushered in another far different from anything most people could have imagined in 1776 or even in 1865. From our beginnings as a second-rate country with a tiny navy and army, we have grown to become a global economic and military superpower. We are a democratic republic in which democracy weighs far more heavily in our constitutional and societal calculus than the framers would have endorsed. We vest government with the responsibility for safeguarding our prosperity, health, safety, and welfare in ways alien to the experiences of the founding generation.

As our circumstances have changed, so has our Constitution. It does not mean now what it did in its first expression. The document is not a legal straitjacket, nor is it a timeless framework for government. It is the product of practical revolutionaries who sought to institutionalize radical ideas, popular sovereignty—the people as rulers—chief among them. The framers feared power and they trusted liberty, yet they knew that these two forces would always operate in tension. The issue was how to reconcile them so the new nation would benefit from both order and freedom. Citizens of the founding generation found the compromise for their time, even as they continued to debate its terms. And ultimately they trusted that we, the people, would answer for ourselves how best to strike the balance that would further their goal of a more perfect union.

1

Antecedents

In early September 1620, a small ship set sail from Plymouth, England, bound for the New World with a band of 102 religious dissenters. Known as Separatists, they believed that the Church of England was not a true church of Christ. Their remedy was to abandon England and its corrupt church, and in 1609, at peril to their fortunes if not their lives, they settled in Leiden, a Dutch commercial center whose pursuit of wealth left its residents no time to harry dissenting pilgrims. But Holland proved too worldly to be an acceptable haven to these English pilgrims. To preserve their own salvation, they decided to escape Europe and settle under a royal patent, or charter, in the northern part of what then was known as Virginia. A non-separating group, the Strangers, joined them to make up the company of voyagers. Their commitment was risky: not only had an earlier effort by fellow religionists failed, with the loss of 130 lives, but the experience of two earlier English settlements in Virginia at Roanoke and Jamestown reminded them that death and economic ruin were constant companions of adventurers to America.

After a miserable sixty-five-day voyage, the settlers arrived off the coast of what is now Massachusetts and disembarked at Plymouth Rock. The Strangers and Separatists had nothing to bind them into a common enterprise, but both groups recognized that a lack of unity would be disastrous. Their solution was a formal agreement, the famed Mayflower Compact, named for the ship that brought them to a new land. By it, they consented to "covenant and combine themselves together into a civil body politic." The goals of public order and fidelity to their mission, they recognized, would require them to "enact, constitute and frame such just and equal laws, ordinances, acts, constitutions and offices," as required, for the "general good of the colony." The agreement ended with the pledge of "all due submission and obedience" to the government and laws they would establish.

The compact became an icon of American history. In the new United States, it was celebrated as a seminal document, ranking behind only the Declaration of Independence and Constitution as a touchstone for the young republic. In 1802, the young John Quincy Adams, son of founding father and former president

John Adams and later a president in his own right, told a Forefathers' Day crowd in Plymouth that "this is perhaps the only instance in human history of that positive social compact, which speculative philosophers have imagined as the only legitimate source of government. Here was the unanimous and personal assent by all the individuals in the community to the association by which they became a nation."[1]

It was an exaggerated claim. What is remarkable about the compact is not its uniqueness—similar agreements occurred in the colonies of Rhode Island, Connecticut, and New Haven—but its thoroughly English nature. It rested implicitly on assumptions about government and society that had formed over centuries, some of which dated to Magna Carta (1215). It also was not a modern document: its aim was not democratic, as we understand the term. The views of the forty-one men who signed it often were closer to those of the medieval world than to ours. In fact, many of the ideas that came to define American constitutionalism had their genesis in a time we perceive only dimly today. Questions about the construction of governments and the responsibility of citizens, among others, are age-old issues that have occupied the thoughts of philosophers and rulers in all societies. What is instructive about the Mayflower Compact, and the other charters like it, is the English belief that free people had the right to consent to their government.

Histories of American constitutionalism often begin with the English colonial settlements and the arrangements they made to accommodate life in a new world. This choice is not wrong, but it gives rise to an exceedingly complex story. The narrative must embrace different types of colonies, diverse streams of immigration, the adaptation of English forms of law and government to a new environment, and the development of an empire. It is easy to become overwhelmed by detail and to fail to recognize that these developments were part of a long-standing discussion among the English about the nature of power and liberty.

From this conversation—and the word "conversation" admittedly hides the bloody struggles that accompanied it—came the ideas we claim as our constitutional inheritance. They far predate the American Revolution. Scholars have discovered their roots in Greek democracy, Roman republicanism, medieval ideas about natural rights, the civic humanism of the Renaissance and the Enlightenment, Scottish moral philosophy, the writings of John Locke, the judicial decisions of Sir Edward Coke, the English commonwealth tradition of the seventeenth century, and eighteenth-century radical Whig ideology. These ideas were not mere speculations or philosophical musings. They were fodder in a political conflict that consumed the English nation while it simultaneously settled a new world. For the generation that created the United States, they were both part of their history and their lived experience.

The sixteenth and seventeenth centuries especially were times of conflict between the monarchy and Parliament over questions of power and liberty, defined in terms of sovereignty, or who held ultimate authority, and of rights. Colonists were rarely at the center of these struggles, but they were eager students of history and politics. They found instruction about government in the debates that surrounded the English reformation, the Stuart assertions of the divine right of kings, the English civil war of the 1630s and 1640s, and the Glorious Revolution of 1688, all traumatic events that reshaped how they thought about government. But the colonists were more than observers. By the time of the American Revolution, they had had more than a century of experience in governing themselves, never completely or without check, but always with more authority than any theories of government allowed for subordinate colonies within a burgeoning empire.

The conflict over the proper division between power and liberty was a fault line that ran through English history during the centuries of American settlement. It was especially active during the decades when the vocabulary of independence was forming in the colonies. Whether the issue was religious belief, trade, property rights, criminal justice, or the role of magistrates and governors, the debates that animated the Anglo-American political world centered on the exercise of power and its corresponding impact on liberty. Given their importance when the colonies were coming to maturity, it is not surprising to find the same themes in American constitutionalism.

The prominence of liberty in this struggle is peculiarly Western, and even more directly English. Although concepts of power are common to all societies, most non-Western cultures did not have a term for freedom or liberty until they encountered Europe. Significantly, Western languages had words for either one or the other but not both. English was the exception. In it, liberty and freedom had separate, but linked, meanings. Freedom was the absence of arbitrary restraints. It belonged to the group, whether a tribe or a common people; it was their heritage. Freeborn people stood equal before the law regardless of the inequalities or differences that divided them into classes. They had certain rights or entitlements simply because they belonged to the group of free people. When the rights of Englishmen became a rallying cry for colonists who perceived themselves treated unequally under the laws of the British Empire, their claim was one of belonging: they did not lose their Englishness or forsake their English heritage by migrating to the New World.

Liberty was not a synonym for freedom. It implied separation, independence, and autonomy for individuals or groups; the rallying cry attributed to Patrick Henry in 1776, "Give me liberty or give me death," was in fact a demand for independence. What confused the distinction between liberty and freedom was their interchangeable use in common speech. The Protestant Reformation and its aftermath added a new meaning of liberty that English Puritans expressed as "soul freedom," a priesthood of all believers, a direct connection or oneness with God that did not require mediation by any other person or institution. This liberty of conscience—the freedom to do God's work in the world—further muddied any distinction between the words. Yet if in common usage liberty and freedom were interchangeable, over time liberty became the touchstone, or proving ground, of freedom because it pointed more to the autonomy of individuals, their ability to live unfettered by the commands of others.

Theories about power were equally complicated and equally contentious. Most, if not all, cultures embrace the need of some unifying or overarching authority to provide order and cohesiveness to society. In medieval Europe unity ideally came from the church, not the state or government, with allegiance to the papacy and its secular arm, the Holy Roman Empire, serving as common bonds for all territories. But government in fact was a series of personal and reciprocal obligations among the nobility, with noblemen claiming rights over lands they owned while also recognizing obligations to higher lords. The rise of the nation-state signaled the impending end of this feudal system. With nation-states came monarchs who claimed complete political and social power and who did not recognize the existence of any other legitimate authority within the nations they ruled.

This transition to a modern conception of sovereignty, or supreme power, occurred from the fifteenth through seventeenth centuries, but in England especially it developed in fits and starts. English monarchs faced continual challenges from rival lords and from a representative legislature, Parliament. The issue was not the need for ultimate power within the state, but rather who should exercise this sovereignty: king or Parliament. The struggle for control led to rebellion, civil war, the execution of a king, and a peaceful revolution, but by the eighteenth century the answer for England was clear: Parliament was the supreme authority. The process of reaching this conclusion also led to the rise of constitutional theories that justified the new arrangement, most notably by John Locke. These theories and the debates around power—and especially about its proper relationship to liberty—profoundly influenced American conceptions of government.

English ideas about power and liberty, while often framed philosophically, were not abstract. They emerged as responses to specific events, many of which far antedated the troubled seventeenth century yet had great symbolic importance for constitutional developments. Magna Carta is a prime example of this phenomenon. After losing a disastrous war in 1215, King John sought to impose new taxes on the lesser noblemen. In response, the barons marched on London and forced the king to agree to the "Articles to the Barons" at Runnymede, a nearby meadow, in June 1215. This document, affirmed thirty-six times thereafter, most notably in 1225 and 1297, became known as Magna Carta, literally the Great Charter. Its clauses contained bedrock claims of the rights of Englishmen; for instance, four clauses contain the essential elements of the right of habeas corpus. Clause 29 was especially celebrated. It guaranteed due process: no freeman could be deprived of his liberty except by "lawful judgment of his Peers, or by the Law of the Land." Embodied in this phrase was a core contribution to the English understanding of power and liberty—the concept that no one, not even the king, was above the law. Although the document applied only to the king and barons, the most powerful class in English society, over time its guarantee of rights became understood as a commitment to all English citizens.

In the English imagination, Magna Carta stood as strong evidence of an ancient constitution that existed before the Norman invasion of 1066. Under this myth, which influenced English thinking well into the nineteenth century, their Anglo-Saxon forebears lived in a state of near-perfect freedom that William the Conqueror sought to destroy, unsuccessfully, by imposing a "Norman yoke" of French despotism. Magna Carta was a pivotal step in a centuries-long struggle to reclaim ancient liberties and restore the right of Englishmen to participate in government. Its premier role as a restraint on government was signaled by its position as the first entry in all later statute books. The reality was far different. The English monarchy, plagued by debt and instability, was far weaker than was continental royalty. Still, the ancient constitution and Magna Carta were powerful symbols, an easily grasped shorthand, of the liberty and rights that were part of the endowment of the English people.

Migrating Englishmen proudly carried this heritage with them, but the political convulsions that wracked the mother country also meant that claims of power were never distant. Not only was England engaged in a commercial and religious rivalry with European nations to exert influence and control over the Americas, it also was witness to a battle between king and Parliament for supremacy at home. In the sixteenth century, Tudor monarchs, notably Henry VIII (1509–47) and Elizabeth I (1558–1603), relied on Parliament to provide revenues and support for the consolidation of royal authority during the break with Rome. But when the Stuart kings James I (1603–25) and Charles I (1625–49) asserted prerogatives similar to those held by their counterparts in France and Spain, they faced resistance from a much-strengthened Parliament dominated by Puritans. These religious dissenters found alarming the new monarchy's evident sympathies toward Roman Catholicism, which newly Protestant England associated with absolutism and tyranny. Secret courts (such as the Court of Star Chamber), arbitrary imprisonments, inquisitorial tactics, forced loans, bills of attainder (legislative punishments without benefit of trial), excessive fines and punishments, and other Stuart actions raised alarms that the crown was intent on subverting the ancient constitution.

Parliamentary resistance met only royal contempt. An acrimonious tug-of-war between king and assembly came to a violent climax during the reign of Charles I. In the Petition of Right of 1628, Parliament forced Charles to abandon compulsory loans and arbitrary imprisonment in exchange for new taxes, after which the king suspended the body for eleven years and sought to rule alone. When Charles reluctantly called Parliament back into session to raise taxes to quash a Scottish rebellion, he came under immediate attack. Anti-royalist members impeached his advisors, reformed the church, abolished secret courts, and severely restricted monarchical power before Charles once again sought to dissolve Parliament. An eight-year civil war followed, beginning in 1641, with the supporters of Parliament, led by Oliver Cromwell, a Puritan, defeating the royalists and, in 1649, trying, convicting, and executing the king.

The Commonwealth and Protectorate (1649–60) that followed, a period sometimes labeled the English Revolution, was a seedbed for ideas that influenced later English and American constitutionalism. Radical religious groups with names such as Levelers, Agitators, Ranters, and Diggers sought to reform government, usually along Puritan lines. Debates over the limits of power, the rights of Englishmen, and the demands of liberty, especially freedom of conscience, were commonplace. Proposals for separation of church and state, freedom of religion among Christians (but not Catholics), equality of all before the law, and expansion of the franchise (right to vote) to all adult male property holders, among other rights, were published widely in such pamphlets as *The Agreement of the People*, a document that sought to establish a new framework for representative government and ensure basic rights for all Englishmen. It was during this heady time that John Milton wrote *Aeropagitica* (1644), his celebrated attack on censorship: "Let [Truth] and Falsehood grapple; who ever knew Truth put to the worse in a free and open encounter?" Of course, for Milton and all other good Puritans, such freedom extended only to Protestants, but it was the ferment of such revolutionary ideas that fueled American debates on power and liberty a century later.

An even more important development occurred three decades after the fall of Charles I. The Commonwealth collapsed in 1660 and the monarchy reclaimed power, supported by new laws asserting the king's supremacy and requiring adherence to the Church of England. The "Restoration" Stuart kings, Charles II and James II, seemingly oblivious to the conflicts that had led to their father's execution, pushed their royal prerogatives—and their pro-Catholic policies—until Parliament finally rebelled. It deposed James II—peacefully but with the hint of war if the king resisted—in the Glorious Revolution of 1688 and required his successors, William and Mary, to agree to a Declaration of Rights, or Bill of Rights, the next year. Not only did the document make clear that the king governed under common law but it also guaranteed rights of English subjects threatened by the overweening claims of the Stuarts. The right to petition the king freely, the right of Protestants to bear arms, and the restatement of common-law protections such as trial by jury and prohibition of excessive fines and cruel and unusual punishments were among the protections afforded all Englishmen. An accompanying Toleration Act of 1689 granted freedom of worship to all dissenting Protestants who accepted the divinity of Christ. An earlier act in 1679 had strengthened the right of habeas corpus, which allowed judges to free prisoners held wrongfully by the government, and later measures enhanced press freedom by halting the practice of licensing publications, a process that allowed governmental censorship.

But rights were only part of the calculus of power and liberty during this period. The location of sovereignty also changed when the 1689 Declaration of Rights explicitly acknowledged the supremacy of Parliament. The king had to call Parliament into frequent sessions, he could not punish its members for what they said there, and he could not make or suspend laws nor levy taxes without its consent. A later statute, the Act of Settlement (1701) that vested the throne in the Protestant Hanoverian line—the Stuarts were too tainted by their fealty to Catholicism—made royal ministers responsible to Parliament. The same law also established an independent judiciary by granting judges lifetime tenure. These changes made clear that the king was subject to the law—and, more important, that Parliament was the ultimate source of law, with the power to override even common law. By implication, Parliament also was the source of rights, a claim that sparked resistance when its full significance became apparent to American colonists in the 1760s and 1770s.

The decades-long struggle for supremacy spurred important writings that sought to make the case for opposing views of sovereignty. These works later would influence American conceptions of liberty and power. Royalist philosophers supported the Stuarts' contention that the king was the divinely anointed embodiment of the state who could rule unchecked. Especially influential were the writings of Thomas Hobbes, whose masterwork, *Leviathan* (1651), described a pre-social state of nature—"no Arts; no Letters; no Society"—where the constant condition was a "war of all against all" and people lived in "continuall feare, and danger of violent death." Life before government was "solitary, poor, nasty, brutish, and short." To escape this hell-on-earth, men formed a social contract, ceding their rights to a king who exercised absolute authority in exchange for protecting their lives and property.

This view was unacceptable to advocates of representative government who fashioned a counter-argument during the years of parliamentary resistance to Stuart actions. Most prominent among these philosophers was John Locke, whose *Two Treatises of Government* (1689) was a response to Sir Robert Filmer's *Patriarcha*, which defended royal absolutism as a divine right, granted by God from the beginning of society. Locke also imagined a chaotic state of nature that threatened the lives and property of men, but his solution was radically different. He agreed that men formed a social compact and ceded their natural power to government in exchange for security; unlike Hobbes and Filmer, he argued that human nature was characterized by reason and tolerance, not brutishness. People formed government rationally to advance legitimate ends, such as resolving conflicts civilly or promoting their enjoyment of life or property. Government's power was not absolute, Locke argued. The people retained at least some of their natural rights, including a right to renegotiate the social contract if government threatened the interests it was formed to protect. Here was an implied right of revolution. For all their differences, however, royalists and supporters of Parliament agreed on the location of sovereignty: it rested with government. Though Hobbes and Filmer placed it in the king and Locke in Parliament, no one could imagine it residing any place other than government itself.

In the eighteenth century, the political turmoil that had plagued England for two hundred years finally ended, at least in its bloody forms. With it came consensus on the structure of the English constitution. The result was called the King-in-Parliament, a manifestation of the "mixed and balanced constitution" that made the nation not only the most powerful on earth but also made the English the freest of all people. In this new configuration, the monarchy worked in and through Parliament—but always as a subordinate—to project the nation's power, secure its emerging empire, and promote its economic interests. The form of government itself protected English liberty, or so Englishmen believed. It contained the three classical forms of government—a monarchy in the person of the king, an aristocracy in the House of Lords, and a democracy in the House of Commons—but blended them in what became known as "a monarchical republic," and it operated to allow the strengths of each form to emerge and the weakness of each to be checked by the others.

Balance was the key to liberty. Too much power in the monarchy would be tyranny, whereas an overweighting of control toward the aristocracy would be oligarchy, the tyrannical rule of the few, and toward democracy, anarchy. This conception of the balanced constitution represented the final defeat of royalists—indeed, it often is called the Whig constitution after the group that advocated parliamentary supremacy—and by the middle of the eighteenth century all English men and women considered it their national glory.

The principles of this new English constitutionalism were difficult to define because they were considered organic, subject to growth and capable of change. Then and now, any mention of the English constitution was a necessary fiction. It was not a single document, as is the U.S. Constitution, but rather a mix of common-law cases, statutes, and royal decrees that defined the contours of power and liberty. It also was (and is) malleable; it changed whenever Parliament acted legislatively in a way to amend, alter, or otherwise recalculate a traditional element of government. For example, the constitution changed with the Act of Settlement of 1701, when Parliament removed any pretense that the king's ministers were independent of its authority. In the eighteenth century this flexibility was thought to be the constitution's strength, yet it also raised the troubling prospect that Parliament could take away liberties as easily as it could enhance them.

John Locke sought to answer this concern in his *Second Treatise of Government*: people could not give up their natural rights, such as a right to life, and if government broke this social contract, then people could dissolve the government and begin again. People also possessed civil liberty, which was the right to live under laws that protected life and property from the arbitrary decisions of others. Consent was the key to this arrangement. In forming a government, people gave to government the power to create the laws that protected them. The course of English history had vested this consent in the people's representatives to Parliament.

Popular consent and parliamentary sovereignty were important constitutional principles because they protected the rights that belonged to all Englishmen. Rights guaranteed liberty and as such were central to a proper conception of the eighteenth-century constitution, especially in the colonies. When English settlers migrated to the New World, they came with a royal guarantee, announced in their charters of settlement, that they would continue to have the "rights and privileges of Englishmen." The pledge was important because it promised continued ownership of the long tradition of English liberty.

The early history of rights centered on protections for property and for individuals accused of crimes, because in these areas the state most often exercised arbitrary power. Rights of the accused offer the clearest example of what the English people understood to be their heritage. By the time the earliest American colonies were established, many guarantees already existed to ensure a fair criminal trial. The Massachusetts Puritans, for example, included many of these protections in their first law code, the Body of Liberties, in 1641: the promise of speedy trial and equal justice, protection against being tried twice for the same crime (double jeopardy), and the prohibition of torture, among others. The long seventeenth-century struggle between king and Parliament for supremacy further limited the power of government and confirmed or added to the rights of Englishmen, including habeas corpus, the right of petition, a limited form of freedom of speech, a right to release from detention upon a guarantee to appear at trial (bail), and prohibition against excessive fines.

State documents defined only some of the rights of the English people. Much of what English settlers to the New World considered to be their rights was found in the common law, the amassed case law of English law courts, not in statutes or parliamentary declarations. Common law contained what had become customary practice in English society. It emphasized due process, the procedures the government must follow in exercising its power. The rights of the accused were prominent in this customary law: the promise of a speedy and public trial by jury; prohibition of ex post facto laws, or laws that criminalized behavior after it had occurred; and the guarantee of habeas corpus, a procedure that required government to bring a person under detention before a court to determine if legal reason existed to hold him and to release him if the court deemed the cited reason insufficient at law.

But common law was about more than criminal due process. It also offered some protection for the rights of widows and children, the right of compensation for the taking of private property, and the openness of courts to all citizens. Colonial assemblies and courts adopted common law and looked to

English law books for further instruction on what it meant for their rights and privileges. Especially important was the four-volume *Institutes of the Laws of England*, the masterwork of Sir Edward Coke (1628–44), Lord Chief Justice of England in the early seventeenth century, which supported the rule of law against arbitrary government and royal claims of supremacy.

It is ironic that the royal patents and charters granting the colonists permission to settle—and which migrating Englishmen trusted to secure their liberty—often were unclear on matters of power: what laws applied to the colonies and who had the power to make them? The language used by the charters was ambiguous. Laws were to be "as near as conveniently they may be, agreeable"[2] and not contradict or be repugnant to the laws of England, but what did this mean in practice? Equally murky was who or what body had law-making authority. Usually this power rested with the company or proprietor that sponsored the colony, as long as new laws conformed to English precedent. Problems arose when settlers landed outside the area granted to them, as in the case of the Plymouth Colony: did the language of the charter continue to apply to them, especially its guarantees of their rights?

Charters also did not anticipate how inadequate their proposed models of governance, based on English practice, would be in the radically different environment of a new world. What happened in response was that colonists adapted English forms to changed circumstances: for example, the Virginia Company, faced with bankruptcy, in 1619 granted the settlers the right to make local laws through a representative assembly composed of two houses. This model of local, representative government quickly became standard. Other colonies differed in some degree—a unicameral or one-house assembly in Pennsylvania, for instance—but all ultimately mirrored the arrangement of the mother country, with a governor who stood as the king's surrogate in the colony and a representative assembly that colonists took to be a small parliament. This practice meant that the conflict over power in England had special relevance for the colonists, who often saw the same drama played out in their provinces.

Concerns over power and liberty in the new world mirrored what had occurred earlier in England, but colonial experience ultimately was more important than English history in shaping American constitutionalism. Several developments were especially important—the experimental nature of English colonization and the inconstant attention of the English government to colonial matters, the emergence of the British empire, and the growing demographic, economic, and social differences between the colonies and mother country, as well as the diversity within the colonies themselves.

The grouping of English colonies into three types—charter, proprietary, and royal—makes the process of establishing government appear more orderly than it was in fact. Each form represented a different approach to the problem of how to catch up to Spain's century-old lead in tapping the wealth of the new world. The constraint was the relative poverty of the English crown: unlike the

Spanish king, the English monarch did not have sufficient wealth or revenues to finance the effort alone. Both charter and proprietary colonies sought to induce private investment in this cause. When the companies failed, as they all did eventually, the charter reverted to the king. By the eighteenth century, royal colonies were the dominant form.

Regardless of the type, establishing a colony was messy work and made even more difficult because what the English tried to do, understandably, was to recreate the old world in a new environment. But too much was different. Not all social classes joined the migration, the rich because they had no need to leave and the poor because they had no means, which resulted in colonies that were much more middle class than the mother country. They also were more diverse; the colonies were attractive to many more nationalities and religions than existed in England. Land was abundant and much cheaper than in the old world, making it impossible to replicate a social and political order based largely upon its limited ownership. Finally, distances were too large and communication too uncertain, both across the Atlantic Ocean and within the colonies, to sustain more than an increasingly tenuous connection between the old world and the new.

Over time these conditions produced a remarkable similarity among the three types of colonies, at least in the degree of local authority each allowed, often by necessity. In some measure, this localism recapitulated English conditions, in which magistrates had considerable latitude to accommodate the peculiar circumstances of village life. But the physical separation from England and the absence or inattention of high-ranking officials magnified colonial autonomy. Colonial charters did not allow wholesale revisions of law, but they permitted colonial legislatures to transfer law selectively and to innovate where necessary, so long as laws were consistent with English practice. Settlers were free to reform what many migrating Englishmen saw as an archaic and capricious legal system by creating rational laws and simplifying court and governmental structures. A study of early Massachusetts revealed that the creation of the Bay Colony's legal institutions closely paralleled the ideas put forth by English reformers. Enhancing this authority was the scarcity of law books and the paucity of men trained in the law. The absence of lawyers, in particular, invited experimentation with legal and governmental forms.

If the new world provided an opportunity to reform law and government, change did not occur for its own sake. Colonists did not forsake their past or forget their experience simply because they were on a new continent. An analysis of early colonial law reveals that lawmakers followed traditional practice as they recalled it. Their major goal was to simplify the law, removing its obscure and contradictory provisions and making it knowable. They deviated from English law to mitigate its harshness. In these aims, colonists largely succeeded. They restated the law in English, abandoning its Latin forms, and published it for widespread distribution, often requiring that it be read before certain public gatherings. The law also became less bloody and cruel. The early Puritan colonies, for instance, abolished capital punishment for any form of theft, in contrast to the mother country's easy resort to the gallows for as many as 200 property crimes. Moral and material considerations influenced the change. Radical Protestants, including Puritans, valued all life as sacred and would not take it without divine authority. More earthly types recognized the shortage of labor and wanted to do nothing to diminish its supply.

Rights were an important part of colonial codes. Unlike the common law, which buried these safeguards in the great mass of precedent, known primarily by judges, colonial laws gave them prominent attention. Colonists put their liberties into writing as a way to prevent royal encroachment, and they often extended these liberties beyond those claimed by their cousins in the mother country. The Massachusetts Body of Liberties (1641) early on symbolized the shift in emphasis. Although the colony's first leaders resisted popular government, the people, Governor John Winthrop wrote in his journal, "thought their condition very unsafe while so much power rested in the discretion of magistrates." A major objective of the colonists, he noted, was the framing of "a body . . . of laws, in resemblance to Magna Carta."[3] The resulting document was by no means democratic (as we understand the term) but it did contain an extensive list of rights, with many specific provisions—trial by jury, right of counsel, prohibition of double jeopardy and cruel and unusual punishments, for example—having counterparts in the federal Bill of Rights a century later. The Pennsylvania Charter of Liberties and Frame of Government, both written in 1682, also protected the rights of colonists from government interference, as did the New York Charter of Liberties and Privileges enacted the following year.

Religious liberty was chief among these rights, and in this area differences with England were most pronounced. The turmoil of the seventeenth-century civil war had convinced the majority of the English people that religious diversity was dangerous. Adherents held to their beliefs too passionately to permit peaceful resolution in most matters of faith. The response of the Stuart kings after 1660 was to suppress both Roman Catholicism and dissenting Protestants, or sects that did not support the Church of England. Although the Toleration Act of 1689 permitted greater religious liberty for Protestant dissenters, it did nothing to change the privileged position of the established Anglican Church.

But the colonies had a separate religious history. Puritans arrived in New England with the aim of religious liberty for themselves and their goal of reforming the Church of England through their holy City on the Hill. Within the first decades of settlement, however, schism occurred in Massachusetts Bay, with Roger Williams fleeing the colony to establish Rhode Island, which to the disgust of Puritans made separation of church and state a major principle of the new settlement's government. Later colonies, notably Maryland and Pennsylvania, provided guarantees of toleration, if not freedom of practice, in their charters. Even without these protections, the flood of sects that arrived in the eighteenth century—French Huguenots, Dutch Reformed, Presbyterians, Quakers, Jews, and others—made it impractical to supervise religion tightly. The Great Awakening of the 1730s and 1740s so multiplied the number of sects that what once was impractical became impossible. With the exception of Rhode Island, no colony ever disestablished the Church of England, but in all other ways North America was a haven for religious liberty in ways that English people elsewhere could not fathom.

By the eve of the Revolution the safeguards of regular process in criminal law and tolerant practice in religion had become part of a shared language about the liberties of Englishmen who resided in the New World. But it would be a mistake to draw a direct line of descent from the colonial understanding of liberties and rights to our understanding today. The words are similar, but their substance is not. Due process of law, for example, held a sharply different meaning in the seventeenth and eighteenth centuries than it does in the twenty-first. Then, personal rights were important, but the good order of society took precedence over individual liberty. Still, colonial contributions to modern ideas about rights were significant, not so much as a list of rights but more as a set of attitudes about individual liberty. The colonists by necessity had adapted English laws and customs to a new world and, in the process, claimed full ownership in the great tradition of English liberty. But they went further than mere imitation. They had simplified the law and made it accessible in written form to all settlers. They had been willing to reform the law and had added rights not recognized in the British Isles. Their biggest contribution, however, was a pragmatic willingness to mold law to social needs and circumstances.

What made these lessons from experience problematic were dramatic changes in the circumstances of power. During the decades of settlement, England became the United Kingdom of Great Britain as a result of its political union with Scotland in 1707; by the mid-eighteenth century, it emerged as the world's dominant empire. Imperial theorists assumed that an empire was unitary and hierarchical by definition, with authority flowing uniformly from the center to the peripheries, or from the King-in-Parliament through imperial officers to subjects of the empire's most remote territories. Imperial Spain was the model for this conception, but as with so much of the English experience in the new world, reality intruded on this elegant symmetry. The Spanish monarch financed voyages of exploration and conquest, with colonies designed from the beginning as extensions of the crown. In England, the royal purse was too bare to adopt a similar strategy, so the monarchy had used grants of land to induce private investment in the new world. Many of the colonies, as a result, existed before the empire began.

It was not until the mid-sixteenth century, four decades after the founding of Jamestown in 1607, that the colonies were deemed permanent enough to bring them into some formal relationship with the mother country. Even then, the basic impetus came not from the monarch, deposed in the civil war, but from Puritan merchants who controlled the government during the Commonwealth. The economic theory of the day was mercantilism, which argued that the wealth and power of a nation depended upon its ability to accumulate more specie, gold and silver, than its rivals. It assumed that these assets were finite, as was the volume of international trade, so the best way to secure wealth was for a nation to be self-sufficient. The implications for England were obvious. England enriched its treasury and enhanced its power if it exported more than it imported, but as an island nation with few natural resources and a small population, it could achieve this favorable balance of trade only if it had an empire. Colonies would be the source of raw materials, perhaps the means of manufacture, and certainly a market for finished goods. Without colonies, England could not be self-sufficient, but unless the colonies served a national interest it could not be powerful. In an era when rival Catholic powers threatened England's treasury, security, and souls, the nation's survival depended upon an empire.

Beginning in 1651, Parliament passed a series of Navigation Acts that collectively formed the skeleton and sinews of the empire. The principles of each law were similar, all designed to make England the middleman of trade between its new empire and the rest of the world. Not surprisingly, merchants dominated Parliament and these measures directly benefited them. Each successive act in 1660, 1663, and 1673 added a new layer to the imperial structure. Goods to and from the colonies had to be transported in English ships, with English masters and English crews. Certain commodities, such as tobacco, and sugar grown in the Americas (so-called enumerated goods because the act numbered them), could be exported to the American colonies only through ports in England. Customs levied on these goods were to be collected by officials stationed in the colonies, a provision designed to stop smuggling. The final element came in 1696 with the creation of the Lords (later Board) of Trade, the body charged with regulating the British Empire, managing the affairs of the crown in the colonies, instructing and overseeing governors and customs officers, and approving all colonial legislation. In brief, the Navigation Acts outlined a closed commercial system designed to benefit the mother country. As such, a basic assumption was at the heart of the imperial system: the colonies existed for the benefit of England and always were inferior to England. Here, in its baldest form, was the assertion of power.

Historians have long debated whether the colonists suffered under the empire. Was burdensome administration a cause of the American Revolution? In purely economic terms, perhaps not; the cost was less than one-half of one percent (0.5 percent) of colonial income annually. Even though the burden fell disproportionately on certain groups—in particular, planters, manufacturers, and merchants—the colonies prospered to an unusual degree, largely because, as Englishmen, they could build ships and haul cargo, act as middlemen, and benefit generally from the closed circle of imperial trade. Also, the laws were loosely administered. America was a big place and rigid enforcement of the regulations would cost dearly—and likely for not much gain, because most of the trade naturally flowed to England under any circumstance.

But "salutary neglect," as this deliberate policy of lax oversight became known, had other consequences. It allowed the colonists to act in ways other than what the theory and laws of empire prescribed. Notably, it encouraged localism and self-government under an arrangement whereby the practice of government—who exercised authority and when—was continuously in play. Much of colonial life fell outside imperial control under any circumstance, and the casual administration of the empire permitted colonial legislatures to maintain a large degree of autonomy over their own affairs. The presence of crown officers in the colonies, such as royally appointed governors, did not strengthen the British hand because they tended to side more with the assemblies that paid them and with local elites, including most colonial legislators, than with a distant imperial government. Only when the imperial crisis of the 1750s and 1760s threatened this local power did American colonists began to perceive a threat to their liberty. It mattered little to them that the British understanding of empire did not admit such a large degree of local control. From the colonial perspective, the empire worked in the way they assumed it should.

The colonies also benefited to an unusual degree from unique geographies of liberty. The zone of settlement, which ran no more than two hundred miles inland from the coast, was immense by English standards. Transportation and communication were difficult, and many areas never felt the hand of imperial government, except lightly. The openness of this land for exploitation and escape also was a powerful magnet for peoples of many nations, resulting in a polyglot population, one far more heterogeneous than in Europe. By the mid-eighteenth century, one of every three residents of the British Empire lived in the North American colonies, yet the spread of population was much greater than in Britain, a circumstance that permitted refuge for diverse beliefs and encouraged the development of local cultures of control. Merchants and artisans, farmers and lawyers, churchmen and liverymen all had access to space and resources that encouraged freedom of action. The absence of British officials in many areas contributed to the sense of self-determination. So did greater popular participation in government: the easy availability of land allowed many more men to vote at a time when voting depended upon meeting certain minimum property qualifications. In addition, the colonies existed on the borderlands of two empires, British and French, which warred frequently during the eighteenth century for dominance of the continent, thus providing fault lines and pressure points that colonists could exploit to ensure greater autonomy for themselves.

In one of the tragic ironies of American history, a land with a culture that encouraged freedom to a degree unknown elsewhere also was the place that denied liberty in the form of slavery. Bound or contractual service was not an unknown concept in English law—many early settlers came as indentured servants, obligated to serve a master for a period of time to work off their cost of passage to the New World—but forced service, or slavery, was not recognized legally, except for prisoners. When captive Africans first arrived in Virginia in 1619, custom and law treated them as indentured servants, but this arrangement did not last. Africans were not English, and many Englishmen and colonists thought that Africans therefore could not claim freedom as a birthright. First Virginia and then other colonies began to restrict the liberty of imported Africans so that by the 1660s they had become lifetime, hereditary servants—slaves—who could be bought and sold as property, or chattel.

Racism was at this heart of the developing law of slavery, which, in turn, made the law increasingly harsh. Slaves had none of the rights belonging even to white men and women of low status. But in a society in which labor was scarce they were increasingly valuable property. This circumstance and the need to control a potentially dangerous slave population defused debates about the morality of slavery for most colonists, especially slave owners. American freedom, American slavery: it was the paradox of English colonial experience that later became the new nation's dilemma. Its effect on American constitutionalism was large. Slavery's existence—and its aftermath—contradicted both explicit and implicit claims about liberty and equality that generations of Americans, including the framers, imagined were at the heart of the Constitution itself.

By the mid-eighteenth century a number of themes important to American constitutionalism were well established, even if they were not all formally recognized. Consent of the governed through representation, popular participation especially in local government, and written charters reinforced and extended traditional English conceptions of limited government. The centrality of common law and liberties defined as rights also were legacies from England that took on new form and substance in the colonies. No similar understanding existed concerning the claims and extent of governmental power, a circumstance made evident by different conceptions about how authority operated within the British Empire. Imperial officials assumed that the King-in-Parliament was supreme in all matters, even when they allowed colonial legislatures to exercise authority in purely local matters. Colonists interpreted this acceptance of local control as recognition that authority required their consent, which they gave through their elected legislatures. They presumed a quasi-federal system of divided authority, with the British government responsible for those concerns that touched the empire as a whole while colonial assemblies took care of local issues. As the imperial crisis of the 1760s and 1770s revealed, their presumptions were not shared by the British. The conflict that followed proved irresolvable except by war and revolution.

2

Revolution

Long after retiring from public life, two former presidents resumed an extraordinary correspondence that had begun decades earlier. John Adams and Thomas Jefferson had been leaders of the American Revolution. These two allies were present at the creation of the republic and served as brothers-in-arms until the partisanship of the 1790s made them rivals and ruptured their friendship. Now in their old age, they reconciled and started a fourteen-year exchange of letters on a wide range of topics, always seeking perspective on the tumultuous events that too often had divided them. Adams put the issue squarely in a letter to Jefferson: "You and I ought not to die before we have explained ourselves to each other." One question especially held them captive: "What is meant by the Revolution? The War?" Adams asked, and then, typically, answered without pause: "That was no part of the Revolution. It was only an Effect and Consequence of it. The Revolution was in the minds of the People, and this was effected . . . in the fifteen years before a drop of blood was drawn at Lexington."[1]

On this matter, Adams and Jefferson agreed, as have most historians, but even this consensus obscures an important point. The revolution was more than a movement for independence from Great Britain. It was also a profound redrawing of the relationship between power and liberty, a redefinition of human nature and its capacity for self-government, and the invention of "we, the people," as the ultimate source of authority, the sovereign. These themes, and others, had profound implications for American constitutionalism, then and now. They also remind us that the Constitution, so often viewed as a conservative charter, was the product of a revolutionary age.

We often overlook the radical nature of the American Revolution because so much of the constitutional argument between the colonies and Great Britain was couched in familiar terms. The debate at first was a refrain in the centuries-old conversation about power and liberty that had occupied the English since Magna Carta, and especially in the formative decades of American settlement. It focused explicitly on who was to govern the colonies: Parliament or the various colonial assemblies. But if the struggle with the mother country began as a familiar tension, it ended, in the words of a ballad reputedly played upon the British surrender at Yorktown in October 1781, with the "world turn'd upside down."

A new ideological order emerged from the Revolution, one that used an older vocabulary to advance a new and markedly different conception of reality. The political philosophy that embraced and supported a unitary sovereignty exercised by the King-in-Parliament gave way to a new constitutional scheme of divided power. An optimistic appraisal of man's rational nature and his ability to control his baser instincts began to supplant traditional views of man's capacity for evil, a flaw traditionally thought to require the controlling hand of government. Much of the movement toward change was hidden by a conservative rhetoric that called for the restoration of the ancient constitution. Such language should not obscure the extent of the shift to a new foundation for government: a desire to return to a mythical golden age that the present threatens to destroy is a hallmark of revolutionary minds. Independence in fact produced what Americans proudly proclaimed as a "new order for the ages," a radical restructuring of government to control power and enhance liberty.

The imperial crisis that led ultimately to American independence began when Great Britain found itself unable to command reliable support from colonists during the Seven Years War with France (1756–63), the fourth and final conflict between the two European powers for control of North America. Saddled with heavy debt and eager to re-impose its will on the colonies that it deemed insubordinate, Parliament aimed to tighten its grip on the empire through a series of measures designed to stop smuggling and force trade into lawful channels, whereby it could be taxed. It also sought to lessen the cost of administering the empire by limiting expansion west of the Appalachians, which relieved the British from actively defending or governing the frontier it had won from the French while preserving friendly relations with Indian allies in that region.

But more was at stake than economic considerations. Parliament was keenly aware of how close to defeat the empire had been before rallying to victory in 1763. The theory of empire had failed—the parts did not work for the benefit of the whole, as intended—and now the imperial government was determined to remedy its defects. To the British mind, the war was fought largely in the colonies and for their defense, yet they believed that the colonists not only failed to contribute to the war effort but instead sought to enrich themselves as illegitimate middlemen by selling goods to both sides. The colonists disagreed, citing their significant contributions to the war, but Parliament concluded it was necessary to reorganize the colonies, reassert its control, and ensure that the empire functioned as theory and law required. Beginning with the Sugar Act of 1764 and running through the Coercive Acts of 1774, Britain repeatedly tried to pull taut the strings that bound the colonies to it.

The colonists cast their response as a constitutional argument: the various imperial measures violated rights protected by the British constitution and guaranteed to the colonists by their charters. The goal of this position was not to separate from England—the colonists considered themselves loyal Englishmen until the eve of the war for independence—but rather to force the British government to abide by its own constitution as the Americans understood it. The security of their constitutional rights as English subjects became the focal point of colonial protests against the mother country. Scholars have long debated the issue, but it is difficult to imagine a rebellion without the colonists' conviction that their rights as Englishmen were in grave danger of extinction. This theme was too constant, the argument too insistent, to doubt the primacy of this issue to the revolutionary cause.

Colonists entered the struggle to protect their liberty with a seventeenth-century view that rights were customary and immemorial restraints on power. These guarantees had a dim and ancient history, or, in the quaint phrase of English legal commentators, since a time "to which the memory of man runneth not." In this meaning, rights were immutable: they existed because they were fundamental to the very conception of liberty itself, not because a monarch or a legislative body granted them. Rights were necessary to secure property and promote a responsible liberty, which meant to be free from arbitrary rule. They were the community's protection against unwarranted interference in its affairs by the agents of a distant, central authority; they did not free the individual from community norms or change the local character of justice. The belief that rights liberated individuals, not the community, was the product of a later age.

Changes in eighteenth-century English political theory challenged this conception of inalienable, community-based rights. The triumph of Parliament in the century-old struggle with the Stuart monarchs gave rise to the view that the British constitution was malleable; rights existed at the pleasure of the sovereign. This argument became increasingly common as the ministry at Whitehall abandoned the policy of salutary neglect toward the colonies and attempted to create an empire more responsive to central direction. Although never as extreme as the rhetoric of resistance imagined, the new imperial policies bred colonists' fears that the demands of power would soon require the sacrifice of English rights in America.

Feeding this anxiety was the resurrection of a political theory first advanced in England to oppose the development of parties in Parliament. During the early eighteenth century, Britain became increasingly more aristocratic, with power wielded by great landowners who dominated Parliament and the ministries. Although known as Whigs, the name originally given to seventeenth-century opponents of the crown, this "country party" was not suspicious of royal power and its menace to liberty. Rather, its ruling cliques within the ministries and Parliament used royal favors to enlist lesser gentry as allies. Sir Robert Walpole exemplified this new way of governing. A member of the House of Commons who became First Lord of the Treasury in 1721, upsetting the tradition that only noblemen could be royal ministers, Walpole organized Parliament in support of his policies by offering patronage in the form of royal appointments, pensions, and other inducements in return for votes.

It was, in many ways, the beginning of the modern legislative politics in Britain, but to his opponents, Walpole's actions threatened the mixed and balanced constitution and its protection of English liberty. The beauty of the King-in-Parliament, the product of the Glorious Revolution of 1688, was its careful balance among the three classical forms of government—monarchy, aristocracy, and democracy—whereby each form canceled out the weaknesses of the other two and allowed only their strengths to remain. Walpole's opponents, known as Radical Whigs or Commonwealth men, charged that the new prime minister had upset this calculus. He was the crown's minion who, they believed, would use the king's purse and prerogatives to restore the monarchy, a proven source of tyranny.

The Commonwealth men were strengthened in this fear by their interpretation of history, set forth from 1720 to 1723 in a lengthy series of newspaper essays by Thomas Gordon and John Trenchard. Written under the pen-name "Cato," a pseudonym chosen to remind readers of the ancient Roman senator who warned against the rise of Julius Caesar, these essays described how all of history could best be understood as a cosmic struggle between power and liberty. Power possessed masculine attributes: it was greedy, rapacious, and never satisfied. It resided in government and always sought more power. Liberty, at home with the people, was described in feminine terms: it was weak, vulnerable, and always in need of protection. It was easily lost. For the Commonwealth men, the English past demonstrated that liberty could resist power as long as the people remained vigilant. But with the rise of Walpole, conspiracy entered English history. Power no longer sought to subdue liberty directly through such abuses as standing armies, exorbitant taxes, or denial of due process, all easily detected actions. Now, it operated surreptitiously, using secret plans and underhanded schemes, all comprised within the term "corruption," to upset the balanced constitution in favor of the king. Walpole's success could result only in tyranny, the result of an unchecked monarchy.

Cato's Letters found no great audience in Great Britain, but it became a best seller in the colonies. Published in six editions by 1755, the collection of warnings ranked second in popularity only to the Bible, with its bound volumes in an estimated half of all colonial homes on the eve of the Revolution. The essays promoted the consensual and limited government outlined by John Locke, and they prescribed the existence of rights as the ancient remedy for tyranny. They also provided colonists with an interpretive framework for understanding the actions of the British: parliamentary measures increasingly became evidence of a corrupt conspiracy to deprive colonial Englishmen of their liberty.

Three rights were central to the colonial understanding of liberty: trial by jury, due process of law, and representative government. Jury trial was especially important. Without it, all other rights would ultimately fail. Only a local jury, unfettered in its judgments, formed an impregnable shield against arbitrary government. The general verdict—a simple reply of guilt or innocence to a charge of wrongdoing—was the people's most effective weapon against tyranny. The presence of jurors precluded secret trials and offered protection against corrupt judges, purchased testimony, threatening officials, and other abuses of power. The jury's power to free as well as to convict also assured that government would follow its own procedures or risk defeat in its efforts to apply power: due process was a formidable barrier to arbitrary government.

Representation was another key element of liberty. Government rested on consent, which in practice could be given only by the people's delegates. What made this right especially meaningful in the colonies was the widespread franchise. English law restricted the vote and officeholding to property holders who paid a minimum tax, which meant that at most only one in six adult males was part of the electorate. The connection among consent, representation, and local control was far more direct in the colonies, where abundant, cheap land opened the ballot and elective office to two-thirds of adult males.

The Revenue Act of 1764, more commonly known as the Sugar Act, was the first parliamentary measure to raise colonial concerns. It decreased the tax on imported molasses but stiffened enforcement against smuggling, which effectively raised the cost of sugar in the colonies. The ensuing debate among the colonists produced a memorable phrase, "no taxation without representation," signaling a belief that the British had violated the constitution, yet Parliament's undoubted power to regulate trade muddied this conclusion. Most protests—and only a few legislatures registered formal complaints—centered on the feared impact on colonial purses. The colonists were mired in a postwar depression, and their preoccupation with the economy disposed them to couch their objections primarily in economic rather than constitutional terms, thereby blunting their challenge to the act.

The next year, a new imperial measure met a much different response. The Stamp Act of 1765 provoked a major outcry. For the first time, Parliament imposed an internal tax on the colonies, one designed not to regulate trade but to raise revenue. Because the stamp tax applied to virtually all paper goods—the extensive list included legal documents, newspapers, bills of lading, pamphlets, and playing cards—it affected almost everyone. Even though the government had imposed and collected a stamp tax in England for years, American colonists viewed the levy as a shocking violation of their right not to be taxed without their consent. The problem was not the tax, which was slight, but the lack of colonial representation in Parliament, the body that levied it. The Virginia Resolves, offered by Patrick Henry in May 1765, almost as soon as the Virginians received word of the new act, expressed a common sentiment: the royal charters guaranteed that colonists could be taxed only by their legislatures. Any attempt to evade this requirement had a "manifest tendency to destroy British as well as American freedom." In October the eight colonies that formed the Stamp Act Congress advanced the same argument when petitioning the king in protest—their rights as Englishmen were violated by any taxation without representation.

The British response rebutted this claim: all Englishmen were represented in Parliament virtually, even when they had no vote or lived in an area that had no delegate. After all, the people of Manchester and Birmingham sent no representatives, but no one questioned Parliament's authority to tax them. Every member of Parliament had the duty to represent all the king's subjects and to consider all their interests; this obligation was the linchpin of virtual representation. But the British argument did not persuade the colonists, who rejected the theory out of hand, arguing that only local delegates, elected by district, shared the mutual interest with voters that made representation real. Colonists rebuffed as nonsensical an off-handed offer to allow them to elect some representatives to Parliament. A person from one place could not represent the people of another place. A delegate from Massachusetts could not represent Connecticut, much less Virginia, because he could not possibly have common interests with the people from those colonies. Representation by definition was local; it occurred properly within geographically defined communities. From this perspective, Parliament's argument was a heretical innovation.

The Stamp Act also included an assault on the jury. Refusal to pay the tax resulted in prosecution before the vice admiralty court, a civil-law tribunal established seventy-five years earlier to enforce trade regulations. Next to taxation without representation, Boston voters proclaimed, "the Jurisdiction of the Admiralty, are our greatest grievance." These civil-law courts operated without juries; a judge appointed by the crown determined all questions of law and fact. As a result, local communities forfeited much of their ability to blunt encroachments on their rights by means of a general verdict of guilt or innocence, and local citizens lost the prized assurance of a fair trial under common law by their peers, or neighbors. The colonists equated civil-law courts with the tyranny of the Byzantine Empire and denounced them as hostile to English liberty. "[W]e are obliged," the people of Newburyport complained, "to submit to a Jurisdiction . . . where the Laws of Justinian [civil law] are the measure of Right, and the Common law, the collected Wisdom of the Ages, is not admitted." Civil law, all Englishmen knew, was the tool of arbitrary government; common law, with its local juries, was the protector of liberty.[2]

Resistance to the Stamp Act was widespread and often violent. Organized groups such as the Sons of Liberty forcibly blocked the tax in many communities, at times tarring and feathering collectors and tying them to Liberty Trees or riding them out of town on a rail. This extra-legal resistance was not unusual—popular protests and mob violence were common features of eighteenth-century culture in both the mother country and the colonies—but it made enforcement of the act too difficult and too costly. An even more effective campaign against the Stamp Act, a boycott of British goods, induced British merchants to lobby Parliament to abandon the unpopular and self-defeating measure.

After a bitter debate, Parliament finally repealed the Stamp Act in March 1766. The same day, however, it enacted the Declaratory Act, which asserted the "full power and authority [of Parliament] to make laws and statutes, of sufficient force and validity, to bind the colonies and people of America, subject to the crown of Great Britain *in all cases whatsoever* "(emphasis added). The claim was not new. William Blackstone, whose *Commentaries on the Laws of England* (1765) captured a common view on Parliament's power, observed, "[Parliament] can, in short, do everything that is not naturally impossible. . . . So long as the English constitution lasts . . . the power of Parliament is absolute and without control."[3] Yet, jubilant over the demise of the Stamp Act, the colonials paid little heed to the Declaratory Act's naked assertion of power until later events suggested it, too, was part of the British conspiracy against their liberty.

Repeal of the Stamp Act did not lessen Parliament's determination to exert authority over the colonies or to abandon its goal of making the colonists help to pay the costs of empire. In 1767 it passed the Townshend Revenue Acts, which levied duties on various articles of imperial trade such as paint, lead, and tea. Chancellor of the Exchequer Charles Townshend insisted that the colonists could not protest these taxes because he had followed their distinction between internal and external taxes. By this logic, Parliament had unquestioned control over the empire as a whole, so taxes to regulate trade were acceptable, whereas only colonial legislatures could levy local taxes to raise revenue from its citizens.

It was perhaps a willful misunderstanding of a confusing proposal made by Benjamin Franklin during the height of the Stamp Act crisis, but the ploy appeared to work. The Townshend duties did not meet the same level of organized and unified resistance that greeted the Stamp Act. A show of force by the British in 1768, when it sent four thousand troops to Boston, a city of only fifteen thousand, stirred little protest. Two years later, on March 5, 1770, the Boston Massacre highlighted the tepid colonial response, when not even the loss of five colonial lives at the hands of British soldiers provoked mass resistance. The colonists had not changed their position—no Englishman could be taxed without representation—but they also counted themselves as loyal Englishmen. They simply were asking that Great Britain honor their right to consent to the laws that governed them.

Popular consent and representation were at the center of how the colonists defined their relationship with Great Britain. Colonists drew lessons on these matters primarily from the historical development of limited government in England, which is why they kept insisting that their view of direct representation was a settled constitutional principle. Yet what the colonial position implied was something new, a sort of divided power within the empire, with the British government responsible for matters affecting the whole but not the individual parts. The idea had antecedents in various plans for colonial union, dating back to the New England Confederation of 1643 and the Dominion of New England (1685–91). Although both efforts were stillborn, they proposed a degree of divided governmental responsibility, especially in matters of trade and defense, by creating a proximate body between England and the individual colonies.

More immediate was the Albany Plan of Union of 1754, drawn up by Benjamin Franklin at the outset of the French and Indian War, that outlined a colonial union "under one government as far as might be necessary for defense and other general important purposes." It, too, failed to receive approval, although some of its provisions later found expression in the Continental Congress and Articles of Confederation. Significantly, this scheme did not challenge existing understandings of the imperial relationship, including the ultimate supremacy of Parliament. It was, in fact, designed to draw the colonies more closely to the empire.

Frustrating efforts to draw the distinction between what was properly colonial and what was properly imperial was the general belief that sovereignty could not be divided, even though most people acknowledged that the empire functioned this way in practice. The dilemma was straightforward: if Parliament represented all Englishmen, including Americans, then its power was unlimited within the empire; if Americans were not represented in Parliament, then did the British have any sovereignty over the colonies? Based on the representative principle, could Americans deny power to Parliament, and if so, did not this make the colonies sovereign and therefore independent? The question surfaced directly in an exchange in the mid-1770s between John Adams and Thomas Hutchinson, the royal governor of Massachusetts. Hutchinson, the first native-born colonist to assume this position, addressed the legislature in 1773, arguing that "no line can be drawn between the supreme authority of Parliament and the *total* independence of the colonies." In a report penned by John Adams, the legislators replied, "If there be no such line, the consequence is either that the colonies are vassals of Parliament, or that they are totally independent."[4]

The colonies in fact were groping toward a definition of what became federalism, a system of divided sovereignty, which they finally reached in late 1774. The catalyst was a sharp rise in tension between the colonies and the mother country over the question of power within the empire. In 1770, Parliament repealed the Townshend Acts—the taxes had generated far less revenue than expected—but retained the tax on tea as a symbol of its authority. Given the easy availability of smuggled tea in the colonies and the lack of enforcement, this tax was of little consequence until a financial crisis in the East India Tea Company led Parliament to pass the Tea Act, granting a monopoly on tea throughout the empire to the struggling company. The tax and the price of tea were set low enough that Parliament believed the colonists would buy the tea and pay the tax while ignoring the constitutional issues the act raised. No longer was the debate about power and liberty theoretical. Even more ominous was the evidence of conspiracy: as the Americans saw it, Parliament was seeking to trick Americans into abandoning their rights.

The tea ships met resistance and hostility upon arrival in American ports. In most cases, the captains chose not to offload their cargoes and returned to England, but at times opposition was forceful and destructive. In December 1773, colonists in Boston costumed as Indian warriors ruined East India tea by dumping it into the harbor. They treated the tea as contraband (illegal property), carefully repairing the locks of the holds of the tea-ship to display their respect for lawful property. But the British made no such distinction, treating the attack as a direct challenge—and an ominous one because the security of property was one of the highest aims of government. Infuriated, Parliament passed a series of acts to force colonists to acknowledge its authority. Significantly, the collective statutes were known commonly by two different names—they were called the Coercive Acts in Britain and the Intolerable Acts in the colonies.

Parliament focused its punishment on Massachusetts, the most egregious offender, as an example to the other colonies. The acts closed the port of Boston, revoked the Massachusetts charter, named the British army commander in North America the royal governor with orders to move the capital from Boston to Salem, and authorized a change in venue to another colony or to London for British officials who were brought before a local jury. An unrelated measure, the Quebec Act, sought to incorporate Canada, acquired from France in 1763, into the empire. It allowed Catholicism to have semi-official status in Canada, established a government without an elected legislature, and retained French law, which did not guarantee a jury trial. Suspicious colonists viewed this measure not as the enlightened approach to a conquered province praised by later scholars but rather as part of the same repressive regime as the Intolerable Acts. Equating Catholicism with tyranny, they feared that this statute offered the blueprint for their own eventual loss of liberty.

For many previously reluctant colonists, these acts were conclusive evidence that a plan was under way to deprive them of their rights as Englishmen. Instead of dividing them, the punitive imperial response was a catalyst for unity. All colonies except Georgia, which was too poor, responded to a call from Massachusetts in 1774 to send delegates to a continental congress in Philadelphia in September to "determine upon wise and proper Measures . . . for the Recovery and Establishment of their just Rights and Liberties civil and religious, and the Restoration of Union and Harmony between Great-Britain and the Colonies."[5] Conservatives wanted only to send a remonstrance to the king, but radicals prevailed when the congress endorsed the Suffolk County (Massachusetts) Resolves with its call for resistance. The Intolerable Acts were the "attempts of a wicked administration to enslave America."[6] The metaphor of slavery was not accidental. It was a common refrain in colonial protests, intended to emphasize the dire urgency of the moment. For a society in which slavery existed in fact, it was a powerful reminder for the colonists of the threat to their birthright, freedom.

By late 1774 the congress had gravitated to a dominion (or federal) view of empire set forth by two leading lawyers and constitutional advocates, John Adams of Massachusetts and James Wilson of Pennsylvania. In this scheme, sovereignty was based on the principle of representation. Parliament governed England alone because only voters in England elected its members; its acts bound Great Britain uniquely. The same rule applied to the separate colonies; each colonial assembly, acting in concert with the king, was the sole authority for its citizens. The empire existed because both Parliament and the various colonial legislatures embraced a common king. The dominion view was an attempt to maintain the connection between the mother country and the colonies, but from this position, the dissolution of the empire was one short step away. If the king proved unworthy of allegiance, nothing would exist to hold the colonies within the empire.

The king soon demonstrated his unworthiness by commanding his troops to subjugate the colonists—the battles at Lexington and Concord in April 1775 were proof—and then, four months later, by declaring them rebels and outside of his protection, refusing to receive a petition for reconciliation (the "Olive Branch Petition") adopted by the Second Continental Congress on July 5, 1775. But still the colonists hesitated. Finally, in July 1776, the Continental Congress abandoned its reluctant pose, and, citing prolonged abuses of royal power, declared American independence.

The colonists delayed this step for over a year both because they did not agree on the question of independence but also because they had no plans for a new government. Thomas Paine addressed this concern in *Common Sense*, a tract published in January 1776 and soon a best seller. Paine urged his countrymen to toss out the complex divisions and balancing of the British constitution and to form the "noblest, purest constitution on the face of the earth" by eliminating the dead hand of monarchy and hereditary rule and establishing a republic based on popular choice with a one-house legislature. The pamphlet's arguments had a catalytic effect on the movement toward separation. It "struck a string which required but a touch to make it vibrate," Ashbel Green, a New England minister, observed. "The country was ripe for Independence and only needed somebody to tell the people so, with decision, boldness, and plausibility."[7] *Common Sense* also made it clear that revolution, not merely separation, was at work, with the goal of creating universal liberty. "The cause of America," Paine reminded his audience, "is in a great measure the cause of all mankind."[8]

This radical aim was plainly evident in the Declaration of Independence, adopted six months after the appearance of *Common Sense*. Although it is not a formal constitutional document, the Declaration is an American scripture that provides both moral imperatives and an interpretive framework for the nation. Its preamble expressed ideas that by 1776 were entirely conventional among the American revolutionaries: these "self-evident truths" encompassed natural rights, including life, liberty, and the pursuit of happiness, the latter a felicitous recasting of the right to property to suggest the broader sense of freedom and security that made happiness possible. It embraced a proposition that "all men are created equal," which also conveyed what had become a commonplace idea. These phrases were part of an everyday political vocabulary but had no settled definition. This characteristic allowed later generations to treat them as expansive promises to be redeemed, notably by extending them to previously excluded groups such as women and blacks.

Yet if the Declaration is not strictly constitutional, it is foundational and embraces a political principle of the first order—popular consent. This idea was at the heart of the argument for separation. Governments rested on the consent of the governed and had an obligation to secure and defend their rights. If they did not, people had the right of revolution, the ability to alter or abolish the government and create a new one in its place. The notion that people could resist the sovereign echoed John Locke's social contract theory. It also reflected an English belief in the right of collective resistance to a tyrannical monarch. Even William Blackstone, a staunch conservative, hesitantly accepted this recourse in his *Commentaries* by acknowledging that a "law of redress against public oppression" existed, which he characterized as an extraordinary action available to the people whenever the monarch violated his contract with the ruled.[9] The litany of grievances in the Declaration of Independence demonstrated how the king had broken his bargain. Both the right of revolution and the law of redress were community rights that reflected the belief that legitimate government rested on the people's authority and consent.

In invoking this belief, Americans plowed no new intellectual ground, but in acting on it, in actually creating a new government, they departed dramatically from past practices. Most governments of the world were monarchies and had come into being through war or usurpation. Americans were in the unique position to invent their governments—"Before us," a South Carolina writer observed, "no people were ever so intirely [*sic*] relieved from the control of hereditary rulers and arbitrary force"[10]—and they seized the opportunity to create governments of limited power and maximum liberty.

Independence, Thomas Paine recognized years later in his 1792 pamphlet *Rights of Man*, was "accompanied by a revolution in the principles and practices of government."[11] Although the Declaration was silent on what form the new government should take, local debates suggested an answer. In the months preceding July of 1776, American towns and colonies adopted over ninety declarations and resolutions on the issue of separation. In none of them was independence an end in itself. Far more important was the purpose of government:

it had to ensure liberty. It also should be one, a South Carolina grand jury argued, by which "the rights and happiness of the whole, the poor and the rich, are equally secured."[12] For the revolutionaries, only a republic offered such guarantees.

Republics were best suited to the preservation of liberty because they limited power and rested firmly on popular consent, but history proved them to be short-lived forms of government. Ancient Rome, the longest-lived republic known, was the telling example. Though its republic had flourished for at least two centuries, it succumbed to the imperial temptation both symbolized and put into place by Julius Caesar when Roman citizens became self-absorbed, corrupt, and decadent. The lesson was plain: to succeed, republics required morally responsible citizens who held a higher regard for the common good than for their own self-interest. Public virtue was essential because people would have to obey the law in the absence of coercive government, and they would have to maintain the proper order of society without a hereditary aristocracy. They also had to select wise leaders who would act for the good of the whole, and the minority on any issue would have to defer to the judgment of the majority.

These requirements meant that, by definition, republics were fragile forms of government. They succeeded only when the people were unified—partisanship and factions destroyed republics—which implied they were suited only for a small geographical area, certainly no larger than an existing state. Unity was necessary for another reason: monarchies hated republics, just as power despised liberty. American republics would exist in a world filled with monarchies. The only way they could survive was by maintaining a virtuous citizenry unified in the common cause of liberty.

Although history provided no comfort to anyone who worried about the longevity of republics, the American revolutionaries were optimistic nonetheless about the suitability of this form of government for their great experiment in liberty. America offered certain advantages for republics. Its distance from Europe offered protection, and its natural abundance allowed Americans to live comfortably and independently as political equals. The new states lacked the hereditary aristocracies, all-powerful churches, and standing armies that typically buttressed tyrannical regimes. In this environment, citizens could unite in the cause of liberty. They already had demonstrated their courage in resisting tyranny; now they could prove their virtue by fashioning a successful government based on limited power. Republicanism would succeed because, in the most radical of acts, Americans could reject history. Government would have no need to force people to be good. This moment and this place offered a new beginning. The belief that America was an exception to historical and temporal processes stretched back to the earliest settlements, and now the revolutionaries confidently asserted its claim: "We have it in our power," *Common Sense* announced, "to begin the world over again."[13]

In creating the various state republics, it was necessary to address several novel constitutional issues: How do the people give consent to the governments that were being created? How can a people rule collectively as sovereign, when, as John Jay of New York (later the first chief justice of the United States) noted, they were "sovereigns without subjects" who "have none to govern but themselves."[14] What functions should be entrusted to government? How could the rights of the people be protected? All of these questions pointed to the central problem of the Revolution: how to restrain power in government. For the revolutionaries, the republican formula was simple enough—act with popular consent and develop public virtue—but applying it proved more difficult.

Almost simultaneously with the proclamation of American independence, the new state legislatures transformed colonial governments into republican ones. They accomplished this shift through what became a touchstone device, the written constitution. Not only did such a text grant, define, and limit the extent of governmental power but it also embodied the explicit will of the people. This great feat of constitution-making, with eight such charters adopted in 1776 alone, was unparalleled and marked a burst of revolutionary creativity. The shape and role of government they prescribed is a guide to American thinking about power and liberty in the era of the Revolution.

History taught that the greatest threat to liberty came from executive power and the aristocracy, so the first constitutions sharply limited the roles of these two branches. The constitutions created two-house legislatures and made the lower, popularly elected house stronger than the upper house, which in the colonial period had represented the propertied elite. Pennsylvania even adopted a unicameral, or one-house, legislature. The new state constitutions also limited governors to a single one-year term and diminished their power considerably; these executives had limited or no veto powers, sharply reduced powers of appointment, and restricted command of the state militia. The legislatures in turn became more representative, with annual elections and districts apportioned according to population. Finally, more men gained the right to vote and hold office, although the franchise was not made universal, even among adult white men. Only property-holding males could vote, except in two states, Pennsylvania and North Carolina, where any man who paid taxes could cast a ballot.

These new states were republics, not direct democracies, the form of government associated with anarchy. They still practiced a politics of deference and anticipated the selection of wise men from the upper classes to govern. Even so, nine constitutions echoed the Declaration of Independence and contained an undefined statement about the equality of men, a principle that soon enough provided momentum toward a leveling of government and society.

Colonial experience had taught the wisdom of spelling out carefully what liberty meant, so nine of the new constitutions included separate bills of rights that served as preambles, whereas the other four incorporated clauses protecting specific rights into the body of their documents. Many of these constitutions followed the example of Virginia's Declaration of Rights, drafted by George Mason with the aid of James Madison in June 1776, which contained a powerful statement of the nature and extent of fundamental rights. Because criminal justice vividly revealed the awesome power of government, most rights addressed procedural protections available to the criminally accused—an injunction against cruel and unusual punishments, the guarantee of due process, the right of trial by a local jury of peers, protection against general warrants and self-incrimination, and right of counsel. Many of these protections existed previously as common law but now were written, an action that both enshrined them and made them more accessible to ordinary people. What is more striking is the expansion of rights following 1776. The guarantee of counsel at trial was a prime example of how far the founders were willing to go to advance individual liberties. Under British law, an individual charged with a felony had no right to the advice or assistance of counsel until 1836, but under the new American charters the right to counsel became commonplace.

Experience was a great teacher, but more was at work than continued reliance on past grievances to define rights. In part, the newness of their enterprise demanded that the framers of these state constitutions take great care in specifying rights, and their inquiry into what was necessary for the protection of liberty inevitably took them beyond the realm of history. What rights were necessary to effect happiness and advance the great experiment in liberty? Were civil rights and natural rights the same? Could rights be added to or subtracted from? Even if one accepted Thomas Paine's commonsense formulation that rights should be a "plain, positive declaration ... a sort of common stock, which, by the consent of all, may be occasionally used for the benefit of any,"[15] there still was need to identify what rights should receive such endorsement.

British legal commentary, Enlightenment philosophy, and the Great Awakening shaped the new understanding of fundamental rights. The seventeenth-century writings of Sir Edward Coke exalted the common law, which proved attractive to Americans who valued their heritage, but the equally authoritative *Commentaries* of Sir William Blackstone proved more useful in identifying the common law as it existed immediately before separation. Blackstone did not inspire new rights as much as confirm old ones; his work allowed the revolutionaries to tie their cause more closely to the protection of long-standing English liberties, even though Blackstone in fact opposed American independence. Whereas the various declarations of rights used general language to identify rights, the *Commentaries* defined specifically what they meant in practice.

Enlightenment philosophy also influenced American revolutionaries who sought to create a new society and to identify new rights. This decades-long search for the natural laws that governed the world led to an explosion of knowledge from the late seventeenth to the mid-eighteenth century, notably in science. Its great advances—from Sir Isaac Newton's laws of motion to Benjamin Franklin's experiments and inventions—stirred people's imaginations and gave them a sense of mastery, as well as a belief in continual progress. It also led to the scientific method and a willingness to experiment in the course of discovery. When considering human affairs, Enlightenment thinkers sought the natural laws that regulated society and government. Their belief in reason spurred an attack on earlier generations' pessimistic appraisal of human nature. People were rational, theorists argued, and would respond positively to humane and intelligent government, a circumstance that provided an opportunity to reform civil society in conformity with logical and discoverable natural laws.

These ideas emphasized the prospect of creating a new order, which appealed to revolutionaries who were full participants in the American Enlightenment that occurred in the decades leading to independence. Their thirst for new knowledge, including lessons derived from history, impelled them to "read, think, write, and speak," as a young John Adams urged his countrymen in his first major work, *A Dissertation on Canon and Feudal Law* (1765). One goal of their intellectual inquiry was to discover the natural laws and natural rights suitable to a new order. The religious revival that swept the colonies in the 1740s, known as the Great Awakening, cemented this understanding. The wide-spread evangelical mind-set that followed in its wake gave ordinary Americans a deep belief in their God-given rights and reminded them of their individual accountability for protecting them. This quest for rights—and its rootedness in different intellectual, religious, and cultural traditions—became a hallmark of American constitutionalism.

Despite the apparent success of the initial wave of state-making, with its firm guarantees of rights, a constitutional problem remained. Republics required popular consent for their legitimacy, yet each of the constitutions was the crea-ture of legislatures that had been colonial one day and independent the next. How did the people give consent? This question obscured an even more impor-tant development that had been a century in the making, namely, the invention of the people as sovereign. From the days of Magna Carta, political theorists had linked the principle of representation, by which people gave consent to their government, to the idea that the English were a common people. It was this assumption that underlay the British claim that Parliament represented all Englishmen no matter where they lived.

The dispute with Great Britain had revealed problems with this belief, but the first state legislatures still acted on it in writing their constitutions. Repre-sentatives assumed that they acted for all communities in the new state, even though not all of these communities were in fact represented. Yet how could anyone know that sufficient unity existed among these communities to allow the parts to stand for the whole, especially in highly diverse states like Penn-sylvania and New York? And if this assurance were not forthcoming, how would the people give consent to their government? How could the people as a whole exercise the power to create government? How could the people be truly sovereign?

Massachusetts developed the answer in 1780 with the adoption of a new device for creating government: a constitutional convention. Two years earlier, in 1778, the General Court of Massachusetts, the state's legislature, had drafted a constitution, but it met overwhelming rejection when submitted to a statewide vote by all adult males. The objection was simple: the legislature had been elected to govern, not to create government. Only a constitutional convention, a separate body chosen by voters for the sole purpose of writing a fundamental charter and whose work must be ratified by the voters-at-large, could act with the people's consent in creating a government. This move was a logical progression from earlier occasions when Americans had acted directly to implement policies that the government was slow to adopt, as, for example, when they gathered in inter-colonial or interstate assemblies to set trading policies or to block unpopular laws. It was a small next step from such direct action to the idea of conventions elected solely to create government. With this development, it now was possible to talk about the authority of the people, or popular sovereignty, and not merely popular consent.

The constitutional convention and ratification process made it possible to distinguish popular sovereignty from governmental sovereignty and fundamental law from ordinary or legislatively enacted law. Only the people acting in a constitutional convention could propose fundamental law and even then it had to be ratified separately by the people-at-large. But this development, as central as it was to a theory of American constitutionalism, did not solve the problem of how to change the fundamental law when necessary or how to maintain the supremacy of constitutions against legislative or executive encroachments.

States groped awkwardly and incompletely toward a process of amending a constitution. Early constitutions, with the exception of the constitution of Delaware, did not include any process other than a legislative vote for revising fundamental law. Virginia explicitly acknowledged a right of revolution in its 1776 charter but it was not to be invoked except for the most serious circumstances. New York established a Council of Revision composed of the governor, members of the legislature, and judges to veto any legislation that violated the state constitution. Pennsylvania created a Council of Censors and charged it with a formal review of governmental actions every seven years. Most states, however, relied on the restraint and moderation of the legislature, the people's representatives, which later events proved was an inadequate protection.

That problems remained should not hide how much the constitutional process had matured since 1776. Written state constitutions, separate recognition of inviolable rights, constitutional conventions, the distinction between popular and legislative sovereignty, and methods to protect the supremacy of fundamental law were all important developments that shaped a theory of American constitutionalism. Each measure limited the power of government, which should have guaranteed liberty. But events in the various states soon demonstrated that these steps were not enough to promote or protect revolutionary ends.

To the dismay of the revolutionaries, the adoption of republican governments did not lead to virtuous government and disinterested politics. Factions
remained, and legislative majorities continued to use their power to pass laws
that favored one class or group over another. Debtors sparred with creditors
over whether speculators should be able to collect on discounted war bonds and
other loans; westerners fought with easterners about the adequacy of protection provided by the states for their lives and property and the systems of representation and apportionment that seemed to favor the more populous east over
the thinly settled west; dissenting religious denominations protested the taxes
they paid to support established churches that were vestiges from the colonial
period. In most instances, state constitutions asserted the rights of citizens over
legislative majorities, yet continuing confusion between legislative and popular
sovereignty meant no certain remedy existed to protect these rights.

By the early 1780s, a new problem, democracy, had emerged to threaten republicanism. People had taken too much to heart the notion of popular sovereignty.
Everywhere they were pursuing their self-interest by enacting laws that benefited
a majority but threatened the rights of minorities, especially their rights in
property. Such factious politics distressed some revolutionary leaders, who had
counted on the rise of public virtue to overcome the divisions that historically
destroyed republics. Evidence of decay in republican values seemed ever present,
but nowhere was it more disturbing than in the scarcity of sober-minded, virtuous citizens. Instead, the revolutionary rhetoric of equality had birthed a social
upheaval that, if not halted, would lead to anarchy, the dark side of the democracy. Republicans from the governing elite also became alarmed at the increasing
influence of men from lower classes. In the best governments, John Adams had
written in his *Thoughts on Government* (1776), "a few of the most wise and good"
were chosen to act for the many.[16] Revolutionaries from the upper classes shared
his view; they believed leaders from below posed a threat to stable republics.

Debate quickly focused on finding a constitutional solution to the problem
of excess democracy. The question was how to replicate in republican states
one of the advantages of the British mixed and balanced constitution, in which
each part of government served as a check on an illegitimate use of power. The
answer lay in rebalancing the state constitutions to shift power from the legislature, the seat of democratic ambitions and majoritarian politics, and provide
checks on efforts to override fundamental law and protected rights. A new wave
of constitution-making strengthened the governor and judges at the expense
of the legislature. In such states as New York (1777) and Massachusetts (1780),
governors became elected directly by the voters and received increased powers to
appoint officials, including judges. More important, they gained the right to veto
legislation, which could be overridden only if a supermajority of the legislature
agreed. Courts began to declare laws unconstitutional, prompting protests that
judicial review transferred sovereignty from the people's representatives to an
unelected judiciary.

These reforms responded to a serious disillusionment with republicanism that jeopardized the Revolution and its experiment in liberty. Threats arose from external and internal circumstances alike. There was growing concern that the thirteen states, loosely bound into an alliance, remained vulnerable to the voracious appetites of European monarchies. The British surrender in 1781 left the United States outside the empire and its protected markets, vindicating American independence but at the same time undermining the basis for American prosperity. The Continental Congress, which served as a surrogate for national government during the conflict, had financed the war with a flood of paper money, which boosted commerce at first but then led to inflation and economic contraction. The phrase "not worth a Continental" was a painful reality for many Americans, who also suffered from a surfeit of state-issued paper currencies.

Speculation in debt instruments made matters worse. Revolutionary state governments had borrowed money to finance the war effort but third parties often had purchased these loan certificates from distressed bondholders, many of them veterans, for cents on the dollar and now were demanding payment in full. Many voters, judging such speculation to be immoral—how could profiteers get wealthy while veterans remained poor?—and worried that it would add to their tax burden, pressed state governments to deny repayments in full. Another problem arose when legislatures, under pressure from debtors, suspended the collection of debts or changed the terms of loans, causing an outcry from creditors. Both matters troubled revolutionary leaders, who were often heavily involved in commercial ventures and who believed such legislative tampering violated their property interests and was unsound economic policy.

The crisis of republicanism also affected other national interests. In an effort to protect their merchants and farmers, states imposed tariffs on goods from other states. New Jersey even created its own customs service in an effort to stop being the "cask tapped at both ends," as James Madison described the effect of predatory duties imposed by its neighbors, Pennsylvania and New York. Boundary disputes, protection of western settlements, and many other disagreements among the states threatened to destroy any prospect of national unity. The general government was ineffective in halting these practices, but it was weak for a reason on which all revolutionary republicans agreed: centralized power was the greatest threat to liberty.

The first national constitution, in fact, was based on this premise. On March 1, 1781, Maryland, the last of the thirteen states, had finally agreed to the Articles of Confederation proposed by the Continental Congress nearly four years earlier, on November 15, 1777. The Articles established an alliance—"a firm league of friendship"—among the states. It was only a pale shadow of a true national government, but the Confederation was firmly in line with the goals of the Revolution, especially its aim to promote liberty by sharply restricting centralized power. Composed of a unicameral, or single-house, congress in which each state had one vote, the Confederation government had few powers, most important the ability to conduct foreign relations and declare war, to settle disputes between states, administer a postal department, and borrow funds, raise taxes, and coin money. Even these limited functions were hedged with restrictions: Congress could not act to resolve disputes unless states requested it, for instance, and states were free to decide how to collect any national levies from their own citizens. Congress had no authority to regulate interstate or foreign commerce or to enforce its laws directly on the people of the several states but rather had to rely solely on each state to enforce one of its measures. Each of the states also had to agree to any amendment to the Articles.

Although it had a few successes, such as winning concessions in the Treaty of Paris (1783) and developing a policy for western lands, the failures of the Confederation were legion. It was a government of limited powers with no independent enforcement power. In sum, it lacked sovereignty, and for good republican reasons. Republics by definition were small, but, equally important, no one imagined that governmental power could be shared or divided. Even the dominion theory of empire, advanced as a last-minute effort to reconcile with the British, did not admit the division of sovereignty but only separate sovereigns for separate spheres. This understanding meant that no national government could exist independent of the sovereign states, the proper republican governments.

By the mid-1780s many ardent republicans believed the experiment in liberty was in grave danger of collapse. The difficulty was in identifying the cause of this decline. Almost everyone agreed the fault lay with state legislatures, but Americans divided sharply over what had gone wrong. Commercially minded revolutionaries with a national outlook, such as merchants and planters, believed that narrow parochial interests posed a barrier to union or, more pointedly, a national market. The Confederation Congress could not smooth the course of interstate trade; it could not enforce the Treaty of Paris; and it could not protect vital western lands to which many wealthy Americans held title. The Articles also had proven inadequate to secure the right to private property, long touted as the guardian of every other right.

Although nationalists at times proclaimed the powers of Congress as superior to the states, neither the theory of sovereignty nor the language of the Articles permitted this interpretation. Even if it had, it is doubtful that Americans who were not wedded to a national outlook would have agreed with the implied remedy. In their view, state legislatures were not democratic enough; they were captives of special interests and did not represent the people as a whole. This conclusion also rested on economic evidence but of a different sort from that offered by advocates of a national market. The war debt and its economic fallout had resulted in a tax burden that, for most Americans, was higher than the one they had experienced under the British Empire. Americans had to contend with increasingly harsh efforts to collect these high levies—and at a time when the only acceptable form of payment, gold and silver, was scarce.

This tax burden, added to a depressed economy, seemed to fall unevenly on farmers and led to rising unrest marked by angry protests and even angrier demonstrations. In one instance in 1786, Shays' Rebellion, unrest became armed resistance as farmers stormed the courthouse in Springfield, Massachusetts, in an effort to prevent foreclosures on their land. This event troubled republicans of both camps. "We are far gone in everything bad," George Washington, a nationalist, lamented when he heard the news. The plain people of Greenwich, Massachusetts, ruefully recalling their earlier disputes with Great Britain, sadly concluded that "our Grievances Ware Less Real and more Ideal then [sic] they are Now."[17]

By 1786 the crisis of revolutionary republicanism had come to its head. Using a well-settled approach, Virginia invited the states to send delegates to a convention in Annapolis, Maryland, to address the inability of the Confederation Congress to settle commercial disputes. Too few states attended the Annapolis Convention to resolve the problem; only five of the thirteen sent delegations, with four lagging behind and four spurning the invitation. Before disbanding, however, the delegates from the five represented states called for a new effort the following year to make the Articles "adequate to the exigencies of the Union." They then sent their report, drafted by Alexander Hamilton of New York with the aid of James Madison, to all thirteen states. At the same time, Shays' Rebellion was under way, providing an ever-present reminder of popular discontent that threatened the Revolution from a different direction, one that nationalists judged to be potentially toxic to the American experiment in liberty. When in February of 1787 Congress endorsed the call for a convention, the stage was set for the gathering in Philadelphia that would produce the U.S. Constitution.

The Federal Convention developed the structure of government we recognize today. In doing so, it tackled the problems of republicanism that had plagued the founding generation, but it did not abandon the Revolution. The framers instead reached a pragmatic consensus that built upon the experiences and advances of the previous decade. Their aim was to save the Revolution, not to reject it. In the process, they would make innovations in constitutional theory that allowed a republican past to embrace an expansive democratic future.

3

Mechanics

At the beginning of 1787, George Washington was uncertain whether he should attend the Philadelphia Convention called to address problems with the Articles of Confederation. He was tired, sick, depressed after the death of his brother, and worried about the fortunes of his sizable Mount Vernon estate. He knew the Revolution was in grave peril. The armed, anti-tax uprising in Massachusetts, Shays' Rebellion, was especially troubling: it was a "triumph for the advocates of despotism," he thought. Although in despair about the unraveling of the great experiment in liberty, Washington was concerned about squandering his reputation on a hopeless cause. He also had pledged to retire from public life in 1783 when he resigned as commander-in-chief of the Continental Army. Would attending the Federal Convention break that promise? Even though his old friend Henry Knox predicted that his service would entitle him to the "glorious republican epithet—the Father of your Country," he still peppered his friends for advice. Were the people ready for a radical change in the nature of their government? Would his absence be seen as a dereliction of duty or a lack of faith in republicanism? What if the Convention failed? He finally decided to attend so no one would think he wanted a military solution to the crisis. "Nothing but the critical situation of his country," Knox wrote later, "would have induced him to so hazardous a conduct."[1]

By Friday, May 25, 1787, enough delegates had arrived in Philadelphia to satisfy the required quorum of seven states. The Convention's membership fluctuated continually as delegates came for brief periods and then went home to tend to business, but collectively the fifty-five delegates from twelve states (Rhode Island did not participate) were, as John Adams characterized them, men of "Ability, Weight, and Experience."[2] They ranged in age from twenty-six (Jonathan Dayton, New Jersey) to eighty-one (Benjamin Franklin, Pennsylvania), with twelve of the delegates thirty-five years old or younger. By no means were these delegates representative of the larger public. They were men of wealth and education. Their perspective was cosmopolitan, not provincial. At least thirty-four had studied law, but soldiers, planters, educators, ministers, physicians, financiers, and merchants were present as well. Nearly all were men of considerable wealth; twenty-five were slave owners. Together, they had extensive experience in government; forty-two had served in the Continental Congress, an experience that gave them a unique perspective on the crisis of the mid-1780s.

The delegates also shared common concerns. They worried about the weakness of the national government, the destructive bickering among the states, and popular discontent so strong that it threatened both anarchy and a tyranny of the majority. These men were not ordinary citizens—no yeoman farmers or shopkeepers attended—but they were no less committed republicans for their elite status. They sought a republican solution for the problems that confronted the United States, which in 1787 most people still considered a plural noun, not a singular one. What they achieved was a radical restructuring of republicanism by reimagining power as an ally of liberty instead of its implacable foe. In the process, they invented a constitution, created a national republic, previously thought to be impossible, and paved the way for a modern democratic state.

Their aim was to save the Revolution from its excesses by fashioning a government that did not depend on virtuous people to function well. This task was made easier by the absence of republicans who did not share their nationalist perspective or their critique of what had occurred since independence. Some well-known figures were serving elsewhere: Thomas Jefferson and John Adams were representing American interests in France and Great Britain, respectively. Early firebrands, such as Samuel Adams and Thomas Paine, were not selected by their states; they were propagandists whose rhetorical skills were not the traits needed for nation-building. Other champions of the Confederation, such as George Clinton and John Hancock, either chose to skip the Convention or, like Patrick Henry, boycotted the gathering. Their experience had been in the states and, as a result, they did not share the sense of urgency about the fragile condition of the Union felt by their colleagues. They were more concerned about the dangers of centralized power than they were about the potential for mob rule. They favored more democracy, not less. Their absence later made it more difficult to convince a wary public that the constitution they were asked to ratify offered sufficient protection for their hard-won liberty.

In an assembly with many talented members, it is misleading to point to any one person as the key to success. George Washington was essential because he lent his great reputation to the Convention as its president, providing assurance that its work would not undo the victory he had won. Benjamin Franklin offered not just his international prestige but also his perspective, based on years as a diplomat and a veteran of inter-colonial and interstate politics. James Wilson had a brilliant legal mind. James Madison, who kept the most complete record of the proceedings, provided intellectual leadership. Later in life he rejected any effort to identify him as "father of the Constitution," yet most scholars have identified Madison as an important architect of the Constitution and, later, of the Bill of Rights.

Even though he was a young man, thirty-six at the time the Convention assembled in Philadelphia, the diminutive, sickly, and introspective Madison already was an experienced revolutionary leader. More theoretical than most of his contemporaries, Madison nonethelss combined an ability to think abstractly with a real-world understanding of how the world of government and politics worked in practice. Despite his reputation as a "gloomy stiff creature," he had served as one of Virginia's representatives to the Continental Congress from 1780 to 1783 before returning to his home state as a member of its House of Delegates.

Early on, Madison formed a deep and lasting friendship with Thomas Jefferson, but he did not share his fellow Virginian's radical utopianism. Jefferson was an optimistic visionary who trusted a free people, symbolized by the independent yeoman farmer, to resist power and protect liberty. Like Jefferson, Madison feared governmental power, but he never had the unquestioning faith in the common people that Jefferson did. He worried about the excesses that could occur when popular passions went unchecked. The differences between the two friends appear clearly in their views about the power and role of legislators. Jefferson trusted the majority, and he sought to ensure that representatives always acted in accord with the wishes of the people who elected them. Madison was more concerned about the rights of the minority, which he feared legislatures would deny in the face of public pressure.

Madison arrived at the Convention with a diagnosis of the problems that ailed the nation. Throughout the 1780s he had wrestled with the deficiencies of the Articles and outlined several schemes for overhauling the Confederation. His experience as a Virginia legislator convinced him that the real crisis did not lie with the weaknesses of the current government but in the popular politics of the several states. His fellow legislators were not filled with the public virtue that republicanism demanded. In Madison's view, they were petty, venal, and small-minded, nothing at all like the enlightened gentlemen that he and others had assumed would guide republican governments. Most of them, he concluded, appeared only to have "a small interest to serve."[3] He submitted carefully drafted bills for consideration only to have them shredded by ill-informed debate and crude political bartering. Even worse for republican government, the fault did not rest wholly with legislators. The problem was too much democracy. Representatives only reflected the parochial, short-sighted interests of their constituents. For Madison, the potential for a tyrannical majority was real and ever present. How could a republic of liberty survive under such conditions? It was a question shared by most of the delegates to Philadelphia, who had similar experiences and reached similar conclusions.

Madison was not content only to diagnose the problem. A keen student of history and philosophy, he came prepared with a remedy. It centered on a new understanding of American politics, one that challenged conventional wisdom about the nature and structure of republican government. For him, the only solution was a strong central government capable of vetoing all state legislation that threatened the sanctity or supremacy of the Union itself. Working quietly, he soon had the support of other nationalists for his plan, including the agreement of George Washington, who shared Madison's diagnosis and encouraged him.

The Convention, which kept its proceedings secret, initially divided between states that simply wanted to do what Congress authorized by revising the Articles and states that sought to render the constitution of government adequate to the needs of the Union, as proposed by the Annapolis Convention the previous year. Quickly enough, however, the delegates decided to focus on a new constitution rather than reform the deficient Articles. Seizing the initiative, Governor Edmund Randolph, another Virginia delegate, offered a set of resolutions embodying Madison's ideas of a nationalist agenda.

Known as the Virginia Plan, it proposed a strong central government with sovereignty over the entire United States and authority to act directly on the people rather than through the states, as the Articles had required. Central to this scheme was a bicameral national legislature, with one house chosen by the people, voting in districts apportioned by population, and the second elected by the first. The executive and judiciary would be chosen by the legislature. Because it represented the people instead of the states, the national government would enforce its laws directly through its own courts. This representative principle also meant that it would possess the rightful authority, granted by the people, to veto state legislation at odds with the constitution. It was a bold vision with support from a strong majority of the delegates. Voting by states, they decided seven to one, with one abstention, to create a truly national union instead of another federation similar to the Articles.

In abandoning state sovereignty for national sovereignty, the delegates addressed the Convention's immediate problem but in the process raised other issues. States did not disappear under the Virginia Plan, but no one understood how authority could be divided between them and the central government. A national solution also raised other questions. Was it possible to grant this government sufficient power to act decisively without also providing it the means to subvert liberty? Both English history and colonial experience warned against the dangers of centralizing power in a distant government. A republican government would solve this problem because it required the active involvement and close supervision of public-minded citizens, but this condition was impossible except within a small geographical space. Could a large nation also be a republic? Few people in 1787 thought so.

An answer, Madison believed, lay in the mechanics of government. A proper structure was critical in freeing power to act without threatening liberty. History had shown that the British style of mixed government had not restrained tyranny because its power, although divided in theory, was undivided in practice. Borrowing an idea from the French political theorist Baron de Montesquieu, whose book *The Spirit of the Laws* was well known to the delegates, Madison suggested that separating the functions of government into three branches—legislative, executive, and judicial—would prevent the concentration of power. Massachusetts already had adopted this arrangement in its 1780 constitution, and other states had debated a similar scheme.

But it was not clear what role each branch would play or even how each would be structured. For every question of form, the Convention faced a problem of power: Was there to be a single chief executive or several? How long would he serve? Who would elect him: the people or the legislature? Would a single executive lead to monarchy? Would the judiciary be elected or appointed, and what would be the scope of their jurisdiction? Vesting the national government with power to act decisively also posed a potential threat to the liberties the Revolution had sought to ensure. A national judiciary with the ability to impose laws through national courts, for example, could undermine the local character of justice, especially the trial jury that was prized as a defender of individual rights.

The longer the debate continued, the more uneasy delegates from the smaller states became. They favored a stronger national government but worried that proportional representation would lead to a tyranny of large states over small ones. The problem, once again, was the concentration of power. If anything was consistent in the chaos of convention debate, in which delegates embraced a solution one day only to shy away from it the next, it was a fear of power. Whenever they circled back to an issue, they had discovered the potential for abuse in the first solution and wanted to consider a different strategy. So it was with the small states, which now advanced a different notion of union to blunt the threat from large states.

Almost three weeks after the Convention opened, William Paterson from New Jersey proposed what became known as the New Jersey Plan; he had the backing of the smaller states and New York, which at the time was a state large in territory but small in population. The plan sought only to revise the Articles of Confederation, thereby maintaining state sovereignty. But it made several concessions: the national government could collect taxes directly instead of relying on the states; in cases of conflict between state and national law, acts of the central government, adjudicated by a national supreme court, would be "the supreme law of the respective States"; and the executive branch, actually an executive board, could call out state militias to enforce obedience if necessary.

The New Jersey Plan's small-state supporters readily conceded the flaws of the Confederation, but they were not willing to consign the states to a meaningless role to remedy the Articles' failures. What entity besides republican states could represent the interests of the people and protect their liberty? Pledges from large-state champions that differences among the most populous states would keep them from conspiring against small-state interests were not enough to calm fears of concentrated power. A delegate from Delaware, Gunning Bedford, the state's attorney-general, put it bluntly: "I do not, gentlemen, trust you," he charged. "If you possess the power, the abuse of it will not be checked."[4]

The New Jersey Plan was voted down, seven states to three, but it was a pyrrhic victory because the small states remained firm in their opposition to the Virginia Plan. A long stalemate followed. The choices, it seemed, had been framed too starkly: the union was to be either a sovereign national government or a federation of sovereign state governments. Rufus King of Massachusetts suggested a way out of the dilemma. Why, he asked, did sovereignty have to reside in one government? What if it were divided between governments? Precedent existed for such a practice. Not only had the colonists made such a claim in 1774 when they proposed a dominion theory of empire—the Confederation operated with divided power. Under the Articles, he noted, states did not have exclusive authority; they could not make war or negotiate peace, for example. "If they [the states] formed a confederacy in some respects—they formed a Nation in others."[5]

King's formulation was a catalyst for compromise, and delegates quickly sought ways to reconcile the two plans. They experimented with language to express this new notion of divided sovereignty or federalism, a term increasingly defined as a system of shared power rather than its previous meaning as a federation of sovereign states. The phrase "national government" in the Virginia Plan became simply "the government of the United States," a small but symbolically important shift. The New Jersey Plan's requirement that state courts enforce national law was more suited to the new meaning of federalism than was the Virginia Plan's proposal for a national veto of state law, especially when linked to a provision that made national law and treaty obligations supreme.

Roger Sherman of Connecticut, backed by his fellow delegates Oliver Ellsworth and William Samuel Johnson, proposed a way to solve the problem of representation. In what came to be known as the Great or Connecticut Compromise, one house of the bicameral legislature, the House of Representatives, would be proportioned by population and directly elected by districts, while the other chamber, the Senate, would represent the states equally, with each state allotted two senators. With this agreement in hand, the new Congress of the United States could be trusted with the authority belonging to a national government, especially the power to tax and the power to regulate interstate and foreign commerce.

But this compromise raised another issue—how to count slaves. The difficulty was not primarily moral, even though some northern delegates opposed the "peculiar institution," but economic and political. Slaves were valuable property, and southerners were afraid that excluding them from the census used to calculate representation would allow the more populous northern states to tax them. Northerners wanted to restrict representation only to free people. Here, a deal was readily available. The Confederation Congress already had grappled with the problem and had proposed an amendment to the Articles that counted three slaves as the equivalent of five white persons for purposes of taxation. The three-fifths rule now became the basis for representation in the lower house and for taxation.

Yet another compromise later in the Convention forbade taxes on exports, a desire of northern states, and limited any import duties on slaves to ten dollars each while also barring any federal interference with the slave trade for twenty years after ratification. Antislavery advocates in the mid-nineteenth century would condemn all these provisions as bargains with the devil, but they were neither explicit endorsements of racial hierarchy nor forerunners of a militant proslavery ideology. They were instead an answer to the Convention's continuing struggle to define important governmental functions, especially to protect rights in property and to distribute and balance power fairly.

After the delegates adopted the Great Compromise in mid-summer, they faced the last major hurdle, establishing the structure and role of the executive branch. It was a difficult problem because history provided no satisfactory model. The Articles, for example, created a President of the United States in Congress Assembled, who held a one-year term, to preside over Congress, with a Committee of the States exercising most executive functions, an arrangement the delegates judged ineffectual. Also, the solution had to answer the question that had preoccupied the Convention from the beginning: How much power could be entrusted to government, or in this case, to the chief executive? Throughout history, tyranny appeared most often in the form of a single figure, the despotic monarch, but the revolutionary experience had demonstrated that the legislature also could pose a threat to liberty. As the embodiment of popular sovereignty, a role made possible by its representative nature, the legislature was to be the great engine of government, but the separation-of-powers principle required a counterweight to its broad authority. Was it possible to create a chief executive with sufficient energy to administer the affairs of government and with power to check the legislature while also halting the inevitable human tendency to accumulate and use power to aggrandize one's self?

Republican theory assumed that leaders would be filled with public virtue and act without consideration of politics. Only a few wise men would meet these criteria—George Washington, of course, was on everyone's mind—but what was the best procedure for ensuring that such men were chosen? At first, delegates considered granting the legislature authority to select the executive, but ultimately they were not satisfied that it could act dispassionately. Gouverneur Morris of Pennsylvania put this fear in terms that Protestant America clearly understood: "If the legislature elect," he argued, "it will be the work of intrigue, of cabal, and of faction; it will be like the election of a pope by a conclave of cardinals; real merit will rarely be the title to the appointment."[6]

Such a scheme also upset the principle of separation of powers. The new basis of government, popular sovereignty, implied election by the people, but how—directly or indirectly? A direct popular election raised concerns: would the people know enough about the candidates to choose wisely? Would it lead to the rise of the man on horseback, the heroic figure who had no other qualification for office, the fear that kept most delegates from seriously considering election of the president by the people. Other questions were in play as well: What would be the length of term and the specific powers of the office? How many terms could the executive serve?

In August the Convention received a plan for the executive branch from the Committee on Detail: the president of the United States, the title of the new office, would be elected by both houses of the legislature for a single seven-year term; he would have veto power over legislation, subject to reversal by a two-thirds vote of the Congress; he would be commander-in-chief of the military in time of war; he could be impeached and removed from office through indictment by the lower house and conviction by the Supreme Court; and he would have authority to appoint all government offices whose selection had not been specifically delegated otherwise. The president was to be addressed as "Your Excellency." Later debate and a further revision by the committee added a council of advisors, similar to the Privy Council in Great Britain. These latter two items, which smacked too much of monarchy, sparked intense debates that reopened all questions relating to the office. Finally the frustrated delegates referred the entire issue to the Committee on Postponed Matters, which had one representative from each state.

That committee's report in early September produced a compromise, the most important having to do with the scheme for election. Following a plan initially advanced by James Wilson of Pennsylvania, the president would be chosen by an indirect election. States would have a number of electors equal to their representation in Congress, with each state legislature to determine whether these electors would be chosen through popular ballot or by the legislature itself. The electors would cast individual votes for the two people they considered the best qualified to serve as president and vice president, as long as one of the candidates came from a state other than their own.

The electoral college, a name that appeared first in the early 1800s and became a legal designation (the "college of electors") in 1845, was a carefully crafted, if awkward, compromise between advocates of popular election and champions of a more deliberative process. Its immediate value was that it broke a month-long stalemate and allowed the Convention to close its work. More important, the process made the presidency a popularly elected office, albeit indirectly. It forged a relationship between the president and the nation as a whole—a claim first made by Andrew Jackson in 1832—unlike Congress, whose members represented local districts or states only. Popular election allowed the president, in time, to become the unrivaled symbol and executor of the national will.

The Committee of Style began to prepare a final draft of the proposed constitution on September 8; four days later, it presented a polished document for the Convention's approval. What had been twenty-three wordy, sometimes clumsily phrased sections emerged from the committee as a plainly written document of seven articles. The first three articles, on the legislative, executive, and judicial branches, respectively, outlined a deliberate hierarchy, with the legislature, the body most directly aligned with the people, assuming first rank. The remaining four articles dealt with a variety of subjects, including the relationships among the states (IV), the process for amendments (V), the supremacy of the Constitution (VI), and how voters would ratify the Convention's work (VII). A preamble, initially conceived as a list of the states that acted to produce the new union, modeled after the Articles, became instead a statement of purpose, proclaimed in the name of the people of the United States. Although without any legal force—it neither grants nor restricts authority—this opening paragraph announced that the people in their sovereign capacity were vesting power in government for certain, specified ends.

At every turn, the text revealed a different understanding of the relationship between power and liberty than was possible in 1776. Experience had tempered the revolutionaries' expectations and blunted exuberant assumptions about radical changes in human nature. But if the turmoil of the past decade had sobered them, the delegates remained committed republicans who sought to redesign government to ensure the success of their experiment in liberty. The central question was the same as in 1776: How much power can the sovereign people trust to government without risking their liberty?

Unlike the first, heady days of independence, the delegates no longer made the easy calculation that restraining power alone was the answer. It was not enough to trust the people or their representatives, even though the people always were sovereign. What was required, the delegates concluded, was a government that could protect liberty even if the passions of the moment might seek to deny it. Here was a different understanding of power and liberty, one that turned earlier assumptions on their head: instead of power and liberty as unyielding enemies, power in government, properly limited, could serve to promote and protect liberty. The trick was to create a government that proved this case, and the key was separating and balancing of authority within a government of delegated powers.

The proposed constitution divided power among three branches of government and between the central government and the states. Article I addressed the makeup, election, and powers of Congress, a bicameral body with each branch chosen by different means. The House, with a membership based on population (including the three-fifths rule for slaves) and more directly representative than the Senate, had one exclusive power—impeachment (an accusation of misconduct)—and one it had to exercise first—all bills raising revenue taxes had to begin in the lower chamber. The Senate, with two senators from each state, was indirectly representative of the people; elected state legislatures chose senators. It was designed as a more reflective body—the minimum age for membership was greater, thirty years instead of twenty-five years for the House, and the term of service was longer, six years instead of two—and it had the exclusive power of approval ("advise and consent") for presidential appointments.

Acting as a Congress, the two branches possessed seventeen categories of specific powers, detailed in Section 8; the most important were the power to tax and to regulate interstate and foreign commerce, thereby addressing two problems under the Confederation. Reflecting concerns about the need to limit power explicitly, Section 9 contained eight clauses denying Congress the power to act: for example, it could not suspend the writ of habeas corpus except for invasion or rebellion, make any ex post facto laws or issue bills of attainder, or pass any export taxes. Section 10 prohibited the states from infringing the powers of Congress in matters of taxation, war, and diplomacy; otherwise, the states were free to exercise whatever powers were permitted by their respective constitutions. The Constitution, in brief, established a federal system, with power divided between the national and state governments but only through an explicit delegation from the people, the ultimate sovereign.

Articles II and III formed the executive and judicial branches, respectively, yet together these sections were only half the length of Article I, with the judiciary (Article III) outlined in far briefer scope than the presidency. The language defining the executive branch is both precise and frustratingly vague. The article begins with a simple declaratory sentence: "The executive Power shall be vested in a President of the United States." What did this vesting clause mean? It differed from Article I, which referred to "legislative powers herein granted," so did the Constitution transfer inherent executive authority to the executive while delegating only specified powers to Congress? Presidents since George Washington have made variants on this claim. In doing so they have relied as well on the prescribed oath of office to "faithfully execute the Office of the President of the United States and . . . preserve, protect and defend the Constitution." Clearly the framers desired a more energetic executive—they set a four-year term in office when all state governors, except New York, served one-year terms—and the new division and balance of powers required an office with more power than republican theory traditionally admitted. Throughout history, after all, despotism had been the province of the executive, not the legislature, but now the requirements of liberty required a rebalancing of power.

This executive power was not unrestricted, however. After fixing the electoral process, itself a check on power, and other requirements (minimum age of thirty-five and a natural-born citizen), the article outlines more specific duties and obligations of the president, many of which mimicked royal prerogatives. He was commander-in-chief of the armed forces, had to assent to legislation and could veto bills (a power granted in Article I), held the power of appointment for federal officeholders and judgeships, could make treaties, and had the power to pardon. But in these functions, the president's power was limited. Treaties and appointments to office required the advice and consent of the Senate (a two-thirds vote for treaties); Congress could override a veto by a two-thirds vote in both houses; and the pardon power did not extend to impeachments. The president also had to report periodically to Congress on the state of the union. Nowhere does the document define the president's war powers, yet here, too, there were limits and a division of authority—Congress had the power to declare war, appropriate money, and establish rules for the military; the president was commander-in-chief—that soon became a subject of heated and continuing debate. Revolutionary fears about executive power also can be seen in the final clause outlining the method of removing a president or vice president by a Senate trial following impeachment by the House.

The article on the judiciary was noticeably brief and general, but it likewise rested on republican assumptions and revolutionary experience. In Britain, dispensing justice was an obligation of the king, and judicial power was part of executive power. The American revolutionaries separated these functions in their various state constitutions, making the judiciary a separate, inferior part of government. The Constitution shifted this calculus by providing for a fully equal branch, with federal judges eligible to hold office indefinitely on "good behavior," an effective lifetime appointment. This change made possible a professional bench, in theory insulated from the passions that often ruled ordinary matters of government. It also provided the impetus for judicial review, already a well-established practice by the late eighteenth century, to ensure that their actions of the other branches of government did not breach the Constitution.

Judicial authority extended to all cases arising under the Constitution and the laws and treaties of the United States, including disputes between states and citizens of different states. The Supreme Court had limited original jurisdiction, however, and generally could exercise its power only on appeal. Other provisions required a jury trial for all crimes except impeachment and strictly defined the terms of treason to prevent its use as a means of prosecution for political ends. For all its specifics, Article III was either mute or sketchy on such matters as how many justices would sit on the Supreme Court, how many lower courts would exist, what would be the extent of their appellate authority, or how cases would be managed. Following the precedent of state constitutions, all these decisions were left to Congress, which provided the basic structure for the federal courts in the Judiciary Act of 1789, passed during its first session. What was certain, however, was the ability of the new government to enforce national law through its own courts, as the Confederation could not.

One major problem under the Articles of Confederation was the ability of sovereign states to decide on their own authority to accept or reject the actions of other states. Article IV addressed this issue through the principle of reciprocity (the legal term is comity). States had to give "full faith and credit" to the acts, records, and judicial proceedings of other states; the citizens of each state would have "all privileges and immunities" of citizens of other states; states were bound to return escaped prisoners and slaves to states from which they had fled. The aim of these specific provisions was clear—the Constitution created a singular United States, with equal citizenship, although initially for free whites only. A separate clause extended this principle to the states by providing for admission of new states on terms equal to existing states. With this provision, the framers rejected all claims to an empire. They were republicans, not imperialists, and to reinforce this point, Section 4 guaranteed to each state a "Republican Form of Government," even though it provided no definition of one.

Articles V and VI also reflected the lessons of revolutionary government under the Confederation. The amending process became somewhat less onerous, requiring supermajorities rather than unanimity to change the constitution (Article V); and national law and treaties were declared supreme over state law, including state constitutions, with state courts required to enforce federal law (Article VI). Other provisions contained lessons from English history, such as the prohibition of religious tests for public office (Article VI), the only mention of religion in this secular framework for government. The final article (VII) set the terms for ratification.

It was not a perfect document, and the delegates knew it. Benjamin Franklin, the oldest member of the Convention, addressed this matter squarely before the vote. "I confess there are several parts of this constitution which I do not at present approve, but I am not sure I shall never approve them," he said, in a speech read aloud for him by James Wilson. Old age made him "more apt to doubt his own judgment, and to pay more respect to the judgments of others," and it was in this vein that he asked the delegates to set aside their differences and accept the document as a successful compromise, one that solved problems without sacrificing revolutionary gains.[7] The important thing, he urged them, was to present an appearance of unity, which he thought would be best accomplished by signing as state delegations, a step that would obscure the decision of some delegates not to endorse the Convention's work.

Acting as Franklin suggested, all twelve state delegations and thirty-nine of the original fifty-five delegates signed the proposed constitution. It was a brief document, especially when compared to modern constitutions, and its 4,500 words effectively hid the long debates and countless concessions required to produce it. Every word of the final draft had been forged by compromise. Repeatedly, the debates in Philadelphia led to positions that no one had proposed initially. Three delegates present at the final session refused to sign because they disliked the omission of a bill of rights (George Mason of Virginia), or the creation of the presidency (Edmund Randolph of Virginia), or the failure to safeguard sufficiently the representation of the people and to prevent the abuse of federal power (Elbridge Gerry of Massachusetts).

But for most delegates compromise did not mean an abandonment of principle or purpose. The delegates who gathered in May had faced a crisis of confidence in republican government. The Revolution had not led to a populace willing to sacrifice self-interest in pursuit of the public good, even though republics depended on virtuous people. Republics required unity to withstand the threats posed by tyrants elsewhere who sought to destroy them, but nowhere did this unity exist. Faced with the loss of all they had fought for, the delegates could have abandoned the Revolution. They did not. The constitution they proposed for ratification was a pragmatic response to the dilemmas of revolutionary republicanism. In the process, the framers rescued republicanism by reinventing it.

Not everyone agreed with this assessment. For many people, the proposed constitution was a betrayal of the Revolution, not its salvation. When it went to the states for ratification—nine states, acting through specially elected ratifying conventions, had to accept the constitution before it became effective— opponents mounted attacks that called into question whether the work at Philadelphia had been in vain. The critique came from all quarters. A member of the Virginia delegation who refused to sign, George Mason, circulated his "Objections to the Constitution" even before he left Philadelphia. Opposition mounted early in Virginia and New York, an especially disturbing sign because defeat in these two states could doom ratification. Men who had made their mark as leaders of the revolutionary cause—Patrick Henry in Virginia and Samuel Adams in Massachusetts, for example—and powerful state politicians, such as New York Governor George Clinton, were vigorous spokesmen against ratification. Farmers, artisans, and backcountry settlers, many of them from small states, suspected that the new constitution was the product of ambitious, commercially minded men who were eager to sacrifice liberty for a government powerful enough to advance their selfish interests. What many opponents feared, in brief, was the emergence of an aristocracy that would subvert the rising democracy unleashed by the Revolution.

Deeply concerned by the voices raised against ratification, proponents of a strong general government undertook a campaign to persuade Americans of the virtues of the new Constitution. They used newspaper essays and pamphlets to defend the Convention's work. Chief among their efforts was a series of eighty-five newspaper essays written by Publius, the pseudonym chosen by Alexander Hamilton, the instigator and primary author, and the colleagues he recruited to help him, James Madison and John Jay.

Writing as many as four essays a week, Hamilton and Madison especially (Jay became ill and contributed only five essays) defended the Constitution and explained how its provisions met the requirements of republican theory. They shrewdly took the name Federalists, signaling their desire to strengthen the federal government while not abandoning the states, which still stood as protectors of liberty under the new arrangement. It was a clever move, but it obscured a transformation in the understanding of republicanism, a shift that stood definitions on their head and laid the foundation for a national republic to emerge.

The central problem of classical republicanism was the need to protect liberty by restraining power. The first state constitutions tried to solve this problem by sharply limiting what government could do and by trusting the people's representatives to protect liberty. *The Federalist*, as the essays collectively came to be known, noted the failure of these restraints and argued instead that the Constitution rightly made governmental power the chief protector and promoter of liberty. No one suggested that power had lost its aggressiveness or its acquisitiveness. It still was a threat to liberty in societies without a means to turn it to useful ends. But the classical solution was inadequate, as the disastrous experiences of the 1780s had demonstrated.

The revolutionaries initially had trusted too much to fallible men. Officeholders were innately corrupt, experience proved, and could not be trusted with power. The Constitution's system of check and balances—separation of powers, federalism, and its grants of specific power, as well as its explicit restrictions on power—made it safer to vest authority in imperfect men burdened by passions, ambitions, and prejudices. For this problem, the Constitution offered a mechanical solution, one suited to the age of scientific enlightenment. Just as Deists imagined God as a master watchmaker, devising a universe that ran on its own internal rules, so the framers, many of whom shared this theology, believed that the right architecture for government would not require perfect men. "Enlightened statesmen will not always be at the helm," Madison noted in *Federalist No. 10*. The structure of government would correct what the weakness of men could not.

Dividing and balancing power in so many ways offered protection from cabals and plots against liberty because conspirators would not be able to act unless they controlled all parts of the government; conversely, requiring all parts of the government to agree on an action made it more likely that power would not be used irresponsibly. Notice how many ways the framers had divided power, *The Federalist* urged. A majority of legislators from two branches, elected under different schemes, had to agree to pass a bill, which the president had to sign before it became law. The president had a veto to check the misuse of power by the legislature, but lawmakers could check the executive by a two-thirds vote to override a veto and, in cases of extreme abuse, by impeachment and removal from office.

The division and balance of power went beyond the structural arrangement of the national government alone. It also extended to the allocation of authority between the state governments and the national government, with some power reserved for the states and some for the central government. The Constitution, in brief, incorporated a central lesson from the 1780s: undivided governmental power, even when entrusted to the people's representatives, was dangerous. The only sure way to trust power was to divide it.

What made this trust possible, of course, was a new understanding of popular sovereignty and the extension of the representative principle to the central government. The first republican governments confused legislative sovereignty and popular sovereignty. State legislators wrote the state constitutions on the assumption that they were the people's representatives, which was true but not in the way they supposed. Voters elected them to enact ordinary legislation, not to establish fundamental law. The Massachusetts constitution of 1780 corrected this misconception through the invention of the constitutional convention and ratification process. Now the people acted directly to create government. In the process, they defined governmental authority explicitly and denied other powers, and they reserved all remaining power for the sovereign people.

The proposed federal constitution adopted this new understanding of popular sovereignty. It made an explicit, written grant of delegated powers from the people to the government, which further protected liberty, *The Federalist* argued, by preventing government from acting in areas the people had not authorized. In addition, the Constitution made the central government representative of the people, both directly and indirectly. The House of Representatives was elected directly, by district; the Senate and president were elected indirectly. This extension of the representative principle to the national government had two important implications. It allowed the government to enforce its laws directly on the people, whose representatives had given their consent, rather than indirectly through the states as required under the Articles. It also created a national republic.

The idea of a national republic, previously thought to be a self-contradictory term, required a new understanding of the nature of a republican state. Under the classical conception, unity was essential for the republic's survival. Factions, or special interests, weakened the republic and made it susceptible to internal collapse or to aggression externally by tyrants, its natural enemy. For this reason, republics were small states. Only within a small, homogeneous area could sufficient unity exist to allow a republic to succeed. By definition, a nation as large and diverse as the United States could not have a republican government.

In *Federalist No. 10*, an essay more celebrated later than at the time, James Madison attacked this conception head-on and reversed its logic. Even if it were possible to create homogeneous states, a result he deemed impractical, experience had demonstrated the error of trusting unity and direct democracy to protect liberty. Not only had the states been riddled by factionalism, but they also had suffered tyranny of the majority and denial of rights to minorities. It was too easy for factions to form majorities that could suppress individual rights, especially in small states. "[In] a pure democracy [citizens voting directly on laws] . . . a common passion or interest will be felt by a majority, and there is nothing to check the inducements to sacrifice the weaker party," Madison wrote.

The solution was not to eliminate self-interested groups, which could not be done with threatening liberty—"liberty is to factions as air is to fire," Madison recognized—but rather to control their effects. No form of government could remove the threat of self-interest—it was part of the human condition—so the best way to blunt its influence was to lessen the opportunities for factions to become permanent majorities. How? By increasing the number of factions, Madison argued. A national republic vastly expanded the number of interest groups, making it much more difficult for them to come together into anything other than temporary majorities. A large and diverse republic also produced other advantages. It expanded the number of candidates available to represent the people and, because they had to appeal to larger constituencies, it was more difficult for corrupt or unqualified candidates to bribe voters or use trickery to win office.

Madison conceded that a large republic produced its own problems, such as choosing representatives "too little acquainted with local circumstances," but another structural innovation, federalism, provided a corrective by giving scope and voice to both national and state interests. Yet how could the nation maintain a balance between sufficient diversity to check factions and the commonality needed to allow a true union to exist? Here, John Jay, in *Federalist No. 2*, reminded readers that America already was "one united people—a people descended from the same ancestors, speaking the same language, professing the same religion." The nation could enjoy the blessings of both unity and diversity.

Anti-Federalists were not convinced: "this unkindred legislature . . . , composed of interests opposite and dissimilar in their nature, will in its exercise, emphatically be, like a house divided against itself," wrote "Cato," a pseudonym likely used by Governor George Clinton, a leading opponent of the proposed Constitution.[8] Clinton and his allies operated from the older, classical conception of republicanism that had served as the first template for revolutionary government. Relying on Montesquieu, whose treatise *The Spirit of the Laws*, also had influenced Madison although he challenged its arguments in his *Federalist No. 10*, Anti-Federalists believed only small republics (at most the size of states) could produce the harmony of interests required for effective government. The wide disparity in economic interests in a national republic was a matter of special concern. The focus on commerce and shipping in the north and plantation farming in the south would inevitably lead to conflict. Even if these interests could be reconciled, the experience of the Greek and Roman republics, noted "Brutus," another Anti-Federalist pamphleteer, demonstrated how expansion beyond a small state began an irreversible descent into tyranny.

The names "Cato" and "Brutus" recalled ancient Roman senators who opposed first the Etruscan tyrants of Rome and later Julius Caesar, and the use of these identities signaled to readers a continuing concern over the dangers of power. The Anti-Federalists remained committed to the Commonwealth man and early republican views that so influenced the movement toward independence and the first stage of the Revolution: power and liberty were intractable foes, and an ever-vigilant, united, and virtuous citizenry, devoted to the common good, was essential to repel rulers who sought only to further their own interests.

Like the Federalists, Anti-Federalists produced voluminous writings in an effort to defeat ratification. Their essays often were brilliantly argued and contained prescient warnings about the problems of government under the new constitution, but, unlike *The Federalist*, they had no coherent message. The essays reflected the disorganization of the opponents, all of whom had different reasons for campaigning against approval. Some people feared the Constitution was a disguised attempt to reintroduce a British-style central government. Others objected to the diminishment of state authority; in their view, states were closest to the people and more protective of their proper interests and liberties. Some acknowledged the weaknesses of the Articles but believed the powers assigned to the new central government were too strong, while others thought the Confederation simply needed time to mature into a more effective government.

The most consistent theme in opposition was the perceived threat to individual liberties. The proposed Constitution contained no bill of rights, nor, Anti-Federalists charged, did it include any guarantee of the most basic individual liberties. The Federalists explained that the Constitution made explicit grants of power only; any power not given to the central government remained with the states or the people. The Constitution did not require a bill of rights because it granted the central government no power to restrict individual liberties. In *Federalist No. 84* Alexander Hamilton not only catalogued all the rights-protecting provisions of the proposed Constitution but went so far as to oppose a bill of rights on the grounds that it would unduly restrict the rights of the people. Drawing heavily from an influential speech by James Wilson seven months earlier, Hamilton argued that, under the Constitution, "the people surrender nothing, and as they retain everything, they have no need of particular reservations." Wilson had asked, "Who would be bold enough to undertake to enumerate all the rights of the people?" and Hamilton extended this theme. He feared that, once the rights were written down, later generations would assume that the Constitution contained all the rights belonging to the people, and rights not codified would be deemed forever excluded from legal protection. He preferred to leave the identification of rights to the common law, which historically had functioned to expand liberty, and to state constitutions.

Anti-Federalists were not persuaded. They countered that since the laws of the United States were superior to state laws, state constitutions offered little protection. Without a bill of rights, they concluded, government could quickly slide into tyranny: the Pennsylvania Anti-Federalists feared the consolidation of power in the national government "must necessarily annihilate and absorb the legislative, executive, and judicial powers of the several states and produce from their ruins . . . an iron handed despotism."[9] They likewise rejected Hamilton's claim that later generations would consider an enumeration of rights to be exhaustive and would not add to them.

Writing from France, where he was serving as the American minister, Thomas Jefferson warned James Madison that the absence of a bill of rights was a serious deficiency of the new constitution. A listing of rights, he argued, "is what the people are entitled to against every government on earth, and what no just government should refuse or rest on inference."[10] Enough people agreed with this position that the lack of a bill of rights quickly became a threat to ratification. Five states already had endorsed the Constitution when Anti-Federalists in Massachusetts seized on growing discontent to demand that a bill of rights be added to the document. The contest pitted defenders of the text as written, who dismissed any talk of amendments as a ploy to undermine the Constitution, against advocates who wanted to rewrite the charter or to ratify it only if a bill of rights were added.

A compromise finally emerged that proved vital to the Constitution's success in the ratification controversy. In a close vote, Massachusetts approved the Constitution but attached a recommendation to add a bill of rights; the other states that had not yet ratified followed suit, voting yes but with similar proposals. Virginia and New York were the critical final votes. Earlier, New Hampshire's vote had provided the required ninth state in favor of the Constitution, but everyone understood that the support of these two states was vital to the success of the new union. When both states ratified, also with recommendations for a bill of rights, the Constitution was a political as well as a legal reality. So was the necessity to amend it immediately with a bill of rights. In what became a pattern of American history, the central role of rights in American constitutional law was due more to the demands of an insistent citizenry than it was to the framers' design.

As a newly elected member of the House of Representatives in the First Congress, James Madison assumed responsibility for fulfilling the pledge made to add protection for rights to the Constitution, in part because his political future in Virginia depended on it; his promise to work for a bill of rights in the new government was vital to his narrow electoral victory in early 1789. During the ratification debates, he at first resisted a declaration of rights because he feared it would be a "parchment barrier," a mere paper incapable of protecting liberty. Now, he had changed his mind.

Four factors influenced Madison: his recognition that the promise of amendments had been critical to the Constitution's success; his belief that he had to keep the promise he had made during the ratification controversy and repeated during his campaign for the House in 1789; his belief that, if he did not take charge of the campaign, others would propose amendments damaging to what President George Washington called "the just powers of the general government"; and, finally, Jefferson's volley of arguments in favor of a bill of rights, written in letter after letter crossing the Atlantic. In a day-long speech in the House of Representatives in June 1789 Madison acknowledged that he now believed written constitutional guarantees were necessary because they would remind people of "the fundamental maxims of free government," especially the close link between individual rights and personal liberty. They would serve as "good ground for an appeal to the sense of community," he concluded, if states or oppressive majorities threatened liberty. He worried much about majorities running roughshod over the rights of minorities, especially in matters of conscience, and he feared states would not be able to resist this kind of tyranny.

As a result, Madison initially proposed that the Bill of Rights apply to the states as well as the central government, a condition rejected by Congress because of its implications for state sovereignty. Not until the twentieth century would rights be nationalized in this way—and then by the courts, not Congress. This development likely would not have surprised Madison, who sought to answer the question of who would enforce the Bill of Rights on behalf of individuals whose rights were threatened? Here, influenced by his correspondence with Thomas Jefferson, he believed that an independent judiciary, operating through courts open to all citizens, would come to consider themselves "the guardian of these rights." They would "resist every encroachment on rights expressly stipulated for in the constitution," forming an "impenetrable bulwark against every assumption of power in the legislative or executive." Whereas most of his contemporaries viewed the Bill of Rights as a standard that enabled people to judge their government, Madison believed that it promoted self-government by enabling citizens to resist any impulse—fear, selfishness, and prejudice, among others—that threatened America's great experiment in liberty. Enforcement of rights by an independent judiciary, he argued, provided a means to correct injustices that were sure to occur in any human society but which could not be allowed to exist in a society dedicated to liberty.[11]

Madison submitted nine amendments to the First Congress in 1789, based on his review of the more than two hundred recommended amendments adopted by the state ratifying conventions. In all, his proposals covered twenty-six paragraphs. Over the next month the House and then the Senate and finally a compromise committee molded these proposed safeguards into twelve amendments; by 1791, the states had ratified ten of them. (The two unapproved amendments were not about rights but rather about congressional apportionment and pay; in 1992, two centuries after Madison had introduced it, the states finally approved what became the Twenty-seventh Amendment, delaying the effect of any change in congressional compensation until after the next congressional election.) These first ten ratified amendments became known as the Bill of Rights, a designation made possible by their posting at the end of the Constitution rather than added to the text in various places, as Madison initially preferred.

The amendments borrowed heavily from the Virginia Declaration of Rights and the various state bills of rights, all of which had resulted from a rich mix of

English history, colonial experience, and revolutionary ideas. It was the product of a society far different from our own: American Indians who had not sworn fealty to the United States and African Americans did not benefit from its protections—Indian tribes were separate nations and African Americans were not considered U.S. citizens until the Fourteenth Amendment—and white women could not claim its guarantees completely, but even these groups were not specifically excluded from its protections.

For all the flaws of its creators, the list of rights was far advanced for its time. The amendments included two types of guarantees: rights necessary for representative government, such as freedom of speech, press, and peaceable assembly, and rights of the accused, including protections against double jeopardy and self-incrimination as well as the right to counsel and trial by jury. Reflecting Hamilton's objection to a bill of rights, the Ninth Amendment reserved any unnamed rights to the people. It was, in fact, the most original of the amendments, by which Madison sought to solve the problem he had highlighted in a letter to Jefferson worrying that an attempt to codify rights might omit some, leaving them unprotected. To satisfy an Anti-Federalist concern, the Tenth Amendment reserved any unspecified powers to the states or the people, although Madison removed the word "expressly" from the initial wording, "The powers not expressly granted to the United States," thus blunting its future impact as a limit on central power by opening the potential for implied powers.

With the ratification of the Bill of Rights in 1791, the revolutionary Constitution was complete. The framers had adopted an innovative structural solution to the ages-old problem of power and liberty. They had not created a "machine that would go of itself," as poet and diplomat James Russell Lowell reminded his fellow citizens in 1888 at the centenary celebration of the Constitution's ratification. It was necessary for citizens to involve themselves in the work of government but it was not essential that men and women be free from self-interest or individual ambitions. Rather, the framers had designed the Constitution to work with imperfect men and not to depend on a never-to-be-realized virtuous citizenry.

The emphasis on structure should not obscure the radical nature of the Constitution itself. For more than two decades the founding generation had struggled to understand the meaning of liberty and the obligations of power. They had begun with lessons learned from English history and then, with independence, briefly imagined a world of growing perfection that did not require government to provide order or to protect the common good from the vanity and self-interests of its subjects.

In this new republican environment, Americans would move from being subjects who required a king to being free and independent citizens capable of ruling themselves. This change would lead increasingly to a refinement of the public realm by producing people filled with public virtue who sought the common good before their own self-interest. When this moral transformation of man did not occur, when people continued to pursue their own selfish ends, there was no conservative counter-revolution, no abandonment of the republican ideal. The men who wrote the Constitution did not reject the Revolution, as the French did a few years later. Rather, they sought to rescue and sustain republicanism in a world fraught with corruption and inhabited by flawed human beings.

The Constitution they produced was the product of compromise, and as such, it left fundamental questions unaddressed and unanswered. It did not mention equality, even though this idea had animated the Declaration of Independence by identifying the nation's highest aspirations. Nor did it include the word "slavery," except by implication. The constitution rested on popular sovereignty—"We, the people"—yet its practical meaning was ambiguous. This foundational principle underwent a metamorphosis during the Revolution, shifting from an assumption that legislative sovereignty and popular sovereignty were the same to one that clearly distinguished between the two. Government no longer was something that happened to people; it became something that people created.

Yet when the people acted collectively to fashion a government, they invoked only one expression of popular sovereignty. At least one other meaning was present, the people acting collectively to rule as sovereigns. The constitution established a representative process—and it required a supermajority for amendments—but did it rule out the people acting directly? Both the procedural view and the democratic view shared the general consensus that the people were sovereign. They differed over how much power remained with the people and how much power the people had surrendered to government. It was a difference that mattered because of the questions it raised: Who were the people? How could the people be both ruler and ruled?

The framers also left other constitutional definitions unsettled. In the early 1790s a bitter debate arose over the meaning of the "necessary and proper" clause of the Constitution. Contained in Article I, Section 8, the words come at the end of a series of seventeen clauses detailing the powers of Congress: the eighteenth clause reads, "To make all Laws which shall be necessary and proper for carrying into Execution the foregoing Powers, and all other Powers vested by this Constitution in the Government of the United States, or in any Department or Office thereof." The drafters of the document were trying to make it clear that Congress could pass laws required to carry out its powers, but what made a law "necessary and proper"? Common law provided no guidance, and common usage was not as certain as the delegates to the Federal Convention might have supposed.

When faced with the proposal to establish a national bank in 1791, the two most prominent figures in the administration of President George Washington differed vehemently over the meaning of these three words. Secretary of State Thomas Jefferson argued that "necessary and proper" meant something that was absolutely essential for exercising the granted power; Secretary of the Treasury Alexander Hamilton, principal architect of the bank bill awaiting Washington's signature or veto, believed that decisions about what was necessary should be left to the judgment of Congress, unless a given power or mechanism was explicitly prohibited. In the end, Washington, having read both Jefferson's and Hamilton's opinions, adopted Hamilton's viewpoint and signed the bank bill into law.

The argument over interpretation, important in its own right, also was emblematic of what would follow because the Constitutional Convention and ratification debates left a long list of unsettled meanings and unaddressed questions. How far does the power to regulate interstate commerce extend (Article I)? What powers are assumed under the president's constitutional duty to serve as commander-in-chief of the military (Article II)? Does the constitutional requirement for Senate approval of presidential appointments in Article II imply that the president may not remove these officers without its consent? Does the silence of Article III (judiciary) on the power of judicial review mean that the Supreme Court cannot declare an act of Congress, a co-equal branch, unconstitutional? What constitutes freedom of speech: Does it have to be words or can it include signs or symbols (First Amendment)? What is an establishment of religion or free exercise of religion (First Amendment)? What is meant by the right to keep and bear arms (Second Amendment)? What constitutes a "search" that requires a warrant (Fourth Amendment)? What distinguishes a cruel and unusual punishment from one that is not (Eighth Amendment)?

From the moment of its adoption, the powers and rights set forth in the new Constitution came into dispute. The tension between power and liberty did not disappear—if anything, it became stronger—as people grappled with the practical problems of government. Over the next two centuries, the Constitution would be challenged, amended, reinterpreted, circumvented, ignored, and, at times, subverted. It would be a weapon in political and class warfare, its phases used as cudgels to advance or beat back change. It would be expanded and contracted by court decisions, congressional acts, and presidential orders. It would be excoriated by scholars who found the framers' self-interest within its clauses, and venerated by generations of Americans who had never read its contents.

What is most striking about the nation's endless constitutional controversies is how often they circle back to the themes debated in Philadelphia. The founders could have seen only dimly, if at all, the triumph of democratic capitalism as the dominant motif of American society. They were fearful of partisan strife and would have been stunned to hear modern political scientists laud the rise of the party system as necessary to the government they created. They never imagined a future where women or blacks could vote, much less rise to the nation's highest offices. They could not have foreseen the enormous expansion of federal authority or the prominence of individual rights in American society. Neither could they have known how often the nation would divide over the same questions that had divided them.

What they could see, what they knew, was the absolute need for the rule of law and for a government that rested on the consent of the governed. They understood the foibles of people and the corruptions of power. Still, they trusted people to be able to rule themselves and to chart their own future if they had a proper frame of government, which, for them, meant one that checked power and embraced the revolutionary principles of individual liberty and political equality they fought to establish.

Federalism

Atwood, Kansas, is a small county-seat town thirty miles from Colorado and Nebraska. Nothing sets it apart from hundreds of small communities on the Great Plains or elsewhere in rural America. Its 1,092 residents worry about the loss of population, declining economic prospects for their children, the price of food and fuel, and how long they can afford to keep their local schools. They are conservative fiscally and politically and take pride in their self-reliance and middle-class values. The only way the town can be considered unusual comes from the long perspective of constitutional history. The weekly newspaper, the *Rawlins County Square Deal*, reveals why. Amid its standard fare in a recent issue—news of the upcoming prom, church programs, library acquisitions, and crop reports—were two stories that would have surprised the founding generation: separate departments of the national government had provided funding for a new water source and a dental clinic. Elsewhere, an announcement of a farm auction noted that the successful bidder would receive approved federal price support for the current year's crops. Few people in 1787 could have imagined that the central government would help a small town pay for its water or guarantee farmers a fair price for their wheat. In the twenty-first century, no one considered it unusual.

Federalism was the most novel doctrine to emerge from the Constitutional Convention. It addressed two pressing issues: how to expand republican government to a national scale and how to grant national government sufficient power to act with energy and dispatch yet limit its ability to threaten liberty. One solution, James Madison explained in *Federalist No. 10*, was to encourage diversity, a result accomplished by giving a national scope to republican government; the more diverse the society, the less likely that any group or cabal could seize power. Another was federalism, a division of authority between national and state governments, even though according to classical political thought it seemingly embraced a contradiction, *imperium in imperio*, a sovereignty within a sovereignty. This logical inconsistency could be resolved only by another innovation, popular sovereignty, that vested ultimate power in the people, who became both rulers and ruled.

For advocates such as Joel Barlow, poet and essayist of the new nation, federalism was the middle course between "the two dangerous extremes of having the republic too great for any equitable administration within, or too small for security without." Others, whom history has dubbed the Anti-Federalists, were more doubtful: a tavern keeper from Massachusetts described it as "a fiddle with few strings, but so that the ruling Majority can play any tune upon it they pleased."[1] For these skeptics, the Philadelphia Convention had dramatically revised revolutionary republicanism to favor the interests of the few at the expense of the many. One difficulty for supporters and opponents alike was that no one knew how this complicated new arrangement of government would work. It rested on abstractions and subtleties, which made it easier for opponents of the proposed constitution to charge that, in fact, the new structure was a ploy for centralizing power.

Today, we judge the Anti-Federalists' fears to be exaggerated, not because their warnings were necessarily wrong but because they were on the losing side of history. Federalism has proven to be a highly malleable scheme for a nation in which change was continuous. Its development reflects how closely the doctrine in practice has met the demands of a diverse, highly mobile society and a dynamic economy. What began as a partnership of equal governments, each operating in different realms and possessing different powers, shifted to a powerful national government with widespread authority to safeguard (or threaten) liberty for its citizens, working sometimes in tandem and sometimes at odds with state governments.

This change from federalism's origins could not be more dramatic nor could the result seem more ordinary. The twenty-first-century United States, with its massive economy, armed might, and global reach, is so far removed from the small eighteenth-century federal republic whose states hugged the Atlantic seaboard that, in retrospect, the morphing of federalism appears inevitable. Nothing could be further from the truth. Federalism's path of development was far from certain. Although a modern consensus might suggest otherwise, few constitutional issues have been as contentious.

The framers created a federal system of government in part because they had no choice. They sought to address the glaring weakness of the Articles of Confederation by investing power in a central government, but they could not ignore the existence of the states. Neither could they slough off the tension between power and liberty inherent in republicanism. Federalists saw danger to liberty in the democratic excesses and state rivalries of the Confederation period. They wanted a strong central government to preserve both the Union and revolutionary republicanism, as well as to command international respect. Opponents believed that only state governments could restrain the natural tendency of centralized governments to swallow liberty in an unbridled quest for power.

The uneasy compromise was to divide authority between state and general governments. The Constitution granted specified or enumerated powers (or denied them) to the central government. Article I, Section 8, detailed those powers, Section 9 imposed limits on congressional authority, and Section 10 listed powers prohibited to the states, primarily in areas of commerce. Some powers, such as taxation, could be exercised concurrently. This careful parsing of power was, simultaneously, both logical and new. In *Federalist No. 14*, Madison eloquently defended it as a solution drawn from Americans' "own good sense, the knowledge of their own situation, and the lessons of their own experience," but he also acknowledged in *Federalist No. 39* that it was "in a manner unprecedented. We cannot find one express example in the history of the world:—It stands by itself." This novelty was its problem. No one had a guide to how this theory would work in practice, a condition that made the doctrine a source of argument and division.

The history of federalism reveals how much the framers' unique arrangement of government reflected their understanding of power and liberty and in turn shaped ours. The founding generation understood well the classic tension between center and periphery. The theory of empire adopted by the British had imagined power flowing from a central government to subordinate and loyal colonies, but experience suggested a different dynamic: center and periphery, empire and colonies, exercised power within their own realms, with occasional friction arising between them. Federalism sought to harness this insight and make the tension between the two parts creative rather than destructive.

The framers' aim was to control power and enhance liberty, but the path to this end was uncertain. Two primary arguments emerged about the direction to take. For advocates of state sovereignty, vesting power in a large and distant central government posed too great a threat to liberty. For champions of a strong national government, such as Alexander Hamilton, power exercised from a vigorous center was the best way to advance the cause of liberty. Although these positions are not value-neutral, over time they have not tracked neatly or consistently with political ideology, party affiliation, or regional identity. At various points, proponents of one view or the other have embraced arguments they once rejected, depending on circumstances and who controlled which level of government. There is no easy symmetry to be found in the history of American federalism.

Changing social and economic conditions and shifts in American culture made the expansion of central authority a major thread of the American constitutional narrative. The demands of capitalism and an expansive national market, the rise of democratic politics with its emphasis on inclusion and reform, and the problems of security and war have been seedbeds for a rebalancing of federalism, with power sliding from states to the national government. This result was not foreordained; it came only in response to politics, broadly construed, as people sought advantage for their individual and collective interests through one institution of government or another. Advocates of states' rights have aided this shift by being wrong, morally and politically, on matters of race and equality. Too frequently they tainted legitimate claims for state sovereignty by insisting on its use to maintain untenable regimes of slavery and segregation or to exclude laborers, women, and immigrants from the democratic process.

It would be incorrect, however, to conclude from this checkered past that states over time have become irrelevant appendages to an all-powerful central government. An opposite view is more accurate. In matters of education, criminal justice, public health, and public safety, among other areas, state and local governments have long been important, and at times preeminent. States are now less visible in textbooks or national media, yet they still are important: they license businesses and cars, tax property and sales, regulate insurance carriers, inspect restaurants, and fund schools, as well as govern many other functions of everyday life. They have served as laboratories of reform: "It is one of the happy incidents of the federal system," U.S. Supreme Court Justice Louis D. Brandeis wrote in 1932, "that a single courageous state may, if its citizens choose, serve as a laboratory; and try novel social and economic experiments without risk to the rest of the country" (*New State Ice Co. v. Liebmann*). Experiments in universal health care, tax-subsidized economic development, recognition of same-sex marriage, and charter schools are only a few among many recent state initiatives that illustrate Brandeis's optimistic view. These examples remind us that the story of federalism is incomplete unless we recognize how much the narrative of national power contains a counter-narrative of local control.

The political drama of federalism, which on two occasions pitted the president and vice president against each other publicly, occurred primarily during the first century of nationhood; by the end of Reconstruction, its arc was set. Although it took over a century, civil war and the transformation of the national economy changed the United States from a plural noun to a singular one, from a confederation to a modern nation-state. The history of federalism since then has been an elaboration of this theme, with the impetus for the growth of national power coming more from actions of Congress and the executive than from judicial decisions.

Scarcely had the ratification process ended in 1788 when disagreements emerged about what the new constitution meant. The dispute in the early 1790s over Hamilton's economic program, and especially his debate with Jefferson over whether the "necessary and proper" clause of Article I, Section 8, permitted Congress to create a national bank, signaled the first major split on what the Constitution permitted. The differences in interpretation soon became embedded in political alignments that were forerunners of the party system that emerged in the 1820s and 1830s. The Federalists, centered in the administration of President George Washington, favored a strong national government based on an expansive reading of the Constitution, whereas the Republicans, followers of Jefferson and Madison, opposed it.

The framers never imagined such a partisan outcome. In revolutionary thought, the presence of factions revealed a lack of civic virtue and unity, qualities required for successful republics. The emergence of party politics was an unwelcomed development, and both sides sought to eliminate them or at least to lessen their influence. No one conceived of a modern system in which organized parties or, more accurately for the early national republic, partisan alliances competed for the right to govern, and few people embraced the notion of a loyal opposition.

Under these circumstances, the results were predictable. The Federalists judged Republicans to be at best naïve in their faith in the common man and reckless in their desire to limit government and keep decision making closely bound to local communities. Excess democracy and states' sovereignty, they believed, almost brought about the collapse of the Union under the Confederation, and they were keen to prevent it from wrecking the new nation. For Republicans, centralization was the threat; history had demonstrated its tendency to consume liberty in a quest for more power. The struggle between these views took an apocalyptic tone at times, but for both sides the stakes were high. Federalists and Republicans alike knew how vulnerable their experiment in liberty was, especially in a world of despots, and the bitter rhetoric that both parties unleashed in the 1790s raised doubts about the experiment's ultimate success. Always alert to the consequences of failure, Federalists in 1798 sought a solution by suppressing their opposition. It was this choice that led to the first crisis of federalism.

During the 1790s the United States became embroiled against its will in the imperial war between Great Britain and its monarchic allies and revolutionary France. By 1798 French interference with American neutrality and a scandal in which French officials had sought bribes from American diplomats (the XYZ Affair) had turned the state of relations between France and the United States battle-hot, sparking an undeclared naval conflict known as the Quasi-War. Federalists seized the opportunity to pass the Alien and Sedition Acts, a series of measures to restrict the influx of immigrants, who tended to vote Republican, and to punish criticism of the government or its officials, a crime known as sedition.

Even though the prosecution of sedition generally has faded from modern law, many eighteenth-century lawmakers and jurists considered it a necessary tool of effective government. Federalists argued that the law was necessary to secure the authority and stability of the government, which was tied to the reputation and character of its leaders, a view that found support in republican theory, and they used their control of the central government to suppress opposition by Republicans. They also pressured President John Adams to muster an army of 10,000 men to protect against a rumored invasion but also to back up Federalist policies with force against the real or perceived threat of domestic dissent. Jeffersonian Republicans were convinced, not without reason, that they were the real targets, citing as evidence the eager Federalist prosecutions of Republican newspaper editors, including a representative from Vermont, despite the First Amendment's guarantees of free speech and free press.

The Alien and Sedition Acts were an early test of the nation's commitment to republican principles—and an early test of federalism. It was an awkward moment because Jefferson was the sitting vice president. Open opposition would put him in direct conflict with the administration headed by his old friend, John Adams, and might result in his own prosecution under the law. Much more worrisome was the apparent Federalist plan to consolidate power in the national government—and, not incidentally, to destroy the Republicans—but under what authority could Republicans resist? Although vindication ultimately came at the ballot box when Jeffersonian Republicans won the national election of 1800, an appeal to the states offered more immediate shelter. Led secretly by Jefferson and his ally, James Madison, the state legislatures of Virginia and Kentucky adopted resolutions expounding a state-compact theory of federalism that, in a more extreme form, served decades later as justification for southern secession.

The Republicans emphasized the role of the states in forming the nation. The Kentucky Resolution of 1798, drafted by Jefferson, declared that the Constitution was a compact "to which the states are parties." Each state had "an equal right to judge for itself" whether actions taken by the central government were legal. Invoking this authority, the Resolution proclaimed the Alien and Sedition Acts unconstitutional, declaring them "unauthoritative, void, and of no force" within the state's boundaries. The Virginia Resolution, written by Madison, announced a doctrine known as interposition. States could stand between its citizens and the national government to block the enforcement of unconstitutional measures, reaching out to the other states for their assistance in resolving the controversy. States "have the right and are duty bound to interpose for arresting the progress of evil," he argued, and "for maintaining within their [boundaries] the authorities, rights, and liberties [belonging] to them." In the Kentucky Resolution of 1799, Jefferson took the final measure. The states formed the Constitution, and "being sovereign and independent, have the unquestionable right to judge of its infraction; and, *That a nullification, by those sovereignties, of all unauthorized acts done under color of that instrument, is the rightful remedy*" (emphasis in the original). Significantly, no other state embraced the standard Madison and Jefferson offered. But the protests of 1798 and 1799 had advanced three ideas—interposition, nullification, and the state compact theory of union—that ultimately proved to be a seedbed for disunion.[2]

The line of descent from the Resolutions' language of interposition and nullification to the fiery rhetoric and actions of southern secessionists (and much later to southern segregationists) is unmistakable, even though Jefferson and Madison never endorsed or desired disunion. Yet the argument for a state-based resistance was neither illogical nor unreasonable. In the 1790s federalism was a novel arrangement of power, and it was unclear which level of government, state or national, had final authority. A state-sovereignty posture seemed natural for a people in whom ideas of localism ran strong and deep.

Opposition to central authority also was part of the young nation's heritage, with state-sovereignty advocates making ominous analogies between Great Britain in the 1760s and the United States government in the late 1790s. Loyalty to the United States—and its new Constitution—was still new and feeble. In this environment it is not surprising that states jealously guarded their prerogatives. For example, when the U.S. Supreme Court in 1793 ruled against Georgia's claim of sovereign immunity in a case brought by a citizen of South Carolina (*Chisholm v. Georgia*), an action permitted under a broad reading of Article III, advocates of state sovereignty pushed for a new Eleventh Amendment, ratified in 1798, reversing the Court's decision and preserving the idea that state governments were immune to such suits.

The revolutionary idea that the people granted power to government, that they in fact held ultimate authority, made resistance to national authority on state-sovereignty grounds appear legitimate. Both state and federal constitutions acknowledged the sovereignty of the people, so logic suggested that the people could exercise their will legitimately in both forums. It also was unclear what recourse other than the states was available to protect liberty if the national government violated the Bill of Rights. Even the great proponent of national power, Alexander Hamilton, thought the people could turn to the protection of the states. In *Federalist No. 28*, he argued that state and national governments would check usurpations by the other: "If [the people's] rights are invaded by either, they can make use of the other as an instrument of redress." The idea that states could not act independently to protect the liberty of their citizens appears foreign only from a modern perspective.

Another circumstance made the state-sovereignty argument plausible. It was unclear what the framers intended. No good record of the debates in Philadelphia was publicly available; the official *Journal* first appeared in print in 1819 and James Madison's extensive *Notes* were not published until 1840, four years after his death. The Constitution itself embraced abstract concepts and principles—rights, sovereignty, representation, federalism—that raised a host of questions: Which rights? For whom? Who were the people? This last question begged another one: What was the relationship between popular sovereignty and the Union created by the Constitution? Had the people acted through the states or had they acted as a national people? The question seems arcane today only because the Civil War answered it definitively, but it was a matter of great consequence from the 1790s through the 1860s. If the Constitution was the result of the people acting nationally, then the reach of the central government was unlimited in the exercise of its delegated power, except as restrained by the Constitution, Bill of Rights, and other amendments. If it was the product of the people acting through the states, then state sovereignty remained as a check on national power.

In many ways, the constitutional arguments about such issues grew more abstract and more heated as the social and economic consequences of policies became more apparent. The result was a peculiarly American style of political debate: policy differences found expression as matters of great constitutional significance, with all political factions claiming faithfulness to the founders' original meaning. In no context was this result more apparent than that of federalism, a term never mentioned in the Constitution but only inferred from the arrangement and sorting of governmental powers between the general government and the states. This lack of clarity made it easier to elevate the state-sovereignty argument into a matter of constitutional principle, thereby giving it more traction and making political compromise more difficult.

Although logic and circumstance emboldened state-sovereignty advocates, most Americans did not accept interposition and nullification as appropriate responses to the dilemma of federalism. No other state endorsed these concepts in the late 1790s, even though both the Kentucky and Virginia legislatures reached out to the other states for support. Every northern state denounced the resolutions, with Rhode Island, deeming them fraught with "evil and fatal consequences." For Jefferson and Madison, the state compact theory made a virtue from necessity—faced with abuses of national power, retreat to the protection of the states was logical in a federal Union—but it also reflected a common assumption about the nature of the Union. Among the states, only Vermont insisted that the Union was formed by the people of the United States.

The inauguration of Thomas Jefferson as president in 1801 effectively settled the matter as politics—the Alien and Sedition Acts had expired by their own terms on the last day of John Adams's presidency—but not as a constitutional claim. Early in the new century, New England states resorted to notions of state sovereignty when confronting national actions with which they disagreed. The entanglement of foreign affairs with domestic concerns again intensified the arguments. In 1803 Jefferson accepted Napoleon's offer to sell the Louisiana Territory even though the Constitution granted no explicit power to purchase land. Jefferson long had opposed any notion of implied powers, but he allowed the acquisition of Louisiana to be settled by treaty, even though he questioned whether the Constitution authorized this means for the purchase of land. The Louisiana Purchase was a defensive act—it removed Napoleonic France from the nation's back door—but it also opened the western part of North America to expansion. This new territory allowed Jefferson to proclaim, in justification, that the United States was creating an empire of liberty, a way of providing enough land for the expansion of the nation's small, independent farmers, whose self-sufficiency he believed was necessary to resist wage-labor enslavement by northern industrialization.

The Louisiana Purchase did not suit New England Federalists, who otherwise supported an expansive reading of the Constitution. They worried that the new territory would drain population and political clout, as well as cheap labor, from their states. They also opposed the introduction of slavery into the newly acquired region. More immediately consequential was Jefferson's effort in his second term to keep the United States isolated from the Napoleonic Wars in Europe. He pushed Congress to enact the Embargo of 1807, a prohibition of Atlantic trade with enforcement resting on a bold, Hamiltonian assertion of centralized power. Now in a minority in the national government, New Englanders resorted to the state-sovereignty arguments that they had opposed a decade earlier. With the regional economy in tatters, they threatened secession, but the effort was stillborn and disappeared completely with the Embargo's repeal in March 1809.

State-sovereignty arguments came closer to fruition four years later. Regional opposition to the War of 1812 led to a gathering known as the Hartford Convention, sought by the Federalist remnant in New England and New York to consider how best to resist a foreign policy they believed was ruinous to their economic interests and their liberties. Talk of state power, interposition, and secession was common. Even the young Daniel Webster, who as senator from Massachusetts later became an ardent defender of national power, angrily adopted state-sovereignty rhetoric when confronted with a federal proposal to conscript state troops into the U.S. Army: "Where is it written in the Constitution. . . . ? It will be the solemn duty of the State Governments to protect their own authority . . . and to interpose between their citizens and arbitrary power," he thundered.[3] The compact theory of the union and ideas of state sovereignty had found a new home in the party and region that, twenty years earlier, had touted the virtues of an energetic, powerful national government.

News of Andrew Jackson's victory at the Battle of New Orleans in 1815 and the Treaty of Ghent drew the fangs of the Hartford Convention, which ultimately adopted a moderate stance; the war's end discredited state-sovereignty radicalism—and with it, the Federalist alliance. The brief-lived and misnamed Era of Good Feelings produced a burst of enthusiasm for national action, especially to address weaknesses revealed by the near-disastrous war with Great Britain. In the flush of prosperity following the economic dislocations of war, Congress quickly adopted a protective tariff and chartered a national bank. No one raised the concern for state authority that had so animated Jefferson two decades earlier, but the National Republicans, now the only party, were not cynics or charlatans when they embraced a program of constitutional nationalism. Their actions were pragmatic: a national emergency required national power. It was an early riff on a consistent theme in the history of American federalism.

Important support for national supremacy within the federal system came from the Supreme Court under the leadership of Chief Justice John Marshall. A Virginia Federalist who became the longest-serving chief justice in American history (1801–35), Marshall was an early supporter of the Constitutional Convention's remedies for problems encountered under the state-centered Confederation government. He shared the Federalists' belief in a strong general government, in the need to encourage economic development, and in the rights of property holders. He also sought a role for the judiciary as an equal branch of the federal government—and for the Supreme Court as the final arbiter of the Constitution, unless the people acted to amend it. In these goals he was supported by colleagues of like mind, most notably Joseph Story of Massachusetts, who became the youngest-ever justice when he joined the Court in 1811 at age thirty-two. The Marshall Court, more than any other, set the terms of federalism, with national supremacy over the states the hallmark of its jurisprudence.

One of Marshall's great challenges was creating a serviceable public law that blended constitutional principles and common law to suit the needs of a developing national economy. During his tenure, the nation experienced rapid economic growth, marked by a nascent shift from an agricultural to a manufacturing economy. Northern and southern interests began to diverge, with the South dominated by plantation agriculture and slave labor, the North by wage-based commerce and industry. Politics followed suit, with the Republicans fracturing into regional groupings, each with different views of the role of the central government in promoting and managing these changes. Complicating the problem was the emergence of a full-fledged state-sovereignty constitutionalism, designed to protect slavery and the class-oriented version of liberty it made possible. The cases before the Supreme Court inevitably reflected these political, economic, and cultural divisions, with disputes pitting state legislatures and state courts against national courts. It was within this context that Marshall fashioned his constitutional nationalism. It was the best remedy he knew to the nation's greatest threat, which he believed would not come from "the overwhelming power of the National Government, but by the resisting and counterbalancing powers of the State sovereignties."[4]

Questions of federalism appeared gradually and with increasing frequency before the Marshall Court, which at first was more concerned with establishing its authority as the interpreter of the Constitution. Not until 1819 did the Court tackle a case that posed this issue squarely, and it led to one of Marshall's greatest judicial opinions. After Congress approved its charter in 1816, the Second Bank of the United States set up a branch in Baltimore. Maryland then passed a tax on all banks operating within its borders that lacked a charter from the state legislature. James McCulloch, the branch president, refused to pay the tax. Maryland's highest court ruled that the Constitution did not grant the power to create a bank, but the U.S. Supreme Court overturned that decision on appeal.

In what remains the leading decision on the power of the national government, Marshall accepted Alexander Hamilton's formula (and his language) of implied powers in declaring that the necessary and proper clause allowed Congress to charter a bank: "Let the end be legitimate," he wrote in his opinion for a unanimous Court in *McCulloch v. Maryland* (1819), "let it be within the scope of the constitution, and all means which are appropriate, which are plainly adapted to that end, which are not prohibited, but consist with the letter and spirit of the constitution, are constitutional." Citing the supremacy clause, the Court also ruled that the state could not tax the bank's branches because "the power to tax is the power to destroy and may defeat and render useless the power to create."

Other decisions of the Marshall Court further expanded national power. In *Gibbons v. Ogden* (1824) Marshall wrote again for a unanimous Court, defining broad congressional power to regulate interstate commerce. Once more, the issue was a conflict between national and state power. New York had granted a monopoly license for all steam navigation within the state, which a ferry company operating a service from Manhattan to New Jersey used to block competition from a federally licensed ship. The state claimed sovereign authority to regulate trade within its boundaries, but Marshall declared that congressional authority to exercise its delegated powers was complete and unqualified. Any incompatible state laws had to give way. Three years later, in another decision, *Brown v. Maryland* (1827), Marshall held that a state could not use even its legitimate powers to promote public health and safety, so-called police powers, if they burdened interstate commerce, which was for Congress alone to regulate.

The commerce cases went directly to the question of federal-state conflict, but they were not the only instances in which the Marshall Court limited state sovereignty. In fact, it declared state laws unconstitutional on an average of one per year. The Court especially used the contract clause of Article I, Section 10 (forbidding states from enacting "law[s] impairing the obligation of contracts"), to restrain state legislatures. A stable national economy could not exist, the justices reasoned, if states could change the terms of contracts at their discretion or as voters demanded. But more was at stake for Marshall than economic growth. The national government represented the will of the people, he argued, and in the areas of its delegated powers, its authority was unrivaled. "America has chosen to be, in many respects, and to many purposes, a nation," Marshall wrote in *Cohens v. Virginia* (1821), in a case rejecting state sovereignty, "and for all these purposes her government is complete; to all these objects, it is competent. The people have declared, that in the exercise of all powers given for these objects, it is supreme."

Taken collectively, Marshall Court decisions enhanced the power of the national government to promote a national economy, but in fact state legislatures were more active and unbridled agents of political and economic change than was the national government. The early decades of the new nation were by no means a period of laissez-faire capitalism, with government and business occupying separate spheres. Government, by habit and design, kept its hands on the economy, promoting, subsidizing, and steering change. Legislatures issued charters, established monopolies, made grants of land and money to private interests, forgave debts, changed banking laws, and engaged in countless other acts to encourage rapid economic growth. Courts also used the law as an instrument of economic policy, favoring property in motion over property at rest. But these entrepreneurial policies came primarily from the states. Hamiltonian visions aside, the federal government did not engage in the large-scale economic promotion that characterized the states. The national road stands as an almost solitary example before the Civil War of a major, federally funded, economic development project (or internal improvement, to use the language of the period), whereas many states went bankrupt or heavily into debt subsidizing canals in the 1830s and railroads in later decades.

This economic promotion meant the debate over the nature of the federal union was not about what government did as much as which government did it. The nationalistic sentiment that followed the War of 1812 had collapsed during the depression of 1819, and hard-hit southern and western states turned against an expansive role for the central government. On a number of issues, the programs of constitutional nationalists such as Henry Clay of Kentucky, whose American Plan mirrored the earlier aggressive agenda of Alexander Hamilton, appeared to be antagonistic to the interests of these regions. Banking, debtor laws, internal improvements, ownership of Indian lands, westward expansion, and tariff policies all were matters on which sectional interests diverged sharply. The tariff, a national tax on imported goods, was the most explosive of these issues. Almost uniquely, it symbolized the threat that national power could pose not only to the South's economic interests but also to its peculiar institution, slavery, and to the way of life it supported. The controversy over the tariff set in motion a debate that, over time, raised questions about the meaning of liberty and whether state power could be used to protect and promote an institution that denied freedom.

In 1828 Congress passed a new tariff designed to protect American manufacturing by increasing the price of British finished goods, especially textiles. Southerners objected strenuously. This import tax, they protested, was unfair and benefited the manufacturing North at their expense. It raised the cost of manufactured goods, on which they were dependent, and it led to retaliation by the British, who reduced their purchase of cotton from southern planters. Also, tax revenues went to improve transportation in the North and West instead of the South, which already had many navigable rivers.

But the South's pivotal concern had to do with slavery. If the national government could adopt measures that otherwise threatened their economic well-being, what was to stop it from curtailing or abolishing slavery? The problem was not merely a threat to southern investments in human property. White southerners feared that the ending of slavery would leave them vulnerable to uncontrollable and vengeful freed blacks, a warning made early on by Thomas Jefferson in his widely read *Notes on the State of Virginia* (1787). A successful revolt in Haiti in 1800 and several notorious—and brutally suppressed—rebellions in the southern states heightened these fears and made southerners more insistent on denying the constitutionality of any governmental action that threatened their control over their slaves.

From 1828 to 1833 federalism was the grand motif in a riveting political battle, later known as the Nullification Crisis, that again set a president and vice president against each other—and with as much consequence as the late 1790s conflict between Vice President Thomas Jefferson and President John Adams. South Carolina enlisted its then-senator but soon-to-be vice president, John C. Calhoun, a former nationalist, to slay the tariff and, with it, the monster of national power. He secretly wrote a 35,000-word report, commonly known as the *Exposition and Protest*, that resurrected the doctrines of interposition and nullification and gave them new force. The tariff could be used solely to generate revenue, he contended, not to protect American industries from foreign competition. Not only was the tariff of 1828 unconstitutional on these grounds, but it also favored manufacturing over agriculture, a choice that Congress had no power to make. Under these conditions, a state, acting in a popularly elected convention, retained power to veto any act of the federal government that violated the Constitution. It was a provocative argument because Calhoun rested his case not solely on state sovereignty but on popular sovereignty as well. The states were not acting as states alone but as agents of the people.

Calhoun's claim reminds us of how often Americans appealed to the revolutionary tradition of popular sovereignty when dissenting from the actions of their government. In this sense, the Virginia and Kentucky Resolutions, the Hartford Convention, and the Nullification Crisis were all of a piece. Each conflict raised the question of how the people created the nation: Did the people act collectively as states to create the union or did they act as an undifferentiated national body? For slaveholders, the answer to these questions became progressively tilted toward an extreme version of state sovereignty.

In the ratification debates, Madison had noted three meanings of the term "states": individual state governments, the people within a state as the sovereign of that state, and the people of the nation who lived in geographic units known as states. When creating the Constitution, he argued, it was the people collectively who were sovereign; they also exercised their sovereignty in creating the separate state constitutions but in these instance their actions were limited to each state. Consistent with this position, the Virginia Resolution, which Madison wrote, did not claim state sovereignty to block the effect of an unconstitutional law; only the people acting as a whole had this power.

The Hartford Convention gave impetus to this understanding. In its first resolution, the delegates called on the five represented states to "adopt all such measures as may be necessary" to protect their citizens from acts unauthorized by the Constitution, in this instance a military draft.[5] Its *Report* also implied that a state legislature, the agent of the state's sovereign people, could frustrate the operation of a national law, a view that differed from Madison's earlier argument that this power belonged only to the people of the nation.

During the Nullification Crisis, South Carolina took the final step in this argument: a sovereign people operating within a state had the authority to nullify an unconstitutional law within the boundaries of that state, regardless of whether other states followed suit. It was a theory of the single-state veto, which took Jefferson's theory of nullification beyond an action of the collective states to a veto by one state. Significantly, Calhoun's theory of nullification also rested on a claim of popular sovereignty, except here the will of the people of a state trumped the will of a national people as expressed in the central government.

The sectional drama ended with the passage of a compromise tariff in 1833 but not until after President Andrew Jackson threatened to use federal troops to enforce national power. As events unfolded, it became clear that no other state was willing to stand with South Carolina. Jackson was characteristically blunt in his denunciation of the doctrine of nullification. It was "incompatible with the existence of the Union, contradicted expressly by the letter of the Constitution, unauthorized by its spirit, inconsistent with every principle on which it was founded, and destructive of the great object for which it was formed," he declared. "The Constitution . . . forms a government, not a league. . . . To say that any State may at pleasure secede from the Union is to say that the United States are not a nation."[6]

Jackson's position was unambiguous, but it also was limited. He was both a unionist and a champion of state sovereignty; he was not a constitutional nationalist in the lineage of John Marshall. He believed that the Constitution had established a permanent union based on popular sovereignty but the power of the national government was limited to its delegated powers, strictly construed. His veto of the 1832 bill to re-charter the national bank as unconstitutional captured his view. Heir to a Jeffersonian philosophy, he believed the national government had no authority to charter a bank, which he believed favored the wealthy and manufacturers, thereby undermining the agrarian society that promoted equality and fostered liberty. Unionism, states' rights, limited government, and entrepreneurial liberty: these tenets of Jacksonian democracy were well suited to the aggressive economic and political individualism that marked much of American society during the 1830s through the 1850s.

The post-Marshall Supreme Court, led by Roger B. Taney, once Jackson's attorney general and secretary of the treasury, was much friendlier to the exercise of state power than the Marshall Court had been. In a capital-scarce economy, the Marshall Court had used the contract clause to protect the interests of private investors against competition and state interference, even if a monopoly resulted, but the Taney Court (1836–64) saw the danger of allowing older forms of commerce and transportation to block progress. In *Charles River Bridge v. Warren Bridge* (1837), Taney's opinion for the Court agreed that public grants such as charters were contracts but they had to be interpreted narrowly and in the public's favor or they would impair innovation. If older companies were allowed to assert monopoly rights from public charters, the country would "be thrown back to the improvements of the last century, and obliged to stand still."

Here, the interests of states, capitalism, and constitutional law converged. State legislatures and courts had moved aggressively to use law as an instrument of economic development by promoting individual competition within a free market. They subsidized turnpikes, canals, and railroads and rushed to lessen the oversight and involvement of government. At the national level, the Taney Court relaxed the Marshall Court's assertion of exclusive federal control of interstate commerce. If the subject of commerce was more national, the justices decided in *Cooley v. Board of Wardens* (1851), federal power is exclusive even if Congress had not passed a law on the matter; if the subject was local in character, states could act on purely local matters until Congress passed a law inconsistent with the regulation.

At play was a new doctrine, dual federalism, which succeeded Marshall's constitutional nationalism. Dual federalism rejected state sovereignty but embraced the notion that each government, state and national, was supreme in its own sphere. Government at all levels had only a limited role, and between the two primary levels of government, a bright line existed. The Supreme Court served as an impartial referee, ensuring that competing state and central governments did not intrude into each other's sphere of authority.

This pragmatic rule worked reasonably well in economic matters; the nation's business was too dynamic and diverse for a small central bureaucracy to monitor, much less control. The Taney Court was relatively even-handed in its role as umpire, and dual federalism freed the states to promote economic development and advance democratic reforms. The opening of the trans-Mississippi west and rapid economic growth allowed the United States to blend Hamiltonian industrialization and Jeffersonian agrarianism. Political parties differed on the respective roles of state and national government—Democrats favored state action, Whigs pushed a national agenda—but a national consensus was clear: free-market capitalism, with its emphasis on individualism, equal access, and freedom of action, and its political equivalent, democracy and limited government, were the twin pillars of national progress.

In matters relating to slavery, the Court's role as referee did not work as well. When the Taney Court addressed rising sectional tensions over the peculiar institution, it found itself at odds with the public temper in the populous northern and western states. Plantation slavery rested on a denial of liberty and fostered a class society conflicting sharply with American values of freedom and equality. As the antebellum commitment to liberty became stronger, proslavery advocates became more entrenched and intransigent. By the 1850s they insisted on their right to expand slavery into the territories as a test of their liberty, specifically the liberty to own private property, including slaves. Their antislavery opponents rallied around a platform of free soil, free labor, and free men, insisting with equal force on keeping the territories free of slavery.

Above all, the issue of fugitive slaves—and the constitutional and legal obligation for northern states to return them, as provided under Article IV and congressional enabling statutes in 1793 and 1850—was the open, festering sore on the body politic. When the national mood finally turned against the proslavery position in the late 1850s, slaveholders again picked up the banner of extreme state sovereignty and nullification, with increasing threats to secede from the Union. The problem was never about money and power alone, although southern wealth was tied up in fixed assets of land and slaves, nor was it solely about the nature of the Union. It also was about race. Slavery was a system of social control and not simply a system of labor. Without it, white southerners feared their way of life would end in a cataclysm of black insurrection and violence.

Dual sovereignty could not provide the answer to the irreconcilable conflict of slavery and freedom, even though the Court in its role as referee vainly tried to make it so. Article IV required all states to "give full faith and credit" to the laws and decisions of the other states, and both northern and southern courts sought to use this principle of comity (reciprocity) to force acceptance of their positions on slavery. Feeling compelled to choose, a fractured Supreme Court settled on state sovereignty. By a 7–2 vote in *Dred Scott v. Sandford* (1857), with nine separate opinions, Taney and the other proslavery justices tried to remove the territorial question from politics by denying the federal government's authority to act, not even to allow people of the territories to decide the question of slavery on their own.

The majority opinion, written by Taney, sought to end the case by declaring that Dred Scott, as a slave, had no right to sue for his freedom in federal courts. He was not a citizen. Under the doctrine of dual federalism, national and state citizenship were separate and distinct, with national citizenship conferred on all residents at the time of ratification. No blacks qualified under this definition, their status as citizens in most northern states notwithstanding. Dred Scott could not bring a suit in a federal court; as a non-U.S. citizen, he had no rights the federal government must protect.

The Constitution did not define citizenship, so Taney could argue from its silence, but, writing only for himself, he went further. He sought to crush antislavery constitutionalism by denying federal authority over slavery: "the right of property in a slave is distinctly and expressly affirmed in the Constitution," he asserted, incorrectly. The Constitution in fact acknowledged slavery indirectly and did not contain any language explicitly to recognize or protect it. Yet Taney interpreted the Fifth Amendment's due process clause as a substantive protection for the property rights of slave owners, including the right to move their property, thus making it unconstitutional for Congress to restrain the spread of slavery in the territories.

For many northerners, the decision was wrong as a matter of law and morality, and it was politically unacceptable. The election of Abraham Lincoln as president in 1860 by a solidly united North and West promised to reverse the repulsive calculus of *Dred Scott*, but this result was one that the southern states, now committed to the defense of slavery by any means, could not accept. War came in large measure because federalism defined as dual sovereignty could not accommodate the nation's growing distaste for slavery.

The Union's victory in the Civil War settled the constitutional crisis over federalism by repudiating the compact theory of union, with its emphasis on state sovereignty and an implied ultimate right of secession. The war also redefined the national Union, first as Abraham Lincoln gave voice to a new meaning and then as the Reconstruction amendments fixed its terms. The United States was singular, not plural; it was a unified sovereign state, not a league of sovereign states. No state could withdraw from it. In his first inaugural address, Lincoln declared that common experience and common culture, as well as "the mystic chords of memory," unified Americans. They had existed as a national people since 1774, well before the Constitution, which was written "*to form a more perfect Union,*" words that Lincoln italicized for emphasis. The people created the Constitution directly, not through the states, and ultimately they, not the Supreme Court, fixed its interpretation; otherwise "the people will have ceased to be their own rulers."

Here was the essence of a new understanding of federalism, one that rested on popular sovereignty stemming not from a Lockean social contract or a compact among the states but from an indissoluble Union based on a common national culture. The national government, exercising the people's authority, represented the nation completely, and in doing so its power was complete and unrivaled. The wartime government soon gave evidence of this new meaning. It adopted measures heretofore considered unconstitutional, such as a draft and an income tax, but it also provided direct aid to the states through such measures as the Morrill Act of 1862 that established land-grant universities to promote the useful arts. More striking was the national government's unilateral recognition of a new state, West Virginia, carved in 1862 out of Confederate Virginia when residents of the state's western counties refused to secede from the Union and instead separated from Virginia.

Reconstruction of the Union—the political and constitutional challenge facing the American people after the Confederate surrender in 1865—provided the opportunity to make this new meaning of federalism a permanent part of the nation's fundamental law. The goal was to improve the Union, to make it more perfect, by removing the scourge of slavery and, in the process, to realize the promise of equality before the law. What it required was a redefinition of federalism to prevent states from denying liberty or rights to their citizens. The Reconstruction amendments accomplished this aim by abolishing slavery (Thirteenth Amendment, 1865), defining citizenship (Fourteenth Amendment, 1868), and expanding political participation to freedmen (Fifteenth Amendment, 1870).

The Fourteenth Amendment was especially important because it changed the traditional relationship of national and state governments by making clear the terms and meaning of citizenship, a subject the original Constitution did not address. Previously, Americans were citizens of their states and of the United States; these categories of citizenship were independent and exclusive. Most people looked primarily to their state constitutions for the expansion and protection of their rights, and few legal commentators thought that the national government had the authority to interfere with a state's administration of its own affairs. Even the constitutional obligation to guarantee a republican form of government (Article IV, Section 4) did not change this belief, as the Supreme Court had made clear in *Luther v. Borden* (1849) when it refused to become involved in an effort to overturn an anti-democratic Rhode Island constitution, judging the painful controversy a "political question" best left to the citizens of the states. But if the nation continued to embrace this understanding, then newly freed African Americans would be vulnerable to abuse, as in fact occurred in 1866 when reconstituted southern states passed the infamous "black codes" to deprive ex-slaves of most rights beyond their mere freedom from enslavement.

The Fourteenth Amendment addressed this problem by establishing national standards for citizenship. It made every person born in the United States both a citizen of the United States and of the state where he or she resides. The amendment also declared that "equal protection of the laws" and "due process of law" were guarantees for all citizens. For the first time, the national government was responsible for protecting the rights of citizens. But with few exceptions federal courts did not interpret the Fourteenth Amendment in this way, nor did they view it as changing significantly the system of dual sovereignty. In this regard, courts reflected public assumptions about federalism; most people looked first to state governments to protect their rights.

Congress reflected this understanding as well. Moderate Republicans, who controlled all three branches of the national government, did not intend for the Fourteenth Amendment to restructure federalism but to restore it. The reason was simple: the Civil War extended the meaning of liberty but it did not lessen the traditional concern over power. Even had the aim been otherwise, the federal bureaucracy was too small to provide effective oversight of the states. Rather, the architects of Reconstruction sought to increase political participation by granting blacks the right to vote (Fifteenth Amendment) and trusted that their participation would lead to state governments responsive to their demands for equal rights under the law. If the states could not or would not provide this guarantee, citizens could appeal to federal courts, with the federal government punishing state actions that violated the rights of their citizens.

At times, this assumption produced the anticipated result. In *Yick Wo v. Hopkins* (1886), for instance, the U.S. Supreme Court ruled that a California statute in practice denied Chinese laundrymen the equal protection promised by the Fourteenth Amendment even though the law as written was neutral. More common, however, was the Court's acceptance of local standards and state differences in the rights of citizens. The classic case occurred when butchers from New Orleans sought relief from a law requiring them to use a central slaughterhouse, alleging it deprived them of their right as citizens of the United States to work freely in their occupation. The justices, 5–4, rejected the claim and drew a sharp distinction between state rights and national rights. The Fourteenth Amendment protected only the more limited set of national rights. States could regulate the conditions of employment as part of their traditional power to protect and promote the health and welfare of their citizens (*Slaughterhouse Cases,* 1873), although in fact the U.S. Supreme Court later began to limit this authority, as Justice Stephen J. Field foretold in his dissenting opinion.

Subsequent decisions narrowed the set of national rights even further. The threshold standard was clear: states could not treat their citizens unequally, but even this criterion was interpreted strictly. When the Civil Rights Act of 1875 sought to block racial discrimination in public accommodations, the Court held that the Fourteenth Amendment protected individuals against the actions of state government, not against discrimination by private individuals (*The Civil Rights Cases*, 1883). The next year, in *Hurtado v. California* (1884), the justices ruled that indictment by a grand jury was not a right included in the Fourteenth Amendment's due process clause. The result affirmed the antebellum understanding that the Bill of Rights did not apply to the state governments (*Barron v. Baltimore*, 1833) and effectively limited the scope of rights that Congress could protect against state action. From such cases, it was a short step to *Plessy v. Ferguson* (1896), in which the Court held that state-mandated racial segregation of railroad cars did not violate the equal protection clause of the Fourteenth Amendment as long as the separate facilities provided were equal. The doctrine, known as "separate but equal," justified the widespread racial segregation and discrimination that finally ended as a matter of law in *Brown v. Board of Education* (1954).

Dual federalism remained alive for decades after Reconstruction but, except for individual rights, it began to fade by the twentieth century in response to the demands of an expansive and increasingly integrated national economy. The problems brought on by the rapid growth of monopolistic industry as well as by the emergence of a national market and the rise of big cities, transcended state borders. Reformers demanded expansion of government's power to regulate the marketplace, ensure fair competition, and promote equal opportunity. In response, states relied upon their traditional police powers to protect the health, safety, and welfare of their citizens. Northern and western states especially adopted progressive laws to regulate issues affecting labor, fair prices, public health, and urban housing, but these measures often proved inadequate because the problems were not local but national. Corporations evaded regulation by incorporating under the laws of the least restrictive states and by using their economic power to lobby against regulation. They also challenged state power in federal courts, where they found an increasingly receptive audience.

Toward the end of the nineteenth century, the Fourteenth Amendment took on new life as a check on the power of states to regulate economic activity.

States traditionally had used taxation, eminent domain, and police powers to spur economic development, and at first the Court upheld their broad authority in these areas. In the *Granger Cases* (1877), for example, the justices accepted regulation of prices charged by grain elevators as a legitimate use of a state's power to act in the public's interest. They soon changed their views. First, the Court defined corporations as persons under the Fourteenth Amendment, a new legal doctrine that gave these entities protection against arbitrary state action (*Santa Clara County v. Southern Pacific Railroad*, 1886). Then, in *Wabash, St. Louis & Pacific Railway Company v. Illinois* (1886), it invalidated an Illinois law fixing railroad rates as an improper regulation of interstate commerce. Congress responded the following year, 1887, with the creation of the Interstate Commerce Commission, a regulatory body charged with ensuring reasonable rates. The national government, first by judicial decision and then by statute, was beginning to assert its power to regulate the economy—and to deprive states of the ability to do so. Increasingly, dual federalism offered too uncertain a standard to be useful in charting an effective response to new economic conditions.

This situation could not last. Reformers charged that the wealth and power of monopolistic corporations threatened liberty. Ample evidence existed to prove their point. Muck-raking journalists and governmental commissions revealed widespread corruption in the form of bribery and vote buying, as well as the use of private police forces to stop union organizing and break up strikes. These corporate abuses made judicial restraints on state power more troublesome and they recast the traditional dynamic between power and liberty. Many voters became concerned that the power that most threatened liberty now came not from government but from corporations. This belief changed the debate about federalism. It was evident that the problems posed by corporate monopolies exceeded the ability of any single state or even groups of states to resolve. The only option was to increase national authority to control the abuse of private power. The Sixteenth Amendment (1913), which authorized a national income tax, helped to make this goal possible. With the revenues to create a strong national bureaucracy, the calculus of power began to change.

The twentieth century became a testing ground for how far the national government could go in the use of its countervailing authority. It was no idle exercise. Large questions were at stake: the Great Depression, two world wars, the Cold War, international terrorism, and global financial crises all produced demands for the national government to act and raised concerns about the effect of federal exercises of constitutional power on liberty. Did the national government have the power to interfere in the economy to whatever extent required to stave off financial collapse? Could it stay the hand of the market by limiting profits, setting wages, and mandating employment? How much power could the national government claim to maintain security? Could it move minority citizens against their will to ensure greater public safety? Could it mine personal data to spot criminal activity? The questions and concerns were real and urgent. They also were beyond the ability of the states to address.

Federalism did not disappear as an important constitutional principle—but it took a different form. World War I brought an unprecedented expansion of national power, which served as precedent when the collapse of laissez-faire capitalism in 1929 led to the nation's greatest economic crisis. A vigorous response by the administration of President Franklin Delano Roosevelt met initial resistance by a Court intent on preserving traditional restraints on national power, but by the mid-1930s the justices had retreated. The crisis left the Court little choice but to free national power to save capitalism. From the mid-point of the New Deal onward, few restraints existed on the ability of the federal government to regulate the economy.

Wickard v. Filburn (1942), an otherwise small case, was telling on this point. Roscoe Filburn was a farmer who argued that the wheat he raised for his personal use was beyond the power of the national government to regulate. The Supreme Court rejected the argument: if Filburn did not use his own wheat, the justices reasoned, he would have to buy it on the open market. The potential impact on commerce would not come from one small farmer but from the thousands of farmers in similar circumstances; collectively, their decisions would affect supply and demand significantly. In brief, the federal power under the commerce clause reached virtually all economic activity, a result that echoed John Marshall's constitutional nationalism in *Gibbons v. Ogden* over a century earlier. The Court affirmed its retreat by declaring the legislature, not the judiciary, the final arbiter of whether a law or regulation was reasonable.

Under the broad authority of the commerce clause, Congress had an almost unlimited field of action, with the ballot box the only check on its power. The result was a wide array of laws and regulations that defined activities as within the "stream of commerce" and therefore subject to national authority. In the Civil Rights Act of 1964, for example, Congress relied on the commerce clause rather than the equal protection clause of the Fourteenth Amendment to ban discrimination in public accommodations because Supreme Court opinions limited the meaning of the amendment designed for this purpose but accepted almost unlimited federal power over commerce.

Judicial acceptance of virtually unlimited congressional power to regulate anything Congress declared to be commerce marked a transformative point in the history of federalism. Or so it seemed until the Court under the leadership of Chief Justice William Rehnquist (1986–2005) revived the notion of state sovereignty as a limit on national power. A conservative jurist who became an associate justice in 1972 before being elevated to chief justice under President Ronald Reagan, Rehnquist initially advocated using the Tenth Amendment— "The powers not delegated to the United States . . . nor prohibited to it by the States, are reserved to the States respectively, or the people"—to limit the power of Congress. In 1976, he was part of a 5–4 majority that used this amendment to overturn an act of Congress based on the commerce clause for the first time since the late 1930s (*Usery v. National League of Cities*). But the Court abandoned this approach in 1985 by deciding that the structure of the federal government and the political process were sufficient to protect state interests (*Garcia v. San Antonio Metropolitan Transit Authority*), although Rehnquist in dissent served notice that the issue would arise again when new justices were appointed.

By 1992 four new justices were on the Court—Sandra Day O'Connor, Anthony M. Kennedy, Clarence Thomas, and Antonin Scalia—all appointed by conservative Republican presidents and all supporters, with Rehnquist, of what came to be termed the "new federalism," which critics claimed was nothing more than dual federalism under a different name. A series of cases revealed new limits on national power. In *United States v. Lopez* (1995), the Court restricted congressional use of the commerce clause as blanket authority in state-federal conflicts when it decided that regulation of handguns on school property was too far removed from the stream of commerce to limit the states' traditional authority in this area. Two years later, it ruled that Congress could not compel states to enforce a federal regulatory program, such as requiring local officials to conduct background checks on gun purchasers, because it was "fundamentally incompatible with our constitutional system of dual sovereignty" (*Printz v. United States*, 1997).

In both cases, as well as in a case striking down the Violence against Women Act (*United States v. Morrison*, 2000), the Court's majority refused to accept a congressional finding that the matter was within the stream of commerce; the evidence developed by Congress to support this claim, the justices decided, was inadequate to justify the intrusion on state sovereignty. Elsewhere, the justices also limited the reach of federal power to override the state immunity provisions of the Eleventh Amendment (*Alden v. Maine*, 1998) when they invalidated a provision of the national Fair Labor Standards Act that had permitted state employees to sue state governments for violations of its overtime-pay requirement.

Lopez and the cases that followed were small victories for advocates of states' rights; they did not reverse the trend toward greater national power, nor did they fundamentally restore state power or redefine post–New Deal federalism. In part, the Court was inconsistent in applying the new federalism. At the same time it accepted the claim of state sovereignty to limit national power, for example, the Court also invalidated a Colorado constitutional amendment barring local governments from enforcing anti-gay discrimination ordinances, upheld as constitutional a congressional statute mandating that employers provide leave time for family purposes, and, in *Bush v. Gore* (2000), intervened to override the Florida Supreme Court's orders for a recount of the state's presidential vote in 2000. In each instance, the majority set aside claims that these areas traditionally were reserved for state control.

A larger explanation for the limited reach of the new federalism, at least to date, is that the American people are divided about the proper extent of national authority. In many areas of modern life, dual federalism is impractical. Localism remains a core cultural value, but it means little in an economy where Wal-Mart standardizes brands and McDonald's franchises food. States have not clamored for change because they have come to rely on federal funds to solve the increasingly complex problems they face. Education, crime, economic development, immigration, public health, and a host of other issues have local expressions, but few people argue seriously that any state could tackle these issues alone. Moreover, the superpower politics of the 1950s through the 1980s and economic globalism thereafter persuaded Americans that only the national government has the scope of authority and the resources to address such large concerns.

The result is cooperative federalism, a twentieth-century trend, with the national and state governments working in partnership to weave together uniform guidelines, national funding, and local discretion to solve matters of government for a complex, highly diverse society. It is this form of federalism that produced the new water system for the small town of Atwood, Kansas, and similar projects for countless other local governments. The framers may not have foreseen this model of divided government, but the forces that produced it would not have surprised them. In *Federalist No. 34*, Alexander Hamilton predicted that the centralizing impact of war and economic crisis would restrict the power of the states to a "very narrow compass" while the demand for national solutions would prove "altogether unlimited."

In another area, individual liberties, the constitutional tide also ran against the states. Beginning in 1896, the Supreme Court extended the due process protection of the Fourteenth Amendment as a restriction on state action, first by redefining due process to mean a fair result and not simply fair procedures. Known as substantive due process, this approach found early expression in antebellum state courts as a protection against legislative interference with property rights. In his dissent in the *Slaughterhouse Cases*, Justice Stephen J. Field introduced it as a limit on state authority under the Fourteenth Amendment. He argued that the amendment's due process clause guaranteed an array of unnamed but inalienable liberties, including the right to engage in lawful pursuits, for instance, to practice an occupation, without unreasonable interference by the legislature, even when lawmakers invoked their legitimate police powers to protect public health and safety.

Under Field's standard, which gradually gained support from his fellow justices, judges, not legislators, would decide when a measure was unreasonable. Although federal courts first employed the guarantee to strike down state regulation of corporate monopolies as unreasonable, by the mid-1920s the Supreme Court had included the First Amendment rights of speech and press "among the fundamental personal rights protected by the due process clause of the Fourteenth Amendment" (*Gitlow v. New York*, 1925). Soon rights of the accused began to be incorporated as restraints against the states, as case after case revealed the states' too-casual concern for individual liberties, especially in matters involving African Americans, labor unions, and political dissenters.

This nationalization of the Bill of Rights became almost complete by the end of the 1960s, as the Court under the leadership of Chief Justice Earl Warren incorporated most of its provisions via the Fourteenth Amendment's due process clause. Many of the cases departed sharply from traditional American federalism and brought protests against activist judges who were subverting the Constitution. Politicians profited by promising to restore the states' right to control such matters as prayer in public schools, police procedures, and pornography, but later courts only trimmed, not reversed, the controversial decisions. Too many instances of injustice had caused citizens to look for protection from the national government rather than from their states; rights, they concluded, could not be dependent on accidents of geography. History had vindicated James Madison, who in 1789 had tried in vain to persuade the First Congress to extend the Bill of Rights to the states and not the national government alone because he feared state legislatures would not be able to resist a tyranny of the majority.

"States' rights" as a bulwark against federal authority no longer has the heft it once did, even though it surfaces occasionally, as in the modern "tea party" movement, especially in protests against the exercise of national power. A succession of southern governors sought to resurrect it during the 1950s and early 1960s to defeat desegregation, but their use of it was little more than political theater. When in 1963 George Wallace stood at the schoolhouse door to block racial integration of the University of Alabama, his administration was at the same time eagerly accepting federal funds for the interstate highway system. States were not powerless, however. They were represented equally in the Senate, which provided them with leverage to influence, impede, and, at times, block policies, as southern senators especially did when they delayed civil rights measures by filibuster and other legislative tactics. They deployed these tactics in an unworthy cause, but their use signaled an important shift in the practice of federalism. It finally had become a matter of ordinary politics.

Federalism as a matter for democratic politics will not end controversies over the proper allocation of power between national and state governments, just as cooperative federalism will not halt the further centralization of power. States will continue to have meaningful roles as incubators of new policies, including new experiments in liberty, in matters ranging from health and welfare to the definition of marriage and the use of otherwise illicit drugs for medical purposes. Federal courts will be sensitive to the policies and practices of the states in determining when a national consensus exists to justify a reinterpretation of law, as the Supreme Court does on a variety of issues from capital punishment and criminal process to educational policy. Congress cannot ignore the wishes of states because its members reflect state and local constituencies. In all of these ways and more, states will continue to matter. Americans will insist on this result not because of a constitutional doctrine but because we all live locally, and we remain uncomfortable as a matter of history and preference with government that lacks a local face.

Federalism has changed not because of fundamental shifts in doctrine but because the nation has changed. When transportation and economic markets assumed a national dimension, the meaning of federalism shifted. When the demand for equality became politically irresistible, Congress and the courts responded by vesting power in the national government to remedy inequalities fostered by state and local control. The national government's current role and power did not arise because of a statist philosophy imposed from above; rather, it grew in response to democratic choices and national, even global, challenges. Citizens demanded a national response to the problems of the elderly and poor and handicapped; they marched for national enforcement of civil rights laws; they lobbied for consumer and environmental protections; and they supported national science, education, and industrial policies vigorous enough to protect American leadership internationally. Advocates for an increased national role have come from both major parties, even when they disagree about what the central government should do.

Questions remain about whether national power is too great and whether it is time to restore authority to the states, but, in fact, states are neither powerless nor inconsequential. The governmental actions that affect citizens most directly remain under the control of states and localities. Experiments in social democracy often occur first in the states. In 2010 five states accepted same-sex marriage, for instance, even though the federal Defense of Marriage Act of 1996 recognized only unions involving a single male and a single female. The Massachusetts Health Care Reform Act of 2006 was a model for the national health insurance system, with its large role for the states, passed by Congress in 2010. States also have the power to grant new rights to their citizens, such as public education and individual dignity, two rights mentioned in several state constitutions but not in the Bill of Rights, which establishes only a floor, not a ceiling, for personal liberties.

The twenty-first century has witnessed renewed and vigorous debate over the proper allocation of authority between state and central governments. After the passage of the Patient Protection and Affordable Care Act of 2010, which established national standards for mandatory health insurance, attorneys general of twenty-seven states filed suit to have the law declared unconstitutional, in part because of their belief that it intruded improperly on state sovereignty. Fifteen states in 2010 permitted the sale and use of cannabis for medical purposes, even though it violates the ban by the federal Comprehensive Drug Abuse Prevention and Control Act of 1970 on the use of marijuana for any reason, including for medical treatments, which the Supreme Court upheld in

2005 (*Gonzales v. Raich*) as a valid exercise of the commerce power. Although the U.S. attorney general in 2009 chose not to prosecute the use of medical marijuana in states that permit it, the same decision may not apply should any state decide to make the sale of marijuana legal, which an unsuccessful 2010 referendum in California proposed to do. In another recent conflict between state and federal power, the state of Arizona enacted a law in 2010 to control illegal immigration, an action promptly challenged by the national government as a matter beyond the authority of states to address.

In these instances and others, as has so often been the case in American history, proponents of states' rights and local control can be found along the entire political spectrum. For some citizens, the scope of authority exercised by the central government threatens their liberties too much; for others, the policy choices made by the various states deny rights of minorities. This debate is the one constant in the changing meaning of federalism. As a nation, we continue to search for the right balance of power and liberty. The revolutionary mantra of divided power remains central to this search, as does the framers' bet that power vested in central government, with proper limits, furthers the growth of liberty. It is this original gamble that continues to give life to federalism itself.

5

Balance

"Tell 'em to read the Constitution. . . . The president has the power to keep the country from going to hell."[1] Such was President Harry S Truman's response to editorials condemning his seizure of the nation's steel mills on April 8, 1952, under an executive order. For the nation's thirty-third president, the case for taking control of the mills was clear. American troops were at war in Korea and the steel companies were threatening to shut down the mills rather than grant union demands for a wage increase. The mills were too essential to the war effort to allow them to close. It was a bold decision, but Truman did not doubt either the need for it or his power as chief executive and commander-in-chief to take an unprecedented action to defend the nation. His former attorney general, Tom C. Clark, who now sat on the Supreme Court, had assured him that the president had inherent authority to prevent paralysis of the nation's economy in a time of war. Other legal advisors agreed. So did Fred M. Vinson, chief justice of the United States, who regularly played poker with Truman and confidentially assured his friend that the president had legal grounds to seize the mills.

Reaction to Truman's order was swift and hostile. The seizure had produced a constitutional crisis, pundits agreed. Even friendly newspapers condemned the takeover as an abuse of power. For some people, the response was more visceral. The CEO of Inland Steel wrote later in his memoirs that he "felt physically ill. . . . [A]ll that I had believed in with respect to the balance of power in a republic was gone, all the safeguards conceived by our founding fathers for the preservation of our democracy, had suddenly been swept away. One man had coldly announced that his will was supreme, as Caesar had done, and Mussolini and Hitler." Although public opinion was more mixed—polls revealed a split largely along party lines—most legal commentators agreed that Truman's action raised major constitutional concerns. The president did not back down. Calling the outcry "a lot of hooey," Truman argued that "the President of the United States has very great inherent powers to meet great national emergencies." He cited Jefferson, Tyler, Polk, Lincoln, Andrew Johnson, and Franklin D. Roosevelt as presidents who had taken actions for which there had been no specific authority but which provided great benefit.[2]

The Supreme Court did not agree with Truman. Within a month the case was before the justices, who heard one of the nation's premier attorneys, John W. Davis, unsuccessful Democratic Party candidate for president in 1924, argue that the Democrat currently in the White House had exceeded his authority. The steel dispute was transitory, he cautioned, but the extent of executive power was not. The seventy-nine-year-old Davis concluded by citing Thomas Jefferson's words in the Kentucky Resolution of 1798: "In questions of power let no more be said of confidence in man but bind him down from mischief by the chains of the Constitution." Solicitor General Philip B. Perlman, presenting the president's case, claimed that "necessity, the vital necessity" of national defense justified Truman's action.

The justices were not persuaded. A majority, 6–3, invalidated the seizure of the steel mills. Justice Hugo L. Black, an appointee of Franklin D. Roosevelt, wrote the Court's opinion, hewing to the Constitution's strict and exact separation of powers: only Congress had the power to take possession of private property, not the president. In a concurring opinion, Justice William O. Douglas acknowledged the inefficiencies inherent in the system of checks and balances but warned what could happen if the Court ignored the constitutional framework of power: "Today a kindly President uses the power . . . to keep the steel furnaces in production. Yet tomorrow another President might use the same power to prevent a wage increase, to curb trade unionists, to regiment labor as oppressively as industry thinks it has been regimented by this seizure."

In *Youngstown Sheet & Tube v. Sawyer*, more commonly known as the *Steel Seizure Case*, the Court's decision to strike down an executive order undercut any claim that the separation-of-powers doctrine left each branch of government free to interpret the constitutionality of its own actions. It also reaffirmed the proposition that the president was not above the law. Equally important, it asserted the Supreme Court's right to be the final interpreter of the nation's foundational document, unless the people overturned a decision by amending the Constitution. The case became an important precedent. Its most visible effect came in the justices' unanimous decision in *United States v. Nixon* (1974), rejecting President Richard M. Nixon's argument that the Court could not review a president's claim of executive privilege, a decision that led to Nixon's resignation when transcripts of his tape-recorded conversations revealed that he had obstructed justice in the Watergate affair.

Yet as significant as *Youngstown* was in establishing the limits of executive authority, what is most striking about the decision was not its rejection of a presidential claim of power—even in the age of an imperial presidency, Truman's action seems extreme—but the difficulty the Court had in reaching its conclusion. The justices wrote seven opinions; only two embraced the limits on power voiced by Black and Douglas. Justice Felix Frankfurter was willing to accept as constitutional a "systematic, unbroken, executive practice" if Congress knew about it and never objected, whereas Justice Robert H. Jackson believed that the claim of inherent power was dangerous, as the experience of Nazi Germany demonstrated. For the three dissenting justices, two of them Truman appointees, the Constitution made a broad grant of executive power to defend the nation. Only a "messenger-boy concept of the Office," Chief Justice Vinson argued in his dissenting opinion, joined by Associate Justices Stanley Reed and Sherman Minton, would require the president to seek congressional approval for all his actions, regardless of the circumstances. The facts demonstrated that Truman was no dictator, so why deny him the authority to save the nation? For the dissenters, the Constitution did not impose a straitjacket on presidential power.

The division in the *Steel Seizure Case* was not unusual. From the beginning of the nation, Americans have agreed that power is dangerous to liberty, but they rarely have been of one mind when confronted with its use. No easy formula exists to identify when matters of power become problematic. Power in government historically has been what Americans have most feared, until the specter of concentrated corporate power, fears of an economic collapse, or threats to national security made the exercise of government authority appear both necessary and desirable. The issue assumes its starkest form when it becomes personified, and in those occasions we can see most clearly the nation's ambivalence. In recent history, Democrats have favored a vigorous presidency, cast in the mold of Franklin D. Roosevelt, at least until the party lost the White House in all but three elections from 1968 to 2008. Then they worried about too much power in the executive branch. Republicans, who since the New Deal had resisted an activist president, suddenly found bold assertions of executive power more acceptable when presidents from their party occupied the Oval Office.

The problem of power is the longest-lived issue in American constitutionalism. It was a central focus of the American Revolution; it became the critical problem of the Constitutional Convention; and it is a constant refrain in American politics. Two perennial questions govern debates on the subject: How much power can be trusted to government? What restraints on power are necessary to protect liberty? These questions framed the debates in Philadelphia in 1787, but they were not asked abstractly. Liberty depended upon order, which a strong central government could provide. But how would it do this without vesting too much power in imperfect men who, as events had demonstrated, might follow their own self-interests? How could the new central government have enough power to provide stability, energy, and direction to the young nation without threatening liberty?

Although the solutions offered in the Constitution embraced the demands of practical politics, they also reflected revolutionary principles. History and experience converged to suggest a guiding theme, the division of power, which popular sovereignty, or the people as ultimate authority, made possible. Federalism was one division of power; another was to separate and balance the powers of the central government among its branches.

The principle of separation and balance of powers stemmed from several sources but was popularized by the French theorist Montesquieu, who derived his scheme from a misinterpretation of the British constitution. The notion nevertheless inspired the framers, especially James Madison, who discovered in it another way to stymie the aggrandizement of power. Montesquieu's cautions about the dangers of legislative tyranny, in particular, resonated with those delegates who worried about excessive democracy as much as they did about an overweening executive: "Were the executive power not to have a right of restraining the encroachments of the legislative body," he warned, "the latter would become despotic; for as it might arrogate to itself what authority it pleased, it would soon destroy all the other powers."[3] Montesquieu's prescription for separating and balancing power had the benefit of curbing both legislative and executive threats to liberty.

A constitution, the celebrated American federal judge Learned Hand wrote in 1942, is "primarily an instrument to distribute political power."[4] The Constitution's apportionment of authority was much easier to conceptualize than to put into effect; achieving a balance of powers in fact was infinitely more difficult. The framers, recognizing this problem, did not believe that a bright line separated the branches of the central government. Montesquieu did not mean that "departments ought to have no partial agency in or control over the other," Madison wrote in *Federalist No. 47*, but that "the whole power of one department [should not be] exercised by the same hands which possess the whole power of another department." In fact, power exercised by the central government has played out in two spheres—the limits and purposes of national power and the roles and responsibilities of the various branches in exercising the government's authority.

These domains had a different narrative arc from that of federalism: no signal event defined and settled them, as the Civil War did for questions of national-state power. Instead, they unfolded in a continuing political drama. In a typically American pattern, each act mixed law and politics, with factions and parties claiming constitutional justification for advancing or, more often, opposing the use of power, a circumstance that made compromise and change more difficult to achieve. Complicating the narrative, each of the three branches, at various times, has made large declarations of power, and each in turn has experienced stinging rebuffs to those demands. By the mid-twentieth century the Supreme Court, as the *Steel Seizure Case* suggests, had seized the role of final arbiter of constitutional meaning. But this stance rarely has gone unchallenged, especially in matters on which the American public remains divided, as the recent unhappy histories of abortion, gun control, affirmative action, and any number of other controversial issues make clear.

Too much emphasis on the judiciary also obscures the demands for power in the other branches. The authority of the executive especially has undergone such expansion that commentators have fretted for decades, legitimately, about the rise of an imperial presidency. In earlier years, Congress appeared too dominant. No simple scheme explains the continual struggle over the nature, legitimacy, and locus of governmental power, but what is apparent is how much the issue remains alive in American culture. In this sense, the revolutionary fear of power and its proposed solution of balance has never died but instead has taken on new dress.

The Constitution makes a grant of power to the central government, but it is oddly constructed in its details. It devotes as much attention to what the government cannot do as it does to what it may do legitimately. Here, we see clearly the Philadelphia Convention's compromise over power: the new government had delegated powers only. It had dominion to act in some well-defined areas; in other areas, it had no explicit authority. Above all, the framers sought to create a nation by removing barriers imposed by the parochialism of the states. But nowhere did they allocate unlimited power to the central government; everywhere the Convention hedged what it granted. The seventeen specific grants of congressional power outlined in Article I, Section 8, are followed in Section 9 by eight clauses denying the power of Congress to act in certain areas; six of these clauses begin with the word "No." Section 10 follows the same negative formula, this time denying states the authority to exercise power in certain areas. The delegates had learned well from the crisis of the 1780s, and the document they crafted addressed the major problems of the Confederation era. They also learned the Revolution's central lesson: do not trust power. It was this lesson that the ratification process reinforced, as the subsequent Bill of Rights imposed even more restrictions.

Yet for all the document's careful delegation or denial of powers, the Constitution contains language that granted power more generally. Section 8 begins with an elastic clause, "Congress shall have Power to . . . provide for the common Defence and general Welfare of the United States," and it ends with a provision allowing Congress "To make all Laws which shall be necessary and proper for carrying into execution the foregoing Powers and all other Powers vested by the Constitution in the Government of the United States." Much of the expansion of national authority has occurred by reference to these general grants of power, and much of the resistance to national power has focused on efforts to interpret these words strictly.

A classic battle over constitutional interpretation took place soon after George Washington assumed office as the nation's first president. The vigorous debate between Alexander Hamilton and Thomas Jefferson over the meaning of the "necessary and proper" clause of Article I, Section 8—did it permit Congress to charter a national bank?—proved to be a dialectic that has framed many of the constitutional controversies in American history. Today this debate often centers on what is known as originalism, a relatively recent perspective that seeks to settle all constitutional questions by reference to the public meaning the text had at the time it was ratified. What did the average informed American think the Constitution meant in 1788? (A popular version of originalism focuses less on meaning and more on the intentions of the framers; for example, the 2010 *Pledge to America*, a campaign document prepared by Republicans in the U.S. House of Representatives, promised "to honor the Constitution as constructed by its framers and honor the original intent of those precepts.") Most notably associated with Supreme Court Justices Antonin Scalia and Clarence Thomas, originalism argues that judges have an obligation to reach a decision that reflects the meaning the document had for those who gave it authority because it is the only legitimate expression of popular sovereignty, the trump card in any constitutional matter. It also reflects a Jeffersonian insistence on strict construction intended to restrain federal judges, uniquely unelected officials, from writing their own views into the document.

An opposite view, often called the "living Constitution," is more Hamiltonian. Articulated most forcefully in recent decades by Justices William J. Brennan Jr. and Stephen Breyer, it argues that the founders were realists who expected the document to adapt to changes in society. Judges have an obligation to reach decisions in line with the values and principles of the Constitution. They are not free to substitute their own judgment on matters before them but rather are to weigh carefully what outcome is most consistent with the Constitution as ratified and amended. In this sense, the document's meaning evolves in a manner analogous to the common law—slowly and incrementally, using precedent (how previous judges had interpreted the law) to guide the application of constitutional values to new situations.

In many ways the debate is a futile one. Evidence from the Federal Convention is too limited—and from the ratification debates too contradictory—to provide convincing proof of a given reading of the Constitution. Even if these writings were unvarnished records of proceedings instead of arguments meant to persuade, problems exist with a bipolar framework that insists on either one view or the other. The debate in the 1790s between Hamilton and Jefferson and their followers reveals the difficulty in trying to reach a clear-cut decision. Not only did these two revolutionary leaders disagree by the interpretive standard of contemporary meaning, but if we were to surmise which was more likely to be right, it might logically be Hamilton, who was at both the Federal Convention and the New York ratifying convention, and not Jefferson, who was at his diplomatic post in France in 1787–88. For much of American history, however, at least until the New Deal, the accepted restraints on central power marked the triumph of Jefferson, not Hamilton.

Even this conclusion is complicated by Jefferson's radical view, expressed in a 1789 letter to James Madison, that constitutions were written for the living and required revision or rewriting by each generation. Madison, who was both

Jefferson's friend and a central figure in crafting the Constitution, shied from this stance. Madison valued the importance of constitutional tradition in shaping a shared culture and in providing a necessary stability to government; he also insisted that ties of obligation and indebtedness bind generations across generational lines, and thus that generations cannot be seen in grand isolation from their predecessors or successors. What has resulted from this contradictory lineage is a politics in which we argue about policy choices as if they were the constitutional principles themselves. We have embraced Madison rhetorically but often act as if we accept Jefferson's notion of generational change. In this sense, our emphasis on constitutional restraints on power exists, in part, because we are uncomfortable with our policy choices or remain too divided as a society to act decisively.

Every decade contains evidence of this debate over the limits and locus of power exercised by the national government, but several periods in American history reveal its dimensions more plainly than most—the Jacksonian Era (1829–37), the Progressive Era (1900–1920), the New Deal (1933–45), and the twenty-six-year span from Lyndon Johnson to Ronald Reagan (1963–89), a tumultuous and discordant time that still echoes loudly in modern constitutional politics. What distinguishes these periods is the sharpness of the lines drawn to define the extent of national power and the constitutional theories invoked to support policy choices. These years also were unusual in their attention to questions of individual liberty, which suggests how entangled questions of liberty and questions of power are in American constitutionalism. They were decades as well when the issue of which branch of government most suitably wielded power was intertwined with debate over the proper limits of power itself.

Matters of constitutional power most often focus on activities of the national government, and the general government, as it was often called early in the nation's history, appears weak before the Civil War. The modern administrative state already was emerging in Europe, and by its standards, the U.S. government was small and exercised limited responsibilities. It had fewer than three thousand employees spread across a vast nation, and, except for the postal service, it had little direct interaction with the citizenry. Much of the era's rhetoric suggested that nobody wanted or expected much from the general government, yet it was during the antebellum decades that a powerful national state emerged.

The national government was a government out of sight: it did not fit our modern conception of power administered from Washington, D.C., but it was active and vigorous nonetheless. Not only did it extend authority over the entire continent and add twenty-four new states but it also expanded the number of executive departments from three to six, created a Patent Office to spur innovation, subsidized the development of railroads, and distributed millions of acres of land. The central government asserted its supremacy over the states as well. We have accepted the notion of limited government advanced by President Andrew

Jackson and his followers in words that already were commonplace—"the government that governs best, governs least"—without examining whether, in fact, the nineteenth-century general government was as restrained in its exercise of power as this shibboleth suggests.

What hides this history is the nation's early politics. During the nation's first decades, Americans believed that centralized power posed the most serious threat to liberty, so any thrust toward a vigorous national government nearly always gave rise to partisan resistance, which often made the opposing party the dominant force in American public life. Hamilton's energetic nationalism led to no permanent increase in the general government's authority; in fact, Federalist excesses in prosecuting the retributive Alien and Sedition Acts reinforced Republican demands for limits on power at the center. A few years later, President Jefferson interpreted the treaty-making power liberally to permit the purchase of the Louisiana Territory and asserted broad authority under the Embargo Act of 1807. But these actions did not recast executive power, just as the national schemes of the Era of Good Feelings did not inaugurate a lasting expansion of federal authority but foundered on the shoals of localism and regional interests. Even the strong nationalism of the Marshall Court was moderated by the Taney Court's more accommodating stance toward state-sovereignty arguments. In this arena, as in others, what was feared was often more consequential than what occurred. The one exception was the division of power between central and state governments. It was this axis of power, starkly cast as a referendum on the nature of the Union, that occupied national debate, in large measure because population growth and territorial expansion continually pushed it to center stage.

The limits and purposes of delegated national power and the roles and responsibilities of the three branches of government underwent significant changes in the antebellum years as well, but the consequences were less apparent immediately. Part of the reason is that the primary claim to power remained with Congress throughout the nineteenth century. It was, in fact, the most representative of the branches under a republican constitution based explicitly on representation. Even so, the Supreme Court and the president early on claimed authority equal to Congress by seizing opportunities to define their own constitutional powers.

The first instance revolves around a seminal case in American history, *Marbury v. Madison* (1803), which confirmed the principle of judicial review. The Articles of Confederation made no provision for a national judiciary, and the Constitution remedied this omission only in the barest language, leaving the first Congress to flesh out Article III by creating a court structure. The resulting Judiciary Act of 1789 is one of the most significant measures ever passed by Congress. It essentially carried on the work of the Constitutional Convention and established a three-tiered hierarchical federal court system—district courts in each state that served as special trial courts for customs cases, circuit courts that were the main federal trial courts, and the Supreme Court as the appellate court of last resort. (The current structure, in which district courts became the main federal trial courts, did not emerge until the Judiciary Acts of 1891 and 1925.)

Like the Constitution, the Judiciary Act of 1789 was a compromise. Federalists wanted courts strong enough to impose a uniform national law as a necessary foundation for a stable and orderly commercial and financial system. Advocates of state and local power viewed federal courts as a threat to the sovereign rights of states and to individual liberty, notwithstanding Alexander Hamilton's argument in *Federalist No. 78* that the judiciary would be "the least dangerous branch" because it controlled neither the sword nor the purse. Section 25 of the 1789 statute offered an important concession to calm this fear: state courts initially would hear so-called federal questions, or cases arising under the laws and treaties of the United States. Federal courts would become involved only after the highest state court had ruled.

The power to declare a state law unconstitutional already had been decided; in *Ware v. Hylton* (1796), the Supreme Court voided a Virginia statute conflicting with the Treaty of Paris of 1783, which ended the War for Independence. Left unclear, however, was the extent to which the Court could review the acts of Congress and determine their constitutionality. In *Hylton v. United States*, also decided in 1796, the Court upheld a federal tax on carriages against constitutional challenge, implying that the justices could also strike down a federal statute it deemed to be unconstitutional, but in the first decade under the new Constitution this assumption remained untested.

Marbury v. Madison provided an opportunity to address this question. The Judiciary Act of 1801, passed in the last months of the Adams administration by a lame-duck Federalist Congress, had expanded the authority and scope of federal jurisdiction. It had created a new set of district courts as general trial courts, transformed the circuit courts to appellate courts, established various justices of the peace for the District of Columbia, and, not insignificantly, made possible the appointment of many Federalists to these new judicial offices. But in the rushed final days of the Adams presidency, then-Secretary of State John Marshall failed to deliver judicial commissions to four new justices of the peace for the District of Columbia, in part because Adams had also named Marshall as chief justice.

After the electoral triumph of Republicans in 1800, Congress repealed the 1801 act, abolished the various judicial offices it created, and reestablished the previous federal court system. One of the newly appointed justices of the peace affected by the repeal, William Marbury, filed suit in the Supreme Court to compel the new secretary of state, James Madison, to deliver his judicial commission. The case seemed to offer Marshall a no-win situation. If he ordered Madison to deliver the commission and Madison refused, Marshall was powerless to enforce his decision; if Marshall admitted that he could not compel

Madison to deliver the commission, he would acknowledge his (and the Court's) lack of power.

In the first case in which he delivered the sole opinion of the Court, Chief Justice Marshall found a solution to his dilemma. It was a Delphic answer: Marbury had a right to the commission, but the justices had no authority to compel Madison to deliver it because the statute on which Marbury had relied was unconstitutional. The Constitution granted the Court original jurisdiction in certain matters only—all other cases had to come to it on appeal—and the Judiciary Act of 1789 seemingly had extended this authority beyond the limits of the Constitution. Given the conflict between the statute and the Constitution, the Court had no choice but to vindicate the Constitution and strike down the statute. Marshall's politically shrewd decision established the principle of judicial review of congressional acts and also protected the Court from partisan backlash.

The importance of *Marbury* was institutional and structural: it gave life to the framers' design and confirmed the Court's role as a separate but equal branch of the central government. The power to declare a law unconstitutional was not an obvious judicial function—under English practice, for instance, courts then and now could interpret a law of Parliament but not overrule it— but doing so unleashed the Court's potential to develop a uniform national law by vindicating the supremacy of the Constitution. Even so, a judicial override of federal law was more posture than practice throughout the antebellum years. In only one other case, the infamous *Dred Scott v. Sandford* (1857), did the pre–Civil War Supreme Court declare an act of Congress unconstitutional. For much of the nineteenth century, the justices engaged in a long and tedious process of elaborating federal law, especially in commerce and contract, two areas in which the Constitution's grant of power was unambiguous and in which the demands from business were most insistent. The Marshall Court, led both by the chief justice and the equally capable associate justice, Joseph Story, a fellow nationalist, set the tone with a series of decisions that restricted the states' ability to interfere with the development of a national market in which goods and capital flowed freely.

Two cases in 1819, *McCulloch v. Maryland* (forbidding states from taxing entities of the national government) and *Dartmouth College v. Woodward* (forbidding states from interfering with the sanctity of contracts), and a third in 1824, *Gibbons v. Ogden* (1824, forbidding states from regulating interstate commerce), are only a few of the better-known instances among many in which the justices laid the foundations for the development of a national economy. This development continued with the Taney Court. Led by Chief Justice Roger B. Taney, the Court faced a new capitalist order that sought to spur innovation and create wealth by destroying outdated forms of enterprise. Its challenge was how to make the law both flexible and predictable in the midst of great change. Its answer came in the 1837 case of *Charles River Bridge v. Warren Bridge* (construing grants of monopoly strictly in the public interest), which made clear that the Court would not let laws protecting property, heretofore a guardian of established wealth, stand in the way of economic progress.

These decisions were not part of a grand design, but through them the Court steadily expanded its jurisdiction. In a diverse and partisan republic, a stable legislative consensus was not always possible, so courts provided ballast by taking on questions that Congress could not resolve. A French visitor, Alexis de Tocqueville, remarked on this practice in his *Democracy in America* (1835–40): "there is hardly a political question in the United States," he wrote, "which does not sooner or later turn into a judicial one."[5] Antebellum lawyers and the business community fostered acceptance of an active role for courts by their demands for a uniform commercial law: a national market demanded national law. Congress could not satisfy this need because of competing political and sectional interests, but the Court tackled it in decisions such as *Swift v. Tyson* (1842), which affirmed the federal judiciary's authority to develop a federal common law of commerce. Justice Story, in his other identity as Dane Professor of Law at the Harvard Law School, especially fostered this evolution by turning out a series of learned and exhaustive commentaries on the full scope of commercial law, as well as an authoritative set of *Commentaries on the Constitution of the United States*. By contrast, the justices had early rejected the notion of a federal criminal common law as conflicting with republican principles—and because no national need could be served by usurping a traditionally local function (*U.S. v. Hudson*, 1812).

The Court's opinions also provided the framework within which Congress and state legislatures responded to new forms of corporate capitalism by applying the commerce clause to promote state licensing agreements and regulatory measures. It recognized regional differences by affording state courts and legislatures great leeway to structure laws affecting the economy, especially in labor law and the laws affecting debtors and creditors. The needs for cheap labor and easy credit were too great and too diverse to be satisfied by a single uniform national policy. In all these areas, the Court assumed power because Congress, divided by separate regional interests, found it expedient to leave difficult matters of public policy to the legal rather than the political realm, a circumstance that finally invited the justices to address the question of slavery in the territories, with disastrous consequences.

The Civil War and Reconstruction greatly expanded the size and scope of national authority. Except for President Lincoln's wartime actions, it was a period of congressional dominance, until corruption and incompetence eroded public trust in elected federal senators and representatives. Without a tradition of a strong presidency—and with a succession of weak incumbents—the Court filled the vacuum of power, establishing its role as the preeminent branch of the general government for the last three decades of the nineteenth century.

The justices were especially active in reconstituting market relations to accommodate the rise of corporate capitalism, even when that effort meant recasting congressional statutes. For example, they sharply limited the terms of the Interstate Commerce Act of 1887 and the Sherman Anti-Trust Act of 1890, which Congress passed in response to popular demands that the federal government restrain market inequities and dislocations caused by monopolistic railroads and industrial corporations. By 1891, the Court also had persuaded Congress to give it the power to choose which cases to accept; some cases still reached it by appeal as of right, but others had to await a vote of the justices to grant review by issuing what was known as a *writ of certiorari.*

This process reflected an implicit accommodation with Congress—the Senate was especially eager to promote the interests of big business—and served to enhance even more the judiciary's role in economic matters. Regardless of whether the aim of the pro-business Court was to restrain the power of the central government or, as some scholars claim, to protect the power of the states to regulate manufacturing, the effect was the same: the federal government had limited authority to halt the dramatic concentration of wealth that occurred in the late nineteenth and early twentieth centuries. Not until the mid-1930s, with unfettered capitalism in retreat everywhere, did the Court relinquish its check on Congress by dropping its opposition to the New Deal, thus opening the way for a vast expansion of federal power to regulate the economy.

As political pressure for a national response to financial collapse shifted the constitutional balance of power in economic matters from the Court to Congress and the executive, that balance moved toward the justices on matters of individual rights. Beginning in the 1920s and with a great rush in the 1950s and 1960s, the Supreme Court extended the protections of the federal Bill of Rights to the states by "incorporating" its various guarantees, one after another, by means of the due process clause of the Fourteenth Amendment.

The Court found encouragement for this role, as well as for its earlier protection of economic liberty, in a new way of thinking about law and the role of judges. In a series of lectures in 1881, Oliver Wendell Holmes Jr., then a prominent Boston attorney with scholarly leanings, argued that "the life of the law has not been logic but experience." By this, he meant that social and economic change—"the felt necessities of the time"—influenced the ways that we interpret the law; reaching the right decision in a case was not simply a matter of reasoning from abstract principles but also recognizing how to apply the law to changing circumstances. Advocates of legal philosophies known as "sociological jurisprudence" and "legal realism" argued that judges had to look beyond legal rules, including precedent, to understand how the law would work in the world outside the courtroom. In this view, courts had a responsibility to keep law abreast of the times. This new understanding of law and courts was instrumental in strengthening protection for individual rights in the twentieth century.

The federal judiciary came under sharp attack in promoting economic consolidation in the nineteenth century and in nationalizing rights in the twentieth. Critics raised serious questions about the role of unelected lifetime appointees to set policy in a representative democracy. "Judicial activism" was the label that opponents slapped on unpopular decisions of whatever stripe. Progressives challenged the pro-corporate judgments of the 1890s with as much fervor as segregationists later resisted *Brown v. Board of Education* (1954) or law-and-order types condemned *Miranda v. Arizona* (1966), which required the police to inform a person in their custody about his or her rights. Judicial philosophy became a touchstone for supporters and opponents in Senate confirmation of federal court appointees. Liberals and conservatives both identified fidelity to the law and Constitution as the sole criterion of a candidate's fitness for judicial office, even though one senator's standard of faithfulness was another senator's proof of betrayal.

The debate was important, but in some ways it was beside the point. The Civil War and Reconstruction had brought about a sharp increase in federal power, with national citizenship, a national bank, a national draft, a national income tax, national monetary controls, and a national welfare and educational bureaucracy for former slaves. Many of these measures did not survive the immediate post-Reconstruction years, but the need for them (or equivalent measures) remained—indeed, many of them reappeared in various forms later—because the nation had undergone, and would continue to experience, dramatic economic and demographic growth.

With Congress sharply divided in its politics and the presidency held by men of limited vision, the federal judiciary became a logical forum for resolving many of the issues related to the development of a new American state suited to the demands of a dynamic industrial economy and an increasingly diverse population. Would giant corporations be dismantled in the name of local control or would the power of the national government grow to balance this new form of power? Would regulation of nation-spanning industries (or, later, globe-spanning corporations) be carried out through some sort of new administrative agencies or would this power remain with the courts? Did the Constitution permit such an expansion of the state or did it restrain the size and function of government? Who would be the appropriate guide: Hamilton or Jefferson?

At times by default, at times by the implicit consent of the other branches, and at other times because the questions were posed as legal not political issues, the federal judiciary interpreted the Constitution in ways that buttressed and extended the modern regulatory and welfare state. It is difficult to know how the framers envisioned the balance of powers in practice but what emerged was not contrary to their understanding of the document they crafted. When urged by the president, Congress addressed the leading issues of the day—the creation of a host of regulatory agencies, a new governmental form, is itself evidence of an active legislature—but more frequently both presidents and Congresses deferred to judges on the most hotly contested problems. What this meant, in fact, was a court-sanctioned, often court-led, incremental redrawing of social and political boundaries, many of which were left to private litigants who pressed their claims and not, as happened in Europe, to public agencies.

The founders had feared rapid change and too much democracy, and the emergence of a judiciary sufficiently strong to balance the other branches made real the system of checks and balances they hoped would allow progress—but not too much or too soon. For reformers, then and now, the pace of change was too slow, the need for agreement among all three branches of government too much an impediment to necessary change. It was a complaint that Supreme Court Justice Louis Brandeis rejected by reminding impatient citizens what was at stake: "the doctrine of separation of powers was adopted not to promote efficiency," he noted in his dissent in *Myers v. United States* (1926), "but to preclude the exercise of arbitrary power."

The Supreme Court increasingly claimed the power to say what the Constitution means, and in one instance, *Cooper v. Aaron* (the 1958 Little Rock desegregation decision), the justices unanimously declared that their decisions were the "supreme law of the land," a distinction the Constitution reserves for itself and for the "laws and treaties of the United States." In large measure, this assertion in *Cooper v. Aaron* was no exaggeration because the Court is the most independent and least-checked branch under the Constitution. It can and does act in ways that would be impossible legislatively, as when, in recognizing a constitutionally protected right of privacy, it removed virtually all existing restraints on abortion in *Roe v. Wade* (1973). Two circumstances bear witness to the Court's unique position: no justice has ever been removed from office by impeachment, and only four of its constitutional decisions have been overturned by amendments—XI (1798) overturned *Chisholm v. Georgia* (1793); XIII (1865) and XIV (1868), *Dred Scott v. Sandford* (1857); XVI (1913), *Pollock v. Farmers' Loan and Trust* (1895), and XXVI (1971), *Oregon v. Mitchell* (1971).

But these facts also are misleading. The Court's use of its power of review has rarely gone unchallenged by the Congress and president. The tug-of-war between these two latter branches of government often has been more significant in developing the axes of national power than decisions from the nation's highest bench. This struggle resulted in an executive power much more vigorous and a legislative power both more democratic and, at times, more conservative than the framers believed they were constructing.

The Constitution enumerates the powers of Congress explicitly; it is much less exact in describing presidential authority. The Philadelphia delegates (and even some Anti-Federalists) agreed on the need for a single executive, but their experience with monarchy before 1776 convinced them to proceed cautiously in defining the office. The title itself, president, was a neutral designation: it was a familiar term (used by social clubs more than governments, as John Adams complained), merely indicating, from the Latin, someone who sat in front of or at the head of a body. Although its traditional use in 1787 might suggest passivity, the new constitutional office was not ceremonial. The balance-of-powers doctrine required an executive strong enough to restrain the legislature, as well as someone to convey the strength of the nation without threatening its republican foundations. Someone like George Washington, the indispensable man of the Revolution, whom scholars agree was the model for the office. Delegates were confident they could trust him to give proper substance to the two broad roles outlined in the Constitution—administer the government and conduct foreign affairs—and the specific powers assigned to them, the most important of which were the powers of appointment and veto and the role as commander-in-chief of the nation's military. In brief, the presidency outlined in the Constitution emerged in the shadow of two Georges—the model Americans wanted, George Washington, and the one they feared, King George III.

Left unanswered in the Convention and ratification debates was whether the initial sentence of Article II made an even more general grant of power to the president: "The executive Power shall be vested in a President of the United States of America." By contrast, the language of Article I granting legislative power is precise: "All legislative Powers *herein granted* shall be vested in the Congress of the United States" (emphasis added). Other provisions of the Constitution suggested some intermixing of roles: the president was the commander-in-chief, but Congress established "Rules for the government and regulation" of the military, with similar authority under the necessary and proper clause to set the terms of power for all departments of government. The meaning of the vesting clause has been the source of much debate over the intervening two centuries: Does it give the president inherent, unilateral power to protect the safety and well-being of the nation? It was this question that was at the heart of the *Steel Seizure Case* in the 1950s and at the center of the policies of President George W. Bush following the terrorist attacks of September 11, 2001.

The working relationship between Congress and the executive began with uneasy efforts to establish proper boundaries. The First Congress spent days debating what to call this new office, rejecting "Your Elective Highness" and other monarchical forms of address in favor of the simple "Mr. President." George Washington, always alert to the precedents that he would set, read straightforwardly the words of the Constitution to secure the advice and consent of the Senate in making appointments and dutifully appeared before the upper chamber, much to the embarrassment of both parties. It was a practice he soon abandoned. Despite this initial awkwardness, Washington set the tone for future holders of the office: he intuitively understood that a single national executive had two functions, that were administrative and ceremonial. His aim, as he noted in his Farewell Address, was to build loyalty to the office, not the man, a necessary stance in a nation moving from monarchical to republican forms of government. He embraced republican simplicity, demanded respect for the president, adhered scrupulously to constitutional principles, and limited his tenure to two terms.

The latter precedent was so powerful that it lasted until the presidential election of 1940, when Franklin Delano Roosevelt defied tradition by seeking and winning a third term of office, and a fourth in 1944, dying in office in the spring of 1945. (The Twenty-second Amendment, ratified in 1951, limited the president to two full elected terms, in part as a vengeful Republican slap at Roosevelt's memory but also in recognition that the demands of the office were too grueling to warrant a longer tenure.) Washington also acted vigorously in both domestic and foreign matters. He provided Hamilton the support for his bold economic plan; unilaterally declared American neutrality in the conflict between Great Britain and France; suppressed the Whiskey Rebellion, a populist revolt against federal excise taxes on liquor; and secured approval of the controversial Jay's Treaty. But for all the energy he manifested, Washington deferred to the actions of Congress as the most representative branch of government, accepting its judgment on legislation unless he believed it clearly violated the Constitution. Here, too, he set a precedent that lasted for a generation.

The language of the Constitution permits either an active or passive executive. A sufficiently vigorous president can overcome the various checks and balances of the document without violating its design of limited power; likewise, executive restraint often results in congressional government or an activist judiciary. At first, the presidency largely conformed to the scheme laid out by the framers, captured neatly in the shorthand phase taught in all civics classes, "The president proposes and the Congress disposes." Washington and John Adams would call matters to the attention of Congress but did not think it proper to propose legislation. Jefferson asked for specific laws because he believed the president "could command a view of the whole ground" better than Congress, and he used party discipline, especially the caucus, to achieve his ends. Still, he, too, deferred to Congress and did not act outside of its approval. For example, he exerted power to an unusual degree in the Embargo of 1807 but he did so by authority of a law enacted by Congress at his suggestion. Madison also took strong, if unsuccessful, measures to avoid the War of 1812, yet he always sought congressional approval and never exceeded his constitutional mandate in foreign affairs. Early presidents expanded the federal bureaucracy, thereby creating a base of power because most officers were executive appointments, but in this matter, as in their deference to Congress as the law-making body, the separation-of-powers principle suffered little, if any, erosion.

The same cannot be said for Andrew Jackson, the seventh president, who, on several occasions, asserted new powers for the office, making it into what we recognize as the modern presidency. He was the hero on horseback, the victorious general of the Battle of New Orleans, the final battle in the War of 1812, and he symbolized the emergence of a new democratic order based on individualism and market capitalism. Imbued with a strong sense of the rightness of his actions, Jackson identified the presidency with himself and demanded loyalty from his Democratic Party and his subordinates in the executive branch.

It was in his role as political actor that Old Hickory (the nickname bestowed by ardent supporters to symbolize his strength and rectitude) first reconceptualized the presidency. He enlarged its roles to three by adding head of party to the functions of ceremonial head of state and executive head of government. Jefferson had been an active party leader, but Jackson far surpassed him in the use of patronage to control the federal bureaucracy, which he expanded greatly during his two terms. Unlike his predecessors, Jackson made political operatives part of his inner core of advisors, the famed Kitchen Cabinet that rivaled the executive Cabinet composed of the department secretaries.

Jackson also defended his right to remove executive officers at his discretion, even though the Senate had confirmed them under its constitutional right to advice and consent, a decision made by the First Congress in 1789 in creating the executive departments. (Years later, in *Myers v. United States*, 1926, the Supreme Court upheld the president's power to remove executive branch subordinates without senatorial consent.) Jackson's control of patronage and the efficiency of his political machine allowed him to make a bold claim: the president, he argued, was the only office that represented the nation as a whole. Congressmen served more limited constituencies, either legislative districts (in the House) or states (in the Senate), but the president was elected by the people at large, a position strengthened by the adoption throughout the states of universal white adult male suffrage in the 1820s, thereby setting aside previous qualifications based on property or income.

The role of president as sole national leader allowed Jackson to reshape executive power in yet another way, by using the veto as a legislative weapon instead of a constitutional one only. Previous presidents had vetoed legislation sparingly and always with the belief that Congress had exceeded its constitutional authority when it passed the law. Jackson followed this course early in his first term when he rejected an appropriation to build a road in Maysville, Kentucky, identifying the building of such roads as a state responsibility. But when opponents passed a re-charter bill for the Second Bank of the United States in an effort to spoil his reelection bid in 1832, Jackson vetoed it. The measure was not only unconstitutional, he argued, it was unwise: it was "incompatible with the Constitution *and sound policy*" (emphasis added).

Jackson asserted as well a departmental theory of constitutional interpretation, borrowed from Jefferson, in which each branch of government had an equal responsibility to judge constitutionality for itself: "The opinion of the judges has no more authority over Congress than the opinion of Congress has over the judges, and on that point the President is independent of both," he insisted. Jackson never went so far as to defy the Court—despite popular legend to the contrary, he never said of the Court's decision in *Worchester v. Georgia* (1832), "John Marshall has made his decision, now let him enforce it"—and his view was not different from those of his predecessors, except by degree. But in combining his departmental theory of constitutional interpretation with his innovative use of the veto, Jackson inserted the executive branch into the legislative process in a way not envisioned by the framers. Congress now had to consult the president on matters before it, a shift in the constitutional dynamic that previously went in the other direction. Today, presidents are deeply involved in the legislative process, often drafting laws to send to Congress, negotiating directly with members, and organizing their party in support. The path to this modern role, although not direct, began with Jackson.

Jackson's striking redefinition of the presidency stirred great political opposition. A new Whig Party, its name recalling earlier English opponents of royal power, united several groups under cries that "King Andrew I" had subverted the Constitution by claiming monarchical authority for the presidency. This charge became a common refrain in American politics, especially under strong chief executives. In fact most nineteenth-century presidents, except for Abraham Lincoln, did little to realize the office's great potential for vigorous domestic leadership of the sort envisioned by ardent nationalists. Many presidents served only one term, and Congress often resisted efforts to advance programs contrary to its sense of what the nation required, a lesson learned at its extreme when Congress rejected Andrew Johnson's plan of post–Civil War reconstruction in favor of its own. Also, reformers succeeded in establishing a merit-based civil service in 1883, following the 1881 assassination of President James A. Garfield by a disappointed office seeker, and this measure, too, blunted the president's authority.

Wars, economic success (and failure), and the personality of the incumbent have shaped the twentieth-century presidency and, in the process, raised serious questions about whether the separation and balance of powers is still a workable constitutional principle. The challenges to national security and economic stability placed great demands on the office, and successful presidents, notably Franklin D. Roosevelt, began to use dormant powers, such as executive orders, to achieve what were in effect legislative outcomes. Traditionally, executive orders were administrative actions to implement laws passed by Congress or to carry out a constitutional function of the presidency. Theodore Roosevelt, for example, used them to expand the national landmarks and monuments permitted under the Antiquities Act of 1906. Franklin D. Roosevelt often invoked this authority to confront economic crisis, as when in March of 1933, days after his inauguration, he declared a bank holiday to prevent collapse of the banking system. More recently, presidents have used executive orders to carry out legislative policies and programs that they could not get Congress to enact.

As a result, the executive order has become a critical tool in presidential policy making. The range of actions taken in this way has included establishing wildlife refuges, placing Japanese Americans in World War II internment camps, firing disloyal civil servants, enlarging national forests, prohibiting racial discrimination in federally subsidized housing, giving federal workers the right to bargain collectively, and sending troops to support peace-keeping efforts around the world. Long-standing congressional acceptance of an executive order gives it the force of law, as happened in 1981 when the Supreme Court upheld a 180-year-old practice of settling claims of foreign nationals through executive agreement. The justices were aware how often the use of executive orders usurped the legislative function, but they believed it was both inevitable and necessary: "We freely confess," the opinion in *Dames v. Regan* admitted, "that we are obviously deciding only one more episode in the never-ending tension between the President exercising the executive authority in a world that presents each day some new challenge . . . and the Constitution . . . which no one disputes embodies some sort of system of checks and balances."

Congress frequently has been complicit in the expansion of presidential power, both because national emergencies of war and depression made it necessary to act swiftly and because the increasing complexity of American life required expertise beyond congressional capacity to supply. Two periods especially, the New Deal and World War II (1933–45) and the 1960s and early 1970s, witnessed the emergence of what now are hundreds of federal agencies. Beginning in the mid-nineteenth century Congress approved the creation of administrative agencies, housed in the executive branch, to apply its general statutes to the diverse and dynamic American economy and society. From the Office of Comptroller of the Currency in 1863 to the recent Administration for Children and Families, these units have broad authority to administer federal statutes. Congress also created federal regulatory agencies, at times modeled on state regulatory agencies, first in the Interstate Commerce Commission (1887) and later in a host of so-called alphabet agencies from the Food and Drug Administration (FDA, 1906) and Federal Communications Commission (FCC, 1934) to the Occupational Safety and Health Administration (OSHA, 1970) and the Consumer Product Safety Commission (1972).

The regulatory agencies are nominally independent of both executive and congressional control and form what scholars have labeled an extra-constitutional fourth branch of government. The president appoints members of these agencies, subject to Senate approval, and Congress can investigate them and change their responsibilities as well as set their budgets, although in fact such actions are rare. They also operate under what often are vague and general guidelines; the FCC, for instance, licenses radio stations in accordance with "public convenience, interest, or necessity." Even though some authorities have argued that this delegation of law-making authority violates the separation-of-powers principle, the Supreme Court has accepted its constitutionality, with only two decisions (*Panama Refining Co. v. Ryan*; *Schechter Poultry Corp. v. United States*) reaching an opposite result—and both occurred in 1935 shortly before the justices dropped their resistance to the New Deal.

This self-inflicted weakening of Congress is not a recent phenomenon. It is cyclical. Congress often has been strongest when a vigorous party system exists, and especially when the same party controlled both executive and legislative branches. This extra-constitutional apparatus historically has permitted Congress to function efficiently and with dispatch. Parties were able to discipline their membership of independently elected representatives and to muster public opinion in support of their platforms. The presidencies of Jackson, Lincoln, Franklin D. Roosevelt, and Lyndon B. Johnson were periods of energetic government because these men were political leaders who worked to manage their parties in Congress; they were not simply chief executives. They also were in office when public opinion demanded solutions to long-festering problems or immediate crises. But more often than not, Congress and president have been divided between the parties, a circumstance that reflects the lack of national consensus and results in inefficiency. Some commentators have argued that, in fact, such division is not accidental but reflects a popularly devised, if informal, set of checks and balances by giving one branch to one party and the other branch to the opposing party.

During these periods of conflict—and the decades since the election of Richard Nixon have largely fit this description—energy has shifted to the president, with the Supreme Court providing a check on power. In turn, this circumstance resurrects twin concerns about power: the presidency is becoming an imperial institution, with no effective checks, and the Supreme Court, an undemocratic institution, is acting to make laws instead of applying law. The accusations come from both sides of the political spectrum, with parties shifting position depending on who is in office and what is at issue. During the great nationalization of rights in the 1960s, conservatives objected to Supreme Court activism, whereas liberals hailed the justices' willingness to define rights as conditions of national citizenship. Under the more conservative Courts of the last several decades, liberals have leveled the same accusations of judicial law making when decisions have trimmed those rights and limited governmental power, while conservatives have been cheered by what they considered to be corrections of earlier abuses of judicial discretion.

Although concern about judicial activism surfaces periodically, many Americans have found the vast increase in presidential power more troubling. The executive branch is replete with well-staffed offices, agencies, and commissions unimaginable even in the mid-twentieth century, all justified by the need to respond effectively to the demands of an increasingly complex global society. The modern president requires a vast apparatus to protect him from threats to his safety. He exists in splendid isolation, protected from public access except through the unrelenting focus of a 24/7 news cycle. This condition, critics charge, has led to trappings of power that rival royalty and that have led presidents to consider themselves above the law. The dual claims of executive privilege and executive immunity have come to symbolize the "imperial presidency," the first referring to the president's power to withhold information at his discretion and the second to his ability to ignore all other processes of law while in office, except for impeachment.

Not everyone agrees with this narrative of presidential power. In the 1980s conservative theorists, concerned that the office had been weakened by vigorous congressional oversight during the last years of the Vietnam War and especially following the Watergate affair, advanced the idea of the strong unitary executive. Under this claim, the Constitution gives the president complete executive authority, and Congress cannot legitimately structure government in a way to diminish this power. As a result, regulatory agencies and independent prosecutors are constitutionally suspect because these offices have administrative or executive functions that can be exercised independently of the president, and their officers cannot be fired at will by him. Also, the president has the right to extend executive privilege, at his discretion, to anyone in the executive branch. Advanced first under President Ronald Reagan and asserted more forcefully by President George W. Bush, the theory seeks to draw a bright line among legislative, executive, and judicial functions, which critics charge is a stricter separation than the framers envisioned.

Executive privilege is an excellent case study in the ambivalence generated by the presidency. Throughout much of American history, presidents usually have accommodated requests for information from courts and Congress alike, although not always. In 1792, for example, the administration of President George Washington declined to supply documents to Congress having to do with the catastrophic defeat by Native American warriors of an American army led by General Arthur St. Clair, a decision that had the support of both Jefferson and Hamilton. In 1807, President Jefferson responded to Chief Justice Marshall's questions in the conspiracy trial of Aaron Burr, for example, though he declined to accept the idea that he ought to testify in person as a witness in Burr's trial. Modern presidents usually have followed Jefferson's example when faced with legal challenges and in responding to Congress, rather than appear before committees as Abraham Lincoln and Theodore Roosevelt did.

Courts have given a wide berth to the president in the performance of his official duties but in recent years have rejected both absolute privilege and absolute immunity. In *United States v. Nixon* (1974), the Court required President Nixon to turn over secretly recorded tapes for use in a criminal case in which he was an unindicted co-conspirator; Nixon complied and soon resigned from office because of the damaging information revealed when he released transcripts of the tapes—information that would have accelerated congressional efforts to impeach him for obstruction of justice. Over two decades later, the justices rejected President Bill Clinton's claim of immunity from testimony in a civil suit unrelated to his duties (*Clinton v. Jones*, 1997), a ruling that contributed to the nation's second presidential impeachment trial. And in decisions from the Civil War to the Iraqi conflict, the Court has rejected presidential authority to ignore rights of persons accused of crimes. Still, these instances have been rare; on the whole, both the legislative and judicial branch have given great deference to the executive, leading constitutional observers to worry that no meaningful check on presidential power exists.

Separation-of-powers issues are never far from the surface in modern American government. Most recently, the U.S. Supreme Court has trimmed the power of Congress in several cases involving the commerce clause, reversing decisions from the 1930s that accepted unlimited congressional authority in this area. The Rehnquist Court, for instance, abandoned an established doctrine of judicial deference to Congress in this area by declaring in *United States v. Lopez* (1995) that insufficient evidence existed in the legislative record to justify a ban on gun possession in a school zone as a matter of commerce. The justices also confirmed the president's appointment and removal power by ruling that Congress can neither appoint nor remove executive officers.

Although the Court most recently has been the arbiter of these conflicts between the president and Congress, its word is not always final, at least as a matter of practice. It struck down the legislative veto, for instance, as an improper intrusion on the power of the presidency (*Immigration and Naturalization Service v. Chada*, 1983), even though it dated back to the early 1930s and had appeared in more than 200 laws by the time of the Court's decision. (The legislative veto allowed either one or both houses to override an executive action if it did not approve of the manner in which the president acted in pursuing the law's objective.) But Congress has continued to exert its authority over executive actions informally by using its budgetary power to require agencies to secure written permission of House and Senate committees before taking specified actions.

It is tempting to view the inefficiencies, tensions, and failures of the systems of separation of powers and checks and balances as a mark of dysfunctional government. If so, it is constitutionally mandated dysfunction. The framers were most concerned about the easy and illegitimate use of power, and they designed government to make it difficult to abuse the authority vested in it by the people, the true sovereigns. The U.S. Constitution contains an elaborate scheme to allocate power and protect liberty—President John Quincy Adams once proudly claimed it was the most complicated government in history—and its complexity proved to be both its strength and its weakness. It has restrained governmental power yet allowed the exercise of this power when required. Checks and balances have slowed the pace of reform but have not blocked innovation; structural restraints have permitted public opinion to develop in support of change. They have not inhibited the growth of a national government much stronger and more dominant than even the most ardent nationalists in 1787 could have imagined. But the expansion of central power, perhaps necessary in a highly mobile nation with a dynamic global economy, has not come without great and continuing concerns about the exercise of national power on individual liberty, concerns that often have led to self-imposed restraints on governmental action.

From the long view of history, the revolutionary influence on our constitutional culture remains active and vital. We still are a nation that fears power, especially in government, and we are willing to live with inefficient government because we sense that we are freer when we do. The Constitution is no longer the same document in practice than it was when adopted, but its essential features are true to the founders' vision. The revolutionaries were realists who understood that men and women were capable of being rulers and being free only when they exercised discipline and patience, but they also understood that these traits were rare in human nature. Knowing that men were imperfect, they experimented with a theory to protect both their sovereignty and their freedom. They established a unique government to divide and balance power because they were convinced, as Madison expressed it, that only radical restraints on power could produce the checks on self-interest that liberty required.

6

Property

In 1913, a Columbia University professor published a book that an Ohio newspaper owned by future president Warren G. Harding blasted as "libelous, vicious, and damnable in its influence." The editorial urged its readers to condemn anyone who purveyed the book's "filthy lies and rotten perversion." The U.S senator from Idaho, William Borah, echoed this attack, calling the author a "hyena" scavenging on the remains of the nation's founders.[1] The book was *An Economic Interpretation of the Constitution*; its author was Charles A. Beard, who later became president of both the American Political Science Association and the American Historical Association and is generally recognized as one of the most influential American historians of the twentieth century.

Beard's sin was to argue that the men who drafted the Constitution acted more from economic self-interest than from disinterested commitment to republican ideals. "They were anxious above everything else to safeguard the rights of private property against any leveling tendencies on the part of the property-less masses," he wrote.[2] The Constitution, he claimed, was the product of a counter-revolution to reverse radical democratic tendencies, to frustrate majority rule, and to protect economic interests. This latter charge was especially potent in an era when populists and progressives were demanding that government use its power to regulate monopolistic corporations and replace the influence of wealth and self-interest with measures to promote democracy and the public good.

Later scholars significantly revised Beard's theme of class conflict by noting that the story was not as simple as rich bondholders versus farmers. Yet no one disputes the prominence that the Constitution gives to property rights and to the power of government to protect and promote economic interests. The framers would have found it unthinkable to exclude the rights of property from the catalog of personal liberties. Anglo-American thought long had judged them essential for the enjoyment of all other rights. The unfettered ability to acquire and own property, best expressed by John Locke in his *Second Treatise of Government* (1689), was considered both a natural law and a fundamental tenet of revolutionary philosophy. It ensured freedom by providing self-sufficiency, the condition that allowed men to resist arbitrary government. Not only was the protection of property "the principal object of Society," a sentiment voiced by John Rutledge of South Carolina and echoed by all the delegates to the Philadelphia Convention; it was necessary for the survival of liberty. "Property must be secured," John Adams wrote, "or liberty cannot exist."[3]

The need to secure the rights of property was especially urgent, the framers believed, because state governments could not be trusted to guarantee them. In response to distressed conditions in the postwar period following the Treaty of Paris of 1783, state legislatures suspended debt obligations and permitted payments of debts in depreciated paper money or worthless property. Rhode Island sought to require creditors to accept useless currency in payment of goods: should the creditor refuse to accept the currency, the debtor could discharge his obligation anyway by giving the paper money to the county sheriff, and any creditor who subsequently attempted to recover the debt in court risked being jailed. Pennsylvania revoked a charter for the Bank of North America, the nation's first chartered bank, under pressure from farmers and local merchants despite protests that it was a contract that the state could not breach unilaterally. These actions and others convinced the delegates to the Convention that the new general government must have the power to protect property or it would not be able to protect liberty.

The concern about legislative misrule and majority tyranny transformed American thinking about property from a right of all citizens into an interest deserving special protection, especially from irresponsible state actions that undermined economic and political stability. This shift found expression in the Constitution. The framers established a number of protections for property, many of which had analogs in the various revolutionary state constitutions. One set of provisions restricted the power of the national government. An important clause shielded landed wealth from federal taxation by forbidding a direct tax unless apportioned by population, a measure that southern slaveholders would block if it were proposed. Other clauses forbade export duties, bills of attainder (imposition of penalties for crimes by Congress rather than by a court after trial), and, most important of all, forfeiture of property upon conviction for a crime.

A second group of clauses strengthened the national government by granting it broad powers of taxation and by vesting it with authority to regulate interstate and foreign commerce. Congress also could establish uniform laws of bankruptcy and protect intellectual property by granting patents and copyrights. Another set of clauses restricted the powers of states, for example, by banning state taxes on imports and exports, a condition that had been the bane of the Confederation government. Much more important, at least in retrospect, was the prohibition against any state law "impairing the obligation of contracts," a clause apparently designed to prevent measures that favored debtors over creditors. Finally, the framers devoted much attention to the protection of property in slaves: Congress could not prohibit the slave trade until 1808; fugitive slaves had to be surrendered to the owners upon claim, with Congress empowered to pass laws carrying this requirement into effect; and three-fifths of a state's slaves would be counted along with its free population for purposes of representation and taxation, a formula that boosted the political clout of slaveholding states.

The Constitution of 1787 contains no broad guarantee of the right to property, despite its acknowledged importance to liberty. The framers relied upon institutional arrangements—the checks and balances of a written constitution—to protect property interests. They also expected property owners to dominate the new government, in part because almost every state required a property qualification for voting and a higher such threshold for officeholding. And, as James Madison explained in *Federalist No. 10*, the multiplication of interests in a national republic would impede the development of permanent majorities bent on limiting the rights of property. "A rage for paper money, for an abolition of debts, for an equal division of property, or for any other improper or wicked object," he wrote, "will be less apt to pervade the whole body of the Union than a particular member of it."

The problem, as Madison recognized, was that government provided the framework for the exchange of goods and the security of property through its law and policies. By definition, it was implicated in all economic matters. It could never avoid regulating the various interests of modern society, and its choices inevitably would affect the rights of one class of property holders over another. Here, the situation was different from other rights; government could safely stay out of matters of religion, for example, but it could not avoid acting on economic policies. His solution was to accommodate factions, the self-interested groups that, under republican theory, threatened the unity necessary for liberty to survive. The more interest groups, he reasoned, the less likely it was that any combination of them could form an effective permanent majority, at least at the national level. He was less optimistic about this remedy for the states, which only recently had posed the greatest threat to property. In fact, Madison had unsuccessfully sought to grant Congress the constitutional authority to veto any state law that violated the nation's fundamental charter.

Opponents of the Constitution focused on its lack of specific protections for individual rights, including property. They also objected to the economic assumptions of the Federalists, defenders of the proposed new government, who stressed the economic utility of private property, especially its role in generating investment capital. The Federalists envisioned America as a commercial society, not an agrarian one, and they proposed to place the new nation in the mainstream of a rapidly developing global market economy. Although Anti-Federalists did not make a sustained critique of these economic assumptions—their central objection was to the absence of a Bill of Rights—they held a different view of the nation's future. Anti-Federalists spoke for local interests, often small farmers, debtors, and backcountry residents, who were less involved in interstate commerce, whereas Federalists represented a national constituency, concentrated on the Atlantic seaboard and intricately connected in trading networks. In many states, the ratification vote reflected this socioeconomic split.

The agrarian-manufacturing divide became a standard trope in American politics. It reflected a fundamental, long-standing disagreement about the shape of the nation's economy and the government's role in economic development, but it also is easy to exaggerate these differences. For most members of the founding generation, private property, free trade, and economic opportunity were hallmarks of a free society; and in 1791, with the adoption of the Bill of Rights, the right to property found explicit protection in the Constitution. In addition to its safeguards regarding criminal procedure, the Fifth Amendment embraced the Lockean idea that protection of property was a central aim of government. It expressed a straightforward principle, even if key terms were undefined: "No person shall be deprived of life, liberty, or property, without due process of law; nor shall private property be taken for public use, without just compensation." Many of these terms were ambiguous—What was property? Due process? Public use? Just compensation?—but the author of the Bill of Rights, James Madison, believed they should be construed broadly. In a brief essay written after the amendment's adoption, he warned against "arbitrary restrictions, exemptions, and monopolies," including indirect takings of property, that denied people both their right to the free use of their property and also the means to acquire it through a "free choice of their occupations."[4]

Modern commentators at times portray the framers as capitalists, imbued with the free-market theories of Adam Smith, whose masterwork, *The Wealth of Nations*, appeared in 1776, the same year as the Declaration of Independence. It is an attractive but inaccurate conceit. The Constitution is agnostic on matters of economic theory; the men who wrote it were not. They were not capitalists who embraced an open and free exchange of goods and services with no interference from government; in fact, the term capitalism, with its connotation of unrestrained competition, did not even enter common speech until the nineteenth century. Rather, they were commercially minded republicans who had come of age in the closed mercantilist economy of the British Empire and shared many of its assumptions that government's role was to foster and manage an economy to ensure a favorable balance of trade. The framers' commercial republicanism placed a different emphasis on the active role of government in the economy from the neutral stance Adam Smith had advocated.

Alexander Hamilton's plans to use governmental power as an economic engine embodied these ideas. Even though he had read *The Wealth of Nations* and preferred its remedies, Hamilton believed the young nation's economy required the active hand of government to improve its self-sufficiency in the face of aggressive European trade policies. But Hamilton and his fellow Federalists did not embrace the full-throated protectionism of the seventeenth and early eighteenth centuries. These men were proto-capitalists whose land speculation and acquisitive commercial instincts suited the coming age. For them, the Constitution empowered government to protect property and secure contractual rights that, in turn, made it possible for ambitious men to create wealth. In their view, wealth and republican virtues were not contradictory, as an essayist with the pseudonym *Citizen* noted in 1785: "The truth is, liberty and . . . the fullest dispersion of luxury . . . are in all degrees and respects compatible with each other."[5] Government had an obligation to trigger economic growth, using its considerable power to develop a national market and stimulate investment in the capital-scarce young republic.

Their Anti-Federalist opponents, and later the Jeffersonian Republicans, were not capitalists, either. They were agrarians who saw little need for government to prod an economy that, for them, focused primarily on small producers and local markets. Capitalism ultimately proved more suitable to the American circumstances of cheap, abundant land, ownership of property by a broad spectrum of society, and a desire to maximize liberty by restraining governmental power, but it is misleading to read the Constitution as an endorsement of this economic theory. More significant is how courts and judges began to reshape the law of property as a capitalist instrument in ways that fit both constitutional republicanism and an emerging democratic order. It was not a neat transition from one era to the next—indeed, the early history of the Supreme Court reveals the tensions between a declining mercantilism and an ascendant capitalism—but by the 1830s Americans and their lawmakers increasingly read the Constitution as a brief for an entrepreneurial free market.

The Marshall Court played a central role in fixing the terms of the Constitution as an economic instrument. The framers had placed protection of property and enhancement of commerce at the heart of the constitution-building process. They limited the ability of a political majority to infringe on property rights by restricting the authority of states to interfere with interstate commerce. Federalism complicated the constitutional protection of property, however, because states retained their traditional police powers, or the ability to pass laws to protect public health, safety, and morality. Such regulations, by definition, affected the enjoyment and use of private property. The Constitution affirmed these powers in several places, including the Ninth and Tenth Amendments, which reserved unenumerated rights and undelegated powers to the people or the states.

In exercising their authority, many states reinforced an American proclivity for local control. They subsidized economic activity, used eminent domain (the power to seize private property for public use), and altered debtor-creditor relations in an effort to spur development. These efforts often had important implications for property rights. At times, states altered existing contractual relationships to make way for new forms of enterprise. Elsewhere, they regulated private businesses to promote the public welfare, for example, by licensing certain occupations. Few people questioned the need for police powers to protect public health and safety, but their use raised questions about the limits of state authority. How to divide competing powers over the economy between state and central governments, especially in matters of contract and commerce, became an important issue in the new nation. The Marshall Court spent much of its jurisprudential energy drawing these lines.

Early on, federal judges signaled an intention to protect existing economic relationships and to curtail state authority to interfere with property rights. The means lay in the extra-constitutional doctrine of vested rights. Under this Lockean notion, mentioned nowhere in the Constitution, the right to property was deemed a fundamental right guaranteed by natural law rather than man-made law. Any law that disturbed property rights was unconstitutional, in this view, because it violated one of the general principles limiting all governments. But the doctrine posed a problem because no fixed standard existed for its interpretation: even sympathetic judges could differ on its meaning when applied to a particular case. It also existed outside the Constitution, which under the theory of popular sovereignty represented the pure expression of the people's will. The solution was to link natural law with constitutional law, a step taken tentatively by Federalist judges in the 1790s but embraced fully by the U.S. Supreme Court under Chief Justice John Marshall, who joined natural rights to the contract clause and made it the centerpiece of the Court's jurisprudence during his tenure.

Marshall sought to promote a national economy, a goal that required both a strengthening of national government and subsequent limits on state power. It was especially important, he thought, to restrain the states' ability to interfere with private property, which he, like all Federalists, believed was the cornerstone of liberty. The contract clause became a linchpin of this effort. It was part of a series of restrictions on state authority contained in Article 1, Section 10—"No State shall enter into any . . . Law impairing the Obligation of Contracts"—but like other constitutional provisions the language embraced a general principle, not a definition or guide to its meaning. Marshall eagerly embraced the opportunity to use the clause to advance a nationalist agenda.

An initial step extended constitutional protection to contracts made by states as well as by private citizens. In 1796, the state of Georgia reneged on a large land-grant contract it had made the previous year to private land companies because the legislature concluded the transaction had resulted from bribery. Marshall declared the repeal an unconstitutional violation of the contract clause when the case reached the Court in 1810 (*Fletcher v. Peck*). The clause was "applicable to contracts of every description," he wrote, and it embraced "the general principles, which are common to our free institutions," a phrase that tied vested rights to the Constitution.

Later decisions extended the contract clause to other state economic actions: a tax exemption that New Jersey granted to a band of American Indians was a non-violable contract (*New Jersey v. Wilson*, 1812); a corporate charter was a constitutionally protected contract (*Dartmouth College v. Woodward*, 1819); a bankruptcy law could not retroactively discharge contractual obligations (*Sturges v. Crowninshield*, 1819). The *Dartmouth College* case was noteworthy because it offered constitutional protection to the corporation, a form of enterprise traditionally used by charitable and public functions but increasingly adopted by businesses as a way of limiting risk. The decision did not offer unalloyed protection, however. Justice Joseph Story's concurring opinion suggested that states could reserve the power to alter or repeal such charters when making future grants. Gradually, many states pursued this course.

Chief Justice Marshall was not uniformly successful in his effort to use the contract clause as a bulwark against state interference with property rights. In 1827, for example, he was in the minority when the Court ruled that laws in effect at the time a contract was made became part of the bargain (*Ogden v. Saunders*)—Marshall wanted the clause to reach state laws that operated prospectively as well as retroactively—but his leadership made the contract clause a keystone feature of national power in economic matters. These decisions also reflected the Court's belief that economic progress depended above all on the security and stability of contracts. This principle was important in facilitating the transition to a free-market economy.

The Marshall Court's contract clause decisions forged a vital connection between capitalism and constitutionalism, but modernizing the law of contract to fit the needs of an emerging market economy was largely a matter for state courts. In English and American law, considerations of equity, that is, concepts of fair value and a just price, influenced the interpretation of contracts. If a judge deemed that one person had taken advantage of another, then he could modify the contract to restore fairness to the bargain. A market economy assumes a more neutral stance, and the idea had emerged in England (but not America) that parties to the contract were capable of agreeing on a fair price, which judges generally should accept except in cases of fraud and coercion. The "will" theory of contracts limited the role of the government by assuming the freedom of individuals to make their own bargains—or to govern themselves. State courts embraced this principle and made it an article of constitutional faith in the public's mind.

The role of the Marshall Court in this development was indirect. The U.S. Supreme Court historically has had little impact on the substantive law of contracts, but the Marshall Court's decisions gave such a broad definition to contracts—and so protected them from state impairment—that individuals have had great freedom to make and enforce their own economic bargains without governmental interference. It was a constitutional stance that tracked well with an emerging capitalist and democratic ethic.

By the mid-1820s Americans had come to believe in the power of the free market to allocate resources, increase wealth, and provide economic opportunities to individuals willing to take risks in the pursuit of profit. The notion of an unfettered market open to all had its political equivalent in democratic individualism, and both strands of this new American ethic grew out of key constitutional themes. For democracy, the demand for universal white adult male suffrage required a recasting of the representative principle; for capitalism, the free market demanded an embrace of the sanctity of contracts as a barrier against government interference with private economic arrangements.

It was not an accidental marriage. Both ideas reflected the triumph of individualism as a primary American value. Contracts, like the vote, resulted from the exercise of free will; they were instruments of a society based on liberty and thereby fostered economic opportunity for all citizens. This sentiment did not correspond to the increasing concentration of wealth, cyclical economic depressions, or disruptions in the labor force caused by the influx of poor immigrants from Germany and Ireland. The market was hardly guided by an invisible hand in allocating resources fairly and equitably, but this reality did little to blunt the widespread belief that capitalism and democracy were essential to liberty. Americans also expected the Constitution to protect, if not promote, the values embodied in these new ideas.

A change in the legal and social meaning of property was prelude to this transformation. At the time of the Constitutional Convention, real property (land) benefited from a well-developed and mostly uniform body of law regarding its sale. But the law and conditions governing other forms of possession varied from state to state. As a result the exchange of personal property, whether in tangible forms such as money or goods or as intangible property such as promissory notes or bonds, rested on less certain footing, which limited its use in the wide-ranging and geographically diffuse transactions common to capitalism. For instance, a creditor could lend money and expect to collect on the note he received from the debtor, who promised to pay in full, but if the lender in turn transferred the debt to a third party, then the new holder of the note might not be able to collect, depending on the jurisdiction and the type of note it was.

Property also acquired a different social meaning. Traditionally it had existed primarily for personal enjoyment rather than as an investment or asset for more productive use, although this meaning was under challenge throughout the late eighteenth century as land increasingly became a market commodity.

By the early nineteenth century, these deterrents to economic development began to disappear as legislatures passed statutes and judges reinterpreted existing law to permit the free, secure exchange of property in all forms. New forms of legal status emerged, such as the limited liability corporation, and new types of non-tangible property, such as franchises, copyrights, and patents, became important as Americans invented new ways to tap the resources of a nation that now spanned a continent. Most of the changes did not touch constitutional issues, but they reflected an instrumentalist conception of law—law should be an instrument to promote economic development—that began to affect the meaning of the Constitution, notably its contract clause.

The mid-nineteenth century witnessed a reinterpretation of the contract clause. A Court with different membership and a new leader sought to harmonize the Constitution with the tenets of the politically ascendant Jacksonian democracy and its emphasis on states' rights and strict construction. A new chief justice, Roger B. Taney, who had served as attorney general and secretary of the treasury under Andrew Jackson, shared his patron's belief in popular will and individualism, as well as Jackson's antipathy toward special privilege. He also served during a time when the nation's dramatic transformation was evident even to the most casual observer. A population that barely exceeded three million in 1790 increased tenfold by 1860, while the nation's western boundary shifted 2,000 miles to the Pacific Ocean. Rapid advances in transportation, with steamboats, canals, and railroads, facilitated demographic and economic growth by opening the interior to settlement and smoothing the emergence of cities as regional trade centers. A new form of economic enterprise, the corporation, began to replace traditional partnerships and single-owner businesses, setting the stage for the accumulation of capital and economies of scale that made later industrialization possible.

These developments were not unmixed blessings. As markets expanded, the economic power and importance of local communities lessened. And the corporation possessed wealth and power that later proved almost as threatening to Americans as the imperial hand of Great Britain had been. It was in this environment that Taney sought to reconcile the interpretations of his predecessor with the new realities of American life. The contract clause was a proving ground for this adjustment.

Taney's opponents attempted to caricature his decisions as a radical departure from those of Marshall, but in fact the two jurists shared fundamental values. Each sought to preserve claims arising from private ownership of property; each supported constitutional limitations on the power of state and federal governments; and each was committed to an independent and powerful federal judiciary. Their differences were generational. Taney and his colleagues inherited the revolution that Marshall and his contemporaries made, and they aimed to preserve and advance those gains within a fully capitalist and democratic society. A classic case, *Charles River Bridge v. Warren Bridge* (1837), gave the Taney Court (seven of the nine justices were Jackson appointees) an opportunity to make this accommodation of old and new. The goal, although expressed in economic terms, was the same one embraced by the revolutionary generation: how best to maximize liberty.

The case represented a clash between two visions of the nation's economic future: one mercantilist and the other capitalist. In 1785, Massachusetts granted the Charles River Bridge Company permission to build a bridge across the Charles River connecting Boston and Charlestown, with the right to collect tolls for forty years (later extended to seventy years). The grant was a classic colonial practice that mimicked actions the English crown had taken since the mid-sixteenth century to induce private investment. In this instance, the cash-strapped Massachusetts legislature promised an exclusive right to collect payment to investors willing to build roads or bridges. The bargain was clear: the state improved its transportation network, and investors received a nice profit (for example, the initial investment of $50,000 in the Charles River Bridge had earned $825,000 by the 1830s).

But within a few years after construction, traffic had increased so much that the state granted another group of investors, the Warren Bridge Company, the right to build a nearby bridge that would become state property after six years. The Charles River Bridge Company filed suit against the new company, claiming that its charter, a contract, implied exclusive rights; otherwise, investors would not have risked their money for an uncertain return. Property rights were at issue, and the Charles River attorney cast the problem in familiar terms: "I look to the law," he argued, "for the protection of the rights of persons and property, against all encroachments by the inadvertent legislation of the states."

Charles River Bridge v. Warren Bridge likely would have been a landmark decision in any number of areas, for it brought together questions of signal importance to the future of constitutional law: What was the status of corporations? What effect would new technologies have? How much control over the economy could states exercise? But it was the reshaping of the contract clause that tied the nation's constitutional past to its capitalist future. Taney did not repudiate Marshall's decision in *Dartmouth College v. Woodward*, in which his predecessor ruled that a charter was a contract that the state could not impair, but he refused to interpret it to include any right "beyond those which the words of the charter, by their natural and proper construction, purport to convey." The real issue was progress: Would contracts be allowed to hinder a state's ability to encourage economic growth? The question was not hypothetical. Railroads already were speeding the flow of goods to market, and a decision for the Charles River Bridge company would only blunt their development, as Taney made clear in a remarkable passage:

> Let it once be understood that such charters carry with them these implied contracts, . . . and you will soon find the old turnpike corporations awakening from their sleep, and calling upon this court to put down improvements which have taken their place. . . . We shall be thrown back to the improvements of the last century, and obliged to stand still, until the claims of the old turnpike corporations have been satisfied, and they shall consent to permit these States to avail themselves of the lights of modern science, and to partake of the benefit of those improvements

which are now adding to the wealth and prosperity, and the convenience and comfort of every other part of the civilized world.

Taney understood that the abandonment of the old to make way for the new—what economists have labeled "creative destruction"—is integral to capitalism. He was part of a major transformation of American law that sacrificed concepts of vested rights and natural law to the demands of progress. The *Charles River Bridge* case was an exemplar of this change. The Court's decision did not undermine the right to property but made it clear that the nation's economic future demanded dynamic, not static, forms of property.

The Taney Court's embrace of law as an instrument of policy fit the temper of a democratic age and provided an adaptable constitutional framework for balancing the individual right to property with legislative determinations of the public interest. The justices also demonstrated their commitment to an American trait of innovation and experimentation in law as in other areas of society. From its beginnings, the nation had jettisoned laws that did not work in the new republican environment, for example, by abandoning primogeniture (inheritance of the entire estate by the first-born son) or eliminating barriers to the easy exchange of land or granting married women title to property through trusts and prenuptial agreements. Taney and his colleagues instinctively embraced this tradition.

As states increasingly sought new ways to promote economic growth, the Taney Court on occasion sought to balance legislative authority with the right of contract. Following Marshall Court precedents, the justices ruled that legislatures could not modify the terms of contract to favor the interests of debtors over those of creditors (*Bronson v. Kingie*, 1843). But they also ruled that the state's use of its power of eminent domain did not violate the contract clause, even when it destroyed the value of a franchise (*West River Bridge v. Dix*, 1848). The Fifth Amendment forbids government from taking private property for public use without just compensation, but in *Barron v. Baltimore* (1833) the Marshall Court had refused to apply this takings clause to the states. The *West River Bridge* decision left states free to experiment with the power of eminent domain, often to the detriment of property rights.

State courts and legislatures gave broad scope to the meaning of public use and took a narrow view of what actions constituted a taking that required compensation. Not only did some states require a complete taking of title rather than a lessening of property value before requiring payment, but they also offset any loss by whatever benefit the property owner received. Under this controversial practice, the value of access to a railroad, for instance, could offset the cost of land taken for the right of way, thus leaving the landowner with much less than market value for his seized property. Critics protested that these benefits often were elusive and could not be calculated. They also argued that state actions in such cases violated due process and forced landowners to subsidize economic development. On the whole, it was an argument that gained little traction until after the Civil War, when some state constitutions banned the practice and some state courts began to insist that payment must be made in money. In another area of property rights, the exercise of police powers, the Taney Court gave wide latitude to states as well. A majority of the justices, after all, were state-sovereignty southerners who shied from any ruling that threatened local authority over slavery or that implied a national power to restrict this most politically volatile class of property.

The right to property and the ability to promote economic development were also at issue under the commerce clause. The framers of the Constitution desired to create a uniform national market by eliminating state trade barriers, and therefore they gave Congress the power to regulate interstate and foreign commerce. The Marshall Court, in line with its policy of economic nationalism, at first adopted an expansive reading of the clause, reserving nearly exclusive powers under it to the national government. But Congress rarely used its powers over interstate commerce, at least before the Civil War, and increasingly the question arose concerning the states' ability to regulate commerce under their police powers. The ownership of human property complicated the issue; an expansive reading of national commerce power potentially threatened the southern states' interest in protecting the internal slave trade.

Dual federalism was the Taney Court's answer. In a decision that lasted nearly a century, the Court determined in 1852 that states had a concurrent power to regulate trade unless and until Congress acted (*Cooley v. Board of Wardens*). This step was not a large one conceptually. Marshall had acknowledged in 1824 in *Gibbons v. Ogden* that federal authority did not extend to intrastate commerce, and his opinion for the Court in *Willson v. Black Bird Creek Marsh Co.* (1829) hinted that a state's police powers might affect interstate commerce. But when state and federal power clashed, national authority prevailed. Such was the case when Congress passed a statute overturning a Pennsylvania court decision ordering the destruction of a Virginia-authorized bridge on the grounds that it impeded steamboat traffic (*Pennsylvania v. Wheeling and Belmont Bridge Company*, 1856). The commerce clause, like the contract clause, promoted new forms of enterprise even if it harmed or destroyed established interests. Only when slavery was at issue did this calculus shift.

Dual federalism and the states' broad role in shaping the economy hid the degree to which unrestrained property ownership enjoyed widespread support among federal jurists. Legal commentaries routinely emphasized constitutional restrictions on government authority over property. "The fundamental maxims of a free government," Justice Joseph Story wrote in *Wilkinson v. Leland* (1829), "seem to require that the rights of personal liberty and private property should be held sacred." These rights found their fullest expression in democracy, economic individualism, and the free market. But capitalism favored property in motion over property at rest, which required a shift in constitutional doctrine.

Significantly, judges assumed this responsibility, prompting Alexis de Tocqueville to observe that the American judiciary, federal and state, was the most powerful in the world. Distrustful of legislative interference, federal judges especially cast themselves as special guardians of property rights, a stance with major implications for the coming industrial age.

Symbolic of their new claim was *Swift v. Tyson* (1842), in which the Supreme Court ruled that a general judge-made commercial law of the United States existed and overrode state-court decisions, in this instance, New York law, even though no constitutional provision or act of Congress established such a federal common law. *Swift* limited the ability of state law to upset the expectations of parties in interstate transactions and was essential in preventing what otherwise would have been a balkanization of commercial law. It also suggested that the Court would decide on a case-by-case basis what the uniform commercial law was. Federal judges, in brief, would become the touchstone for economic decisions, including the right to property, which increasingly they decided was paramount to the protection of the public welfare. In this sense, the laissez-faire jurisprudence of the late nineteenth century stemmed directly from the property-conscious law of antebellum America.

By the middle of the nineteenth century, the United States had fully embraced a market economy, and the Civil War guaranteed that it would be based on free labor. Property and contract rights were the foundation of this market, which depended wholly on credit to finance investment. But the credit market was fragmented and undercapitalized, so Americans leaned heavily on public financing and private lending advanced by merchants and small shopkeepers to expand the economy. Private lending especially assured relatively easy entry into the market for individual entrepreneurs; in turn, the ability to begin a business quickly bolstered popular support for capitalism.

The demands of war—large armies could be sustained only through mass manufacturing—soon changed this formula for success. What took its place were corporate capitalism and national credit markets. It was not an easy transition. Although the United States was the world's second largest industrial power in 1860—Great Britain was first—more than 60 percent of the nation's manufacturers were unincorporated. Both tradition and antipathy blunted the widespread adoption of the corporate form, despite its attractiveness as a means of spreading risk. Antebellum states had dropped special legislative charters in favor of general incorporation statutes that made this form of business organization widely available. But states also taxed and regulated corporations to ensure public accountability, which made them less attractive to investors, especially in matters of corporate governance. Moreover, Jacksonian democracy and the depression of 1839–43 made "soulless" corporations objects of suspicion and distrust: many Americans considered them variants on monopolies, with the power to deny equal opportunity to compete fairly, a belief that rekindled the long-standing fear of power.

War changed the perception and treatment of corporations, at least outside the South, by favoring the efficient organization of material and money in pursuit of victory. Railroads created a transcontinental market for goods, and corporations quickly became the preferred business form, especially in transportation, manufacturing, and energy production, because they facilitated the large-scale investments required by these national enterprises. One result of this development was the rise of corporate capitalism and laissez-faire constitutionalism to bolster the new market economy.

Between 1865 and 1900 the United States changed in ways the framers could not have envisioned. Its population more than doubled, and it made two significant transformations: the nation was becoming more urban, with 40 percent of all inhabitants living in cities by 1900, compared to 20 percent in 1860; and Catholic and Jewish immigrants from eastern and southern Europe replaced northern European Protestants as the largest number of new citizens. For the first time, all African Americans lived free of slavery, if not of racism.

The economy experienced equally dramatic shifts. Work was mechanized, both in manufacturing and agriculture; national markets emerged in food, clothing, and durable goods, with economies of scale reducing costs to consumers but often harming local suppliers and businessmen; and standards of living improved, especially for a rapidly growing urban middle class. These transitions were not smooth or uniform in their effect: steep depressions occurred in 1873 and 1893; labor often clashed violently with owners over pay, hours, and working conditions; urban poverty and crime were major problems; politics was unusually partisan; and government at all levels was overwhelmed, unstable, and often corrupt.

The late nineteenth century also was a time of legal transformation, with rights of property at the center of a new constitutionalism based on free-market capitalism. The change was momentous in both its scope and in the issues it raised about the Constitution's relationship to the nation's economy. The controversies coming before the Supreme Court, in the words of a leading justice, Stephen J. Field, "exceed[ed], in the magnitude of the property interests involved, and in the importance of the public questions presented, all cases brought within the same period before any court in Christendom."[6]

Field scarcely exaggerated. The challenge was how to reconcile a legal framework built for a highly decentralized agrarian society, with its emphasis on restraint of public power, to the needs of an urban, industrial nation in which private or corporate power came to be seen not only as an engine of prosperity but also as a threat to liberty. For decades the Supreme Court grappled with this problem, but the solutions offered by the justices were built on classical theories of law and economics that proved unsuitable for a new age. This result would not change until the constitutional revolution of 1937.

From the time of Marshall, American judges had sought to make law a science, devoid of all emotion and based solely on reason. This effort, known as formalism, involved a separation of law and politics. Politics was based on the temporary and transient will of majorities, but the Constitution was permanent and represented the fundamental will of society. The judiciary was uniquely responsible for upholding its timeless principles, which centered on the restraint of power to protect liberty. Under this framework, jurists believed that law had two branches—public law and private law. Public law embraced the actions of government and ultimately was political. It responded to the popular will and, in economic matters, its tendency was to regulate and redistribute wealth. Private law, such as the law of property and contracts, protected the exercise of individual will and was essential to the functioning of a free market. Only judges, in this view, were in a position to serve as mediators between the conflicting demands of public and private law. They imagined themselves as neutral arbiters, striking a balance between the legitimate powers of government (but ever mindful of its constraints), and the liberty of individuals to act free of the coercive hand of the state.

This notion of the judicial role and the distinction between public and private law were fictions—in a democracy, law always is political—but they expressed a powerful Anglo-American ethical tradition that government should not advance the interest of one party over another. The attacks on vested rights, monopolies, and special interests from Jefferson through Jackson and beyond were part of this legacy that sought above all to promote individual liberty as its highest goal. Any governmental restraints on this liberty were suspect.

Formalism achieved its ascendancy on the Court in the late nineteenth century, beginning with two dissents in the *Slaughterhouse Cases* decided by the U.S. Supreme Court in 1873. The question was whether the privileges and immunities and due process clauses of the Fourteenth Amendment protected the rights of New Orleans butchers to process their cattle outside of a state-chartered slaughterhouse, which had been granted a government monopoly in an effort to ensure sanitary conditions and promote public health. The Court's majority rejected the challenge. It was unwilling to recognize any change in the federal government's authority over the states.

Two dissenting justices, Stephen J. Field and Joseph P. Bradley, used their opinions to fashion the beginnings of a doctrine known later as economic due process. Field attacked monopolies as an encroachment on the right to acquire property and viewed the Fourteenth Amendment as protection for the right to pursue a lawful occupation. Bradley linked liberty, property, and due process in his opinion: "a law which prohibits a large class of citizens from adopting a lawful employment . . . deprive[s] them of liberty as well as property without due process of law."

This stance gradually became a majority position. For a few years, the Court continued to give states a wide berth in regulating private property under their police powers, for example, through so-called Granger laws governing prices charged by grain elevators (*Munn v. Illinois*, 1877). By the 1880s, however, a shift in interpretation was apparent. Influential legal scholars had begun to advance a new theory of due process, linking its ancient requirement of fair procedures to Jacksonian themes of equal rights and hostility to special-interest legislation. In this new formulation, due process became a substantive protection for property rights; the issue was not whether the legal process was fair but whether it produced a fair result. Impartial, objective judges were the proper monitors of due process, not legislators who were beholden to special interests.

Justice John Marshall Harlan the elder, often lauded by scholars for his race-blind jurisprudence, exemplified this new posture. He declared that courts had a duty to "look at the substance of things" and not simply to accept a legislative determination that its actions were necessary to safeguard the public's health, safety, or morals (*Mugler v. Kansas,* 1887). Judges would decide whether state action was reasonable; federal courts, in brief, would supervise state economic policies. Economic due process embraced a straightforward definition of reasonableness: Did the law adhere to free-market principles, which included the right of property not to be subject to state regulation? This approach was a clear expression of laissez-faire constitutionalism: economic liberty and personal liberty were the same, and the right to own and use property unimpeded by government became a judicial touchstone of American freedom.

By the 1890s economic due process (also known as substantive due process) replaced the contract clause as the most important constitutional doctrine protecting the rights of property. The Supreme Court ruled in 1886 that the Fourteenth Amendment's due process and equal protection clauses were meant to cover artificial legal persons, or corporations (*Santa Clara County v. Southern Pacific Railroad*). The decision provided the opportunity to extend the Court's oversight to state economic legislation, especially the regulation of railroad and utility rates. With the definition of reasonableness now a judicial question, the Supreme Court established a formula to determine minimum prices that a utility must be allowed to charge to guarantee a fair return (*Smyth v. Ames,* 1898). The justices also abandoned the two-decades-old *Munn* standard allowing states to regulate railroad prices. The majority in these cases relied upon the dormant commerce clause, an inferred doctrine, first noted in *Gibbons v. Ogden,* prohibiting the states from acting in matters of interstate commerce even in the absence of any federal law or regulation. The effect was to make the judiciary the arbiter of interstate commerce.

Formalism was at play in these decisions, yet so was instrumentalism, the idea that legal doctrines should be interpreted to achieve desired policy results, as the Court was acting to preserve the investment capital that fueled a booming economy. But economic due process was about more than protecting the Court's role or advancing the interests of capital. It also was about a new standard for liberty. In 1897, the Court determined that liberty as protected by the Fourteenth Amendment included the right to "enter into all contracts which may be proper" to pursue an occupation and acquire property. This newly discovered liberty of contract, a right not connected to the contract clause, assumed that both parties freely entered into a bargain on equal terms, a premise that would hardly fit the circumstances of women, African Americans, immigrants, American Indians, the poor, and other disadvantaged groups.

Oddly, at least to modern eyes, this assumption was widely accepted; it fit a new ethic of liberty in which all individuals were the sole proprietors of their skills and talents and owed society nothing for them. This possessive individualism, rooted in Locke's philosophy but fed by American abundance, found its highest expression in the unfettered marketplace, which became a metaphor for liberty itself. Even exploited groups defined their aspirations in market terms: women's agenda for equality, for example, depended to a large extent on their ability to enter into contracts and control property independently of men.

Elsewhere, the Court protected the rights of property by giving an expansive interpretation to the takings and just compensation requirements of the Fifth Amendment, reminding legislators that the assessment of an indemnity payment was a judicial function only. In 1897, the justices unanimously decided to incorporate just compensation into the due process guarantee of the Fourteenth Amendment, thereby making it the first provision of the Bill of Rights to be applied as a protection against state action (*Burlington and Quincy Railroad Company v. Chicago*). The Court used the commerce clause as well to restrict state power to regulate railroads and interstate trade, even as it limited federal authority to intercede in the market. For instance, the Court weakened the first congressional regulatory effort, the Interstate Commerce Act (1887), by denying the Interstate Commerce Commission, the nation's first administrative agency, the power to set railroad rates. It also defined commerce as trade and transportation only, not production (specifically not manufacturing), thereby limiting congressional authority and preserving the traditional state power to regulate business, even though it was apparent that many state legislatures were prisoners of corporate interests.

Finally, the justices interpreted the federal power to tax narrowly, ruling that an 1894 federal income tax was unconstitutional (*Pollock v. Farmers Loan Trust Co.*, 1895). This latter case revealed sectional and class divisions that increasingly became important in national politics. The majority justices, influenced by principles of laissez-faire economics, viewed the tax as an assault on capital and an attempt to soak the rich. Justice Field warned of dire consequences if the tax were approved: "It will be but the stepping stone to others, larger and more sweeping, till our political contests will become a war of the poor against the rich." The dissenting justices decried the Court's denial of political democracy: the decision was "nothing less than a surrender of the taxing power to the moneyed class." At issue was the role of courts in setting economic policy, a question that would not be settled until the New Deal.

It is easy now to criticize the Court's embrace of economic due process and its exaltation of laissez-faire capitalism, but in fact the justices were responding to significant problems that were not being addressed elsewhere. The patch-work of state regulations imposed a burden on corporations that operated in a national market. By imposing standards on the rate-fixing process, the Court protected the accumulation of investment capital. It also sought to remove ob-stacles to interstate trade.

The justices were less involved in establishing a new constitutional framework than in reifying an older one. Theirs was a nineteenth-century jurisprudence blending the constitutional nationalism of Marshall with Taney's accommo-dation of democracy and capitalism and extending it to its logical extreme, making the rights of property and economic liberty a primary object for gov-ernmental protection. Economic due process was the ultimate embodiment of a philosophy that made economic theory an article of constitutional faith. That it appeared to work—the nation became ever more prosperous during this pe-riod—gave credence to this belief, and the weaknesses of the other branches of the federal government removed any serious challenges to it or to the role of judges as its high priests.

Progressives and other reformers assailed the notion that courts, not elected legislatures, were the proper forum for resolving property and contract disputes. They attacked as well the conceit that the Constitution enshrined laissez-faire eco-nomic theory. Reformers also perceived threats to democracy in the growing gap between rich and poor, the economic distress of farmers and urban laborers, the corrupting influence of money in politics, and, above all, the concentration and abuse of private power. Private power, represented by corporate capitalism, had become a danger to liberty equal to the risk posed by overweening government.

The reformers' preferred remedy was the regulatory state, in which adminis-trative agencies staffed by experts with technical skills corrected the imbalance of power in the new industrial order. One goal was to preserve competition in the face of corporate monopolies; another was to alleviate the harshness of industrial employment and urban life. States were laboratories for experimen-tation, with measures such as workmen's compensation, minimum-wage and maximum-hour rules for workers, and health and safety standards infringing the right to property and the liberty of contract as expressed in laissez-faire constitutionalism. The justification for this new regulatory posture could be found in state police power, which Progressives interpreted broadly but which flew in the teeth of economic due process.

The attack on formalism resulted from a reconceptualization of what law was and how it operated. For much of the nineteenth century, jurists had sought to bring coherence to the common law and build it into a tightly organized, highly rational, and stable instrument for its more effective use in a rapidly changing world. This effort represented the convergence of a waning Enlightenment faith in rationality with a new exaltation of science, but it also sought to blunt the increased democratization of American law, reflected, for example, in the belief that lawyers needed little special training.

The disjuncture between a highly formal law and the messiness of life invited a new approach, which the legal philosopher (and later Supreme Court Justice) Oliver Wendell Holmes Jr. offered in his influential treatise, *The Common Law* (1881). "The life of law has not been logic," he wrote, "it has been experience." This view, which came to be known as sociological jurisprudence, argued that law was a product of its time and place; it reflected customs and embraced existing social and economic norms. It was not, as traditionalists maintained, a set of eternal principles from which objective judges could discover equally timeless and value-free rules.

Influential judges, lawyers, and scholars carried this message to a wider public audience and gradually gained acceptance for the argument that law must be judged by its results, not by the application of formal reasoning. Social justice was a hallmark of this new philosophy. Emblematic of this new stance was the "Brandeis brief," a tactic made popular by the progressive lawyer (and also a future Supreme Court Justice) Louis D. Brandeis, who larded his pleadings with non-legal evidence on the social and economic effects of laws and decisions that he sought to reverse. Soon even opponents of reform had adopted this tactic, compiling evidence on beneficial impacts even as they defended a timeless law, judicially determined.

All new beliefs must overcome defenders of an existing faith, and formalists did not surrender easily. In fact, laissez-faire constitutionalism reached its zenith in *Lochner v. New York* (1905), when the Court, by a vote of 5–4, struck down a state law that restricted work in bakeries to ten hours a day and sixty days a week. Writing for the majority, Justice Rufus Peckham acknowledged that states could act to protect the health of workers, but he disagreed with the legislative judgment that baking was unhealthy. He also doubted the legislature's honesty: "It is impossible for us to shut our eyes," he noted, "to the fact that many laws of this character, while passed under what is claimed to be the police power for the purpose of protecting the public health or welfare, are, in reality, passed from other motives." The real reason for the law, he concluded, was to regulate labor relations, which violated the constitutionally protected liberty of contract. Bakers were not wards of the state, he argued, and the state regulation was a "meddlesome interference with the rights of individuals" to decide for themselves if working conditions were acceptable.

In dissent, Justice Oliver Wendell Holmes Jr. fumed that the "Fourteenth Amendment does not enact Mr. Herbert Spencer's Social Statics," referring to a popular treatise that applied the rule of survival of the fittest to economics. The majority relied upon "an economic theory which a large part of the country doesn't entertain," he charged. Elected legislatures, not courts, Holmes argued, were the proper forum for economic policies. Judges should defer to "the right of a majority to embody their opinions in law" on such matters. (In a letter to a friend years later, Holmes pithily remarked: "[I]f my fellow citizens want to go to Hell I will help them. It is my job.")[7] This view of judicial restraint differed from the dissent written by Justice John Marshall Harlan, which embraced the rationale of the New York statute regulating working conditions. Unlike Holmes, who insisted that judges defer to legislative judgments, Harlan reserved for the Court the power to oversee state law making and determine whether a law was reasonable or not.

Of course, the Court is never the sole interpreter of the Constitution, and its claim to be the final arbiter of property rights met stiff resistance. Progressives believed that the federal judiciary had sacrificed the general welfare to the interests of property owners. The Supreme Court especially was an obstacle to necessary reforms: its laissez-faire constitutional doctrines were anti-democratic and allowed unelected justices to exercise vast power over social and economic legislation. Scholars such as Charles A. Beard published work undermining the claimed veneer of judicial neutrality and seeking to reshape public understanding of the Constitution as a venerated object.

Although the Court gave some ground, it did not abandon or retreat much from its reliance on economic due process and liberty of contract to safeguard property rights. It overturned a District of Columbia statute establishing a minimum-wage law for women, arguing that setting wages and prices was a matter for owners and employees, not for government: "Freedom of contract," the majority argued, "is the general rule and restraint the exception" (*Adkins v. Children's Hospital*, 1923). The Court accepted a more liberal interpretation of the commerce clause. It allowed a greater role for federal oversight of contaminated products, for instance. It adopted as well a stream-of-commerce doctrine that blurred its earlier distinction between trade and manufacturing and accepted federal authority over economic matters previously reserved for the states (*Swift and Co. v. United States*, 1905). But it also struck down an effort by Congress to ban goods produced by child labor from interstate commerce on the grounds that the products were not inherently harmful and that the real aim of the statute was to regulate employment, not commerce (*Hammer v. Dagenhart*, 1918). This decision triggered a long-running but unsuccessful effort to overturn it by a constitutional amendment granting Congress the power to ban from interstate commerce products made by child labor; the Court ultimately reversed itself in *United States v. Darby Lumber Co.* (1941).

The Court was not opposed to all reform, as the issue of zoning attests. Zoning arose early in the twentieth century—first in Los Angeles, in 1906—as a progressive response to health and safety concerns posed by dangerous industrial practices. It reflected the penchant for planning at the heart of early twentieth-century progressivism, but in restricting how land could be used, zoning threatened the rights of private property. Of course, it also could enhance property values by excluding racial or religious minorities, as well as the less affluent. In 1926 the Court accepted zoning as a constitutional use of state police powers if it was not arbitrary (*Village of Euclid v. Amber Realty*

Co.), but here the meaning of property rights was more ambiguous, at least to the judicial mind, than it was when corporate interests were at stake.

The election of Progressives to national and state offices—Presidents Theodore Roosevelt and Woodrow Wilson were both reformers—gave rise to new economic regulations and especially the creation of agencies and commissions, such as the Food and Drug Administration and the Federal Reserve Board, that comprised what became known colloquially as a fourth branch of government. The new regulatory state embraced governmental power to restrict property rights and restrain the excesses of corporate capitalism in the public interest.

Reform also came to the Constitution itself. Twice, Congress passed and states ratified amendments that redefined property rights. The Sixteenth Amendment (1913) enabled Congress to tax incomes, which provided the means to fund the regulatory state and lessened the laissez-faire protection of property by taxing wealth. The Eighteenth Amendment (1919) was a more direct assault on property rights by halting the manufacture and sale of intoxicating liquors, effectively destroying its value. A third amendment, the Seventeenth (1913), made the Senate subject to popular vote—previously, state legislatures made the selection—which eliminated a corrupt mode of election too often controlled by corporate interests and forced senators to pay attention to public opinion.

The New Deal (1933–40) marked the end of laissez-faire constitutionalism. Faced with unemployment of 25 percent, unprecedented corporate failures, and a bankrupt financial system, President Franklin D. Roosevelt rejected free-market solutions to the nation's distress—market failure led to the problems, he concluded—and instead embraced unprecedented government intervention in the economy. A vast array of new federal and state programs sought to control corporate behavior, to counterbalance private power by fostering the growth of labor unions, and to provide economic security for the poor and disadvantaged. During its first hundred days, the new administration demonstrated how it intended to use the commerce clause to reshape the economy: Congress passed new laws to regulate the stock market, set wages and prices, create a government-owned energy producer (the Tennessee Valley Authority [TVA]), and provide relief to the poor. Later laws established Social Security and a number of new regulatory agencies.

This new approach owed much to John Maynard Keynes, a British economist who argued for vigorous government involvement to save capitalism from its own excesses. The New Deal was frankly experimental, and its programs failed as often as they succeeded. It did not end the Great Depression, although its approach of massive fiscal stimulus did: World War II spending—and the enlistment of millions of men into the armed services—ultimately solved the problems of widespread under-consumption and unemployment that prolonged the Depression. Even so, the New Deal's constitutional importance cannot be overstated. It embraced governmental power to control private excess in pursuit of public liberty and warred with the rigid notions of limited government, marketplace competition, and respect for property rights that were at the heart of the prevailing constitutional order.

At the end of his classic work, *The General Theory of Employment, Interest, and Money*, Keynes wrote, "Practical men, who believe themselves to be quite exempt from any intellectual influences, are usually the slaves of some defunct economist."[8] New Dealers had the same view of laissez-faire constitutionalism and its champions on the Court, who they feared would block reform. The justices did not disappoint these expectations; only three were sympathetic to the idea that the Constitution should accommodate economic decisions reached by the representative branches of government.

The first confrontation came in 1935, when the Court struck down four New Deal measures. The emblematic case was *Schechter Poultry Corporation v. United States*, otherwise known as the "sick chicken case" because the prosecution of the local producers involved the sale of "an unfit chicken." Under the National Industrial Recovery Act of 1933, a federal agency, the National Recovery Administration (NRA), established codes for various industries, including poultry processing, that regulated hours, wages, working conditions, and marketing practices. The goal was to reduce the free-for-all competition that the statute's architects believed had helped to cause the Depression. Schechter Poultry presented two arguments: it was engaged exclusively in intrastate commerce and therefore was subject only to state regulation; and the fair practices code mandated by the NRA was an unconstitutional delegation of legislative authority to the executive branch. The Court unanimously agreed on both counts, a decision that killed the act.

In 1935 the justices also overturned the Agricultural Adjustment Act, which subsidized farm commodities (*United States v. Butler*); rejected an act regulating the coal mining industry on the basis of the general welfare and commerce clauses (*Carter v. Carter Coal Company*); reasserted its power to review administrative fact-finding; and declared a New York minimum wage law unconstitutional. The Court upheld only the TVA (as a national defense measure), which New Dealers interpreted as a feint to deflect criticism that the justices would undermine all recovery measures. The conclusion did not seem exaggerated. Never before had the Court overturned so many acts of Congress in such a short period of time.

A political backlash against these decisions soon produced a constitutional crisis. Reelected by a commanding majority but still facing a recalcitrant Court to which he had had no chance to name a justice, Roosevelt and his advisors devised a strategy to blunt the Court's power. In 1937, the president unveiled a plan to restructure the Court, an action permitted to Congress by Article III of the Constitution. For all Supreme Court justices over seventy and one-half years of age, which included its four most conservative members, the president could appoint an additional justice, up to a maximum of six. The measure, presented as a reform designed to aid justices who were too old and ill to carry their judicial responsibilities, provoked a firestorm of criticism, with all but the most dedicated supporters of the New Deal deserting the president. Chief Justice Charles Evans Hughes presented a memorable rebuttal, showing that the justices were easily able to handle their workload and pointing out that the plan offered by the president would actually make more work for the Court and leave the expanded panel less able to carry out its job.

Only after Congress passed an uncontroversial aspect of the plan—a system of pensions for retiring federal judges—did one member of the Court's conservative bloc retire. In a still hotly disputed series of cases in 1937, the Court signaled its willingness to accept New Deal measures. Though Roosevelt lost his battle to reshape the Court, within a few years he had named eight of the nine justices, and the new Supreme Court was, for all practical purposes, the Roosevelt Court.

Four cases in 1937 confirmed the new direction: the Court upheld a Washington State minimum wage law (*West Cast Hotel Company v. Parrish*); extended congressional authority to regulate commerce to any intrastate activity that might directly or indirectly affect interstate commerce, including unionization (*National Labor Relations Board v. Jones and Laughlin Steel Company*); and upheld the Social Security Act of 1935 as a legitimate exercise of congressional discretion under the general welfare and taxing clauses in Article I, Section 8 (*Steward Machine Company v. Davis*, upholding the unemployment insurance features of the act, and *Helvering v. Davis*, sustaining its old-age pension provisions). The repudiation of the old order was clearly evident in the minimum-wage decision, which explicitly rejected the doctrine of liberty of contract: "What is this liberty?" Chief Justice Charles Evans Hughes wrote. "The Constitution does not speak of liberty of contract. It speaks of liberty . . . [but] it does not recognize an absolute and uncontrolled liberty." The right of property was not immune from regulation by a democratic majority or the bureaucracy that acted on its behalf.

The level of judicial scrutiny also changed significantly, as a case the following year made evident. In the most famous footnote in American constitutional history, "Footnote Four," Justice Harlan Fiske Stone, writing for the majority in a decision that prohibited filled milk (skim milk with non-milk fats added) from being sold in interstate commerce, introduced the idea of levels of judicial scrutiny (*United States v. Carolene Products Co.*, 1938). When a law or action, on its face, is within a constitutionally authorized power, the Court would assume its reasonableness and apply minimal oversight—but not when a law falls within an area strictly prohibited by the Constitution, as was the case with the Bill of Rights.

The shift could not have been more dramatic, as was clear two decades later when Justice Hugo Black, writing for the majority in 1963, said, "We refuse to sit as a 'super legislature.' . . . [W]hether the legislature takes as its textbook Adam Smith, Herbert Spencer, or Lord Keynes or some other is no concern of ours" (*Ferguson v. Skrupa*). Of course, the right to property was part of the Fifth and Fourteenth Amendments, but the Court in 1938 decided it could no longer apply standards of strict scrutiny and substantive due process to a collapsed economic order. It has not changed its stance appreciably since then. In effect, Congress has had an unqualified power to regulate any economic activity under the commerce clause. It was an inevitable result, given the public temper during the still-lingering Great Depression.

The "switch in time that saved nine," as political wags labeled the reversal, rescued the Court from an untenable stance—the justices indeed had read the election returns—but it provided no alternate explanation for the Court's work. Formalism had failed as a guide to constitutional interpretation: justices were not impartial and neutral, and time and place affected the interpretation of constitutional principles. The collapse of formalism left a void; no standard took its place that recognized the centrality of property rights to American constitutionalism regardless of the economic theory in vogue.

The Court's retreat on economic matters—or its surrender, as some scholars claim—opened the door to the modern regulatory state. Footnote Four's distinction between property rights and personal liberty would have confounded the framers, who thought of the Constitution as a check on threats to property posed by a democratic majority. Critics such as federal circuit judge Learned Hand noted the "strange anomaly" of imagining that the Fifth Amendment "constituted severer restrictions as to Liberty than Property."[9] The Court since the late 1930s has denied that it thinks of the two as separate: "A fundamental interdependence exists between the personal right to liberty and the personal right to property," the justices proclaimed in 1972. "Neither could have meaning without the other" (*Lynch v. Household Finance Corp.*).

In fact, the constitutional double standard instituted by Footnote Four in the *Carolene Products* case quickly became the new orthodoxy. Since the constitutional revolution of 1937, Congress has had free rein in matters of economic policy under an expansive interpretation of the commerce clause. The Court repeatedly has fostered a national market by limiting sharply the states' ability to isolate or protect their businesses or citizens from national regulations, for example, by striking down a state's prohibition on the importation of waste materials or giving its residents preferred access to natural resources. In this sense, it has promoted the liberty of individuals and corporations to conduct business across state lines, an aim clearly in line with the intentions of the Philadelphia Convention in 1787.

In recent decades a conservative attack on this New Deal constitutionalism has emerged among scholars who asserted the superiority of a private market and sought to apply a cost-benefit analysis to public regulation. According to proponents of the so-called law and economics school, all people voluntarily make rational decisions to further their self-interest, as when they give up money to acquire property or liberty to gain security. But in a regulated economy, consumers and small-business interests are shut out of a legislative process rigged in favor of large interests; laws and administrative rules claim to promote the public welfare, when in fact they advance special interests. Judges, as a result, should decide cases in a way that enhances the ability of people to compete in a free, rational market because doing so maximizes the wealth of society.

This philosophy had appeal in a political environment that, by the end of the 1960s, had grown weary of reform and regulation and too often appeared to promote racial or gender preferences. Conservative victories at the polls in all but three presidential elections from 1968 to 2008 produced a host of lower federal court judges who were sympathetic to this view, as well as to a jurisprudence based on originalism as the only legitimate basis for constitutional interpretation. The new appointments made little difference. Despite a few cases invoking the contract clause as a protection against egregious state interference with property arrangements, the Supreme Court has generally followed the course set in 1937, although in the 1980s and 1990s especially it was deferring to a Congress partial to deregulation and to free-market competition.

At times, this stance produced decisions sharply at odds with what many people believed was a Fifth Amendment protection for property, as when the justices upheld the taking of private property for use by private developers who claimed to be working in the public interest (*Kelo v. City of New London,* 2005). A majority of states quickly passed amendments to their constitutions prohibiting the transfer of eminent domain power to private interests, which suggested that state legislatures were not as unsympathetic to individual interests as the law and economics school assumed.

By the latter half of the twentieth century, the so-called takings clause, the subject of *Kelo*, had emerged as the principal constitutional battleground for property rights. At mid-century the Court equated the "public use" language of the Fifth Amendment as equivalent to the state's police powers and gave wide latitude to the legislative determinations of the need to use eminent domain. The justices also accepted land-use regulations as a legitimate exercise of these powers and thereby not subject to the restrictions of the takings clause; for example, it approved New York City's designation of Grand Central Station as a historic landmark even though this action prevented the landowner from modifying the property, which sharply reduced its commercial value. By the late 1980s the Court revisited this stance and strengthened the rights of property owners faced with a loss of value because of a regulatory taking (the term used to signify a governmental taking by means of a land-use restriction rather than seizure of the property). In 1987, the justices struck down a land-use regulation for the first time since the 1920s (*Nollan v. California Coastal Commission*) and two years later reasserted the rights of utilities against the rate-making authority of states when it warned that "the Constitution protects utilities from being limited to a charge . . . which is so 'unjust' as to be confiscatory" (*Duquesne Light Co. v. Barasch*, 1989).

It is unclear whether the attention to the takings clause represents a new direction for the Court on matters involving congressional power over the economy. The Constitution clearly embraces property and contractual rights, and both the repeated political judgments of state legislatures and the Congress since the 1820s and the decisions of countless courts, including the Supreme Court, have linked these rights to capitalism and a free market. But the deep recession that began in 2007–8, and especially the subsequent need for governments around the world to intervene vigorously in financial markets, called into question the assumption of a rational, beneficent market and in the desirability of an unregulated or lightly monitored economy. Once again Americans were reminded that unbridled private power was as much a threat to liberty as unlimited governmental power.

The issue, as it had been in 1787, is one of balance. The United States, indeed the world, has changed radically since the Revolution—then, only 3 percent of the nation was urban; today, eight of ten residents live in a city; then, markets were limited, local, and isolated; today, they are boundless, linked, and international—but the fundamental questions about the role of government remain. What is not certain is whether the system of checks and balances established in Philadelphia still operates in economic policy or even whether it can any longer be renegotiated in a rapidly changing, increasingly global economy with its disregard of national boundaries. What has become apparent over two centuries of constitutional jurisprudence, however, is how often private ownership is in tension with popular sovereignty, democracy, and the general welfare. How to strike an appropriate balance between these legitimate constitutional interests remains a challenge, one that we share with the founding generation, who viewed this tension as a mainspring of American freedom.

Representation

August 1920 was hot and muggy in Nashville, Tennessee. Normally it was a month when residents left the capital city for the highlands of Kentucky or the Smoky Mountains to the east. But this August was not typical. The Tennessee legislature was in session to ratify the Nineteenth Amendment and extend the vote to women. Thirty-five states had approved the amendment, one short of the three-fourths required for its adoption, yet suffragists were uneasy. The state they had counted on for victory, Connecticut, suddenly appeared unlikely to ratify. Now they had to fight the battle in the conservative, unsympathetic South. A defeat in Tennessee, they feared, would deny constitutional protection for women's suffrage.[1]

The town was thick with celebrities and reporters from around the nation. Carrie Chapman Catt, head of the National Woman Suffrage Association, had arrived from New York two months earlier to organize rallies and letter-writing campaigns, with support from women of urban and rural backgrounds, different social classes, and different races. To demonstrate their unity, the pro-amendment forces adopted the yellow rose as their symbol. In response, opponents chose the red rose. The ensuing campaign soon became known as the "War of the Roses," a tag that played on the name of the fifteenth-century struggle for dominance in England.

Initially, legislators appeared to favor passage, but they began to waver under relentless pressure from opponents of the amendment. The Tennessee senate voted overwhelmingly to ratify, but the state's lower house leaned the other way. A simple count of roses worn by legislators to signal their position, 49 red and 47 yellow, forecast defeat for the amendment. "We are up to the last half of the last state," Catt wrote, "[and] opposition of every sort is fighting with no scruple. . . . [They] are appealing to Negrophobia and every other cave man's prejudice. . . . It's hot, muggy, nasty, and this last battle is desperate. . . . We are low in our minds. . . . Even if we win, we who are here will never remember it but with a shudder."

The road to ratification that was approaching its climactic moment in Tennessee had begun in 1848 at the women's rights convention in Seneca Falls,

New York. The Declaration of Rights and Sentiments adopted at Seneca Falls, framed principally by Elizabeth Cady Stanton and modeled on the Declaration of Independence, contained the first serious proposal that women be allowed to vote. Twenty years later, a women's suffrage amendment was first introduced, unsuccessfully, in Congress. In the 1870s suffragists tried again, this time proposing the so-called Anthony amendment, named for Susan B. Anthony, who rivaled Stanton as the century's leading campaigner for women's rights. Modeled after the Fifteenth Amendment, which forbade states from denying the right to vote based on race or color, but not gender, it provided that "the right of citizens of the United States to vote shall not be denied or abridged by the United States or by any State on account of sex." This language entered the Constitution as the Nineteenth Amendment in 1920, forty-two years later.

All the arguments advanced in Tennessee for and against the amendment had been part of the national debate for decades. Supporters emphasized three themes—citizenship, equality, and responsibility. Women were citizens and the American ideals of citizenship, as expressed in the Declaration of Independence and reinforced in the Fourteenth Amendment, required equal treatment under law. The Fifteenth Amendment had extended the vote to previously excluded African Americans, so women, too, especially white women, were due this right. Women also pointed to their contributions to the nation's economy and demanded an equal opportunity to fulfill their civic obligations and to receive their full measure of other constitutional protections. Increasingly they worked in factories and had begun to enter the professions—and yet they still could not serve on juries, for instance, because jurors were chosen from voting rolls, an exclusion that denied women defendants the right to be tried by their peers. Above all, they were among the people of the United States; they deserved representation of their own choosing.

Opponents of female suffrage focused on threats to the family. A woman's place was in the home, they argued; it was her separate sphere, a world of motherhood and domesticity where she exerted a naturally superior moral influence. Admitting women to the nasty arena of partisan politics would sully them, dragging them to the level of the men who were less refined morally and ethically. Ironically, many feminists accepted the notion that women played a superior domestic role, but they argued in rebuttal that by voting, women would uplift the nation's political and moral tone.

The critical vote came in Tennessee's lower house on August 18. Supporters were two votes shy of passage, but then an opponent switched sides, leaving the legislature deadlocked. A second vote on the amendment produced another tie. Tensions mounted as each side lobbied furiously to change legislators' minds. Suddenly on the third roll call, the youngest member of the legislature, twenty-four-year-old Harry Burns, whose district opposed the amendment, dramatically announced his support. In his pocket was a telegram from his mother, a staunch suffragist, who urged him to vote yes, writing, "I have been watching to see how you stood, but have noticed nothing yet. Be a good boy and help Mrs. Catt put 'Rat' in Ratification." The amendment passed, 49–47. With the certification of Tennessee's decision, the Nineteenth Amendment—and a new democratic right—became part of the Constitution. Only one delegate from the Seneca Falls Convention was still alive when the amendment passed. Charlotte Woodward had been nineteen years old in 1848. When she finally became eligible to cast her first ballot, she was ninety-one. It had taken a lifetime for women to achieve the right to vote.

This wait for inclusion was not unusual in American history; a slow, often fiercely contested expansion of the electorate has been the nation's historical pattern. The success of universal adult suffrage resulted in a Constitution markedly different from the one framed in 1787. The worldview of the framers had no room for women as voters, nor did it see blacks, Indians, or the poor as worthy of the ballot. For the men gathered in Philadelphia, popular consent was essential to republican government, but gaining approval from the people, the ultimate sovereigns, did not imply a universal right to vote. Nor did popular sovereignty, the essence of the Revolution, mean democracy.

The original Constitution does not even mention the vote or democracy, yet today most Americans—indeed, most people throughout the world—casually refer to the United States as democratic. This characterization is accurate as a matter of common practice but misleading as history. The Revolution turned subjects into citizens, but the framers worried about their capacity as rulers. Good republicans all, they believed the vote belonged to any adult male with some investment in society, usually symbolized by holding a minimum amount of real or personal property, but they believed as well that most voters should defer to the wisest and best among them for leadership.

The idea of a limited electorate and deference to wise leaders came under sharp attack early in the young republic, but its retreat was slow and reluctant. The right to vote, both the symbol and the animating force of a democratic society, has followed a tortuous path in American history. Far from inevitable, its progress has been tenuous and always attended by opposition and setbacks. It exists as a constitutional right by amendment, not because of congressional measures or court decisions. War has been the catalyst for each amendment that extended the right—the Fifteenth following the Civil War, the Nineteenth after World War I, and the Twenty-Sixth, which lowered the voting age to eighteen, in the midst of the Vietnam War—with mass movements providing the energy to expand the meaning of the people as rulers.

Yet the vote has been only the most visible symbol of the nation's representative democracy. Questions about the people's rule and their consent to all matters of government have fed political unrest throughout American history, from the antislavery crusades of the 1830s to the angry populism of the 1890s and the tea party protests of 2010. The theme also has been at the heart of battles over judicial review, whether concerning *Dred Scott v. Sandford* in

1857 or *Bush v. Gore* in 2000. More than any other constitutional issue, questions of representation have exposed the fault lines of class, race, and gender in American society. Popular sovereignty has always been the touchstone of republican liberty, with the people conceived as both rulers and ruled, but only grudgingly have the rulers in fact admitted the ruled into their circle.

We often fail to appreciate how radical the idea of popular rule was in 1776. Western societies traditionally viewed hierarchical authority as natural, with ancient Greece and Rome the exceptions that proved the case. The people were considered dangerously unstable and irrational; they were the rabble who required the taming hand of a government led by men with the talent, education, and wealth to promote social order.

Revolutionary republican theory embraced a different set of assumptions based on a century of English resistance to exaggerated views of governmental sovereignty. Its premise was simple: the people must consent to government; they could rule themselves. The colonial argument with Great Britain had tied this claim to a sharpened understanding of representation, the means used by the people to express consent. The connection between the representative and the represented must be direct, which meant that it must be local. Without this bond, the people could not give consent. The requirement for direct, local representation justified colonial resistance to imperial authority. Without it, no legitimate representation could exist; without representation, Parliament had no sovereignty over America. After independence, this formula of popular consent and representation became the measure for republican government.

The revolutionary generation was profoundly aware that theirs was the first—indeed, the only—nation created by the will of the people. Government rested explicitly on the consent of the governed. It was no longer something that happened to people but rather was something that the people by their own volition and active participation brought into being. This belief was a central and deeply felt meaning of the Revolution. But who were these sovereign people and how could the people collectively govern a nation larger and more diverse than Europe? Delegates to the Constitutional Convention avoided this first question and answered the second by invoking the concept of representation.

The failure to define "We, the People" was no accident. Popular sovereignty was in fact a convenient but widely accepted fiction, a necessary philosophical and political argument for the new charter. James Madison and other supporters of a strong general government invoked it to trump the authority of sovereign states, whose fractiousness and self-interest threatened the republican experiment in liberty. But it was a momentous claim because of its radical implications for government. Not only were the people the ultimate authority—"As our constitutions are superior to our legislatures; so our people are superior to our constitutions," reasoned Pennsylvania's James Wilson, Madison's ally in Philadelphia—but the national government depended on their participation. Popularly chosen ratification conventions would convey the people's consent for what heretofore was a contradiction, a national republic. Direct election of the House of Representatives would ensure that the general government's legislature continued to reflect the popular will. Congressmen were agents of the people, chosen to act for the people but never to take the place of the collective sovereign. The people were the rulers, and this characterization made democracy part of the new constitution. Wilson again put the point plainly: "All authority of every kind is derived by REPRESENTATION from the PEOPLE and the DEMO-CRATIC principle is carried over into every part of the government."[2]

It was a nebulous link. For all their commitment to popular sovereignty, the framers were suspicious of unbridled, direct democracy. With the unrest of the 1780s fresh in their minds, they created a framework to restrain and guide democracy. The Constitution contains no right to vote, although it guarantees to each state a republican form of government, an implicit recognition of the right, and specifies the nature of the electorate for the House of Representatives. Elsewhere, the institutions of government had only an indirect connection to the people. The Senate represented a different constituency but it was not to be an aristocratic branch: no property qualifications existed for senators, nor did they formally embody a certain social class or interest. It, too, depended on popular consent, albeit indirectly through election by representative state legislatures (direct election did not occur until 1913, after passage of the Seventeenth Amendment). Indirect election through an electoral college likewise characterized the selection of the president. The aim throughout was not to repudiate democracy but to restrain power and enhance liberty. Success ultimately depended upon a careful architecture to balance interests against each other so the people's will could emerge deliberately rather than as an unrestrained impulse.

The idea that the people could be both sovereign and subjects demanded much from the young republic. Regardless of the internal architecture of checks and balances or the mechanics of government, only the people themselves could make government work. They were responsible for seeing that the Constitution was implemented and interpreted properly. But, again, who were the people? The Constitution failed to define national citizenship, leaving the question, by inference, to the states; it likewise left decisions about the franchise, or vote, of citizens to the discretion of the states. The issue came up for discussion in Philadelphia but few delegates supported an expanded vote, much less universal suffrage. Practical considerations were at play. State constitutions already established qualifications for citizenship and voting, and they differed significantly from one another. An attempt to define these terms in the federal Constitution could jeopardize ratification, especially because slavery complicated the question of citizenship, so the delegates left these matters for the states. Most states agreed, however, that only men of property could cast a ballot.

Property qualifications for voting had a long history. Colonists had adopted the English practice of the forty-shilling freehold, which required a man to own property taxed at this value in order to be eligible to vote. In England, this levy restricted voting because few people, perhaps 10 percent of adult males, owned property taxed at this threshold. The franchise was a privilege granted by the state only to people who had a sufficient stake in society, even though representatives were responsible for everyone in society, not simply voters. America was different. Land was cheap and easily bought, and as much as 70 to 80 percent of adult males owned sufficient property to qualify. Not only was the franchise widespread but the link between property and the vote promoted liberty by freeing men from economic coercion in choosing their rulers.

Many republicans also believed the inverse was true: granting a vote to the poor potentially threatened rights in property and liberty itself. These men would have no mind of their own, James Madison argued in Philadelphia. The growth of manufactures (industry), he feared, would leave men without property of any kind, making them "tools of opulence and ambition." The public liberty, he warned, "will not be secure in their hands."[3] Even for the few advocates of a universal franchise—Benjamin Franklin most prominently—the knowledge that as many as 20 percent of adult white men could not vote was not troublesome. The electorate was much larger and more widespread than in England, and it would ensure proper republican fidelity to the Constitution by electing the wisest and most virtuous men as leaders.

Popular sovereignty could not so easily be constrained. The idea of the people as rulers carried an internal dynamic that set it at odds with republican beliefs about the virtues of deference and submission to the public good. The Revolution unleashed a democratic spirit—Alexis de Tocqueville termed it a "habit of the heart"—based on equality but combined with the civic obligations of republicanism. All men had a duty to participate in government. Americans took this obligation seriously. Collective sovereignty suggested that the people might act in at least three capacities in relationship to government. In the most basic meaning, they could act as the sovereign in creating, amending, or even abolishing government. They also could monitor the actions of the government they created, as happened when they voted. Finally, they could exercise their rights to protest the soundness or constitutionality of governmental actions. In all these roles, the people were both sovereigns and subjects.

The republican duty to participate at times led many Americans to seek continuous improvement in their fundamental law. Veneration of the Constitution, which began early in the young nation, obscures how often Americans have sought to change it. At first glance, the number of amendments seems too small to support this conclusion. Since the flurry of amendments adopted soon after ratification (the Bill of Rights in 1791, the Eleventh Amendment in 1798, and the Twelfth in 1804), voters have modified the Constitution formally only fifteen times in 220 years, with three amendments coming immediately after the Civil War and two others in the experiment with national prohibition. This scanty record should not suggest that the amending impulse has been weak, however; more than 12,000 attempts to change the Constitution since 1787 serve as evidence of its vitality.

The question of how permanent to make a particular framework for government animated a correspondence between Thomas Jefferson and James Madison in 1789. Their exchange was speculative and spurred by Jefferson's dismay at the devastation inflicted on France, where he had served as the American ambassador, by a corrupt monarchy and aristocracy. The Francophile Jefferson toyed with an idea about how to avoid such conditions in the future. Expressing an opinion that he would repeat often, although not always consistently, Jefferson reminded his friend that "the earth belongs to the living. . . . No society can make a perpetual constitution or perpetual law." It was a radical democratic vision. But for Madison the idea was fundamentally unsound, in great measure because of the continuities of debt and obligation linking generations. He replied that the idea was fine as theory but not in practice: "A Government so often revised would become too unstable to retain those prejudices in its favor which antiquity inspires, and which are perhaps a salutary aid to rational Government in the most enlightened ages."[4]

As a society we have embraced Madison's view. We celebrate the framers' foresight in balancing change and stability through the elaborate process required to amend the Constitution; we view it as a counterweight to the whims of public opinion by requiring a supermajority of Congress followed by a supermajority of ratifying states to change fundamental law. In this sentiment we share the views of the victorious Federalists, who sought gradual change. But Jefferson's vision captured the imagination of many inhabitants of the young nation who took the notion of popular sovereignty as a good deal more than slogan or shibboleth.

Within a few short years after the Constitutional Convention, Americans came to revere their fundamental charter, yet they continued to debate vigorously whether the people, acting collectively as sovereigns, could change their charters at will rather than follow the process of amendment and ratifications. By this logic, a majority of the people could not be bound by a fundamental law of their own making. Both the procedural view of change by amendment and the democratic view of change by majority will shared the general consensus that the people were sovereign. They differed over how much power remained with the people and how much power the people had surrendered to government. It was a difference that mattered because of the questions and controversies it raised about how people could govern themselves.

We have lost sight of this history because of our tendency to assume that the framers' constitutional vision epitomized American thinking on these questions. What this singular focus ignores are the countless other constitutional proceedings that occurred in the states before the Civil War. In true Jeffersonian fashion, a significant number of Americans believed that one generation could not bind another, even in matters of fundamental law. This sense of an active popular sovereignty took various guises, from the first wave of state constitution-making in the 1820s and 1830s and their removal of property requirements for voting to a series of crises, such as the Kentucky and Virginia Resolutions (1798) or Hartford Convention (1814). Usually considered as disagreements about federalism, the problem in each instance also involved both questions about the Constitution and questions about constitutionalism in general, especially the role and responsibility of collective sovereignty in American government. The belief that the people, acting as one, could challenge federal power did not depend on an established process for redress of grievances.

The Civil War discredited but did not extinguish this claim. Americans traditionally appeal to the same tradition when dissenting from the actions of their government. Popular sovereignty has taken life continuously when invoked by individuals and groups who find themselves in the minority on a particular issue. Protest is made legitimate by an appeal to the people's right to rule, even if the occasion for protest came as the result of defeat in democratic elections. Popular sovereignty, or rather claims of its denial, has been the natural refuge of factions who fail to win a majority at the ballot box or who suffer defeat in legislative chambers. It is at the heart of all populist rhetoric.

While Americans debated the riddle of how the people could be both sovereign and subject and as they pressed for constitutional change, they also viewed voting as the means of ensuring representative and responsive government. In 1787 state constitutions guaranteed the right to vote, and all except Vermont restricted the franchise to adult male property owners or taxpayers. Only in New Jersey could women vote (specifically, unmarried women who met the property qualification), and free blacks who owned property could vote in a majority of northern states.

The electorate expanded dramatically by the middle of the nineteenth century, although to include white men only. Two waves of state constitution-making, the first in the 1820s and the second in the 1850s, led to the abolition of property requirements, resulting in nearly universal white adult male suffrage. By contrast, Native Americans and women were never considered for the franchise except in a handful of places, and many of the states that had permitted free blacks to vote now stripped them of their political rights.

By the mid-1850s few economic barriers to voting existed. Even aliens (foreigners) could vote in most states outside the Northeast, on the belief that it would induce them to settle there and because non-citizen immigrants were a significant percentage of the population, notably in the Midwest. The United States was not alone in this democratic impulse—Western Europe, too, experienced it—but nowhere was the right to vote more broadly defined than in America.

It is tempting to attribute this development to an unalloyed desire to expand democracy. The idea was powerful but, as with most movements, more was at work. One influence was the rapid increase after 1790 in the number of men who were ineligible to vote. The growth of urban areas meant that an increasing number of its residents could not meet property qualifications rooted in conditions of an agrarian society. The practical consequence was that fewer men were eligible to serve on juries or in the militia, thus increasing the burden of government on voters, who formed the pool of eligible men for such civic duties. A limited electorate also raised questions about the legitimacy of government, the exercise of power, and even what it meant to be free: "They alone deserve to be free," a Virginia petition proclaimed, "or have a guarantee for their rights, who participate in the formation of their political institutions."[5] Partisan politics played a role as well. The development of an extra-constitutional party system prompted a competition for votes not envisioned by the framers. Federalists and Republicans and then Democrats and Whigs vigorously sought voters who shared their respective visions for society. Extending the vote to these men was the fastest route to power, regardless of a party's commitment to democratization.

Liberalization of the vote occurred before Americans became concerned about the dangerous classes flooding into the nation's cities. Few advocates of a broadened franchise thought they were extending it to the lower classes, immigrants, and former farm laborers who worked for wages in the nation's new factories. Rhode Island offers a case in point. Alone among the states, it faced the question of expanding the vote after such a demographic shift. This geographically small state was one of the first to move to an industrial economy, and its textile mills and small manufacturing attracted thousands of immigrants to Providence and other urban areas. Rhode Island in the 1840s maintained property qualifications for voting from its seventeenth-century colonial constitution; considered liberal generations before, they now excluded more than half the state's male residents. Under this scheme, landowners controlled state government and were jealous of sharing power with non-propertied men.

Blocked from the ballot box by an antagonistic legislature, in 1841 mechanics and workingmen convened a People's Convention to draft a new state constitution based on universal adult male suffrage. A ratification vote revealed clear majority support for the new charter, but the legislature rejected it as illegitimate. What followed was an armed march on the capital, the arrest of the People's Convention's leaders, and the collapse in 1842 of the insurrection known as Dorr's Rebellion (named after Thomas Wilson Dorr, its leader). Class politics had trumped democracy.

A case stemming from the episode, *Luther v. Borden* (1849), made it to the U.S. Supreme Court, which declined to interpret the Constitution's guarantee of "a republican form of government" (Article IV) to require states to be democratic or more completely representative. This question was political, not judicial, and therefore could be decided only by the state, the Court determined. More than 150 years later, at the beginning of the twenty-first century, following a hotly disputed presidential ballot recount in Florida between Vice President Al Gore and Texas Governor George W. Bush, the justices would not be so deferential.

Dorr's Rebellion was a harbinger of class-based efforts in the late nineteenth century to restrict the vote as waves of eastern and southern Europeans, Jews, and Asians flooded the nation's cities. But during the antebellum decades, democracy, with its emphasis on popular consent, was a new American gospel. It did not apply to women, blacks, and certain categories of white men, most often paupers, migrants, and felons, but few people doubted that the United States had given birth to a new democratic age. A constitutional consequence of this faith was the recasting of the presidency as a democratic office. The framers had deliberately insulated the office from popular pressure through a process of indirect election by electors chosen by state legislatures in proportion to their representation in Congress. The heated antebellum contests between political parties changed the substance, if not the form, of this process.

By the election of 1824 only six states retained property requirements, but the most significant turn came with the presidency of Andrew Jackson (1829–37). Campaigning as a common man, Jackson blended the newly emergent strength of both urban and rural democratic reform movements. He pledged to reform the national government and its atmosphere of privilege, which he blamed for denying him election in 1824, when he won a plurality of electoral votes but lost in the House of Representatives to a candidate from the ruling establishment, John Quincy Adams, son of John Adams, the second president. (Under Article II, Section 1, the House, voting as states, chose the president if no candidate received a majority of the electoral vote.) Jackson especially wanted to cleanse the executive branch, he announced in his First Annual Message to Congress, and make its duties "so plain and simple that men of intelligence may readily qualify" as appointees. As is often the case, this reform served two masters: it widened the circle of executive talent in Washington, and it gave the president more offices to distribute as rewards for his supporters, which in turn strengthened the party system. The spoils system, as Jackson's opponents labeled it, made the president the titular head not only of the government but also of a political machine that continually sought to gain more votes.

Jackson helped to create the democratic presidency as well with his argument that his office alone represented the nation. He accompanied his veto of the re-charter of the Second Bank of the United States in July 1832 with a message designed to win popular support against the supporters of privilege. The bill, he argued, not only was unconstitutional, but it also harmed ordinary citizens: "[T]he rich and powerful too often bend the acts of government to their selfish purposes . . . but when the laws undertake to add to these natural and just advantages artificial distinctions . . . and exclusive privileges, to make the rich richer and the potent more powerful, the humble members of society—the farmers, mechanics, and laborers—who have neither the time nor the means of securing like favors to themselves, have a right to complain of the injustice of their Government."

Jackson's easy reelection a few months later sharpened his claim to be the people's representative, with an ability to act independently of Congress. The result was not a centralization of power as his opponents feared; Jackson's brand of democracy favored local control within a strong Union. But his argument that the presidency was uniquely representative, with its implication that presidential action had popular consent, proved to be a powerful catalyst for the decades-long remaking of the presidency into a different sort of constitutional office than that envisioned by the founders.

In many ways, Jackson's presidential tenure was the ultimate irony. The hero of New Orleans wanted nothing more than to restore the values of the Old Republic. Instead, his presidency—and, perhaps more significant, what it captured and symbolized—both tapped and unleashed a torrent of democratic reforms. Advocates and opponents of change alike used the mass tactics pioneered by political parties, such as popular conventions and petition campaigns, to agitate for widespread changes, from temperance and immigration restriction to women's suffrage and antislavery. This new democracy roiled the nation with its promise of individual equality in a more perfect union: "The country is full of rebellion; the country is full of kings," essayist Ralph Waldo Emerson observed in the mid-1840s. But reform carried with it the seeds of disunion, especially on issues, such as slavery, that threatened the sectional compromises at the foundation of the new democratic politics. The nation may not have reached secession and civil war by an excess of democracy, as scholars once argued, but the reforms entrenched more firmly the opposing ethics of freedom and slavery and exposed their constitutional incompatibility.

The Civil War and Reconstruction embedded representative democracy as the mode of constitutional government in the United States. The 1787 constitution was a charter for a democratic republic, as the founders understood the term, but it was not what later generations would deem democratic. "We, the People" was no literary conceit, but neither was it a guide to how government would operate. The Jacksonian era shifted this expectation with its attacks on elitism and its chants hailing the common man as king; it was the Civil War that established democracy as the governing ethos. Modern warfare has a leveling influence—the battlefield does not honor class distinctions—and the emphasis on equality and democracy as core constitutional values stemmed in part from its effects.

The Reconstruction amendments made this transformation clear in at least two ways: they advanced a new, inclusive definition of citizenship depending solely on place of birth (or naturalization), and they pledged national power to ensure equality before the law for all citizens. The amendments also introduced a new equation that linked liberty, equality, and democracy. Freedom for all people (Thirteenth Amendment), unconditional equality before the law for all citizens (Fourteenth), and guaranteed access to the ballot box (Fifteenth) was the constitutional frame for this turn. President Abraham Lincoln cast the promise poetically in the closing phase of the Gettysburg Address—"that government of the people, by the people, for the people shall not perish from the earth"—but, even as an aspiration, his words were a clear break with the assumptions of 1787. Certainly, later generations understood Lincoln's peroration as a pledge and sought to redeem it: all the amendments from the Sixteenth through the Twenty-fourth (except the Prohibition amendments) were extensions of the power of the people to choose and control their government.

These steps came slowly. From 1850 to 1920, two stories of democratic constitutionalism emerged. One was its formal expansion to excluded groups, as expressed through the right to vote; the other was its restriction in law and practice. For free blacks, exclusion began long before the Civil War, as all but five states added the qualifier "white" to their constitutional or statutory requirements for voting by 1850. The antebellum federal government also prohibited black voting in the territories. Even after ratification of the Fifteenth Amendment, which forbade denial or abridgement of the right to vote for American citizens "on account of race, color, or previous condition of servitude," blacks found their access to the voting booth blunted by literacy tests, grandfather clauses, and poll taxes, not to mention outright intimidation. Early efforts by the national government to protect newly enfranchised African Americans faded after Republicans grew tired of policing a recalcitrant South intent on restoring a social and political regime based on race. By the mid-1870s the Supreme Court had eviscerated key provisions of the Enforcement Act of 1870 (*U.S. v. Cruikshank*, 1876) and held that the Fifteenth Amendment did not confer the right to vote but only prohibited exclusion on racial grounds (*U.S. v. Reese*, 1876).

The result was predictable: throughout the South blacks effectively lost the right to vote. No southern state excluded black voters directly because it was too easy to deny the vote by legitimate means. By the early part of the twentieth century, for example, most of the states in the former Confederacy had amended their constitutions to limit the franchise by requiring payment of a tax to register, an act that kept poor whites as well as blacks from voting, especially if the tax were cumulative. Other legal tactics included lengthy residence requirements, elaborate registration systems, secret ballot laws, and ultimately white-only primaries. And if these restrictions did not work, threats, violence, and manipulation of voting results would. As one black Georgia voter poignantly testified before a Senate committee, "You may vote till your eyes drop out . . . [but] there's a hole in the bottom of the boxes some way and lets out our vote."[6]

In the late nineteenth and early twentieth centuries, racism fed resistance to the black vote in the South, and often in the North, too. A desire to limit voting by class was common everywhere. Few advocates of restrictions denied their aim of keeping black, poor, and illiterate people from voting: "I told the people of my county," a delegate to the Virginia constitutional convention of 1901 said, "that I intended . . . to disenfranchise every negro that I could disenfranchise under the Constitution of the United States." An Alabama leader promised to keep "ignorant, incompetent, and vicious" white men from the polling booth.[7] The efforts to restrict suffrage worked. In the South, voting dropped precipitously from Reconstruction levels; in Mississippi, for instance, turnout plummeted from 70 percent in the 1870s to 15 percent in the early twentieth century, a level that suggests how severely the new limits reduced both black and poor white voting.

The issue in the North was the 25 million new immigrants who flooded its cities from 1870 to 1920. Few arrivals were from Anglo-Saxon stock, and many were not the virtuous, independent farmers who formed the heart of an earlier agrarian republic; rather, they were poor laborers who supported big-city political machines. They were the "dangerous classes" who allegedly threatened social order, and middle-class reformers sought to limit their electoral influence. Historian Francis Parkman put the case bluntly in a widely circulated essay, "The Failure of Universal Suffrage": the city was full of "restless working men, foreigners . . . to whom liberty means license and politics means plunder . . . who love the country for what they can get out of it . . . [and in this circumstance] universal suffrage becomes a questionable blessing."[8]

Faced with this threat, many northern leaders repudiated the notion, so prominent in mid-century, that voting was a right. Like their southern counterparts, they pushed for restrictions on voting to purify the electorate. The means were similar: literacy requirements (use of the Australian or secret ballot, a widely adopted reform, meant that voters must be able to read), exclusion of paupers, residency requirements, and elimination of alien suffrage, among other tactics, were used to limit the northern electorate. In all of these measures, the Constitution, as interpreted by the Supreme Court, posed no barrier. Only overt or blatant racial discrimination by a state, not by individuals (private actors), was barred by the Reconstruction amendments. In most other ways, states could exercise a free hand in determining the shape of the electorate and the conditions for voting.

The campaign to gain the vote for women offered both a confirmation and a counterpoint to efforts to restrict the vote for other Americans. Attempts to include women in the electorate were rare before Seneca Falls in 1848 and, despite growing agitation for women's suffrage in the 1850s, Radical Republicans had no enthusiasm for linking it to their commitment to black enfranchisement. "This hour belongs to the negro," the abolitionist leader Wendell Philips admonished, expressing a common belief that support for women would jeopardize the cause of ex-slaves.[9] Both the Fourteenth and the Fifteenth Amendments made the point clear: the former by specifically guaranteeing the right to vote in federal elections to male citizens over twenty-one and the latter by barring abridgement of the right to vote based on "race, color, or previous condition of servitude," a standard that excluded white women.

The reason was not unalloyed sexism, at least not in the sense of primitive animus against women. American culture simply assumed female inferiority. This premise made the issue more complicated because so much of American law was based on gender distinctions. Married women, for instance, were the legal creatures of their husbands. The cause of women's suffrage implied an equality that went against cultural assumptions and held the unwelcome potential for wholesale restructuring of domestic and property law.

Frustrated with the politics of reform, feminists turned to litigation, but the Supreme Court was no friendlier to women than drafters of the Reconstruction amendments had been. Francis Minor, an attorney and the husband of a suffrage activist, filed suit on behalf of his wife to test his belief that women could vote under the Fourteenth Amendment. (As a married woman, Virginia Minor had no legal right to sue in her own name.) A unanimous Court rejected the argument. Women were persons and might even be citizens under the terms of the Fourteenth Amendment, but its language did not prevent states from restricting the right to vote—"that important trust"—to men alone (*Minor v. Happersett*, 1875). Two years earlier the Court had rejected Myra Bradwell's petition for membership in the Illinois bar, ruling that it was not a privilege of citizenship protected by the Fourteenth Amendment (*Bradwell v. Illinois*, 1873). Justice Joseph P. Bradley, who wrote a concurring opinion, gratuitously cited the "Divine Law of the Creator" for the separate and inferior status of women: "[T]he natural and proper timidity and delicacy which belongs to the female sex evidently unfits it for many of the occupations of civil life," he announced. "The paramount destiny and mission of women are to fulfill the noble and benign offices of wife and mother."

Blocked by the Court and by an equally resistant Congress, women suffragists adopted a state-by-state strategy, with some success. The territory of Wyoming granted women the vote in 1869, and reaffirmed it upon statehood in 1889. By the mid-1890s three other western states—Utah, Colorado, and Idaho—had enfranchised women, in part because it rapidly cut the time territories had to qualify for statehood on the basis of a minimum population of duly registered voters. Other states rejected similar efforts, but women made small gains in state and local elections, such as municipal and school offices, that were not governed by constitutional restrictions.

Although progress was slow, the movement attracted support, in large measure because of the very fear of social disorder that spurred efforts to deny the vote to urban working classes. Some men were persuaded by long-standing republican and natural rights arguments based on popular consent; more accepted it because women were believed to have superior moral qualities, such as industry and sobriety, which would improve governance and politics. Class and race also entered the argument for women's suffrage: white, middle-class women outnumbered the immigrants, blacks, and paupers; they would counterbalance the ballots of these less deserving and less desirable groups. But this anti-democratic argument was not effective because it fit too well with prevailing conservative efforts to restrict the franchise. Among suffragists, the period from 1896 to 1910 became known as "the doldrums" because it produced so few victories.

What slowed reform was its narrow political base. It rested too much on the energies of activists, many of whom did not represent the interests of either elite or working women. Once the movement became more diverse and better organized, it built an irresistible momentum for a constitutional remedy for what ordinary politics and litigation had not accomplished. One key to its success was an ideological shift from xenophobia and class politics to social reform. Suffragists began to emphasize the vote as a way to protect the interests of working women. In doing so, they linked their cause to wider Progressive Era concerns about the concentration of economic power and exploitation of workers. The engagement of working-class women brought new support from trade unions and socialist groups. This coalition began to earn victories after 1910, with eight states granting women the vote by 1913.

In 1915 the various national women's suffrage organizations, which had long differed on strategy, came together with a single-minded focus on securing a federal amendment. The U.S. entry into World War I in 1917 briefly suspended the congressional lobbying and White House picketing that the coalition used to build pressure for passage, but soon the war became a catalyst for victory. President Woodrow Wilson, who had advanced democracy as one justification for American engagement in the European conflict, called for the enfranchisement of women in recognition of their contribution to the war effort. It was a mimetic moment. Just as the Civil War had strengthened the claims of equality for African Americans, so World War I spurred a similar demand for women. Congress quickly passed a constitutional amendment and submitted it for ratification. On August 18, 1920, Tennessee's slim vote of approval provided the necessary thirty-sixth vote, and the Nineteenth Amendment became part of the Constitution.

War proved important in crystallizing support for a more democratic Constitution. Both the Fifteenth and Nineteenth Amendments—and, later, the Twenty-sixth Amendment (1971) lowering the voting age to eighteen— followed conflicts in which excluded groups made important contributions to the war effort. Many white Americans believed that freedom was uniquely an Anglo-Saxon heritage, and they first imagined extending the franchise as a blow against European dictatorships, a way to assert American exceptionalism.

In a limited sense, these amendments were products of the moment. But they also had a long gestation. Democratic constitutionalism was more than an impulse; it was the result of social, economic, and political changes that persuaded the nation to redefine its fundamental law. In each case, the democratic ideal, whether expressed as popular consent, representation, or equality, spurred and sustained a movement for expansion of the electorate against significant opposition and resistance to change. The new amendments threatened to alter deeply held social beliefs about race and sex and to upset existing power relationships. Admitting blacks to the political order as equals also implied a social equality that most whites did not accept. In similar fashion, the right to vote was an expression of male power. It belonged initially to white men and then to all men, but only to men. Women's suffrage challenged traditional male roles, including men's legal dominance over women. Yet with both amendments democratic demands (and practical politics) bested fear.

In neither instance did these larger social transformations occur as anticipated—or dreaded. A brief flurry of black participation in politics during Reconstruction ended in the face of southern white opposition and northern indifference. The Fifteenth Amendment, unambiguous on its face, was interpreted in ways that ignored its plain purpose. By the 1890s segregation was more entrenched and African Americans more marginalized than even the most diehard opponent of black equality could have imagined after the end of slavery. This circumstance did not change until the civil rights movement of the 1950s and 1960s, when African Americans finally gained the vote and realized the representative participation in government that had been pledged a century earlier.

Women did not face the stigma of race but their entry into politics also brought little immediate change. Voting patterns and party alignments remained similar to pre-enfranchisement decades. Social reform, once the hope for women's suffrage, did not happen, at least not at once; bankers and stockbrokers dominated the 1920s, not crusaders. Social welfare became a more prominent concern but few programs engendered by women's interests—for example, maternal and infant care—materialized until the New Deal or later. After their enfranchisement, women were more permanently part of government than African Americans had been earlier, but they, too, had to wait decades before reaping the fruits of their democratic labors.

Constitutional democracy scored another success in the Progressive Era with the ratification in 1913 of the Seventeenth Amendment, requiring the popular election of U.S. senators. The Constitution initially provided for the election of senators by state legislatures in order to secure representation of the states, but for much of the nineteenth century this system instead had fostered corruption and political chaos that often left state legislatures deadlocked. Rejecting the debased system, twenty-nine states adopted direct election, and after the fraudulent election of an Illinois senator in 1909 and his subsequent unseating following a Senate investigation in 1912, a recalcitrant Senate finally supported the measure first proposed in 1893.

The Seventeenth Amendment was part of a package of reforms designed to cure the ills of democracy by creating more democracy, as reformers put it, by which they meant bypassing party caucuses and political machines. Progressives believed that graft, corruption, and corporate power had bastardized the political process and sapped civic virtue. The secret ballot, state-controlled direct primary elections, restrictions on campaign contributions and lobbying activities, and initiatives and referenda were intended to circumvent state legislatures and allow voters to pass state laws directly. Recall of elected officials also was part of the prescription for reform.

These changes usually were aimed at state and local governments, although some had counterparts in federal law (such as restrictions on lobbying and campaign contributions), and they reflected a desire to keep government close to the people. Another amendment, likewise part of the progressive agenda, made it possible for the national government in future decades to become an engine of national reform. The Sixteenth Amendment, ratified in 1913, legitimized a federal income tax, which the Supreme Court had declared unconstitutional in 1895 (*Pollack v. Farmers Loan and Trust Company*) despite the enactment of such a tax during the Civil War. Although its impact was not immediate, the income tax gave the central government the financial means to respond vigorously to important national problems, including demands for an energetic democratic constitutionalism that arose again after World War II. It also democratized the national government indirectly; by making the American people the source of its funding, the government became responsible to them.

Democratic revisions of the Constitution did not end in 1920. The Twenty-third (1961), Twenty-fourth (1964), and Twenty-sixth (1971) amendments all advanced this aim. Two amendments mimicked the negative style of the Fifteenth Amendment by forbidding states to use certain criteria in determining who could vote: states could not levy a poll tax (Twenty-third) and could not prevent men and women eighteen years or older from voting (Twenty-sixth). The Twenty-fourth Amendment granted the District of Columbia a number of electors equal to the least populous state, thereby extending the right to vote in presidential elections to residents of the nation's capital.

These amendments were a clear public commitment to universal suffrage, which now was at the center of the representative principle, while other amendments aimed in part to increase the national government's responsiveness to the people. Shifting the start of a new presidential term from March 4 to January 20 (Twentieth Amendment, 1933), prompted by the emergency of the Great Depression, was an effort to vest authority and accountability more quickly in the people's choice. Limiting the president and vice president to two terms (Twenty-second, 1951), a Republican-led reaction to Franklin Roosevelt's four consecutive electoral victories, mandated a turnover in office that recalled Andrew Jackson's call for democratic rotation.

The voting amendments embraced democracy as a core value, but they were not self-enforcing. The history of the Fifteenth Amendment was illustrative. Throughout the last half of the nineteenth century and well into the twentieth, neither the Congress nor the Supreme Court actively pursued remedies when state actions circumvented the clear federal constitutional intent to provide blacks access to the ballot box. The Court permitted white-only primaries to continue, for example, unless they were approved by state law, and Congress ignored ample evidence that blacks in the South faced insurmountable obstacles when attempting to vote. By the mid-twentieth century, however, the success of the civil rights movement persuaded both legislators and justices to make democratic values part of statutory and constitutional law.

Many of the early voting rights cases decided by the Supreme Court involved the efforts of the Texas legislature to prohibit African Americans from casting ballots in the Democratic primary. (Texas was part of the one-party South that emerged after the end of Reconstruction.) The justices initially had declared the exclusion of blacks by state law to be in violation of the Fourteenth Amendment but accepted as constitutional a decision by the state party executive committee to limit the primary to whites (*Grovey v. Townsend*, 1935), under the notion that the discrimination was private and beyond the reach of the Constitution. Eight years later, in *Smith v. Allwright* (1944), they reversed course: the party, the justices reasoned, was in fact an agent of the state and thereby exercised a public function that must meet constitutional requirements. The Court closed the door completely on white-only primaries in *Terry v. Adams* (1953) when it blocked the use of voluntary white-only clubs to choose nominees, a decision that set an important precedent for later congressional prohibitions of private racial discrimination under the Fifteenth Amendment.

In 1953, Earl Warren became chief justice, and this Californian politician-turned-judge soon led the Court to much bolder and more controversial decisions on questions of suffrage. Most notably, a concern for equality replaced traditional deference to state legislatures in matters related to the franchise. The justices increasingly interpreted the Fourteenth Amendment's due process and equal protection clauses as barriers to statutes and official practices that violated core principles of fairness and representative self-government.

The radical break with precedent came in the early 1960s, when the Court turned to legislative redistricting. The initial case, *Baker v. Carr* (1962), arose in Tennessee. The state had not redrawn its legislative districts since 1901 even though its constitution required reapportionment after every decennial census. The result was disproportionate power for rural districts that had lost population for decades and no longer represented a majority of the state's population. Tennessee, in brief, embraced a system of virtual representation similar in practice to the scheme rejected by American colonists in the years before independence. Ultimately, the issue came down to whether the federal courts had jurisdiction. If it was a political question, then the antebellum precedent in *Luther v. Borden* suggested they did not, but the Supreme Court now decided the question was one of equal protection. Simply put, urban voters in Tennessee did not have representation in the state legislature equal to their percentage of the population.

Baker v. Carr was unusually contentious—the justices debated it far longer and more intensely than usual, issuing five separate opinions—and the decision did not immediately force the state to redistrict, although the majority justices warned that failure to do so would violate the Fourteenth Amendment's equal protection clause. Chief Justice Warren, who earlier had written the opinion for the Court in *Brown v. Board of Education*, called the result the "most vital decision" of his tenure on the Court. Within a year, reapportionment suits had been filed from thirty-six states. Two years later, in *Reynolds v. Sims* (1964), the Court settled on the standard of "one person, one vote" to govern these politically volatile questions. The formula was precise for congressional districts and only slightly less so for state legislative apportionment, but the principle was certain. The Constitution required that each person's vote count the same, or as Warren wrote for the Court: "Legislatures represent people, not trees or acres. Legislators are elected by voters, not farms or cities or economic interests."

The upshot of the decision, part of a series of cases known collectively as the *Reapportionment Cases*, was a vast institutional revolution. At least one house in nearly all the states and both houses in most were judged unrepresentative. Soon the principle of equal representation extended to the local level. These cases involved the Court in a "political thicket," as Justice Felix Frankfurter had warned earlier in his plurality opinion in *Colegrove v. Green* (1946), but they also reaffirmed that "fair and effective representation for all citizens," as Warren asserted in *Reynolds*, was a central tenet of democratic constitutionalism. This principle also reinforced the notion of local, geographically based representation that had been central to the American revolutionaries.

What this principle meant in practice was a more vexing question, especially because *Reynolds* had set the standard as more than one person, one vote. It also had spoken of unconstitutional arrangements that diluted the weight of a person's vote, as, for example, when legislators drew equal but intentionally white-majority districts. In these circumstances, the discrimination was not individual but collective: black and white votes counted equally but whites would always be able to block the election of an African American representative.

The Voting Rights Act of 1965 anticipated some of these issues. President Lyndon B. Johnson, a Texas Democrat who was deeply committed to black equality, pushed the measure, using the harsh public reaction to televised police brutality against civil rights demonstrators in Selma, Alabama, earlier in the year to pressure a reluctant Congress. The act mandated national supervision of voting, especially in southern states where hostile legislatures and unsympathetic federal judges had barred African Americans from the polls. Not only could federal marshals be used to ensure minority suffrage, but states with a history of discrimination had to obtain pre-clearance from the Justice Department for any changes in their election laws.

Challenged by the affected states, the Supreme Court affirmed the measure as a valid exercise of power under the Fifteenth Amendment's enforcement clause

(*South Carolina v. Katzenbach*, 1966). In a separate case (*Katzenbach v. Morgan*, 1966) it also invoked the equal protection clause of the Fourteenth Amendment by upholding the provision that banned New York from using English-only ballots to exclude the large number of Spanish-speaking Puerto Ricans in New York City. Other cases later in the decade upheld the power of Congress to bar literacy tests; and in 1970, the justices ruled that the ban on such tests and other devices to discriminate against back voting extended to the states under the Fifteenth Amendment (*Oregon v. Mitchell*).The Court's decisions clearly affirmed two basic precepts: all racial barriers to voting were illegal, and the national government had the power to ensure race-neutral elections.

The Voting Rights Act also attacked wealth as a barrier to voting by instructing the attorney general to seek a test of the constitutionality of state poll taxes. (The Twenty-third Amendment banned poll taxes only in federal elections.) In *Harper et al. v. Virginia Board of Elections* (1966), the Court reversed a 1937 decision by ruling that the equal protection clause forbade states from using "wealth or fee paying" as a test of voter qualifications. For the first time in the nation's history, a majority of justices, two of whom had grown up poor, rejected all economic restrictions on voting. A congressional ban of unreasonable residency requirements also received Court approval, following its adoption in 1969 of the "strict scrutiny" standard for evaluating the constitutionality of voting statutes. Legislators must meet a high burden of proof in this area, as in race, because these laws, the justices reasoned, "constitute the foundation of our representative society" (*Kramer v. Union Free School District,* 1969). Over the course of a decade, both the Court and Congress had linked the Fourteenth Amendment's equal protection clause to the Fifteenth Amendment's ban on racial discrimination in voting and then extended it to other forms of voting discrimination not expressly forbidden by the Constitution.

Broadened several times to include Latinos, Asian Americans, and American Indians, most recently in 2006, the Voting Rights Act was the most successful civil rights act ever passed by Congress. It resulted in substantial increases in both the number of minority voters and officeholders, but it also raised an important new question about the meaning of representation and constitutional democracy. Did it guarantee group rights as well as individual rights? Were minorities entitled to a proportionate number of representatives or, at a minimum, to districts in which that group was the majority? The questions were not abstract because legislators still had legitimate means to dilute the impact of minority votes, for example, through creation of multi-member districts. Even though the Court heard a variety of cases in the 1970s and 1980s that tested this notion, it never developed a clear standard, in part because proportionate officeholding has never been embraced as a right by most Americans.

Moreover, the nature of representation itself had shifted. From the nation's beginnings, geography had served as shorthand for the mutual interests shared by the representative and represented: people who lived in the same district were assumed to share common bonds. This circumstance was much less likely in the polyglot, economically diverse, and highly mobile society of the late twentieth century, but Americans were too individualistic to be comfortable with the idea that representation could be tied to racially defined groups.

Consistent with this belief, the Supreme Court ruled that racial gerrymandering, that is, privileging race to ensure a majority for any racial group, normally would not be constitutional (*Shaw v. Reno*, 1993). The vote was an individual right that belonged to all adult citizens equally. The true constitutional measure was whether each vote was meaningful. By the twenty-first century, with numerous examples of black candidates elected by majority white electorates, including most significantly the first African American president, Barack Obama, many people found it difficult to argue otherwise.

By the early 1970s, with the right to vote nationalized, the United States had nearly universal suffrage as a matter of constitutional law. Wealth, race, gender, and literacy, among other characteristics, no longer could be used to disqualify adults from voting. The Voting Rights Act nationalized voting requirements, and in 1993 the National Voter Registration Act, also known as the Motor Voter Law, made registration easier by requiring states to enlist voters when they did business with local motor vehicle bureaus or applied for social services. Intended to increase turnout at elections, which had been in decline since 1924, the act was the final step in removing impediments to voting and meeting the demands of democratic constitutionalism. Under its aegis, registrations increased dramatically, disproportionately drawn from the young, black, and high school educated who tended to vote Democratic, the result feared by Republicans who had opposed the bill. Critics of the measure began to charge that it was a cover for voter fraud across the nation.

But turnout did not increase, as hoped, at least not until 2008 when voter dissatisfaction and demands for change in the nation's direction were palpable. Even then, new restrictions appeared in many states requiring official identification to receive a ballot. Supporters justified these measures as necessary to prevent voter fraud, while opponents, usually Democrats, condemned them as partisan efforts to limit the electorate. In 2008, a conservative but sharply divided Supreme Court upheld a strict Indiana law against what the legislature deemed to be the risk of voter fraud, even though the state offered no evidence that fraud was a problem (*Crawford v. Marion County Election Board*). The Republican and tea party sweep in state and national elections in 2010 only intensified this trend, with numerous legislatures, for example, rejecting university-issued student ID cards as sufficient to satisfy the requirement of official identification.

By the turn of the twenty-first century, what had been a long list of restrictions on voting had dwindled to only a few, good behavior chief among them. The largest disenfranchised group was ex-felons, estimated at over four million in 2010, the majority of them African American or Hispanic men. Although in

1974 the Court ruled that felony disenfranchisement did not violate the equal protection clause (*Richardson v. Ramirez*), many state and national restoration efforts sought to end this last major impediment to voting. Other problems remained with the voting process, such as a lack of uniform national standards (or even common standards within a state) on how to count disputed votes. A sharply divided Court halted the bitterly contested recount in the presidential election of 2000 because the majority held that the lack of uniformity in this area violated the equal protection clause, but the decision affected only Florida (*Bush v. Gore*, 2000). Even with these problems, however, the effect of several decades of reform was certain: after two centuries, voting was clearly established as a right of all adult citizens in the nation's fundamental law as well as in public opinion.

Of course, the story of constitutional democracy does not end with universal suffrage. Class, wealth, gender, and race no longer are qualifications for suffrage, but they are not inconsequential factors in shaping what representation means in fact. The power of money is evident in every presidential election and increasingly in state and local elections. Campaign costs in 2008, for example, exceeded one billion dollars, a circumstance that appeared to heighten the influence of wealthy interests.

Congress first sought to control the effects of money on elections in 1907 when it prohibited corporate contributions—previously no federal regulations existed—and it added more restrictions over the next forty years, although the laws were rarely enforced. The first meaningful limits on campaign financing came in 1971, with the Federal Election Campaign Act (1971) and its establishment of a Federal Election Commission to regulate and monitor contributions and expenditures. The Watergate scandals following the election of 1972 led to even tighter limits in 1974. Two years later, in *Buckley v. Valeo* (1976), the Supreme Court rejected an argument that the restrictions controlled conduct rather than speech but decided that the First Amendment's protection of speech could be overcome in part by a compelling government interest in preventing corruption. But it struck down as an unconstitutional restraint of speech any limits on total campaign expenditures from a candidate's own funds, as well as any spending made independently by supporters.

Buckley v. Valeo dramatically increased the use of "soft money" by groups or individuals supportive of or opposed to a candidate. By the beginning of the new century, concern about the pervasive influence of campaign money on elections led to new legislation intended to mitigate its ill effects. In 2002, the Bipartisan Campaign Reform Act, commonly known as the McCain-Feingold Act, placed additional limits on a variety of political activities, including banning third-party broadcast ads about a candidate within sixty days of the election, and extended the regulations to state parties in any election in which federal candidates appeared on the same ballot. The Court upheld the law in 2003 (*McConnell v. Federal Election Commission*). In a decision that effectively overturned the understanding reached in *Buckley*, the justices accepted congressional restraints on speech as legitimate to protect the "integrity of the process," a standard more relaxed than the need to guard against narrowly defined corruption.

Soon, this standard changed dramatically. In 2010, a more conservative Supreme Court, now led by Chief Justice John Roberts, declared unconstitutional any statutory restrictions on the amount of campaign contributions that could be made by corporations and unions (*Citizens United v. Federal Elections Commission*). The controversial decision, based on the First Amendment's guarantee of unrestricted political speech, overturned Court precedents and federal law dating back to the Progressive Era restraints on corporate influence in politics. The congressional election that followed unleashed a flood of corporate money, with early estimates suggesting that the total would exceed the record amount spent in the 2008 presidential election.

The extreme partisanship of the 2010 election obscured any objective assessment of the decision's long-term impact, but the story of political representation in America is more complicated than a simple narrative of corporate power or unbridled campaign finance. Counterbalancing the *Citizens United* case is a decades-long increase in the use of direct democracy to bypass the legislature in states that employ means such as initiative and referendum. Adopted at the turn of the twentieth century to override conservative opposition to regulation and other progressive reforms, today these tools more often serve to restrict the power of state government. In the 1970s and 1980s the trend was to limit property taxes but in the 1990s and first decade of the twenty-first century voters resorted to this device to address social issues such as same-sex marriage, abortion, the use of medical marijuana, environmental justice, and educational requirements, among other causes both conservative and liberal. These developments suggest that the nation's impulse remains toward more democracy.

Sometimes, it helps to step back and take a longer view of the uncertain path of constitutional democracy in the United States. In November 1869, when the ratification of the Fifteenth Amendment was still uncertain, *Harper's Weekly* published a Thomas Nast cartoon in which Americans of all races and colors were seated around a Thanksgiving table. The centerpiece included the words "self government" and "universal suffrage," with "come one, come all" and "free and equal" also prominent. Nast's endorsement of ratification was plain, as was his vision of a democratic America.

By the end of the first decade of the twenty-first century, the vision had become much more real. The framers distrusted direct democracy, preferring instead the indirect form of a democratic republic, but the theories on which they based the Constitution, popular sovereignty and representation, had their own internal dynamic that pointed toward more, not less, citizen participation in government. Democracy was not the inevitable outcome of this citizen involvement, and in fact, democracy, as signified by the right to vote, came only after much resistance from interests bound by considerations of race, class, and gender. But eventually it came and with such force that it redefined the Constitution. Amendments have made democracy central to the nation's fundamental law. In the Cold War, this ideal, so tortuously advanced in America, even became part of a national mission to the world.

The framers may not have forecast these developments, but neither would they have found them inconsistent with their sense of the nation they were creating. Popular sovereignty meant that their singular experiment in liberty would succeed only if citizens participated and continued to give their consent to government through their legitimate representatives. Women, African Americans, and citizens without property were not part of their formula for republican government, but the framers had created a charter capable of amendment, even if change came slowly. Finally, the early dispute between Madison and Jefferson about the character of the nation's fundamental law, permanent and stable or flexible and responsive, had an answer. Madison and Jefferson were both right—but only because a democratic constitution made them so: a permanent constitution was necessary for stability, but only a flexible constitution could become the people's charter.

Equality

It was one of the shortest presidential addresses in American history, a mere ten sentences. Many in the large, restless crowd at the commemoration of the Gettysburg battlefield on November 19, 1863, were not even aware that Abraham Lincoln had spoken, and newspaper reports were divided in their assessment of the speech. The *Providence Daily Journal* praised its "charm and power," but the *Harrisburg Patriot and Union*, based thirty-six miles from Gettysburg, called them "silly remarks," a sentiment echoed by the distant (and anti-Lincoln) London *Times*, which editorialized that the "ceremony was rendered ludicrous by the [President's] sallies."[1] Yet it was not long before the Gettysburg Address was being praised for its beauty and majesty. Today, it ranks as a literary classic, a prose poem built on a structure of past, present, and future time.

The Address began with the nation's founding eighty-seven years earlier, in 1776. It continued with the meaning of the Civil War, which Lincoln viewed as a testing of the founders' ideals and the nation—he used the word five times—and especially "whether that nation . . . can long endure." It ended with the pledge of "a new birth of freedom" based on democracy—"government of the people, by the people, for the people"—that "shall not perish from the earth." Few other American speeches so brilliantly captured the anguish and sacrifice of the war or its higher, nobler purpose.

The Gettysburg Address was memorable for another reason: for a broad public, it redefined the Constitution in light of the other founding document, the Declaration of Independence. It was, in effect, a preamble to the nation's second constitution. Equality joined liberty as a central aim of the American experiment: the United States, Lincoln declared, was "conceived in liberty and dedicated to the proposition that all men are created equal." This characterization was not incidental. The Declaration was no mere time-bound statement of political grievances; it was a timeless charter of universal principles. It offered a rebuttal, he had asserted in the 1850s, to anyone who proclaimed "none but rich men, or none but white men, were entitled to life, liberty, and the pursuit of happiness." The war was more than a defense of the Union; it was also a defense of the Union's republican values of liberty and "equality of opportunity for all." For Lincoln, both the Declaration and Constitution incorporated liberty and equality as a guarantee of freedom and a promise of "hope to the world for all future time."[2] These foundational charters were the inextricably linked sources of American freedom and prosperity: the Declaration's principle of equality ("liberty for all)," he wrote in 1861, was "the apple of gold," and the Union and the Constitution "the picture of silver." The Constitution was made "not to *conceal*, or *destroy* the apple but to *adorn*, and *preserve* it. The *picture* was made *for* the apple—*not* the apple for the picture."[3]

Equality was not an explicit core value of the Constitution of 1787, nor was it embraced as a basic condition of republican governments. From the founding onward, certain groups of Americans were considered unequal on the basis of race, gender, religion, or wealth. Non-whites, women, immigrants, and individuals without property—and in many instances, the categories were not mutually exclusive—could not claim the rights and privileges of citizenship. Yet the ideal of equality, announced as a natural right in the Declaration of Independence, was a powerful weapon for generations of reformers who sought to redeem this promise of American life.

Crusades for equality began early in the nation's history and have never disappeared. Attacks on class and economic privilege were central to Jeffersonian and Jacksonian democracy; challenges to slavery and demands for women's rights and woman suffrage were part of nineteenth-century social reforms; and efforts to secure equality for African Americans, Catholics, Jews, immigrants, labor, and other groups were common in the twentieth century. Rarely have campaigns for constitutional equality been absent from the nation's political and legal discourse, but never have these efforts been embraced easily or without controversy and resistance. Still, by the mid-twentieth century, equality had emerged as a dominant theme of American constitutionalism. It triumphed not because of new amendments, congressional measures, or Supreme Court decisions; these steps were important but often late affirmations of popular opinion. Equality became a constitutional value because of angry, insistent demands by Americans on the margins of public life who believed that the Declaration of Independence applied to them as well.

Parity among citizens was alien to the framers, who lived in a world based on class distinctions. The founding generation chafed under British assumptions about colonial inferiority and rejected a belief in a hereditary aristocracy, but most people casually accepted the idea of a natural aristocracy based on merit. The Constitution originally contained only one reference to equality of any sort, when it guaranteed that "no State, without its Consent, shall be deprived of equal Suffrage in the Senate." Even when state documents from the revolutionary era made a nod toward the idea, the language always was qualified in some way. The Virginia Declaration of Rights in 1776, for example, used a common construction when it announced that "all men are by nature free and independent" and enjoyed rights "when they enter into a state of society," a phrase that by definition excluded slaves, indigenous people, and other groups who were part of society but who did not benefit from many of its legal protections.

Political equality was of course central to the drive for independence—the protesting colonists repeatedly insisted on their equality as subjects under the British constitution—and to the revolutionary republican governments that followed, even though this condition applied only to white men who owned property. Such distinctions among men were natural, the founding generation believed. They were innate to the human condition; "no human legislator can ever eradicate" them, John Adams proclaimed. Even if it could be done, future chief justice John Jay warned, "[P]erfect equality . . . deadens the motives of industry, and places Demerit on a Footing with Virtue."[4] Republican liberty existed to allow merit to flourish, not to create an unnatural order in which the capacities and talents of men counted for little.

Republicanism did not embrace social equality, but it did reject any effort to promote inequality by law. The Constitution banned titles of nobility, for example, as did the various state constitutions. This animus against privilege resulted in abolition by the states of entail and primogeniture, holdovers from English law that limited inheritance to a beneficiary's legitimate descendants and required passing the family estate intact only to the firstborn son whenever the owner did not leave a will. The removal of property requirements for voting, a product of the second wave of state constitution-making in the 1820s and 1830s, reflected this impulse as well.

Reforms elsewhere embodied a similar concern for equality. Jurists made efforts to simplify the common law and democratize criminal justice. Established churches had disappeared by 1833, and the Second Great Awakening led to hundreds of denominations and sects, with each group claiming parity before the law, even when denying it to non-Protestants or radical "new faith traditions," such as Mormons. The anti-bank and anti-monopoly crusades of the 1830s were attacks on economic privilege. Both the antebellum embrace of democracy and market capitalism strengthened this meaning of equality. These creeds led to an individualistic ethic that accepted differences resulting from talent and initiative as long as men had the freedom to compete fairly. All these developments stemmed from the belief that law could not serve to anchor privilege. But this notion was far removed from the modern idea that the Constitution mandates equal protection under the law for all citizens, regardless of their race, gender, or other personal characteristics.

The presence of racial slavery hobbled any impulse toward a more positive expression of equality. In his classic book *Democracy in America*, Alexis de Tocqueville lauded the American commitment to equality and community—in fact, equality was the central theme in his work—but this reading of the American character was incomplete, as even Tocqueville acknowledged.

From the beginning, the Constitution accepted racial inequality as part of the republican experiment in nationhood. The founding generation had made a bargain with slavery, a forced labor system that also operated as a system of racial control. The framers found it necessary to accommodate slavery—in truth, many of them were not sufficiently troubled by the inconsistency of freedom and slavery as bedfellows to force a change—and the three-fifths, fugitive slave, and slave trade clauses, among other proslavery markers in the Constitution, were powerful symbols of the limits of liberty and equality in 1787.

Not only did the Constitution permit slavery, but federalism and the extra-constitutional party system served to promote it. The division of power between federal and state meant that states defined the rights of their citizens virtually without restraint by the federal government. The Bill of Rights did not bind the states (*Barron v. Baltimore*, 1833), and the regulation of morals and behavior, the so-called police power, was the nearly exclusive province of state governments. In southern states, slave codes mandated a separate and inferior status for blacks. Nor did the Constitution's privileges and immunities clause apply. Its requirement in Article IV, Section 2, that "the Citizens of Each State shall be entitled to the Privileges and Immunities of Citizens in the Several States" excluded blacks because many states did not consider them to be citizens. National citizenship was not available to blacks either, as the *Dred Scott* case made clear.

Party politics also protected slavery. The growth of the second American party system, beginning in the 1820s, muted criticism of slavery within the federal government because both Democrats and Whigs sought to avoid actions that would alienate the southern wing of their parties. The Democratic Party, with its greatest strength in the South, dominated national elections on a platform that championed states' rights. As a result, many federal measures promoted slave interests. From 1836 to 1844, for example, the House of Representatives routinely tabled abolitionist petitions without hearing them, in disregard of the First Amendment's clause protecting the people's right to petition for redress of grievances. Congress also enacted fugitive slave laws in 1793 and 1850 requiring northern states to use the standards of slave law to decide the fate of alleged runaways. Under these measures, accused blacks had no right to testify, command witnesses, or retain counsel. The government created by the Constitution too often appeared to be the handmaiden of slavery, and for an increasing number of citizens it seemed tainted beyond repair.

The constitutional and legal contract with slavery, already abandoned elsewhere in the Atlantic World by the 1830s, remained acceptable to most white Americans well into the first half of the nineteenth century. But the nation slowly was changing as a result of the rise of a persistent and growing anti-slavery crusade. From the late 1780s, reformers had considered the Constitution corrupted by slavery and either sought to reconcile it with the self-evident truths of the Declaration of Independence or denounced its inconsistency with the Declaration's principles. They found early success in abolishing slavery in northern states where slaveholders and blacks were few in number. Constitutions in these states either did not authorize slavery explicitly or were silent on the question, although in 1781 a Massachusetts decision interpreted the state constitution's equality clause as a ban on slavery. The Northwest Ordinance of 1787, which prohibited slavery in the territories north of the Ohio River, further ensured that new states carved from this territory would be free states on their admission to the Union. These developments transformed slavery from a national to a local (or peculiar) institution found only in the South. This result, ironically, convinced many northerners that slavery's inability to expand would spell its eventual demise; the seeming inevitability of this hoped-for result drained any sense of urgency from most northern and western opposition to slavery.

The absence of slavery in the North and West, however, did not mean the acceptance of racial equality, either socially or legally. Racial hostility chilled most efforts to extend legal equality to blacks. The movement toward universal white male suffrage generally excluded free blacks, and many local and state laws restricted their access to housing, occupations, public schools, and even mobility. The Indiana Constitution of 1851, for instance, prohibited migration of African Americans into the state; other midwestern states required them to post bonds for good behavior before entering. Most northern states maintained segregated schools, banned interracial marriage, and denied blacks the right to serve on juries or to testify in a case in which a white person was a party.

Sentiment for equality before the law for all races was almost nonexistent. The strongest judicial statement for this position came from Chief Justice Lemuel Shaw of the Massachusetts General Court, who in his opinion for the court in *Roberts v. City of Boston* (1849) accepted equality before the law "as settled and regulated by law" with rights determined by "laws adapted to their respective relations and conditions." For Shaw, however, equality meant only the right to be treated like other blacks, a standard of separate but equal that permitted racial segregation in Boston's public schools. At best, equality before the law was the rule within legally recognized groups, not between groups—and the distinction that mattered most was between white and black.

Equality for white men only was too much at odds with American ideals to remain unchallenged. As abolitionists found their political voice in the 1830s and afterward, they began to create an array of constitutional arguments against the peculiar institution. Their arguments were largely religious—slavery was a sin and all men were equal before God—but they also redefined the republican principle of equality in terms drawn from the Declaration of Independence. A positive legal imperative existed to treat all men the same because each man had the same claim to life, liberty, and the pursuit of happiness. Some abolitionists, most notably the fiery William Lloyd Garrison and his ally Wendell Phillips, condemned the Constitution as "a covenant with death, and an agreement with Hell." Other leaders, such as the former slave Frederick Douglass, sought to reinterpret it to support the elimination of slavery.

By the 1840s antislavery constitutionalism linked new ideas with an older intellectual tradition. Moderates who were willing to accept gradual emancipation argued that the framers anticipated the end of slavery by the constitutional provision allowing Congress to halt the importation of Africans after 1808 (Article I, Section 9). Some even suggested that the Constitution granted the power to ban the interstate slave trade under the commerce clause. They also reinterpreted the due process clause of the Fifth Amendment to guarantee substantive rights that the government could not abridge—for example, liberty of movement or the right to pursue an occupation—and not simply the procedural requirement of fairness. Slavery obviously denied these rights. Free blacks went further and claimed constitutional protection because they were American citizens: "We were born in no foreign clime. We profess to be Americans and republican," the New York Convention of Colored People remonstrated in 1840.

A more radical antislavery constitutional argument was based on natural rights. The "laws of Nature and Nature's God," in Jefferson's phrase from the Declaration, created men with equal and unalienable rights that government was bound to protect. This philosophy, advanced by the American revolutionaries in the Declaration of Independence, imposed an obligation on government to eliminate slavery. The conclusion was innovative but the theory was not. A belief in natural rights was part of the national creed, and the supremacy of natural law over man-made law had gained early endorsement from John Marshall and other jurists who suggested that statutes in violation of natural law were illegitimate.

The natural-rights argument was especially significant because it fused the nation's two founding documents: the Declaration contained the permanent values of the American people, which the Federal Convention incorporated by implication into the Constitution. The framers did not jettison the Declaration in favor of the Constitution; they never proposed "to accept the shell, and throw the kernel away," natural-rights advocates proclaimed.[5] From this perspective, the Declaration was much more than a brief for separation from the empire; it was the constitutional standard for perfecting the Union, the goal announced in the Constitution's preamble.

Both the republican notion of negative equality—the law could not privilege inequality—and the Declaration's promise of unalienable rights lay at the center of other efforts to reconcile American ideals with social and political realities. Women especially were insistent in their arguments for equality. In traditional common law, wrote Sir William Blackstone, the influential English legal commentator, married women were "dead in law" or, in the words of American treatises, "civilly dead"; they could not own property or legally act separately from their husbands.[6] American circumstances changed this status in part—frontier conditions gave women more freedom than their English sisters—but women still generally lacked equal status with men.

Now active in many reform circles, including those committed to antislavery, women sought to extend the abolitionist logic to their own cause: "Are we aliens [non-citizens] because we are women?" a petition from a female antislavery society asked. Other women reformers sought full gender equality. Sarah Grimké, a prominent South Carolina abolitionist, put the issue plainly: "I ask no favor for our sex. I surrender not our claim to equality. All I ask our brethren is that they will take their heels from our necks and permit us to stand upright on the ground which God designed us to occupy."[7]

The women's rights movement made its most famous mark with the Seneca Falls Convention of 1848; its Declaration of Sentiments adapted the language of rights and grievances of the Declaration of Independence in a demand for female equality. It was an important step, but industrialization and the rise of an urban middle class already were pushing the social role of women in a different direction, into a separate domestic sphere where women ruled the hearth while men supported the family economically by their labors in the wider world. Despite such reforms as married women's property rights acts (which allowed wives to own and control property separately from their husbands), female equality was not a priority for most antebellum crusaders. For them, slavery, not inequality between men and women, was the primary blot on American ideals.

The sectional crisis of the 1850s shattered the fragile national consensus on slavery and set in motion events that would lead to the adoption of equality as a constitutional command. The new Republican Party, formed in 1854, embraced antislavery constitutionalism by contending that the extension of slavery into the territories subverted the intentions of the framers and undermined the nation's commitment to natural rights and equality. They argued, as did moderate abolitionists, that the Fifth Amendment's due process clause guaranteed freedom as an individual right in all areas under federal control, which, of course, meant the western territories. Many Republicans also agreed that native-born free blacks were state citizens and thereby under the protection of the Constitution. They embraced as well the principles of the Declaration of Independence and its assertion of natural rights for all men as the foundation of republican government. This stance did not mean social and political equality for blacks—such a position would have been political suicide—but it did accept their right to liberty and to the protection of law.

The Civil War transformed American constitutionalism, although this outcome was not apparent in 1861. The new Republican president, Abraham Lincoln, sought at first to assure the southern states that the federal government had no power to abolish a local institution such as slavery. His goal was to preserve the Union, not to challenge the time-honored interpretation of federalism. But by late 1862 Lincoln had accepted the abolition of slavery as one goal of the war, and he moved decisively in this direction with the Emancipation Proclamation, which freed slaves in areas under federal control. He and the Radical Republicans insulated themselves from charges they wanted only to liberate blacks by entwining a moral imperative—the removal of slavery—with an action that weakened the Confederacy, thereby making emancipation a military necessity. Although its timing was political, the Proclamation freed thousands of slaves as Union troops advanced deeper into southern states and served notice on the Confederacy that the end of slavery had become a goal of the war. It served alongside the Gettysburg Address to suggest a new constitutional framework, with equality at its center.

What we might call the second American constitution had its roots in three amendments adopted between 1865 and 1870. The Thirteenth Amendment (proposed and ratified, 1865) ended slavery and committed the nation to a principle of freedom for all residents. The Fourteenth Amendment (proposed 1866, ratified 1868) set the terms of citizenship, an omission in the 1787 charter, and made state citizenship a consequence of national citizenship. It also made equality a formal part of the constitutional vocabulary. The Fifteenth Amendment (proposed 1869, ratified 1870) guaranteed the right to vote to newly freed slaves and other qualified African American men, designating them as political equals in the national republic. More important, all three amendments gave the federal government the power to enforce these new guarantees, which it did initially in a series of civil rights measures designed to make the nation's promise of equality real.

The Civil Rights Act of 1866 represented a radical departure for American constitutionalism. It repudiated the *Dred Scott* decision by establishing a color-blind citizenship and pledged national protection for individual rights, which states could determine but had to apply to all citizens equally. The Fourteenth Amendment, ratified in 1868, provided clear authority after the fact for this new assertion of national power. It became the keystone of a fundamental commitment to equality. Section 1 defined United States citizenship, prevented states from excluding blacks from the benefits of state citizenship, and established guarantees for individual rights. Its language was pregnant with promise—states could not "make or enforce any law which shall abridge the privileges and immunities of citizens of the United States" or "deprive any person of life, liberty, or property without due process of law" or deny anyone "equal protection of the laws"—but the meaning was unclear. One thing was certain, however: equality of citizens under the law was now a constitutional requirement.

It is easy to dismiss as impermanent the changes outlined by the Reconstruction amendments. Except for a single decade immediately following their ratification, the nation soon stepped back from a guarantee of equality. Political maneuvering and a judicial commitment to formalism and precedent allowed white southerners to ignore federal law and recreate slavery in a different guise. The postbellum sharecropping system resembled slavery in its racism and social control, as did the emergence of Jim Crow laws and strict social segregation. These developments were troubling, yet in fact the United States had changed and so had its constitutional and legal framework. The Civil War had forced the nation to confront slavery. The legal transformations that followed affected every part of American life. In many ways, however, these changes only created the potential for a new era. The revolution in American life was incomplete, and not simply because lawmakers, officeholders, and courts still had to act on the promises. Only when law and popular culture shared the same ground— only when public opinion agreed that race (and, later, ethnicity and gender) had no bearing on liberty and rights—could equality in fact occur.

This extra-constitutional transformation began almost immediately. One notable change was in the conception of the nation itself. In 1787 the nation was a voluntary creation, brought into being by an act of the people. It was an invented nation, the first in history. By 1865, the nation had become organic: it had a history. In his first inaugural address (1861), Lincoln referred to the "mystic chords of memory" as he sought to persuade southerners that all Americans shared a common past and, as a result, were a common people. The nation could no more be dissolved than could England or Germany. Nations represented a solidarity based on collective identification, a bond not only among the living but also between the living and the dead. This identity emerged from history and included a common language, a common culture and folklore, and connection to a particular geography or place. The 1840s had witnessed a romantic celebration of nationhood, with the 1848 revolutions in Europe serving as powerful examples of its hold on the popular imagination. Lincoln and many of his contemporaries shared this sense of what German romantics called the *Herrenvolk*, a common people bound by time and culture, which the poet Walt Whitman celebrated in *America* when he wrote of a nation "Perennial with the Earth, with Freedom, Law, and Love . . . Chair'd in the adamant of Time."

An organic nationhood was significant for what was to follow. It provided an ideal that spurred the struggle of people on the margins of American society— blacks, immigrants, and women, most notably—to claim their legacy. It also provided a standard for judgment, a measure of right and wrong that influenced public opinion. And it gave impetus to an American quest for equality, which Martin Luther King Jr. later identified as his dream that "one day on the red hills of Georgia the sons of former slaves and the sons of former slave owners will be able to sit down together at the table of brotherhood."

It was a dream deferred, of course, but at first it appeared that the new order would hold. Faced with southern hostility to black equality, the Republican Congress passed two acts—the Enforcement Act of 1870 and the Ku Klux Klan Act of 1871—to punish anyone who interfered with blacks' right to vote and to suppress the white terrorism that was rampant throughout the South. These acts broke fresh ground by providing individuals with a federal remedy against private acts of violence and by using federal power, including the army, to punish conspirators, notably Klansmen, who blocked access to the ballot box. The Civil Rights Act of 1875 even asserted federal authority to ensure equality in public accommodations, a measure that struck directly at the idea of social segregation.

The 1875 act marked the final stage of Reconstruction. Democrats in the South already were using the banner of white supremacy to regain political control and repeal state laws designed to enforce equal protection. Republicans became more cautious politically as their revolutionary ardor waned and their position in Congress weakened. The denouement came when the U.S. Supreme Court interpreted the Reconstruction amendments and the legislation designed to carry them into effect, and deemed them less consequential than history would prove them to be. Instead of supporting the efforts of congressional Republicans, the justices, most of whom were moderate northern Republicans, circumscribed national power to protect civil rights and enforce equality.

The reason was federalism. The Court believed the amendments did not change the division of authority between federal and state governments established by the Constitution of 1787. It was not an unusual view. Americans were suspicious of centralized power and clung to the principle of local autonomy. Self-government relied on citizen participation, which most Americans believe occurred most naturally at local and state levels. The issue was not race, at least not on its surface. Instead, like most Americans, the justices could not imagine that overcoming the burdens of slavery would require such an extreme reallocation of governmental power.

Contrary to the expectations of the congressional Joint Committee on Reconstruction, which recommended the Fourteenth Amendment, the Supreme Court soon held that it did not require states and local governments to respect the guarantees of the Bill of Rights. The justices instead followed traditional practice and allowed states wide discretion to protect individual liberty as they saw fit.

The first inkling of the old order's triumph came in the *Slaughterhouse Cases* (1873). Neither the civil rights of African Americans nor the immediate issues of Reconstruction were at stake in these cases. Rather, the lawsuits were brought by white butchers in New Orleans who challenged a new state law requiring them to use one of two central slaughterhouses, for which they would pay a fee to the owners. The regulation today doubtless would be upheld as a legitimate use of state police powers to protect the public health, but the butchers charged that the law deprived them of their right to pursue a trade and to use their land as they wished. Their lawyers argued that Louisiana had abridged their rights as citizens of the United States, rights now protected by the Fourteenth Amendment. They also claimed that the regulations violated the amendment's due process clause, which they wanted to be read broadly to include individual rights and not merely as a mandate to follow fair procedures.

The Justices disagreed, 5–4, with the majority interpreting the amendment's language narrowly to deny the butchers' claims. The amendment, the Court majority concluded, applied to actions required to protect former slaves; it did not commit the federal government to protect the civil rights of all citizens. States, not the central government, continued to define the rights their citizens enjoyed.

The major interpretive hurdle for the Court was the relationship between national and state citizenship. It was a new issue; not until the Fourteenth Amendment did the Constitution identify who was a citizen of the United States. The traditional rule, inherited from England, was that citizenship was defined by place of birth, not blood. By contrast with that traditional rule, *Dred Scott* had made plain that Indians and blacks, both born in the United States, were excluded from citizenship because of ethnicity, their blood or race. With the Fourteenth Amendment's revival of the traditional rule, a direct connection now existed between all citizens—native-born and naturalized, including previously excluded groups—and the federal government. But what was the relationship between the two kinds of citizenship, state and national?

In the *Slaughterhouse Cases*, the Court's majority used an antebellum frame of reference, dual federalism, to answer this question: the amendment had not changed the nature of the Union; it only added what had been omitted. Four justices dissented, and one minority opinion, by Justice Stephen J. Field, was notably prophetic. In the original Constitution, Field argued, several provisions prohibited states from discriminating against citizens of other states, yet no protection was available to citizens from the misuse of power by their own state. The Fourteenth Amendment created parity between these two groups of citizens: national citizenship, in brief, protected individuals from illegitimate actions of their own state government. Field's view was revolutionary—it rejected the assumptions of dual federalism—but not until much later did its potential for interpersonal equality become apparent.

Initially, the Court extended the logic of the *Slaughterhouse* majority in a series of decisions in the 1870s and 1880s, often with tragic consequences for black citizens. An early example occurred at the same time as the *Slaughterhouse* decision. In 1873, armed whites in Colfax, Louisiana, massacred as many as one hundred freedmen gathered to support local Republicans whose claim to office had been challenged by Democrats. The federal government prosecuted three men under the Enforcement Act of 1870, which made it a crime for private citizens to deprive individuals of their civil rights. The indictment specifically accused the defendants of denying rights guaranteed by the Bill of Rights (the right to bear arms and the right of assembly) as well as of violating the Fourteenth Amendment's due process and equal protection clauses.

In *Cruikshank v. United States* (1875), the Supreme Court set the convictions aside, citing dual federalism. States established rights for their citizens and were responsible for enforcing them; violations of these rights were not punishable under the Enforcement Act. The Fourteenth Amendment, the Court determined, simply restricted state action; it did not empower the federal government to punish private individuals who violated the rights of other citizens, the equal protection and due process clauses notwithstanding. By this view, the Civil War and Reconstruction had not redefined the relationship of federal and state governments, even though the Fourteenth Amendment clearly made national citizenship preeminent and provided Congress with power to enforce its guarantees of equality.

The Court made this result even more plain in the *Civil Rights Cases* (1883), in which it struck down the ban on private discrimination in hotels, restaurants, and public transportation in the Civil Rights Act of 1875. The Fourteenth Amendment, on which Congress relied for its authority, prevented only states from discriminating against their citizens. The equal protection clause did not apply to the actions of individuals or private businesses. The meaning of the decision was clear: the national commitment to equality was limited.

But when states discriminated, the justices did not hesitate to hold them to the new standard. The Reconstruction amendments clearly forbade hostile state action, as in 1880 when West Virginia ran afoul of the equal protection clause by unconstitutionally restricting jury service to white men only (*Strauder v. West Virginia*). Four years later, in 1884, the Court upheld federal authority to protect blacks against political terrorism, including exercise of their right to vote (*Ex Parte Yarborough*). The justices also found in favor of Chinese laundrymen in San Francisco who had been excluded from practicing their trade under an ordinance that, while written broadly, applied only to them. "Though the law be fair on its face and impartial in appearance," the Court wrote in *Yick Wo v. Hopkins* (1886), "yet if it is applied . . . with an evil eye and an unequal hand . . . the denial of justice is still within the prohibition of the Constitution."

The Court's decision in *Yick Wo* suggests the power of equal protection as a constitutional ideal, but it mattered little in most circumstances of daily life. Equal protection was left solely to the states' discretion. Although several northern states and cities passed equal accommodation laws, the vast majority of African Americans lived in the South, a region hostile to their claims. For them, dual federalism meant that the protection of their rights was a matter left to state governments. The result was predictable—rigid segregation under Jim Crow laws and an official unwillingness to protect blacks from violence should they breach this social norm.

The Court officially acknowledged the legitimacy of racial segregation in *Plessy v. Ferguson* (1896), in which it enshrined "separate but equal" as acceptable on railroads (and by implication in public schools and elsewhere) under the equal protection clause. In reality, "separate but equal" was a myth: in 1910, for example, the former Confederate states spent three times more per capita on white schoolchildren than they did on black pupils. As a constitutional standard, the doctrine focused on the letter of the law and ignored results, a circumstance that entrenched racial inequality. Stripped of its common-sense meaning, equality for minorities under the Fourteenth Amendment had become an empty promise.

African Americans were not the only group denied equality under the law after the passage of the Reconstruction amendments. So were women, regardless of race. In theory, all men could claim rights under the Constitution; no woman could. For women who had provided energy and leadership during the ferment of reform, this situation was intolerable. State by state and city by city, they pressed for equality with men but had limited success, even though feminists often relied on racism to justify their claim to equality: why should poor, ignorant black men have rights denied to educated white women?

These prejudices made it difficult for women to unite across color lines, but they also distracted women reformers from attacking the social assumptions that blocked their progress. For most white Americans, political equality for black men did not mean social equality. The calculus was not the same for white women, who lived in intimacy with white men as African Americans never could. Granting equality to women threatened to upset the legal dominance of husbands over their wives, which was at the heart of domestic and economic relationships. Allowing black men to vote did not necessarily admit them to social or economic equality, but making women equal with men had the potential to change society fundamentally. In the late nineteenth century, most white Americans, male or female, resisted this possibility.

Throughout most of the nation's history, law has privileged white men. For example, they could do with their property, including their labor and bodies, as they wished. Other groups did not have the same freedom. Married women by definition lacked a control similar to their husbands' because, as one legal commentary noted, "the very being or legal existence of the woman is suspended during the marriage."[8] The poor faced similar restrictions on their freedom. In the South especially, peonage, a form of involuntary servitude for debt, and other forms of contract labor, such as sharecropping, deprived hundreds of thousands of poor citizens, especially men and women of color, of a right to their labor equal to the right enjoyed by middle-class whites. White men exercised legal control in other ways, as well. For instance, property owners, overwhelmingly white and male, could exclude certain groups from residential neighborhoods or allow entry to their business or service only to whites.

Many middle-class people considered these privileges natural to society and beyond the reach of legislation: "stateways cannot change folkways" is how the late nineteenth-century sociologist William Graham Sumner put it.[9] Still, the ideal of equality continued to inspire resistance to socially constructed and legal labels of inferiority. The acts of rebellion were often individual—a woman's refusal to take her husband's name or share his bed, or later, Rosa Parks's refusal to take a seat in the back of a segregated public bus—but increasingly in the late nineteenth and twentieth centuries, resistance took organized form.

As they had done in the fight against slavery, African Americans joined together to demand unfettered access to the voting booth, to lobby for anti-lynching laws (more than three thousand blacks were lynched from the late nineteenth century to the mid-twentieth century), and to demand that the nation honor its formal commitment to equality. At times these efforts were joined by white men and women, including members of such marginalized groups as Jews and socialists. Among the earliest and most influential organizations were the National Association for the Advancement of Colored People (NAACP, 1909) and the American Civil Liberties Union (ACLU, 1920), which sought to use the law itself to bring about the equality promised by the Fourteenth Amendment and the Declaration of Independence. Internal divisions existed over tactics, but no one strayed from a common commitment to the goal of a color-blind society.

Women likewise banded together to promote their cause, although they, too, divided over strategy. They succeeded in gaining the right to vote in 1920 with the ratification of the Nineteenth Amendment, but ultimately their divisions were more problematic. Many women were not advocates of gender-neutral laws because the belief in female inferiority at least offered some protection from the rigors of an industrial society, such as judicial acceptance of wage-hour limits for working women that were not available to men. This difference in approach stymied the movement toward women's constitutional equality for five decades after women gained access to the voting booth.

Equality became the central constitutional issue of the twentieth century, but its role as a core value was slow to emerge. The first decades of the twentieth century suggested that the Court was ready to give substance to the Reconstruction amendments. Bolstered by journalistic exposés of a system of quasi-slavery in southern states, the justices accepted the use of federal power against peonage based on the enforcement provisions of the Thirteenth Amendment, which had abolished slavery. Pressed by the NAACP, they also overturned an Oklahoma statute that required a literacy test for voting based on whether a person's forebears had been able to vote in 1866, a test that barred the large majority of blacks who had been slaves until 1865. They outlawed a Louisville, Kentucky, ordinance that kept whites from selling residential property to blacks, although the justices viewed the ordinance as an unconstitutional interference with the so-called liberty of contract rather than a violation of the Fourteenth Amendment's equal protection clause. Too often, however, these decisions were pyrrhic victories. Other tools, such as poll taxes and literacy tests, existed to keep blacks from voting, and restrictive covenants became a standard way to maintain racially segregated neighborhoods.

Events in the first third of the twentieth century spurred changes in the American politics of equality. The Great Migration that began around 1910 brought more than a million African Americans to northern cities as industrial workers. They became members of powerful labor unions and, in turn, an important part of big-city Democratic political machines; both were vital to the election of Franklin D. Roosevelt as president in 1932, who, with his wife Eleanor, already was committed to civil rights. The New Deal made a place for black Americans, including them among its beneficiaries for poverty relief and providing professional jobs and opportunities for leadership. The vast expansion of federal power occasioned by the economic crisis also benefited blacks, most notably through the growth of a regulatory state that entrusted rule-making and enforcement to professional bureaucrats isolated from direct political pressure. In response, African Americans abandoned the party of Lincoln for the party of FDR, giving Democrats even greater reason to continue their support for black demands for equality. At the same time, public attitudes were beginning to shift toward racial tolerance, thanks to academic research that challenged the myth of white supremacy and to growing concern about the rise of fascist regimes in Europe that were based on ideas of racial superiority.

Although the New Deal did not end the Great Depression, its energetic response to national crisis spurred a dramatic new division of authority between federal and state governments and between public and private spheres. Increasingly, Americans accepted a stronger federal hand in affairs traditionally left to state or local control. They also rejected the laissez-faire constitutionalism that had previously barred government regulation of the market.

This change in public attitude, made evident by Roosevelt's landslide reelection in 1936, had its parallel in constitutional law. By the mid-1930s the Supreme Court was erasing the public-private distinction in matters of economic regulation, albeit reluctantly at first, and permitting government to intervene in areas previously considered private. An expanded view of the commerce power was especially important in justifying regulation of any activity that touched interstate trade. This new role for government had important implications for the constitutional protection of equality. If government now had the authority to intervene in the private sector for the public good, then government also could be held accountable for its failures to intervene. This theory of government's role ultimately prevailed, but not until the 1950s and 1960s was its effect apparent.

At first, the Supreme Court did not incorporate this new sense of governmental responsibility into its decisions about racial equality. The justices unhesitatingly blocked state action to deny black rights, as in 1927 when the Court unanimously overturned a Texas state law denying blacks the right to vote in the Democratic primary. But they were reluctant to go further and intervene in private actions that had the same effect, such as when they accepted as a private matter a state party rule excluding blacks from participating in so-called white primaries (*Grovey v. Townsend*, 1935). By the same logic the justices failed to block private actions that resulted in residential segregation. Here, though, the federal government accepted racial discrimination through means such as restrictive covenants and segregated public housing. The same circumstances prevailed in public schools, with both the Court and the federal government allowing separation of the races as customary and legal.

The NAACP continued to press for a different result, adopting an incremental, case-by-case approach that kept the issue before the Court. A decision in 1938 suggested the potential for change. In *Missouri ex rel. Gaines v. Canada*, the justices deemed it a substantial inequality for Missouri to require black law students to leave the state to receive the same educational subsidy offered to whites who went to a state school. Though not ready to invalidate legal segregation, *Gaines* hinted that the Court would not long accept racial inequality imposed by law. The case, significantly, was argued by a Harvard-trained black attorney, Charles Hamilton Houston, whose presence before the Court, unimaginable in the 1920s, symbolized what blacks could achieve if provided the opportunity.

In criminal justice also, the Court's decisions extended federal power to protect African Americans by incorporating fundamental protections, such as the right to an attorney, into the Fourteenth Amendment's due process clause. These federal guarantees of fairness applied to any criminal defendant, of course, but they affected blacks most, especially in southern states. It is too easy to accept these harbingers of change as emblematic of the decade. The nation was not yet ready for full equality. African Americans in the South continued to experience widespread discrimination, including almost total exclusion from the political process. Although northern blacks were more active politically, segregation and other forms of racial discrimination were still common in all but a few places.

World War II marked an important change in U.S. race relations. Many Americans came to understand the cruel paradox of fighting for democracy with a racially segregated military, especially when the fascist powers made a religion of racial purity and, in Germany's case, white supremacy. "Prove to us," NAACP president Walter White insisted, "that you are not hypocrites when you say this war is about freedom."[10] Vital to both the armed forces and wartime industry, blacks became more militant, joining the NAACP in record numbers and demanding their rights as citizens. Voter registration by African Americans in the South increased fourfold and, with it, their clout in the national Democratic Party grew.

The protests and political action soon paid dividends. In 1941, Roosevelt banned discrimination in defense industries by executive order and established a federal commission to monitor compliance. By the end of the decade, the national government was more active on behalf of blacks than at any time since Reconstruction. The Justice Department vigorously pursued lynching and supported an NAACP effort to end restrictive covenants. President Harry Truman, who was friendly to African American claims and also fearful that these new

Democratic voters might drift back to the Republican Party, urged Congress to pass major civil rights legislation and in 1948 used his executive authority to desegregate the military. More powerful symbols of changed public attitudes were the emergence of popular African American celebrities, such as jazz musician Louis Armstrong, a celebrity since the 1920s, and baseball player Jackie Robinson, who in 1947 broke the major league color line when Branch Rickey signed him to play for the Brooklyn Dodgers.

Aware of this new cultural moment, the Court was increasingly receptive to African American claims. In 1944 the justices reversed course and held the Texas all-white primary was indeed state action and therefore unconstitutional (*Smith v. Allwright*). They also declared restrictive covenants unenforceable (*Shelley v. Kraemer,* 1948) because the states had "made available to individuals the full coercive power of government to deny petitioners, on the grounds of race or color, the full enjoyment of property rights" in violation of the Fourteenth Amendment.

These decisions presaged a litigation assault on *Plessy v. Ferguson*, the totem of legal segregation. Led by Thurgood Marshall, chief lawyer for the NAACP Legal Defense Fund (and later the nation's first African American solicitor general and in 1967 the Court's first African American justice), the NAACP pressed the Court for a reversal of *Plessy*, using the segregated University of Texas law school as its target. It was, by choice, a difficult hurdle to overcome. By most standards, Texas provided a black law school that compared favorably with the white school in terms of facilities and faculty. But in the hearing before the Court, Marshall insisted that the two schools could never be equal because of intangibles, such as the superior reputation of the white school and its more influential alumni network.

In *Sweatt v. Painter* (1950), the justices unanimously accepted Marshall's argument. Although not overruling the 1896 decision, they implied that "separate" could never be "equal." The same day, in *McLaurin v. Oklahoma State Regents*, the Court ordered the University of Oklahoma to cease segregating a black graduate student within its classrooms and library. In tandem, the two decisions, one outlawing segregation within an institution and the other denying it between institutions, left only a faint trace of the legal color line that had separated American society.

Emboldened, the NAACP attacked *Plessy* directly. In 1954, they won. *Brown v. Board of Education,* consolidating four cases into one, outlawed racial segregation in public schools across the nation. It was a landmark decision, the central case in the development of equality as a constitutional mandate. The justices were unanimous in holding that segregation was "inherently unequal," but this outcome was far from certain when the cases were first argued in 1952. All the justices except one were ready to reject *Plessy*, yet collectively they worried about southern acceptance of such a ruling—and about the damage to the Court's reputation if the other branches of government failed to uphold it.

They had reason to be concerned. Although public opinion polls revealed that whites were willing to accept integration in such areas as interstate transportation, public schools were different. In them, the mixing of races was not temporary, as it was in travel; schools also were tightly bound to community traditions, which in the South meant segregation in even the most ordinary matters. Several justices worried as well about isolating their personal views from their decisions. The problem was precedent. The Court's previous decisions accepted the legality of racial segregation. Justice Robert H. Jackson, who as a prosecutor at the Nuremburg trials of Nazis after World War II saw the "terrible consequences of racial hatred," still was troubled by his reading of previous decisions, as well as by the history of the Fourteenth Amendment: almost a century of cases, he concluded, were virtually "unanimous . . . that the Amendment tolerated segregation by state action."

In 1953, in the midst of the Court's proceedings in *Brown*, Chief Justice Fred M. Vinson died suddenly. A Kentuckian, Vinson was opposed to overturning segregation, and the justices had been so deadlocked that the case was held over for re-argument. Vinson's death thus held the promise of changing everything on the Court, as one of his colleagues, Justice Felix Frankfurter, an opponent of legal segregation, recognized; on the morning of the funeral, Frankfurter told his law clerk that Vinson's death was the first proof that he had ever had of the existence of God.

Vinson's successor as chief justice, Earl Warren, was a California Republican who had come to the bench from the governorship of his state and service as the state's attorney general before that. The first appointee named by President Dwight D. Eisenhower (who later concluded that the appointment was the worst mistake he had made as president), Warren brought to the Court a strong commitment to equality before the law and, just as important, the leadership skills necessary to bring his eight quarrelsome and independent-minded colleagues along. He set to work to rally his fellow justices behind a carefully crafted, unanimous opinion. Warren understood that overturning *Plessy* would require a unanimous Court, or southerners would seize on the minority opinion as a reason to resist. He also knew, as did several other justices, that the Court, in this instance, was working with history, not against it.

Brown was not the unvarnished triumph that it appears to be in retrospect. The decision, while leaving no doubt that legal segregation was dead, provided no remedy, and the justices agreed to hear a sequel to *Brown* in 1955. When the Court considered the remedies issue in *Brown II*, it settled on a standard of "all deliberate speed" to guide federal district courts in implementing desegregation locally. Anything more forceful, the justices feared, would expose the Court's fatal weakness—it could not enforce its decisions without the support of Congress and the executive branch, neither of which favored immediate desegregation.

Their concern was not misplaced. What followed was a period of massive resistance in the South, with violence and mob action the popular responses to judicial desegregation orders. White southern politicians revived the discredited mantle of "states' rights" to justify "segregation now, segregation tomorrow, segregation forever," as Alabama governor George C. Wallace angrily threatened in his 1963 inaugural address. Neither Congress nor the president gave much support to the Court's decision; indeed, at first President Eisenhower echoed southern protests by saying that "it is difficult through law and through force to change a man's mind." Ultimately federal troops were required to intervene in places like Little Rock, Oxford, and Tuscaloosa to ensure compliance, but segregation remained the norm across the South—and at times elsewhere—until the late 1960s.

The Court was mostly silent on desegregation after *Brown II*. The exception was *Cooper v. Aaron* (1958), the Little Rock, Arkansas, desegregation case in which the justices unanimously reminded the nation that "the interpretation of the Fourteenth Amendment enunciated by this Court in the Brown case is the supreme law of the land." The actions of segregationists and many politicians suggested otherwise. As late as 1963, less than 2 percent of southern black children attended an integrated school. Segregation was no longer legal, but racial equality was not yet a constitutional reality.

In spite of "massive resistance," *Brown* made a difference in the way that Americans thought about race and equality. It directed public attention to the discrepancy between the Constitution in theory and the Constitution in practice and forced people and their representatives to judge tradition and custom against American ideals. Folkways began to yield to stateways and gradually to a new social reality. No major political party endorsed a return to pre-*Brown* days, and public opinion polls began to show a majority of citizens willing to condemn racial discrimination as morally wrong.

Whites may have been educated about racial disparities by *Brown*, but blacks were motivated by it. It inspired lawsuits and protests: African Americans sought to compel school boards to integrate, and they took action to extend the principle of *Brown* to other areas of life. The Montgomery, Alabama, bus boycott, a catalytic event in the modern history of civil rights, was a direct result of the *Brown* decision, as were the lunch counter sit-ins and freedom rides of the early 1960s. *Brown* taught a valuable lesson: litigation alone was insufficient to bring about change. It was too limited in its effect and too incremental. Success in achieving constitutional equality depended upon a social and political movement.

The 1960s witnessed the political maturity of the modern civil rights movement that cemented black equality as a matter of law, although not always of practice. It also marked the beginning of a white backlash that spilled into the 1970s and beyond. Southern whites blamed the NAACP especially for breaching the wall of segregation and pressured state and local governments to harass or close the organization. Blacks responded by invigorating older associations, such as the Southern Christian Leadership Conference (SCLC), with Martin Luther King as its leader, and later by establishing new ones, such as the

Student Non-Violent Coordinating Committee (SNCC), when change came too slowly. Attempts to register black voters from 1961 to 1965 and civil rights marches met increasingly violent responses. The use of police attack dogs, the bombing of a black church in Alabama that killed young schoolgirls preparing for choir practice, Klan murders of civil rights activists in Mississippi, and police brutality against marchers in Selma, Alabama, finally repelled the nation and provided the opportunity for President Lyndon B. Johnson to demand a congressional remedy for racial injustice.

Three important measures followed. The Civil Rights Act of 1964, which the Supreme Court upheld unanimously later that year in *Heart of Atlanta Motel v. United States*, used the New Deal's expansive interpretation of the Constitution's commerce clause to end legal segregation in public accommodations, including entertainment venues. The act also authorized the U.S. attorney general to file suit against state institutions and facilities, such as schools, and required the cut-off of federal funds to any program that did not adopt anti-discrimination policies. Finally, it banned employment discrimination on the basis of race, color, religion, national origin, or gender. The next year, the Voting Rights Act of 1965 attacked voting discrimination by appointing federal examiners to monitor state and local voter registration and elections and by ending state poll taxes, which the Twenty-fourth Amendment had outlawed the previous year in federal elections.

Significantly, these acts allowed the federal government to prosecute private discrimination under the Fourteenth Amendment, thus freeing Congress to protect individual rights more broadly. They also paralleled Court decisions that incorporated many provisions of the Bill of Rights, especially rights of the accused, into the Fourteenth Amendment's due process clause, thereby checking arbitrary state action against minorities. Faced with these developments, white resistance weakened. Within months after passage of the 1964 act, many southern businesses dropped whites-only policies, schools came under court orders to desegregate, and, by 1966, blacks were voting in larger numbers than at any time since Reconstruction.

These victories were short-lived. As the 1960s unfolded, urban race riots, the rise of black nationalism, and demands for economic equality divided the civil rights movement and soured white willingness to remedy past wrongs. The Vietnam War soon divided the majority Democratic Party, which had led the efforts to write these reforms into law, and the resulting political realignment made the South a vital part of a Republican Party that captured the presidency in 1968. A more conservative Court in the 1970s led by Earl Warren's successor as chief justice, Warren E. Burger, slowed but did not abandon the revolution in civil rights; the justices no longer were united on their reading of what the Constitution allowed.

It is not easy to find a clear pattern in the post–Warren Court decisions. The justices accepted busing as a remedy for school desegregation but refused to extend urban desegregation decrees to include largely white suburban areas without evidence of discriminatory intent (*Milliken v. Bradley*, 1974). This refusal effectively blunted school reform in most cities. The Court also interpreted the 1964 Civil Rights Act to forbid disparate impact in employment but ruled that laws lacking an explicit racial classification scheme would not be subject to the highest judicial oversight. Strict scrutiny applied to race, however, and the justices even expanded its definition to include "identifiable classes of persons who are subjected to intentional discrimination solely because of their ancestry or ethnic characteristics" (*Saint Francis College v. Al-Khazraji*, 1987).

The Court further adopted a policy of affirmative action to remedy past wrongs. In *Regents of the University of California v. Bakke* (1978), a badly divided Court reviewed the admissions program of the medical school at the University of California, Davis, which had no history of racial discrimination; this program set aside sixteen of one hundred seats in its entering class for minorities, some of whom had lower grades and test scores than white applicants. By a narrow 5–4 vote that reflected the division in public opinion, the Court ruled that race could be one criterion for making decisions, but that explicit racial quotas were illegal unless there was a history of racial discrimination. The decision was even closer than it appeared, with the Court splitting 4–1–4: four justices found the school's program invalid under the 1964 Civil Rights Act, and four justices deemed it acceptable under the Fourteenth Amendment's equal protection clause. The swing vote came from Justice Lewis F. Powell, who concluded that the program was invalid under the equal protection clause because its explicit racial quota did not have a background history of past racial discrimination to justify it.

Nearly thirty years after *Bakke*, in *Grutter v. Bollinger* (2003), a different and more conservative Court led by Chief Justice William H. Rehnquist affirmed the use of race in making admission decisions if the purpose was to achieve "the educational benefits that flow from a diverse student body." But the Rehnquist Court also held earlier, in the 1990s, that these programs must provide proof of the discrimination that they were created to remedy and be narrowly tailored to benefit only the persons harmed, two criteria that raised questions about the continued constitutionality of affirmative action itself. The Court refused as well to extend judicially mandated school desegregation, especially when racial separation existed because of residential segregation that could not be shown to be the product of explicitly racially discriminatory public policy.

In 2007 the Court, now under the leadership of Chief Justice John Roberts, went further and ruled that local school districts in Seattle, Washington, and Louisville, Kentucky, could not use race as a tiebreaker in assigning students to a school in an effort to achieve racial balance. For the 5–4 majority, the intentions of school districts to maintain interracial schools violated the Fourteenth Amendment's equal protection clause and did not overcome the right to be free from decisions based on race (*Parents Involved in Community Schools v.*

Seattle School District No. 1, 2007). "The way to stop discrimination on the basis of race is to stop discriminating on the basis of race," the chief justice insisted in his opinion for the majority, which was joined by Justice Anthony Kennedy, who concurred that the programs were invalid because they used race as a determining factor but did not agree that race could never be considered. The minority justices sharply criticized the decision and argued that the constitutional mandate of racial equality at times required the explicit use of race as a criterion to overcome racial discrimination.

These decisions did not signal a retreat on civil rights as much as they did the emergence of more complex issues. By the mid-1970s, few people were willing to defend racial segregation imposed by law but no popular consensus existed on what else constituted racial discrimination or what actions were required to make up for past wrongs. For many citizens, race mattered less in the last decades of the twentieth century and the first decade of the twenty-first century than at any time in the nation's history. Public opinion polls revealed a strong belief in the value of racial and ethnic diversity and the easy acceptance of racial integration as commonplace, especially among younger people in the so-called Generations X and Y. The election in 2008 of Barack Obama, an African American, as president also suggested that the United States had in fact achieved the constitutional equality promised by the Reconstruction amendments. If so, it was an uneasy triumph. Race still looms large in contemporary society, with blacks ranking low on most measures of social and economic progress. But Americans no longer considered this disparity a constitutional problem.

The same was not true of other forms of inequality. The success of the attack on racial discrimination was not lost on women, who looked both to legislation and to the Fourteenth Amendment's equal protection clause as ways to remove inequalities based on gender. In 1920, the women's movement scored a major victory with the ratification of the Nineteenth Amendment forbidding discrimination in access to the polls based on sex, and yet the expected transformation of American life (and the promised purification of politics) did not occur. Women largely voted in much the same way that men did.

Once again, World War II changed what a constitutional amendment did not. As men went to war, women took their places in factories and government, achieving an economic independence that they had lacked as non-working wives. Even though the idealized conception of the family of bread-winning father and stay-at-home mother survived the war intact, the role of women was changing as they entered college and the workforce in increasing numbers. But new opportunities for women too often did not lead to equality with men in matters of pay, working conditions, or career advancement or in the laws that governed both the workplace and domestic life. Continuing discrimination based on gender spurred a third wave of the feminist movement—the first had occurred in the 1830s and 1840s and the second in the early twentieth century—and, like the first two, it drew upon and reflected a widespread sense of injustice. It was this perception of equality denied that propelled major changes in the law of gender.

The 1964 Civil Rights Act provided a wedge to bring about legal change. The act outlawed discrimination based on sex as well as race, an addition made by southern opponents who hoped that it would lessen support for the bill. The statute also established the Equal Employment Opportunity Commission (EEOC) and gave it the authority to investigate and settle claims of workplace discrimination. For many women, these changes were too incremental. They sought more comprehensive change and believed that only a constitutional amendment could bring it about.

This conclusion was not new. The campaign to add gender equality to the Constitution had begun soon after the adoption of the Nineteenth Amendment, which had done nothing to change the vast legal framework limiting the roles of women in other areas of American life. The movement for change, however, divided over its agenda. Not all women reformers accepted the need for change. At times, the notion of a separate sphere for women offered protections to them that were not available to men—for example, in wage-hour and safety regulations. But the internal contradictions of an argument for both equal protection and special treatment soon pushed more militant women toward a constitutional amendment to ensure strict legal equality. In 1923, the National Woman's Party, the militant wing of the suffrage movement, proposed an Equal Rights Amendment (ERA) drafted by its leader, Alice Paul. Its language was straightforward: "Men and women shall have equal rights throughout the United States and every place subject to its jurisdiction." Other women's organizations rejected this approach in favor of an incremental approach that would allow public opinion to change in support of equal rights.

The Court's inconsistent decisions in this area from 1923 to 1970, however, gave weight to the argument that a clear and unambiguous constitutional directive was needed. In the 1940s, for example, the justices allowed separate minimum-hour statutes for women at the state level but approved a single standard at the federal level. By the 1960s, a more aggressive and more political women's movement, symbolized by the National Organization for Women (NOW), pushed for changes in state laws and, with the aid of the American Civil Liberties Union, mounted an assault on gender-discrimination practices in state and federal courts. They also sought ratification of a revised ERA, which used language that tracked its constitutional precursors in the Fourteenth and Fifteenth Amendments: "Equality of rights under the law shall not be denied or abridged by the United States or by any State on account of sex." Feminists considered an amendment necessary for three reasons: it would make the law clear, something the Supreme Court had failed to do; it would place the burden on government to justify any legal distinction between men and women; and it would make the principle of gender equality permanent, not subject to uncertain political tides.

In 1972, Congress passed the Equal Rights Amendment and submitted it to the states for ratification. Thirty-five states ratified before the deadline expired in 1982, three short of the three-fourths vote required for approval. Most of the states acted within the first year after the amendment's proposal, but the measure met determined resistance from conservatives, including many women, who claimed the amendment would mean unacceptable social changes such as gay marriages and women serving in combat. The amendment's opponents also realized that they could slow down the amendment's progress in the state legislatures and run out the proposal's seven-year time limit. An extension by Congress in 1978 of the time limit for an additional three years presented the appearance of illegitimate rewriting of the rules, and the amendment failed in 1982, with five states attempting, unsuccessfully, to rescind their earlier ratifications.

The campaign for the ERA also failed because the Court undermined the impetus for an amendment by changing the standard it used to assess claims of sex discrimination. The shift began with a 1971 landmark decision (*Reed v. Reed*) that deemed an Idaho law arbitrary by automatically preferring men over women as executors of decedents' estates. Two years later, in *Frontiero v. Richardson* (1973), the justices dismantled the law's assumption of female dependency in marriage. Finally, in 1976, the justices announced they would use a standard of "intermediate scrutiny" to evaluate laws that differentiated between men and women (*Craig v. Boren*). This rule, still in use in gender discrimination cases, was less than the strict scrutiny standard applied to issues of race, which required a compelling government interest to justify legal distinctions, but it was a burden of proof that many states could not meet.

Congress also responded by prohibiting practices that the Court had found permissible under the Constitution. When the Court determined that discrimination against pregnant workers was not unconstitutional, for example, Congress made it illegal. With few exceptions, by the 1990s sex discrimination by law had disappeared, symbolized by *U.S. v. Virginia* (1996), a decision that ended one of the last male-only bastions by ruling that Virginia could not deny admission to women at the state-supported Virginia Military Institute.

The ERA had not succeeded, but the cause of women's legal equality had. The Court's very makeup confirmed the shift: Sandra Day O'Connor became the first woman justice on the Supreme Court in 1981, followed by Ruth Bader Ginsburg as the second in 1993. With the appointments in 2009 and 2010 of Sonia Sotomayor and Elena Kagan, respectively, fully one-third of the Court is now female, O'Connor having retired in 2006.

The movement toward constitutional equality for all citizens during the last half of the twentieth century still left areas in which legal discrimination was possible. Equality for gays and lesbians was the new battleground, with marriage becoming its central focus. Traditionally, legal marriage has been the exclusive domain of heterosexual couples, and it had a preferred status under many federal and state laws (such as income tax rates, Social Security and insurance benefits, and inheritance or estate law). In 1996, the Defense of Marriage Act strengthened this standing under federal law. But American culture was becoming increasingly comfortable with gays and lesbians in highly visible roles, and this change in attitudes presaged important constitutional consequences.

By the turn of the twenty-first century, open demands for full legal equality, which had begun in New York City's Stonewall riots of 1969, had resulted in significant changes. During the first decade, supreme courts in six states invalidated heterosexual-only marriage laws as violations of their state constitutions' equal protection clauses, and in 2009 Vermont and New Hampshire became the first states to make gay marriage legal by statute. Private homosexual acts no longer were a crime, except in the military. In 2003, the Court ruled that a Texas anti-sodomy statute infringed individual liberty protected under the Fourteenth Amendment's due process clause (*Lawrence v. Texas*), a ruling that overruled a decision a mere seven years earlier in which the justices denied constitutional privacy protection to sexual acts engaged in by same-sex couples (*Bowers v. Hardwick*, 1986). Predictably, these developments met with strong resistance. More than thirty states responded by amending their constitutions to ban gay unions, one of which, California's Proposition 8, was challenged successfully in federal district court in 2010 as a violation of the Fourteenth Amendment's equal protection clause in a striking reprise of a familiar argument grounded in the civil rights and women's rights movements.

Equality is now part of the Constitution in ways its framers could not have imagined in 1787. It has become a core constitutional value because Americans demanded it, although not without controversy and resistance. Amendments to the nation's charter have been the principal vehicles for this change, but the promises contained in them, especially in the Fourteenth Amendment, were realized slowly. The touchstone of this transformation—due process of law and equal protection of laws—was sufficiently flexible to allow reformers to push for new meanings and opponents to resist by invoking tradition.

In this sense, changes in the direction of greater equality have been no different from other constitutional changes. They have occurred only when a majority of Americans were ready to embrace them. What is different, however, is the impact that these amendments have had on the Constitution itself. The first ten amendments pitted liberty against power; they had restrained government to protect individual liberty. The new amendments made power the friend of liberty and government the guarantor of freedom. In doing so, they created a new constitution in which guarantees of liberty and equality fulfilled the revolutionary pledges of 1776, and it is this constitution we now use to determine what these promises mean in our ordinary lives.

9

Rights

On August 23, 1984, the *New York Times* carried a brief story on an inside page about a disorderly march in Dallas, Texas, the host city for the Republican National Convention. The incident had begun as a protest against the nomination of Ronald Reagan for a second term as president. About one hundred people were arrested for disorderly conduct; among them was Gregory Lee Johnson, who was charged under a Texas law outlawing the desecration of "venerated objects." He had burned the American flag.

Tried and convicted in a Dallas court, Johnson received the maximum penalty of a year in jail and a $2,000 fine. No doubt many people believed he deserved the sentence. Few things stir the emotions of Americans as strongly as an assault on their patriotic symbols. This attack was especially troublesome. Even though he was a native of the nation's heartland, Indiana, and the son of a soldier, Johnson was not a sympathetic figure. He had joined the Revolutionary Communist Party, an avowedly anti-American group. While the flag burned, he and other members of the demonstration had shouted, "America, the red, white, and blue, we spit on you."

Johnson appealed his conviction, and the case reached the U.S. Supreme Court. The justices ruled, 5–4, that the First Amendment's guarantee of free speech protected Johnson's act. He was expressing a political opinion that clearly fell within the protections of the Bill of Rights. "If there is a bedrock principle underlying the First Amendment," Justice William J. Brennan Jr. wrote for the majority, "it is that the government may not prohibit the expression of an idea simply because society finds the idea itself offensive or disagreeable." The minority, citing the value of the flag as a historical symbol of national unity, saw Johnson's actions as an incitement to violence, not the protected expression of an idea: "flag burning is the equivalent of an inarticulate grunt or roar that . . . is most likely to be indulged in not to express any particular idea, but to antagonize others," Chief Justice William H. Rehnquist retorted in dissent.

The reaction to *Texas v. Johnson* (1989) revealed a deeply divided nation. The decision brought a storm of criticism, as well as voices in strong support of the decision. In response, Congress immediately enacted the Flag Protection

Act, and when a bare majority of the Court narrowly ruled that it, too, was unconstitutional, a movement began to amend the Constitution to protect the American flag from "desecration." The House of Representatives passed a flag desecration amendment six times from 1995 to 2005,[1] but each time it failed to obtain the required two-thirds majority vote in the Senate. In mid-2006 the proposed amendment failed by one vote in the upper house from passing to the states for ratification. The American public remains split over what is more important—upholding a symbol of national unity and order or protecting free speech.

In popular versions of the nation's past, the framers of the Bill of Rights codified our essential liberties in the first ten amendments to the Constitution. Many people assume that these rights had self-evident meanings, which judges today simply apply to new circumstances. The truth is far messier. Our rights have never been out of the teeth of controversy, and they never have been the responsibility of courts alone. Throughout American history, rights have been invented and repudiated, fought over and striven for, expanded and violated. Scarcely was the ink dry on the Bill of Rights when debates began about what the words meant. The history of American liberty has this contest at its core. Perhaps more than any other action, the declaring and re-declaring of rights has defined our national politics and led to continual revisions and interpretations of the Constitution. The argument about rights is nothing less than an argument about the meaning of liberty itself.

By the eve of the Revolution, rights were part of a shared English heritage that undergirded and guided American resistance to Britain's efforts to tighten control over its colonies. For centuries Englishmen had considered personal liberties and rights to private property as fundamental principles normally beyond the reach of the king. They were concessions from the sovereign and limits on his power and could be forfeited only by the law of the land. This was the meaning of Magna Carta, the first in a long series of such guarantees. These concepts of liberty and rights carried with them a large set of assumptions about customs, obligations, and rules of behavior that attached to all members and ranks of society, with the common law serving as the guide to how they applied in practice.

Rights and liberties were the inheritance of all Englishmen, and the list of grievances that poured from colonial pens from 1763 to 1776—and were captured in a long litany in the Declaration of Independence—reveals how valuable the colonists considered them. Grievances are rights in reverse—they identify rights under threat—and by this measure the Declaration of Independence is an important gauge of what the colonists believed was at stake. Taxation without representation was an interference with their right to property; trials of alleged smugglers by a judge alone violated the right to a public jury trial by members of the local community; suspension of local courts denied due process of law. British actions, the document charged, robbed Englishmen of their heritage. Each action of the imperial government mocked an essential ingredient of English liberty; collectively, they proved an intention to deprive the colonists of their freedom.

During the revolutionary struggle the vocabulary of rights began to shift from protecting what the English people over centuries had wrested from government to discerning what rights men ought to possess. Rights became defined as natural, not historical. This language was not new; natural rights had entered political discourse with John Locke's defense of the Glorious Revolution of 1688 in *The Second Treatise of Government* (1689). In a distant and unknowable past, Locke argued, people in a state of nature entered into a compact (the social contract) to protect the rights they enjoyed as autonomous individuals (natural men). They did not retain the freedom of nature but rather gave up some rights, notably their executive and legislative authority, to civil government, which then provided security and protection of their retained rights to life, liberty, and property. In Locke's telling, this transfer of power was always subordinate to the true purpose of the social contract, which was "the mutual preservation of their lives, liberties, and estates," and individuals did not lose their right to alter or change the government when it acted to subvert this end.

Locke was vague about which rights were part of natural law, yet he contended that individuals did not give up their innate ability to reason, by which Americans inferred they could discover new rights. Once introduced, the idea of natural rights could not be so easily confined to a list of rights won and now in danger of being lost. It was too expansive; it invited men to consider rights beyond ones derived from tradition and history and to imagine the freedom they enjoyed not by virtue of their birth as Englishmen but by their humanity. John Adams pointed to this sense of rights in his *Dissertation on the Canon and Feudal Law*, protesting the Stamp Act of 1765: "I say RIGHTS antecedent to all government,—*Rights*, that cannot be repealed or restrained by human laws—Rights, derived from the great Legislator of the universe."

Other revolutionaries imagined that Americans were in a unique moment when they could re-enter a state of nature to reclaim their primeval rights. This sentiment was common to the age. The French Enlightenment sage Jean-Jacques Rousseau echoed it in the opening words of his book *On the Social Contract* (1762): "Man is born free," he wrote. Rousseau's natural man, like Locke's, also entered into a social compact for the purpose of protecting his rights, but these rights were not fixed by history. They were whatever parties to the contract agreed they should be. When the social compact broke down, people could renegotiate it, again specifying whatever rights and obligations they chose to include in the new contract. Rousseau did not influence American revolutionary thought as much as he anticipated one of its central ideas: rights could be claimed without limit, as long as men agreed to them.

The years of protest and debate preceding the Revolution were heady times but the abstract quality of the argument begged an important question: What were these natural rights? Here was the rub. The inquiry might result in a greater defense of property, a prospect that would have pleased individuals who saw the right to control property, including women and slaves, as the guardian of all other rights, but it also might slip into claims of equality and democracy, much more radical notions. This elusiveness gave rights a protean quality—there was no limit to their growth—but it also made them a matter of contention. What the wealthy merchant considered a right may not have been the same as what the laborer demanded, so the question often became which rights and for whom?

Rights talk was the fodder of revolutionary politics—no one disputed that rights were essential to liberty—but the initial task of republican leaders was to limit power, not expand rights. Restraints on government were at the heart of the state constitution-making from 1776 to 1780, and to this end, rights became part of fundamental law in almost every state, either as part of the text or listed separately in a bill of rights. The focus was on rights necessary to protect liberty. Most of the guarantees were familiar to Americans because they came straight from the English past—trial by jury, the right to confront accusers, and the privilege against self-incrimination—but the list of rights was more expansive than colonial grievances and included freedom of religion and the press. Their framers discovered rights not in English history alone but in the laws of nature, or natural law. These rights went beyond the common law, and because they existed before societies were formed, rights belonged to individuals, not communities.

The goal in recognizing such rights, however, was to promote the public good, not elevate the individual. The revolutionaries were republicans who were skeptical of private desires and sought instead to promote public virtue. Rights may no longer belong to the community, yet civil society, a Pennsylvania committee reminded citizens in 1779, "requires that every right . . . claimed or exercised by any man . . . be in subordination to the public good."[2] It is this sense of rights as an aid to perfecting society that explains how revolutionaries could uphold the freedom of conscience, for instance, and still be comfortable with an established church, taxing religious dissenters, or barring men who held publicly odious religious beliefs from taking political office. The public good required a balance that could not be achieved by embracing unbridled liberty. The fifteenth article of the Virginia Declaration of Rights of 1776, the model for the federal Bill of Rights, was clear about the public purpose for a listing of rights: "That no free government, or the blessings of liberty, can be preserved to any people but by a firm adherence to justice, moderation, temperance, frugality, and virtue and by frequent recurrence to fundamental principles." This was not the stuff of unrestrained individualism. It was instead a civic republicanism that emphasized individual liberty within the context of community and citizen participation in government.

By the time the Federal Convention met in Philadelphia, concerns about democratic excesses had eroded utopian hopes for liberty secured through a citizenry imbued with public virtue. For the framers, liberty required structural restraints on power—federalism, separation and balance of powers, and the like—but the ratification debates produced another condition: written acknowledgment of the rights individuals could claim against the general government. The federal Bill of Rights (the first ten amendments to the Constitution) was a product of this revolutionary penchant for protecting rights by making them part of fundamental law. It contained twenty-five assorted substantive and procedural rights, many already having found some expression, although not universally, in the various state constitutions and declarations of rights.

The First Amendment, the only one to begin with the words "Congress shall make no law," contains a quintet of guarantees concerning speech, religion, press, assembly, and petition that Supreme Court Justice Benjamin Cardozo described in *Palko v. Connecticut* (1937) as "the matrix, the indispensable condition, of nearly every other form of freedom." These rights allow citizens to participate in public life and to maintain a private faith, free from interference by government. The next two amendments restrain the central government from interfering with an individual's right to bear arms (Second) and from commandeering private homes to house troops (Third). The five amendments that follow (Fourth through Eighth) outline procedural guarantees for individuals who confront the power of government, usually as persons accused of crimes. The Fourth and Sixth Amendments, for example, establish detailed requirements for law officers and courts to follow in matters of arrest and trial, while the Eighth Amendment forbade cruel and unusual punishments, including excessive fines.

The Ninth and Tenth Amendments are more general but they, too, set boundaries on the power of the central government. The Ninth, the handiwork of James Madison, who feared the prospect of omitting rights from the amendments, recognized the potential for additional rights by commanding that the "enumeration in the Constitution of certain rights shall not be construed to deny or disparage others retained by the people." This language not only reinforced the notion of popular sovereignty and the contractual nature of rights but it also opened the door for the judicial discovery of rights, especially in the twentieth century, although a fear of being seen as too activist has inhibited most judges from pursuing this course. The Tenth sought to safeguard rights by limiting federal power: the "powers not delegated to the United States by the Constitution, nor prohibited by it to the States, are reserved to the States respectively or to the people." It, too, was a source of litigation, often unsuccessful, as the role of the national government expanded during the twentieth century. In the congressional debates, James Madison blunted the Tenth Amendment's potential for limiting federal power by refusing a motion to add the word "expressly" ("not expressly delegated") to the proposed text because, he argued, "there must necessarily be admitted powers by implication."[3]

Almost from the moment of their ratification, the rights promised in the new constitutional amendments came into dispute. The desire to safeguard individual liberty did not disappear—if anything, it became stronger—but when faced with practical problems, people disagreed about what government could and could not do. The sharp political divisions of the 1790s, especially the emergence of a highly partisan press, exposed the matter plainly. Party newspapers engaged in vicious personal attacks and routinely challenged the integrity of government officials. The Federalists viewed this development with alarm, especially after the French began to intrude on U.S. sovereignty, first in support of the Jeffersonian Republicans in the presidential election of 1796 and then in the controversy over a French effort to bribe American trade nego-tiators (the XYZ Affair) and an undeclared war with France (the Quasi-War) that began in 1798. The danger to the fragile republic was both obvious and imminent to Federalists, who believed that the federal government was only as strong as the integrity and reputation of its leaders. Vindictive attacks on the general government and its officers would fatally undermine the popular support it needed to survive.

To curb this threat, the Federalist-controlled Congress passed the Sedition Act of 1798. Modeled on an English statute enacted a few years earlier, the act made individuals who criticized the government, officials, or laws in a manner designed to bring them into disrepute or cause a civil disturbance subject to prosecution for seditious libel. Under English common law, truth could not shield a defendant in such cases; in fact, commentators believed it was more damaging because it would lead to greater social unrest, as expressed in the maxim, "The greater the truth, the greater the libel." But the federal statute, reflecting American revolutionary ideas about the importance of free speech, made truth a defense.

Under the cultural and political logic of the period, the act was an effort to reconcile the competing demands of power and liberty. By modern standards, it was a blatant attempt to suppress speech. Prosecutions under the act were strictly partisan, resulting in the conviction of several Republican editors and even one Vermont congressman, also an editor, who had pointedly criticized the Congress and president. Challenges to these prosecutions cited the First Amendment's guarantee of speech and press in defense, along with the truth-fulness of the criticisms.

Here, the uncertain meaning of the First Amendment became apparent. It was unclear what the framers intended, except for their belief that reporting corruption or abuses of power and speaking freely about public matters were vital in a system based on popular rule. But this protection largely concerned prior restraint of the press or speech, which was common in Great Britain yet unpopular in the colonies. No evidence existed as to whether the framers of the First Amendment proposed to outlaw seditious libel. At trial, Federalist judges rejected the argument that the act was unconstitutional. The law expired in 1801 without a definitive judicial interpretation, although the defeat of Federalists in 1800—the party lost both the Congress and presidency to the Jeffersonian Republicans—suggested that the electorate did not support the suppression of speech for partisan reasons.

Even this outcome was tenuous: in 1804, Alexander Hamilton, one month before his death in a duel with Vice President Aaron Burr, successfully defended a Federalist newspaper editor in New York from a charge of seditious libel against a Republican-led prosecution backed by President Thomas Jefferson. (Hamilton argued successfully that truth published for good motives was not libelous, thus ending the life of this weapon for government to wield against its critics.) At the least, these events reveal that the founding generation had sharp differences of opinion about the scope of free speech and free press in practice, a pattern that became a hallmark of Bill of Rights jurisprudence in every period of American history.

On the whole, the concern for rights became more intense in the decades following the Revolution, although its focus shifted from the federal to the state governments. By the 1820s the United States was becoming more democratic, with most states removing property qualifications for voting and officehold-ing to allow all adult white males to participate in government. The nation also had embraced capitalism, which emphasized individual risk and reward. Both developments reinforced the notion of individual rights, especially prop-erty rights, and they strengthened as well a demand for fair procedure, or due process, to ensure equal opportunity in the political arena and the marketplace.

Ensuring these guarantees of liberty, however, was primarily the respon-sibility of the states. In 1833 the U.S. Supreme Court determined, in *Barron v. Baltimore*, that the Bill of Rights restrained the federal government alone, a rule that held sway until the twentieth century. In some ways, this decision had a limited effect because almost every state constitution included the set of rights contained in the federal amendments, and some exceeded the federal safeguards. But the decision also meant that the interpretation and enforce-ment of rights could vary widely from state to state. Establishment of state churches, for instance, remained acceptable in some states until 1833.

Most individual rights in the nineteenth century were protected by state con-stitutions, yet state judges often applied the Bill of Rights to invalidate state laws and constrain state government. Many state courts, but not all, under-stood the federal amendments to establish general constitutional principles that applied to their legislatures and governors even when the state constitu-tion was silent. For example, in the early decades of the nineteenth century the supreme courts of Georgia, Arkansas, and Louisiana upheld the right to bear arms (though not concealed weapons) as protected by the Second Amendment, which Georgia also judged a natural right.

This practice of looking to the federal amendments for guidance was es-pecially evident with reference to rights of the accused. No other part of the law had a more intimate relationship to everyday life than did criminal justice, and, not surprisingly, rights of the accused occupied much of the nineteenth-century attention to individual liberty. Dozens of state cases invoked the Fourth Amendment as a prohibition against unlawful searches and seizures, the Fifth Amendment's ban double jeopardy, and the Sixth Amendment's outline of the requirements of a fair trial. The reason for state courts' references to the Bill of Rights was straightforward, as expressed by J. H. Lumpkin, chief justice of the Georgia Supreme Court: "[O]ur patriotic forefathers, out of abundant caution, super-added these amendments to the Constitution, so as to place the matter beyond doubt or cavil, misconstruction or abuse."[4]

Judges also interpreted guarantees in their state constitutions to offer significant protections to anyone accused of crimes. They insisted on strictness in matters of due process, by which they meant adherence to proper procedures, such as requiring that indictments, or formal accusations of crime, use precisely the words required by law. The goal of such precision was twofold: the defendant needed to have exact knowledge to prepare his defense, and the indictment's strict language ensured that the state could not use the alleged facts to support a second trial for the same offense. Judges resisted any pressure to loosen these safeguards: "The harmless decision of today becomes the dangerous precedent for tomorrow," an Indiana court warned. The regard for proper procedure was no "idle technicality"; "the people have no better security than in holding officers of the state to a reasonable degree of care, precision, and certainty in prosecuting the citizen for a violation of the law."[5] The point was clear: individual rights restrained government, which was a preeminent concern not only for the revolutionary generation but also for nineteenth-century Americans.

Even so, a concern for rights in principle did not always translate into protection of rights in practice. In matters of criminal justice, for instance, an insistence on proper adherence to procedure diminished by the mid-nineteenth century, as fear of crime increased in tandem with the growth of cities. Efforts to professionalize the police met mixed success, and extra-legal or popular justice administered by vigilantes, citizens' associations, and law-and-order leagues was common in all parts of the country.

Public demands for order and security had profound implications for rights of the accused. By the end of the century, states in effect were running as many as three different criminal systems, each with its own standard of due process, as illustrated by Alameda County, California, home to Oakland. At the bottom was assembly-line justice. It was a highly bureaucratic process that used plea bargains—negotiated sentences in exchange for a plea of guilty—to move people accused of minor crimes swiftly from arrest to imprisonment. The handling of ordinary but serious property crimes was marginally less routine, with fewer than half the cases going to trial and the vast majority of defendants being found guilty. Only for the most serious crimes—murder and robbery chief among them—did rights of the accused play any part in the criminal process. These cases grabbed public attention, and the duel of lawyers acted to educate citizens on an idealized version of American justice and the rights of defendants. But, in fact, most crimes proceeded to trial without adequate counsel for the accused and with rights a mere shadow of what state constitutions promised. Of course, for immigrants and blacks even the most ordinary administration of due process was often a mirage.

Religion proved to be an especially problematic proving ground for individual rights. The earliest state constitutions recognized a government-supported or established church (or multiple religious establishments in New England states), but the First Amendment forbade this practice by the federal government and prohibited Congress from passing any law prohibiting the free exercise of religion. These guarantees marked a departure from European practice and raised an important question about how to maintain morality in a secular state.

One answer was apparent by 1830 when Alexis de Tocqueville penned his assessment of the American experiment in popular government. He noted the unusual vitality of American religion and attributed it to the intense competition for adherents among the hundreds of religious groups that flourished everywhere in the United States, a conclusion also adopted by later scholars. This vying for souls promoted diversity and tolerance; it also allowed government to remain neutral regarding official faiths. But diversity and tolerance rested on a shared assumption that America was a Christian nation with a common Protestant culture. Law reflected this belief. Legislatures enacted anti-blasphemy statutes and Sunday closing laws, local school boards required religious instruction, and local governments enacted temperance legislation based explicitly on evangelical Protestant doctrines about alcohol. Courts upheld these measures and were rarely sympathetic to complaints from Catholics, who did not object intrinsically to strong drink, and Jews, who did not share Sunday as the sabbath, about their discriminatory impact.

The U.S. Supreme Court did not consider the First Amendment's religion clauses often in the nineteenth century, but the cases it decided drew a line between belief, which the government could not touch, and action, which was legitimate for government to regulate or prohibit. In *Reynolds v. United States* (1878), for example, the justices rejected the argument that the Mormon doctrine of polygamy imposed a religious duty on believers that government could not breach. Not surprisingly, the decision unleashed a flood of anti-polygamy legislation in the states, and Congress required Utah to adopt such a statute to gain admission to the Union, which happened in 1890 after the polygamists had lost a few more legal battles. What was at stake was how far religious innovation could go, and both federal and state legislative and judicial branches limited it to diversity within a well-established mainstream. The relationship of the government to religion was circumscribed by the conviction that "This is a Christian nation," as the Supreme Court proclaimed in an 1892 decision (*Church of the Holy Trinity v. United States*).

Even though it was applied unevenly to religious and ethnic minorities, the goal of expansive, liberal rights maintained a powerful hold on Americans throughout the nineteenth century. The antebellum decades especially witnessed numerous reform movements designed to extend the federal Bill of Rights and other democratic safeguards of liberty, some of them newly created, to excluded groups. It was a second era of rights invention. Women made one of the strongest demands, as the Seneca Falls Convention in 1848 put their case for voting rights and property rights in the Declaration of Sentiments that borrowed language from the Declaration of Independence. Nine years earlier Mississippi, a state not known for its liberalism, passed the first Married Women Property Rights Act (1839), granting wives significant control over their property. Workingmen used Jefferson's term "inalienable rights" to lobby for fair wages and the ability to use their free time as they saw fit, two rights they wanted to include in the list of individual liberties. The language they used was not the nineteenth-century vocabulary of markets but the revolutionary words of natural rights. The key phrase—and the most explosive—was equal rights, which for most antebellum reformers meant the same rights for all white men. It was a core value not only of revolutionary republicanism but also of the new democracy that now was an American trait.

A demand for equal rights resulted in a measure of success for women and workingmen in the twentieth century, yet it was another campaign of the nineteenth century that had the most profound effect on rights as we know them today. This movement sought the abolition of slavery. It linked equality and rights for all men, not only whites, as a matter of justice and morality. Northern states never extended first-class citizenship to African Americans, but neither did they deprive blacks of individual rights because of their color. The crusade for rights even extended to fugitive slaves. Personal liberty laws—statutes that sought to extend due process to runaways—were not simply antislavery states' protests against slavery. They, too, symbolized an expansive culture of individual rights that by the 1840s and 1850s had become a hallmark of American society outside the slaveholding South.

The 1860s marked the zenith of the second wave of rights invention with the three constitutional amendments adopted during Reconstruction. Each added new constitutional guarantees, and one, the Fourteenth Amendment, contained within it the seeds of a veritable revolution in the American conception of rights by changing the traditional relationship of national and state governments. Previously, Americans were citizens of their states; they looked primarily to their state constitutions to secure their rights. To ensure protection for former slaves, the Fourteenth Amendment defined uniform standards for citizenship and made every person born or naturalized in the United States a citizen of both of the nation and of his or her state. Equally important, it established "equal protection of the laws" and "due process of law" as guarantees for all persons. The choice of the word "persons" rather than "men" was significant, more so in retrospect. The requirement of fairness and equal treatment under a rule of law was no right of citizenship alone but instead was a fundamental obligation owed by the United States to anyone within its jurisdiction.

For the first time, the federal government had the responsibility to protect the rights of individuals—at least in theory. Yet on the whole, federal courts did not interpret the amendment in this way during the last half of the nineteenth century. Contrary to the expectations of some of its framers, the Supreme Court held that the amendment did not require states and local governments to respect the guarantees of the federal Bill of Rights. The justices instead followed traditional practice and allowed states wide discretion to protect individual liberty as they saw fit. In the *Slaughterhouse Cases* (1873), the Court held that the basic civil rights and liberties of American citizens remained under the control of state law and limited the federally protected privileges and immunities of citizens to such narrow rights as travel to and from Washington, D.C.

This pinched interpretation prevailed throughout the nineteenth century, even when the case involved rights of African Americans, the clearly intended beneficiaries of the amendment. For example, in *Plessy v. Ferguson* (1896), the Court held that state-mandated racial segregation of railroad cars did not violate the equal protection clause of the Fourteenth Amendment. The "separate but equal" doctrine justified the widespread racial segregation and discrimination that finally ended as a matter of law in the 1960s.

A concern for federalism as traditionally defined explains much of the Court's stance. During this period, many justices believed that a more expansive reading of the amendment would undermine the role of the states, either through federal legislation or federal court decisions. Most Americans accepted this view. The voices of protests came most often from marginalized groups, notably women and blacks, who struggled to gain the political clout to change cultural and legal norms.

Part of the intellectual difficulty that the justices faced in applying the federal Bill of Rights as a restraint on the states through the Fourteenth Amendment stemmed from the Court's own rules of judicial construction (interpretation), as an 1884 case, *Hurtado v. California*, demonstrated. Joseph Hurtado, a murderer who faced execution in California, appealed his conviction because he had not been indicted first by a grand jury, as required by the Fifth Amendment. Another part of the amendment guaranteed that no one could be deprived of life, liberty, or property without due process of law, the same phrase used in the Fourteenth Amendment. A majority of the justices rejected Hurtado's appeal because the Court's interpretive standard assumed that no part of the Constitution was superfluous—the framers would not have been redundant—which meant that the Fifth Amendment and Fourteenth Amendment could not mean the same thing. Another Court rule, however, assumed that the same words had the same meaning within a document, which implied that the definition of due process was the same in both amendments. This contradiction stymied the justices, who chose not to include any part of the Bill of Rights in the meaning of the Fourteenth Amendment.

By the end of the nineteenth century, the Court was moving away from its internal contradictions, but not to embrace the Fourteenth Amendment as a bulwark for individual rights. Rather, the amendment became a protection for the property rights of corporations. From the late nineteenth century through the first three decades of the twentieth century, big business dominated the American economy as never before. The U.S. Supreme Court proved to be its strong ally, first by declaring that a corporation was a person for purposes of the Fourteenth Amendment (*Santa Clara County v. Southern Pacific Railroad*, 1886) and then by reading the amendment as protecting freedom of contract, an inferred individual right, from state interference under the amendment's due process clause (*Allgeyer v. Louisiana*, 1897). Individual rights noted explicitly in the Constitution, such as freedom of speech, were not included in this interpretation. In effect, this stance prevented most state and federal regulation of economic activity in the name of protecting individual liberty.

But in one case, the Court provided a wedge into the Fourteenth Amendment that later would prove decisive in extending the Bill of Rights to the states. When the city of Chicago opened a street across a railroad track, paying the railroad company only a dollar for the use of its property, the Court decided that the token price violated the Fifth Amendment's requirement of just compensation, which the justices deemed to be included in the meaning of the Fourteenth Amendment's due process clause (*Chicago, Burlington, and Quincy Railroad v. Chicago*, 1898). It was the first time that the Court incorporated a part of the Bill of Rights via the Fourteenth Amendment as a restraint on the states; although economic liberty was the cause in this case, incorporation would become the major vehicle for a liberalization of rights in the twentieth century.

The expanded conception of due process was accompanied by developments in legal thought that encouraged judges to look beyond legal rules, including precedent, to understand how the law would work in the world outside the courtroom. This view reflected the origins in the 1870s of a distinctly American philosophy, pragmatism. Led by Charles Sanders Peirce, William James, and John Dewey, pragmatists sought to reconcile clashes between different ways of thinking by looking to their practical consequences. Theories, as James wrote in *Pragmatism* (1907), were "instruments, not answers to enigmas." Influenced by this approach, progressive legal thinkers such as Associate Justice Oliver Wendell Holmes Jr.; Roscoe Pound, dean of the Harvard Law School; and the reformist lawyer and later Supreme Court justice Louis Brandeis argued that the law as interpreted by judges should not be a mechanical application of theoretical precedents but rather a response to the world as it is. Courts had a responsibility to keep law abreast of the times. It was a view that proved instrumental for protecting individual rights in the twentieth century.

The first step was to challenge the belief that individual property rights were sacred. The U.S. Supreme Court had adopted an exalted view of the marketplace, seeing it as the ideal arrangement for securing the utmost economic liberty, and the justices advanced this interpretation under the theory of substantive due process. Initially, due process meant only that government had to follow its own laws or procedures when making decisions or taking actions. If it did, then the result was thought to be fair. The new interpretation of due process looked instead to the substance and result of the decision-making process: Was it fair, and if not, who decided the right result—legislatures or judges? Under this meaning of due process, government could follow all its established procedures and still deprive citizens (or corporations) of their rights because the decision-making process reached an illegitimate outcome. In such cases, judges had the duty to correct the injustice brought about by the law passed by the legislature or administered by the executive.

Substantive due process represented a shift in interpretation. It came to a head when states sought to regulate the monopolistic practices of corporations, for example, by establishing the rates that railroads could charge. The Supreme Court usually struck down these laws because even if the state followed its procedures to the letter, regulation infringed on the corporation's property rights. Regulation had resulted in a loss of freedom by the corporation to set its rates at whatever price the market would bear. Significantly, the Court did not apply this same logic to individual rights, which remained under state protection—or, too often, as in the case of racial minorities, which were not protected at all.

Even though the Supreme Court ultimately retreated from its belief in the supremacy of economic rights, the concept of substantive due process became embedded in constitutional law as a protection for other individual rights. Increasingly in the twentieth century, progressive reformers took the idea first advanced to protect property and asked whether the guarantees of free speech, fair trial, rights to counsel, and other safeguards of the Bill of Rights were included substantively—were they incorporated?—in the meaning of the Fourteenth Amendment's due process and equal protection clauses.

World War I and its aftermath presented an opportunity to test this idea when the federal government sought to suppress dissent as harmful to the war effort. Much of the government's concern focused on attempts by union organizers, many of them self-proclaimed communists, to use wartime labor shortages to force concessions from business, even if it harmed military production. State courts long had refused to protect radical or offensive speech, and they also suppressed speech if it was accompanied by action that threatened public order, such as might occur at a union rally.

Initially, the U.S. Supreme Court followed this traditional line of reasoning: it upheld convictions under state laws of anti-war protestors, including Eugene

Debs, a candidate for U.S. president (*In re Debs*, 1919), because their speech presented "a clear and present danger" to the war effort. The First Amendment right of free speech did not protect individuals from state laws designed to ensure public order. By 1925, however, the Court had changed its mind, not about the meaning of free speech but about the role of the First Amendment. It ruled for the first time, in *Gitlow v. New York* (1925), that the freedoms of speech and press "are among the fundamental personal rights protected by the due process clause of the Fourteenth Amendment from impairment by the states." It would be several years before the full impact of this decision would become apparent, but it marked the beginning of a new era for individual rights.

By the late 1930s the Court was marching under the banner of incorporation for First Amendment freedoms. In 1937 the justices rejected an argument that the Fourteenth Amendment's due process clause included the Fifth Amendment's ban on double jeopardy, although Justice Benjamin Cardozo, writing for the majority, ruled that it did incorporate all the provisions of the First Amendment. These rights—speech, press, religion, and assembly—were freedoms of expression, which Cardozo called "the matrix, the indispensable condition" for nearly all other freedoms.

Other rights were subject to selective incorporation, or inclusion one by one in the meaning of due process. The Court would apply only those rights that are "of the very essence of a scheme of ordered liberty" and could be considered fundamental because they were so deeply rooted in American traditions (*Palko v. Connecticut*, 1937). This standard meant that the justices would consider individual rights on a case-by-case basis, with strict scrutiny or a "more searching judicial inquiry" applied to laws that appeared to cut harshly against "discrete and insular minorities" (*United States v. Carolene Products*, 1938). Not only did it invite judges to be more active in their oversight and use their discretion more forthrightly than was usual in rights matters but it also divided the justices.

Two justices named to the Court by President Franklin Delano Roosevelt embodied the split. Felix Frankfurter favored selective incorporation. Born in Austria, Frankfurter by his own efforts had risen through education at City College of New York and the Harvard Law School until he was a leading professor at Harvard, from which Roosevelt named him to the Court in 1939 to succeed Justice Cardozo. Frankfurter was openly progressive in his politics, but he also insisted that the Constitution was not a set of abstractions that judges could interpret as they chose. It rested instead upon the evolution of basic principles, each with an array of historical meanings, that the judge must apply carefully in individual circumstances and always with deference to the decisions of popularly elected representatives. In his view, the Bill of Rights could be selectively incorporated only as circumstances required.

Justice Hugo Black took an opposite stance. A New Deal politician from Alabama—he was a two-term U.S. senator when Roosevelt appointed him to the Court in 1937 to succeed the conservative Justice Willis Van Devanter—Black insisted on the total incorporation of the Bill of Rights under the Fourteenth Amendment. As a senator, he had been appalled at the Court's defense of corporations under the doctrine of substantive due process, and he was determined to limit judicial discretion, especially on questions of rights. Total incorporation, he believed, would force the Court to recognize that the whole of the Bill of Rights restrained state and local governments, not simply whichever clauses the justices chose to include as a limit on their power.

The Frankfurter-Black dispute framed the debate over incorporation for the next three decades, yet it scarcely had begun when successive international crises, World War II and the Cold War, plunged the Court into a debate about how to reconcile liberty and security. It was a problem as old as the Constitution itself, and it centered on how far individual rights extended in times of threat. The first cases to test the limits came from an unlikely source, Jehovah's Witnesses, a religious group that claimed First Amendment protection for the refusal of their children, on grounds of religious doctrine, to salute the flag in school as required by state laws. The law breached their right to the free exercise of their religious beliefs, the Witnesses argued, because they owed allegiance to God alone and not to any symbol of secular authority; to do so would be to worship a false idol or graven image, they insisted. The Court disagreed. In an opinion written by Frankfurter, the justices deferred (by a vote of 8 to 1) to legislative judgments: the need to encourage patriotism, they concluded, was sufficiently important to justify a minor interference with a religious belief (*Minersville School District v. Gobitis*, 1940).

When accounts of public attacks on the Witnesses reached court chambers, accompanied by a tidal wave of criticism, several justices reversed course; in 1943, the Court ruled, by a vote of 6 to 3, that the First Amendment protected freedom of religion from state infringement. Justice Robert H. Jackson, usually an ally of Justice Frankfurter in deferring to elected officeholders, wrote the majority opinion (to which Frankfurter filed an anguished and eloquent dissent): if there was any "fixed star in our constitution," Jackson concluded, "it is that no official, high or petty, can prescribe what shall be orthodox in politics, nationalism, religion, or other matters of opinion or force citizens to confess by word or act their faith therein" (*West Virginia State Board of Education v. Barnette*, 1943).

The assault on liberty during World War II, as seen in Nazi Germany, fascist Italy, and militarist Japan, generally renewed Americans' belief in the necessity of individual rights. President Roosevelt used his fireside radio chats to remind the nation of the need to protect "essential human freedoms." He called for a "second Bill of Rights" to include new guarantees, such as the right to a home, adequate medical care, and old age insurance, among others. But this expansive talk was not always consistent with rights in action. In 1942, for example, weeks after the Japanese attack on Pearl Harbor, the federal government ordered the relocation of Japanese Americans into internment camps.

Scholars today agree that the executive order violated the equal protection and due process clauses of the Fourteenth Amendment; it treated one group of citizens differently based solely on their ethnicity and deprived them of liberty and property without due process of law. In 1943 the U.S. Supreme Court decided otherwise, upholding systems of curfew targeting exclusively Americans of Japanese descent and resident aliens of Japanese ancestry (*Hirabayashi v. United States*). A subsequent case, *Korematsu v. United States* (1944), upheld the internment of citizens from these groups. The justices were not willing to challenge the president in time of war, even when the government could produce no evidence of a real threat; in fact, later scholarship has demonstrated that the government altered the record to mislead the justices into believing that there was evidence to justify the internment. In times of crisis, concerns about national security generally trumped individual rights.

The Cold War, the post–World War II struggle between democracy and communism represented by the United States and the Soviet Union, respectively, also raised challenges to individual rights, especially First Amendment freedoms of speech and association. The exposure of domestic spy rings and the communist takeover of Eastern Europe and China persuaded national and state governments to launch massive loyalty programs to purge communist sympathizers. At first the Supreme Court supported convictions under laws designed to punish anyone who belonged to an organization that merely advocated the overthrow of the government. The decisions represented a setback in protection for individual rights because they punished beliefs, not actions, departing from the Court's movement toward a broader view of First Amendment freedoms.

Once public hysteria subsided in the mid-1950s, the justices reverted once again to a more liberal interpretation of these safeguards. They operated under the increasingly accepted view that the due process and equal protection clauses of the Fourteenth Amendment applied to the states as well as the federal government. What remained to be decided were what liberties these clauses included under their protection.

In the 1950s, under the leadership of Chief Justice Earl Warren, the Court began a dramatic expansion of individual rights that lasted through the 1960s, and its decisions shaped a rights consciousness that remains strong today. In some ways the justices' new attention to rights was simply a continuation of a prominent theme in American history. Each decade since the nation's founding had brought some new assertion of rights—a right to freedom, a woman's right to vote, a right to organize. Some of the claims resulted in fundamental law: both the right to freedom (the right not to be enslaved) and women's suffrage were products of constitutional amendments. Other rights, such as the right to organize, were recognized by statute. What was different in mid-century was the leadership of the U.S. Supreme Court in applying the Bill of Rights creatively to new situations.

One explanation for the Court's newfound aggressiveness was the appointment in 1953 of Warren as chief justice. He was a former California district prosecutor, attorney general, and governor. His tenure on the Court signaled a shift in judicial style from restraint to activism. He rejected the belief that judges should make decisions based on narrow facts rather than on broad constitutional principles. Warren specifically dismissed as "fantasy" the notion that justices should be impartial. "As a defender of the Constitution," he wrote in his memoirs, "the Court cannot be neutral." He sought a broad and active role for the high bench: the "Court sits to decide cases, not to avoid decision."[6] More important, Warren believed that the Constitution contained moral truths essential to enlightened government. It was the Court's duty to apply these principles, even if it overturned laws favored by a large majority of citizens. The Court's role, he believed, was to champion individual liberty, especially for people without a meaningful political voice.

Nowhere was this judicial philosophy more evident than in Warren's attitude toward the Bill of Rights. It codified the "sense of justice" that humans were born with and provided the basis for bringing American law "more and more into harmony with moral principles." These views required the "constant and creative application" of the Bill of Rights to new situations. "The pursuit of justice," he said in a *Fortune* magazine article in 1955, "is not the vain pursuit of remote abstraction." It was an active search for a fundamental moral guide to the problems of daily life, led by an independent judiciary. This process suggested continual revision of the catalog of rights, leaving "a document that will not have exactly the same meaning it had when we received it from our fathers" but one that would be better because it was "burnished by growing use."[7]

Acting with unprecedented boldness, the majority of members of the Warren Court promoted a new understanding of individual rights, one that restrained the abuse of governmental power and, in their view, promoted a just society. The reforms came so swiftly that many commentators labeled them revolutionary—and in a sense, they were. What had changed was the justices' willingness to broaden individual rights aggressively in areas where traditionally legislatures had set standards. The Court mandated sweeping reforms of the electoral process, political representation, school desegregation, religious freedom and separation of church and state, obscenity, and free speech, among others, all based on new interpretations of constitutional guarantees.

Free speech was a bellwether for the expanded conception of rights. In 1919 the Court had adopted the "clear and present danger" rule for judging the constitutionality of speech: speech that fit this definition—for example, falsely yelling "fire" in a crowded theater—could be regulated by government (*Schenck v. United States*). Half a century later, a different test prevailed: government cannot regulate the content of speech unless it is likely to incite or produce imminent lawless action (*Brandenburg v. Ohio*, 1969). At the core of the new free speech jurisprudence was an anti-censorship principle. With few exceptions—"fighting words" (words likely to cause an immediate breach of the peace) and obscenity, for example—speech enjoyed the protection of the First Amendment.

The underlying rationale already had a long history when the Court embraced it. In the early twentieth century, Justices Oliver Wendell Holmes Jr. and Louis Brandeis had begun to turn from the "clear and present danger" doctrine (which, ironically, Holmes had created) to one that embraced "the marketplace of ideas," a rationale the two men advanced in dissents in a 1919 case, *Abrams v. United States*, which the Court handed down the same year as *Schenck*. "[T]he best test of truth," Holmes wrote in *Abrams*, "is the power of thought to get itself accepted in the competition of the market. . . . That at any rate is the theory of our Constitution." It was this axiom that led the Court to extend the anti-censorship principle, known in this instance as "no prior restraint," to the press in *Near v. Minnesota* (1931), when it ruled that even the inflammatory, anti-government stories in a tabloid owned by an unsavory and bigoted publisher fell under the protection of the First Amendment.

The modern Court has applied this idea to expressive speech as well, as the flag-burning cases reveal, but this standard does not mean that no regulation is ever acceptable. In 1968 the Warren Court reinstated the conviction of a Vietnam protester who burned his draft card because the government's rule against destroying draft cards was not directed at suppressing protest but at maintaining an army, which the Constitution permitted (*United States v. O'Brien*). Commercial speech and low-value speech, such as pornography, have fewer free speech protections, but they do not fall completely outside the orbit of the First Amendment. But political speech, no matter how troublesome, is beyond government control, even if the aim is to ensure the equality of voices in public debate. It is this principle that explains, in part, the Court's controversial opinions in *Buckley v. Valeo* (1976) and *Citizens United v. Federal Election Commission* (2010), in which the justices struck down congressional limits on campaign spending by individuals, groups, and corporations, even though critics charged that such decisions in an age of expensive mass communication would only make it easier for wealthy interests to drown out other voices.

Other First Amendment guarantees, most notably involving religion and the press, also came under scrutiny by the Court. Few decisions met more continuing criticism than ones involving religion, in part because the Court historically had addressed the issues only infrequently and in part because they affected the beliefs and practices of millions of faithful Americans. The small body of precedent included the nineteenth-century distinction between action and belief and the 1947 incorporation of the religion clauses as restraints against the states in *Everson v. Board of Education*. (The First Amendment contains two clauses concerning religion: an establishment clause banning Congress from establishing a religion by law, and a free exercise clause preventing it from prohibiting the free exercise of religion.) In 1802, President Thomas Jefferson had written to the Danbury Baptist Association in Connecticut citing his belief that "religion is a matter which lies solely between Man & his God," which the First Amendment recognized by "building a wall of separation between Church & State."[8] Beginning in the late 1940s, with *Everson*, the Supreme Court began to cite this phrase routinely to strike down laws affecting religion.

The most controversial decisions came in the 1960s, when the Warren Court overturned a non-denominational prayer prepared by the New York State Board of Regents for use in the public schools (*Engel v. Vitale*, 1962) and rejected as unconstitutional a Pennsylvania statute requiring that at least ten Bible verses be read at the beginning of each school day (*Abington School District v. Schempp*, 1963). The absolutist cast of these decisions met widespread condemnation. Newspaper headlines proclaimed an assault on religion, and prominent Protestant and Catholic leaders decried the rulings as un-American: evangelist Billy Graham charged that "we can no longer appeal to God for help," and Francis Cardinal Spellman in New York denounced *Engle* as striking at "the very heart of the Godly traditions in which America's children have for so long been raised." The Court stood firm in its stance that the First Amendment, as applied to the states through the Fourteenth Amendment, did not permit state mandates involving religion, even when the purported aim of the statute was not explicitly religious, as when it struck down an Arkansas law requiring equal time be given to creationist views when teaching evolution in public schools (*Epperson v. Arkansas*, 1968). But the Court also accommodated other laws that affected religious practice, such as when it accepted Sunday closing laws as constitutional.

Rights of the accused also were fertile ground for the expansion of individual liberties—and, on the whole, they were by far the most controversial actions of the Warren Court. Between 1961 and 1969 the Court accomplished what previous courts had stoutly resisted: it applied virtually all the procedural guarantees of the Bill of Rights to limit the states' administration of criminal justice. Adopting the strategy of selective incorporation, the justices explicitly defined the Fourteenth Amendment phrase "due process of law" to include most of the rights outlined in the Fourth, Fifth, and Sixth Amendments. The result was a national standard that governed all criminal proceedings at both federal and state levels.

Some cases evoked little controversy, such as when the Court extended the right of counsel, at state expense, to indigent defendants charged with serious crimes, as it did in *Gideon v. Wainwright* (1963). More contentious decisions set new standards for search and seizure and broadened the exclusionary rule that barred illegally seized evidence at trial to include state prosecutions (*Mapp v. Ohio*, 1961) and nationalized the Sixth Amendment right of an accused to confront a witness against him (*Pointer v. Texas*, 1965). The justices even extended these rights beyond the courtroom to the nation's police stations and jails, places previously thought to be subject to local control only.

The Court claimed not to diminish states' rights but instead to elevate inadequate state practices to a higher national standard. In the process, however, it ignited a firestorm of criticism that the expansion of these rights favored criminals at the expense of public safety. Everything depended upon the adjective used: rights for white men were not nearly as troublesome as they were when the accused was black or poor or Hispanic. Here, the rights at stake seemed to be not for ordinary citizens but for the outsider, the social misfit, the criminally inclined individual who upset public decency and threatened public order.

Miranda v. Arizona (1966) was the cause célèbre of the new constitutional order. At issue was the Fifth Amendment's protection against self-incrimination. It was an ancient privilege, dating to the fourth century, and its abuse in the sixteenth and seventeenth centuries by special crown courts that used torture to extract confessions resulted in its ban in the Bill of Rights. Early nineteenth-century courts were jealous guardians of the privilege, excluding confessions gained by force, but late nineteenth- and twentieth-century fears of crime led to widespread abuses. In 1908 the Court had rejected a universal right to the privilege against self-incrimination (*Twining v. New Jersey*) and left states to follow their own practices, which, a national commission revealed in the 1920s, had resulted in routine use of the so-called third degree (physical intimidation sometimes going as far as torture) to extract confessions and remove suspected criminals from the streets.

In 1964, in *Escobedo v. Illinois*, the Court reversed its earlier stance and concluded that the Fifth Amendment right was part of the due process guaranteed by the Fourteenth Amendment. Two years later, in *Miranda v. Arizona*, the justices extended the privilege to the station house, requiring the police to warn suspects in their custody of their constitutional rights and even crafting the language they should use. Today, the *Miranda* warning—"You have the right to remain silent . . ."—is well known to all Americans, thanks to countless televised crime dramas, but at the time, critics charged that the Court had handcuffed the police. The conclusion was greatly exaggerated: later studies revealed that less than 1 percent of all convictions had to be overturned for failure to issue the warning.

This 1960s expansion of rights was troublesome to many people, but more problematic were new rights that the justices inferred—invented, critics complained—from constitutional language. Chief among these implied rights was the right to privacy, which the Constitution does not mention explicitly. For eighteenth-century men and women, privacy meant the right to be secure in one's home, safe from the arbitrary actions of government. Social and individual privacy in the sense of isolation and solitude only became an expectation when nineteenth-century economic growth created the wealth that made it possible. By the twentieth century, privacy had entered the social and constitutional vocabulary. Early cases centered on the ability of new technologies—for example, the ability to tap phone conversations—to breach the sanctity of the home without trespassing on physical space. In 1928 the Court applied the concept of physical trespass to rule that wiretapping required no warrant, a protection of the Fourth Amendment, but the dissent by Justice Louis Brandeis pointed the way to a different future. The framers of the Fourth and Fifth Amendments, he argued, "conferred, against the Government, the right to be let alone—the most comprehensive of rights and the one most valued by civilized men" (*Olmstead v. United States*, 1928).

Four decades later, in *Griswold v. Connecticut* (1965), the Court announced a new constitutional right to privacy. The justices rejected a state law that banned contraceptives and prevented anyone from encouraging their use. For the majority, Justice William O. Douglas found the right in various guarantees designed to create "zones of privacy," such as the Third Amendment's ban on quartering soldiers in private homes, the Fourth Amendment's explicit recognition of the right of people to be secure in their homes, and the Fifth Amendment's self-incrimination clause. Douglas wrote of "emanations" and "penumbras" from rights plainly noted in the Constitution—"specific guarantees in the Bill of Rights have penumbras, formed by emanations from those guarantees that help give them life and substance"—but his choice of metaphors opened him to criticism that he was inventing rights.

Douglas and the majority justices sought instead to devise a more limited means of recognizing and protecting unenumerated rights, a category recognized implicitly in the Ninth Amendment. Although the result in *Griswold* was not controversial—it was "a silly law," one justice noted—the way it was reached suggested a liberal judicial activism reminiscent of an earlier conservative activism in such cases as *Lochner v. New York* (the 1905 "liberty of contract" case). It raised questions not only about the proper interpretation of the Constitution but also about whether judicial decisions could establish new rights. The controversy intensified with the Court's decision in *Roe v. Wade* (1973), which guaranteed a woman's right to abortion based on a right to privacy. The continuing, often rancorous, debate over abortion demonstrates how contentious the claims of a court-discovered right of personal autonomy can be, even in a society otherwise dedicated to individualism.

In some ways, the inflamed response to the rights revolution was puzzling. Even though the 1960s had witnessed a dramatic expansion in rights claims—and, in turn, elevated the role of courts in deciding them—the claims most often were appeals to existing values, not demands for new, previously unrecognized rights. The most aggressive litigants, such as the American Civil Liberties Union and the NAACP, sought the protection of established guarantees for their socially marginalized clients. The conditions for the rights revolution also were not new. They could be found in the pragmatic progressivism of the early twentieth century, in which reformers sought to use the power of government to correct the ills of American life for the purposes of expanding equality and liberty. Nor was the goal new to American values: no longer would circumstances of geography, race, and class determine the protections that citizens could enjoy.

What the rapid nationalization of rights revealed, however, was a tension, always present but increasingly apparent, between individual and collectivist understandings of American guarantees of liberty. Rights-based litigation led to interest-group politics in the civil rights and women's rights movements (and soon the gay rights movement as well). The result was that rights claims entered politics, first in a conservative reaction led by law-and-order candidates and then in a liberal counter-response.

By the late 1960s, the remarkable expansion of individual rights was nearing an end. Americans were increasingly uneasy about the course of reform charted by the Warren Court. Critics complained that the liberties of individuals had taken precedence over the order and security of society. The decade's turbulent history appeared to support this conclusion: critics of the Court's decisions cited urban riots, political violence, and increased crime as evidence of this point. Conservatives also charged that judges had upset the constitutional balance by making law, a legislative function, which, in turn, subverted democracy. The Warren Court record became a major issue in the 1968 presidential election. The winning candidate, Richard M. Nixon, promised to appoint law-and-order judges who would interpret the Constitution strictly, as the founders intended, and halt, if not reverse, the trend toward greater liberalization of individual rights. Subsequent elections also featured this theme, with Ronald Reagan in 1980 and 1984 making a similar pledge to stop the creation of "judge-made rights."

Three successive chief justices, Warren E. Burger, William H. Rehnquist, and John Roberts, all appointed by Republican presidents, held similar views, but the courts they led during the last three decades of the twentieth century and the first decade of the twenty-first century left much of the Warren Court's legacy in place. The justices did not abandon the newfound catalog of individual rights but focused instead on what these rights meant in practice. In matters of religion, for example, the Burger Court evoked a three-pronged test to determine when government action violated the establishment clause: it must have a secular purpose; its impact must be primarily secular; and it must create an excessive entanglement between the state and religion (*Lemon v. Kurtzman*, 1971). Under the *Lemon* test, the Court has banned officially sanctioned prayers at public high school events and rejected public financial aid to religious schools. But it also has allowed state laws permitting tax-supported vouchers for individuals to use in the school of their choice, including private religious schools.

These cases, among others, revealed a Court grappling with how to accommodate widespread belief in the public utility of religion with the demands of a highly pluralistic and increasingly secular society. A similar dilemma confronted the justices as they sought to determine what other individual rights meant in practice, especially in a society experiencing a flood of legal and illegal immigration, rapid changes in communication technologies, and a new ethic of personal autonomy.

On occasion, decisions by the more conservative modern Courts brought the same public opposition that had greeted the more controversial cases from the 1960s, as reflected by the flag-burning case *Texas v. Johnson* (1989). In some instances the Court reaffirmed explicitly what had once been viewed as a radical departure: in *Bond v. United States* (2000), for example, the justices upheld the *Miranda* warning in an opinion written by Chief Justice Rehnquist, once a vocal critic of the original Warren Court case. In other areas, the justices went beyond the 1960s decisions to expand or affirm individual liberties, especially the rights of women and affirmative action programs designed to remedy past racial discrimination.

Concern about whether the Supreme Court has overstepped its proper role by its aggressive expansion of protections codified in the Bill of Rights is a recurring theme in American history. Progressive reformers leveled the same criticism early in the twentieth century against judges who cited a right to economic liberty as a shield against regulatory laws passed by democratic majorities. What made this challenge especially contentious in the late twentieth century, however, was a resurgence of what came to be known as "rights consciousness," a widespread willingness on the part of individuals and groups to push for the recognition of new rights. The awareness of rights to be asserted against government and others has long been a hallmark of our national culture. It is in fact a legacy of our revolutionary beginnings, but rights consciousness has rarely been stronger in American history than it has been since the 1960s. Not only has it led to claims of new rights to fit the needs of a modern age but it has raised again questions about the role of rights in American democracy.

As a society we often have debated how far to extend individual rights, but some of the decisions of the 1960s and later, especially those involving civil rights, introduced a new concept, group rights, into American constitutional law. After the Supreme Court's landmark rulings mandating equal treatment regardless of race in schools and public facilities, questions arose about how to remedy or correct racially discriminatory practices. One answer was affirmative action, which focused attention on an individual's membership in a racial or ethnic group and allowed race to be used as a positive factor in decisions about employment and admission to higher education. These programs, which the Court has accepted as constitutional under the equal protection clause, reflected a shift from rights as a protection against government to rights as a way to change social relations.

What began as an effort to correct long-standing discrimination against blacks soon moved into new rights claims for other groups—women, gays and lesbians, ethnic minorities, and the disabled, among others. Social welfare rights were especially prominent in this later-stage rights revolution. Heeding Franklin D. Roosevelt's call for a "second bill of rights," the right to a job, health care, and education became targets of a new generation of social reformers. Significantly, most of these demands were pursued in the political arena and through the legislative process, both at state and federal levels, and not through the courts. The Americans with Disabilities Act of 1990, for instance, established legal rights for physically and mentally handicapped citizens, and the Patient Protection and Affordable Care Act of 2010 advanced the case for a right to universal access to health care.

Not all claims were accepted by courts, legislatures, or voters, however, and moving them successfully to constitutional protection proved difficult. In the 1970s, women's rights advocates pushed hard for an Equal Rights Amendment, only to fall heartbreakingly short of the goal of ratification in 1982. Ironically, the political appeal of group or collectivist rights may have helped to secure the rights revolution by increasing the number of citizens and organizations invested in protecting its gains. But its ultimate constitutional success remained questionable because it stands at odds with the nation's deep historical and cultural commitment to individual rights.

We may be more rights-conscious today than at other times in our history, but we remain divided over how far our rights extend. New assertions of rights and organizations dedicated to promoting them, such as the American Civil Liberties Union, historically have met resistance and angry backlash. In many ways this conflict has made rights talk even more contagious. Rights claims, after all, are made by someone who alleges a denial of liberty against the government or someone else. It is hard to think in terms of common values or community when engaged in rights talk; too much focus on individual liberties can skew our sense of the interests we hold in common. Yet what is most striking about the conflict over rights has been its democratic character. Rights are always a matter of public debate about the proper balance between order and liberty. It is a conversation that engaged the framers of the Constitution, and, as has been the case with each successive generation, we, too, are forever working out the boundaries of what individual liberties are essential for a just and free society.

10

Security

For most people, the day began as most September days begin, with summer fading yet still strong enough to blunt all but the slightest hints of autumn. Farmers were getting ready for harvests, pupils were settling reluctantly into the still-fresh routines of another school year, and commuters were hurrying to their jobs. Everywhere, it was a normal news day. The stock markets were struggling with the effects of an economic slowdown, the baseball pennant race was tightening, and *The Musketeer* was at the top of the Hollywood box-office charts. In the nation's capital, another clash between Palestinians and Israelis had raised doubts about the latest efforts to stage peace talks. The secretary of defense pledged to cut the Pentagon's budget. The president was in Florida, preparing to read to a first-grade class as he promoted his signature education initiative.

Then the world changed. At 8:46 AM on September 11, 2001, a commercial passenger airplane, hijacked by terrorists, slammed into the North Tower of the World Trade Center in New York City. Seventeen minutes later, at 9:03 AM, a second hijacked airliner crashed into the South Tower, this time captured by live television images from crews that had rushed to the scene. At 9:37 AM, a third commandeered airplane crashed into the Pentagon. A fourth jetliner, headed for Washington, D.C., with the intent to strike either the Capitol or the White House, crashed in a field in Pennsylvania after passengers stormed the cockpit in an effort to prevent the hijackers from reaching their goal. It was 10:03 AM. By then, the South Tower had collapsed, followed by the North Tower a half-hour later. Almost three thousand people were dead; at least six thousand were injured. It was the largest loss of life from a hostile attack in American history.

By the time President George W. Bush declared a national emergency three days later, the identities of the hijackers were known. The nineteen men were all Arab followers of Osama bin Laden, a Saudi national who led a terrorist movement, Al-Qaeda, linked to the 1998 bombing of U.S. embassies in east Africa and the 2000 attack on an American warship, the USS *Cole*. Even before the president addressed a joint session of Congress, the House of Representatives and Senate had authorized the president to use "all necessary and appropriate force" against the nations, organizations, and individuals whom he determined were behind the attacks or who had sheltered them. His authority, the joint resolution noted, was granted by the Constitution. Many members of Congress also said publicly that they intended to remove any restrictions imposed by an earlier measure, the War Powers Resolution of 1973, which forbade the president from committing American troops without specific congressional approval unless the United States was under attack. As a result, the newly approved resolution was unusual: it authorized war but left it to the president to decide who the enemy was.

The next several weeks only reinforced the belief that the nation was under siege. Air traffic resumed after a complete shutdown—but only with strict new security procedures in place, and at far lower levels because people feared to fly. In October and November, letters containing deadly anthrax spores were sent to Senate offices and newsrooms, resulting in the deaths of five people. Congressional offices had to be decontaminated, and the Hart Senate Office Building would not reopen until January. Capitol Hill was no longer accessible to the public. The nation had entered what the president called a War on Terror against an unseen, stealthy, and dimly understood enemy.

By early October, the United States and Great Britain, acting under a UN Security Council resolution, had invaded Afghanistan and ousted the ruling Taliban, a conservative Muslim regime, that had sheltered bin Laden and his Al-Qaeda operation. The next year the Bush administration made clear its intentions to extend the war to Iraq, the defeated foe in the Gulf War of 1991. Iraq was part of an "axis of evil," the president argued, and had acquired weapons of mass destruction in defiance of a UN mandate. His response, given in a speech at the U.S. Military Academy in September 2002, was a new strategic doctrine of preemptive strikes. Under it, the executive could order an attack without congressional approval if it was necessary "to forestall or prevent . . . hostile acts" against the United States.

After six months during which the United Nations futilely searched Iraq for weapons of mass destruction, in March 2003 President Bush authorized an invasion of Iraq. Although it fit his newly announced doctrine of preemption, he based his order on a second congressional resolution passed the previous October. In this instance, as in the case with Afghanistan, Congress had not declared war, its constitutional prerogative, but rather had provided the president with the authority to make this decision.

Immediately following the terrorist attacks, the Bush administration began to tighten domestic security. The USA PATRIOT Act of 2001, enacted by overwhelming majorities in both houses of Congress in late October 2001, strengthened the government's ability to conduct criminal investigations by relaxing limits on surveillance. The Justice Department closed immigration hearings and held without bond any aliens who appealed extradition. President Bush issued an executive order establishing military tribunals for terrorism suspects, instead of using the federal judicial system. He claimed sole authority to classify enemy combatants, as these suspects were called, and to hold them indefinitely without charge and deny them access to a lawyer, even if they were American citizens arrested within the United States.

These actions, although initially supported by a large public majority, increasingly met strong criticism. Few members of Congress had opposed the first war resolution in September 2001, with only Senator Robert Byrd (D-West Virginia) lamenting a failure to debate the issue: "What would the signers of the Constitution have to say," he warned, "when they learn about the silence, that is deafening, that emanates from that great Chamber [the Senate] on the great issue of war and peace?" By the presidential election of 2004, with the war in Iraq going badly, the critics were more vocal, claiming that the president not only had far exceeded the authority granted by Congress but was arrogating power to the executive branch in defiance of the Constitution. President Bush defended his actions as wholly constitutional, as a legal brief filed by the Bush administration in 2003 maintained: "The Constitution vests the President with full 'executive Power,' and designates him 'Commander in Chief' of the Armed Forces. Together these provisions are a substantive grant of broad war power that authorizes the President to unilaterally use military force in defense of the United States' national security."

The response to 9/11 divided the nation. For many liberals, the president's actions were illegitimate and marked a constitutional crisis of the first order; for many conservatives, his assertion of authority was not only necessary but well within his power as commander-in-chief. Several challenges to presidential authority reached the Supreme Court by mid-decade, with the justices ruling against the president in each case but splitting sharply on what the Constitution permitted. Four years later, public disillusionment with the wars in Afghanistan and Iraq, the election of a new president who promised a different strategy for fighting terrorism, and the global economic crisis that began in 2007–8 tamped down the debate temporarily but the differences were far from resolved. When the new Obama administration sought to close the notorious detention camp at Guantanamo Bay and try terror suspects in domestic courts, the argument resumed. The constitutional fissures were as evident as ever.

For all their ultimate fury, the controversies following 9/11 were not unique in American history. From the beginning, citizens have rarely agreed over whether war suspends the Constitution or whether the Constitution controls the conduct of the war. War poses an imminent threat to the nation's existence, but so does suspension of the nation's fundamental laws. There are no easy answers because the questions are extraordinarily complex and the stakes are high. Within the American experience, the issues are especially compelling because they are the same ones the founding generations confronted when thinking more generally about the nature of government: What is the relationship of power and liberty? Can the powers of government be limited to protect liberty without hampering the ability of the nation to defend itself? What rights can individuals exercise in a time of crisis?

These questions were present during the nation's founding because the American revolutionaries knew the threat their radical experiment in liberty posed to an established order. They had created a republic in a world of monarchies. History had taught them that it was the nature of monarchical power always to seek the destruction of republican liberty. Their experience confirmed this lesson. The success of the early republic often hides from us the founders' search for security, but even a cursory review of their public and private language reveals the perils they believed they faced. This concern above all fed their sense that the best course for the new United States was to remain isolated from a rapacious Europe. But they also were realists who understood the inevitability of war, so it is not surprising that the Federal Convention of 1787 grappled with the question of how the nation would wage it. What is surprising is that they came up with no clear answer.

The framers fashioned a novel arrangement to limit power in government without handicapping that government's ability to wage war for the protection of liberty. They separated and mixed authority between the legislature and executive in a way that recast European tradition. Executive power was vested in a single person, the president of the United States, but the office did not come with the prerogatives of the monarch, as Alexander Hamilton acknowledged in *The Federalist No. 69*. The royal powers to coin money, regulate trade, raise armies, and declare war, among other powers, were given to Congress, not the president. The president could appoint judges and executive officers but only with the advice and consent of the Senate; his veto power was not absolute but conditional, subject to override by a two-thirds vote in both houses of Congress.

The one area in which the president seemed to have sole authority was as commander-in-chief—but even here he depended upon Congress to appropriate the funds required to supply the army and navy. Everywhere, the framers mixed war powers between the executive and the legislature; the Convention sought to require agreement between the two elected branches before government could act. As the Princeton political scientist and constitutional scholar Edward S. Corwin wrote in his 1957 classic, *The President: Office and Powers*, the Constitution created an "invitation to struggle" between Congress and the president on these contested issues.

But the Constitution only assigned powers; it did not define them, although its debate provides some guidance regarding the intended meaning. For example, the Committee on Detail, which created the first draft of the Constitution, initially had written that Congress had the power to make war, but the delegates changed the verb to "declare." In his notes of the debate, Madison observed that the framers believed only the president could conduct a war, which was the implied meaning of the phase "to make" war. Congress had the power to repel invasions by calling forth the militia, which the president commanded, but did the commander-in-chief's authority extend to repelling sudden or threatened attacks when Congress could not act? This unanswered question would vex the nation for the next two hundred years.

Much less ambiguous was the decision to vest Congress with the power to decide upon war and set the rules for its conduct. All the war-making powers—the authority to declare war, to fund war, to decide how the army and navy would operate, to establish the conditions for use of the militia, as well as the denial to states of the ability to declare war—are contained in Article I, which created the legislative branch. The ratification debates also suggest broad concurrence in the placement of war powers in Congress, not the president. During the Pennsylvania ratification convention, James Wilson, who had helped to frame the Constitution, voiced a common belief: "This [new] system will not hurry us into war. . . . It will not be in the power of a single man, or a single body of men, to involve us in such a distress; for the important power of declaring war is vested in the legislature at large; . . . from this circumstance, we may draw a certain conclusion that nothing but our national interest can draw us into war."[1]

The experience of the early republic confirmed Wilson's view. The first test came quickly in the 1798–1800 Quasi-War with France. Despite an official policy of neutrality, the United States was drawn into the conflict between Great Britain and France that embroiled Europe. Both nations used their navies to seize American ships bound for enemy ports, but the revolutionary French appeared to be the greater threat, at least in the minds of President John Adams and his Federalist allies, who controlled Congress. In 1797 Secretary of State Timothy Pickering reported that the French navy had captured more than three hundred American vessels during the previous year.

The next year, with tensions high because of the XYZ Affair, a French attempt to bribe U.S. emissaries, Congress authorized the president to acquire and outfit ships and attack the French marauders. There was no declaration of war but no one disputed the notion that only Congress could approve these reprisals. Even Alexander Hamilton, an architect of the anti-French policy who had long argued for a vigorous executive, agreed that the Constitution narrowly constrained the president's actions. A case before the Supreme Court reached a similar conclusion: "The whole powers of war," Chief Justice John Marshall wrote in 1801, "being, by the Constitution of the United States, vested in congress, the act of that body can alone be resorted to as our guides" (*Talbot v. Seeman*). The founding generation understood that Congress had the dominant role in deciding matters of war, declared or not.

Congress used its power to declare war only twice before 1860, in the War of 1812 and the Mexican War, but the United States was more active militarily than these two declarations imply. Early presidents on occasion relied upon their role as commander-in-chief to protect American interests, seeking explicit approval from Congress only later. Shortly after Thomas Jefferson took office, the satrapy of Tripoli, a pirate enclave in Northern Africa, declared war on the United States, signified in the traditional manner by cutting down the flagstaff in front of the U.S. consulate. The ruling pasha had discovered that the payment he received from the American government for restraining his Barbary Coast pirates was smaller than the ones given to Morocco and Algiers. Without authorization from Congress, which was not in session, Jefferson dispatched a naval squadron to protect American shipping and gave its commander blanket authority to seek out and destroy Tripolitan ships. Months later, Jefferson informed Congress of his actions, although he exaggerated the threat. With its approval, he then sent a larger fleet to rid the Mediterranean of pirates. Known previously as an advocate of a limited executive power, Jefferson concluded that circumstances sometimes required the president to "assume authorities beyond the law" in keeping with "the laws of necessity, of self-preservation, of saving our country when in danger."[2] It was a justification hesitantly invoked in the nineteenth century; it became a mainstay in the twentieth.

What appeared to be a certain doctrine about exclusive congressional power in matters of war became muddled in the secession crisis of 1861. The beginning of the Civil War presented the nation with a true emergency: the success of the Confederacy would mean the dissolution of the Union. In response, Congress vigorously asserted constitutional power not only to win the war but to reshape the nation. The Republican majority rejected the prevailing philosophy of limited government and especially the southern view of a nation created by compact among the states. The necessary and proper clause gave broad scope, they argued, to their delegated powers to declare war, raise an army, and guarantee republican governments. This expansive reading allowed Congress to compel military service, take control of the nation's railroads and telegraph system, dredge canals and channel rivers, subsidize the creation of universities, and directly control the functions of seceding states, all measures deemed necessary to ensure victory. It was a bold use of power, but only by comparison with traditional limits on federal authority. Congress today routinely exercises a greater array of powers, yet even in the 1860s Republicans had precedent for their position, which recalled the necessary and proper argument used by Alexander Hamilton in support of his economic program during the first Washington administration.

The use of congressional war power during the Civil War tracked closely with its constitutional mandate. Not so with the use of presidential authority. Abraham Lincoln relied upon a more aggressive, innovative, and controversial constitutionalism in the exercise of his power. His actions to save the Union went beyond the Constitution in some instances and ignored its clear injunction in others. In the process, Lincoln transformed the nature and prestige of the office. For several months before taking office in March 1861, he sought to calm the crisis and reconcile a deeply divided nation. But when Confederate forces seized Fort Sumter in April 1861, Lincoln acted swiftly and, with

Congress not yet in session, acted on his own authority to prevent southern secession. He committed troops, without congressional approval, as head of the armed forces; spent funds Congress had not appropriated; ordered a blockade, an act of war; seized private property for military purposes; and called for the mobilization of 75,000 troops from state militias. Once conflict began, he unilaterally declared martial law in certain areas, closed the post office to treasonable mail, emancipated slaves, arrested people without a warrant, and tried civilians in military courts.

In justification, Lincoln offered two sources of constitutional authority: the presidential oath of office requiring him "to preserve, protect and defend the Constitution," and the powers inherent in his role as commander-in-chief. He also relied indirectly yet significantly upon the Preamble, which delegated no powers but instead announced the aim to create a "more perfect union." Lincoln interpreted this language in the light of a newfound sense of nationalism that defined the nation as organic, a people bound together by "the mystic chords of memory" and common ties of language, custom, and culture rather than one created by consent. The nation existed before the Constitution, and "this county, with its institutions," he said in his first inaugural, "belongs to the people who inhabit it." As such, it possessed inherent authority over all subjects within its borders. The president's primary responsibility was to use this power to protect the nation's existence, which secession threatened to destroy. In doing so, he also met his obligation to preserve and defend the Constitution.[3]

Many critics denounced Lincoln's actions as unconstitutional and tyrannical. Northern Democrats, who agreed on the need to preserve the integrity of the Union but not the Republican goal of vesting civil rights in African Americans, were especially vocal in their opposition. So, too, were erstwhile allies. Senator Charles Sumner of Massachusetts, a leading Radical Republican, labeled the justifications as "irrational . . . absurd and tyrannical"; abolitionist Wendell Phillips called Lincoln an "unlimited despot." Many scholars later joined the chorus, at times referring to the wartime presidency as a constitutional dictatorship.

The charge seems exaggerated. Lincoln frequently went well beyond limits accepted by his predecessors, but his habit was to act and then to seek congressional approval. When he suspended habeas corpus in 1861, for example, he invited Congress to decide the question, which it did in 1863; likewise, the Emancipation Proclamation was soon followed by legislation freeing the slaves. In defense of his actions, he reminded his critics that Congress could impeach and remove him from office if it found his conduct of the war unacceptable. Lincoln also was a canny pragmatist who invited Congress to participate in the planning of military strategy, although constitutionally the role was his alone. These steps helped to insulate Lincoln politically, but not always as a matter of law. Within months of the war's beginning, he faced legal challenges to his actions.

The first case occurred in the earliest days of the war, when military authorities invoked Lincoln's suspension of habeas corpus to arrest John Merryman,
a Maryland political leader and Confederate sympathizer who had sabotaged
Union supply lines. U.S. Chief Justice Roger B. Taney received the case in his
role as presiding judge of the federal circuit court sitting in Baltimore. He
issued a writ of habeas corpus requiring the detaining officer to explain why
the prisoner was being held. When the officer did not submit, Taney ordered his
arrest, but the military, under Lincoln's direction, ignored the order. After declaring Merryman entitled to his freedom, Taney then took an unusual step: he
filed an opinion concluding that Congress alone had the constitutional power
to suspend habeas corpus. He ordered the president to submit to judicial authority by executing the laws "as they are adjudged by the coordinate branch
of government" (*Ex parte Merryman*). Lincoln refused. He argued that the
Constitution did not state explicitly who can suspend the writ. (Even though
the power is part of Article I, which outlines the powers of the legislature, the
clause is written in the passive voice, leaving doubt about who wields the power
of suspension.) Nor, he asserted, could the framers have intended to leave the
government without the ability to defend itself until Congress met. Although
he later backed away from the position, at one point he also suggested that a
president would be justified in violating a law to save the Union.

Lincoln prevailed in his dispute with Taney, and in a later case the other
justices, most of them Republicans, signaled that they were not willing to
second-guess the president in such matters. In 1864, they refused to side with
a former congressman from Ohio who had been convicted in a military court
of ignoring a general's order banning declarations of sympathy for the enemy.
The justices concluded they had no jurisdiction over the military and no
authority to review the decision or to issue a writ of habeas corpus to a military commission (*Ex parte Vallandingham*). The Court also upheld Lincoln's
order of a blockade after the bombardment of Fort Sumter in April 1861
(*The Prize Cases*, 1863). Rejecting the views of dissenting justices that the
order was part of a "personal war" by the president until Congress authorized it, a 5–4 majority upheld broad executive power to respond to a domestic insurrection that also had elements of an attack on the United States,
especially when, as in this instance, Congress had retroactively ratified all
of the president's previous military actions. In a pattern repeated often in
American history, the Court was reluctant to interfere with judgments of the
elected branches of government during a time of war.

The Court was not so deferential after hostilities ended, especially on questions of civil liberty. *Ex parte Milligan* (1866) tested the power of the president
or Congress to suspend civil liberties during wartime. In 1863, Congress retroactively authorized the suspension of habeas corpus but ordered that prisoners
be released if grand juries failed to indict them. But what if the military authorities, worried that local courts might release dangerous men, ignored this law?

Late in 1864 a military court's arrest, trial, and conviction of an accused traitor tested this question. Lambdin P. Milligan was an Ohio native who moved to Indiana in the 1830s and turned to law when he could not make a living as a farmer. A respected member of the state bar, he became involved in the anti-war faction of the Indiana Democratic Party. Known as Copperheads (after the treacherous snake), these southern sympathizers in the North were Jeffersonian Democrats who believed in state sovereignty and had no sympathy with abolition. Milligan believed that the Emancipation Proclamation was proof that Lincoln had fallen under the influence of abolitionist New Englanders, so he urged Democrats to defend their rights "at all costs." He also joined with sympathizers to form secret anti-war societies. It is unclear whether his efforts posed any real danger, but reports from army spies suggested that Milligan was conspiring to seize arms and ammunition at federal arsenals and to liberate Confederate prisoners held in several northern camps.

Even though civil courts were open and operating in Indiana, a military court convicted Milligan and sentenced him to hang. He appealed to the Supreme Court, which unanimously agreed that the military lacked jurisdiction. War did not suspend the Constitution, the justices concluded: a military trial of civilians while domestic courts were open denied the accused of their rights to a grand jury indictment and trial by jury. "The Constitution of the United States is a law for rulers and people, equally in war and peace, and covers with the shield of its protection all classes of men, at all times, and under all circumstances," Justice David Davis, a Lincoln appointee, wrote for the Court. "No doctrine, involving more pernicious consequences, was ever invented by the wit of man than that any of its provisions can be suspended during any of the great exigencies [crises] of government." A state of war did not suspend the Constitution or its guarantee of individual rights. The framers knew the nation likely would be involved in wars, but they still chose to restrict what the president could do alone. They hedged the president's authority, Davis reasoned, because "unlimited power, wherever lodged at such a time, was especially hazardous to free men."

The decision was a touchstone for civil liberties, but it often proved to be a thin reed of support during times of war. The Court responded then as it has since, by refusing to second-guess decisions based on claims of military necessity during times of war or national emergency. Individual rights have been especially vulnerable under this standard. The Court acquiesced in the internment of Japanese Americans during World War II, for instance, even though after the war it reaffirmed Milligan's clear principles about the limits of government's emergency power (*Duncan v. Kahanamoku*, 1946). Civil liberties always have been in jeopardy during similar circumstances, as the history of the twentieth century makes clear, but the larger issue initially was the extent of governmental authority: Did war suspend constitutional limits on power?

The Civil War suggested an answer. Acting jointly, Congress and the president could exercise power beyond the bounds of the Constitution if it was necessary to protect the nation. The twentieth-century experience with war affirmed this position but shifted the locus of this authority increasingly to the executive branch. It was not a startling or abrupt transition because a fixed constitutional rule did not exist. Despite the trauma of civil war, the Supreme Court rarely had occasion to decide on issues of war and peace. World War I changed this situation. It was total war, fought on a global stage with mechanized armies and death on a grand scale, and as such it made clear the inherent tension between a requirement for complete command and a constitutional design to limit absolute power. It also brought into sharp focus the difficulty of reconciling executive and legislative authority in time of war.

Neither problem was new, but the circumstances were. Never before had the United States conducted a war that required such total effort from all parts of society. Congress faced the most immediate challenge because total war called into question both the extent of federal power and congressional ability to respond quickly to its demands. In June 1917 the Wilson administration requested authority to control the nation's food and fuel supplies in support of the war effort. The bill, known as the Lever Act, was far broader in its language, however, and gave the president virtually unlimited sway to regulate the entire economy. It also challenged the terms of federalism; many of the functions now assumed by the central government had been the province of the states.

The Lever Act marked a significant change in the constitutional conduct of war. Congress did not abandon its war powers as much as it delegated broad administrative authority to the president, who in turn entrusted these powers to subordinates and commissions staffed by experts. The reliance on professionals was not unusual—it was a hallmark of the Progressive Era that reached its zenith during the war—but the reach of the executive power they exercised exceeded earlier presidents' most expansive claims. Congress gave President Wilson the power not simply to run the war but also to manage the nation's economy. He could regulate the nation's transportation and communication infrastructure, and even seize control of railroad and telephone companies if he thought necessary. His discretion extended to rules governing the conscription of an army, the operation of factories and mines, and the prevention of strikes. In brief, the requirements of modern warfare, Congress determined, overrode the constitutional separation and balance of powers between the legislative and executive branches of the central government and between national and state governments. This understanding soon became the new standard for national emergencies, whether from war or economic collapse.

The Supreme Court accepted the aggressive expansion of national and executive power. Its decisions affirmed the argument that the Constitution imposed no limits on congressional authority in time of war, including the delegation of unchecked discretion to the president. War also set aside the traditional understanding of federalism, as a unanimous Court made clear in 1919: "[T]he complete and undivided character of the war power of the United States is not disputable" (*Northern Pacific Railway Co. v. North Dakota*, 1919). Not even the Bill of Rights was sacrosanct. The Wilson administration, mindful of the *Milligan* precedent, renounced any intention to suspend these constitutional guarantees during the war, but in fact no one believed that civil liberties were the same in war as in normal times. Beyond this, it was not clear how far military necessity could justify government restrictions of individual freedoms, especially the speech, press, and assembly provisions of the First Amendment. No body of constitutional law existed on the subject, in large measure because protection of individual liberty customarily was a state, not federal, responsibility.

The first test of individual rights in war came with the passage of the Espionage Acts of 1917 and 1918, the latter called the Sedition Act by opponents because of its similarity to the disreputable Sedition Act of 1798. These measures imposed a postal censorship of treasonable and seditious materials, made it a felony to obstruct enlistment or incite mutiny in the armed forces, and forbade any disloyal speech or publication. They clearly were aimed at silencing individuals who opposed the war, including socialists and radical unionists as well as a large number of European Americans who were torn between allegiance to their old and new countries.

When the Supreme Court heard challenges to convictions under the acts, it adopted what was known as the "bad tendency test," a standard borrowed from common law. Freedom of speech and press meant only that government could not censor speech or press, a doctrine known as "no prior restraint." Speech or writing that had a tendency to produce an unlawful act was not protected. In *Schenck v. United States* (1919), Justice Oliver Wendell Holmes, offering the analogy of falsely yelling fire in a crowded theater, gave the test a now-classic formulation: "the question . . . is whether the words used are used in such circumstances and are of such nature as to create a clear and present danger that they will bring about the substantive evils that Congress had a right to prevent. It is a question of proximity and degree." This rule ultimately came to express a more libertarian view—"the present danger of immediate evil" is how Holmes expressed it a year later—but not right away. In this instance, war trumped liberties, or as Justice Holmes put it in a much less quoted part of his opinion in *Schenck*, "When a nation is at war many things that might be said in time of peace are such hindrance to its effort that their utterance will not be endured."

The broad assertion of presidential power and congressional acquiescence during war became even more pronounced in World War II. The Supreme Court already had accepted the vast expansion of federal power in a national emergency, most recently with the New Deal, although an increase in executive power still depended on congressional willingness to delegate its authority. A case in 1936, however, recognized an unlimited and exclusive presidential power in foreign affairs that dramatically enhanced the chief executive's statutory authority and ultimately the extent of his war powers.

In the early 1930s Congress authorized President Franklin D. Roosevelt to embargo arms shipments to countries at war in South America. An arms supplier challenged the ban as an unconstitutional delegation of power. In *United States v. Curtis-Wright Export Corporation* (1936) the Court disagreed. It affirmed the "plenary and exclusive power of the President as the sole organ of the federal government in foreign affairs—a power which does not require as a basis for its exercise an act of Congress." The power was restricted only by the Constitution.

It was not the first time the question had arisen. It had in fact been the subject of a debate following George Washington's proclamation of neutrality in 1793. Writing under the pen name *Pacificus*, Alexander Hamilton argued for a sweeping presidential power to safeguard peace independent of the authority of Congress, but, writing to refute Hamilton under the pseudonym *Helvidius*, James Madison insisted that Congress must have a role in such decisions as a matter of its constitutional authority. The Court's acceptance in *Curtiss-Wright* of the argument advanced by Hamilton a century earlier was a watershed moment. It became a cornerstone of unprecedented executive authority in foreign affairs, which inevitably meant matters of war and peace, especially when linked to a decision in 1920 that recognized constitutionally approved treaties as the supreme law of the land (*Missouri v. Holland*, 1920).

The implications of this doctrine soon were apparent. In September 1939 Germany invaded Poland, plunging Europe into a new world war. At first the United States remained neutral, but by 1940 President Franklin D. Roosevelt became convinced that the success of the Third Reich threatened not only Western-style democracy but also America's economic interests and national security. Congress was not persuaded, however, and public opinion did not support any option but continued isolation.

In response, Roosevelt vigorously used presidential power, especially his exclusive authority in foreign affairs, to support the Allied cause. He entered into a number of executive agreements designed to aid nations at war with Germany and its Axis partners, Italy and Japan. Working closely with British Prime Minister Winston Churchill, he announced an Atlantic Charter in 1941 that was, in effect, a military alliance with Britain in anticipation of U.S. entry into the war. This step built upon an even bolder agreement reached in 1940, the "Lend-Lease" deal, in which Roosevelt transferred fifty over-age naval destroyers to the British Navy in return for long-term American leases of British bases in the Caribbean. The exchange ignored a legislative ban on such practices, but Congress essentially affirmed Roosevelt's decision by adopting the Lend-Lease Act the next year.

To bolster the legitimacy of this and other actions, Roosevelt proclaimed a limited national emergency in 1939 and an unlimited one in 1941. Although the constitutional authority for these proclamations was unclear, they activated a long list of presidential powers that Congress already had granted by statute. But in an important sense, Roosevelt felt no need to justify his actions. He believed, as did Presidents Lincoln and Wilson before him, in the president's inherent authority to do whatever was necessary in a national crisis.

The president's power to protect the nation was unlimited, he implied in a remarkably candid message to Congress in 1942, after the United States officially entered the war. When demanding the repeal of a statute, he warned that "if Congress fails to act, and act adequately, I shall accept the responsibility, and I will act." His responsibility was to the Constitution and the people, he argued, and "I shall not hesitate to use every power vested in me to accomplish the defeat of our enemies in any part of the world where our own safety demands such defeat." After the crisis ended, Roosevelt pledged, these extraordinary powers, would "automatically revert to the people—to whom they belong."[4] It was a breath-taking assertion that could be sustained only by assuming that his ability to act in the nation's defense knew no constitutional limits during wartime.

Roosevelt's assumption went untested—Congress quickly repealed the objectionable law—and it remained a working rule, if not yet a constitutional principle. Far more than any of his predecessors, Roosevelt interpreted his war powers liberally and used them aggressively. In many instances, he acted with congressional approval but often went beyond the authority delegated to him. The Emergency Price Control Act of 1942, for instance, permitted the executive branch to regulate consumer prices, which it did by levying fines even though Congress had not granted this power. Taken together, the congressional statutes and presidential assertions of wartime powers resulted in federal command over the economy, including property rights, far exceeding even the control that the government wielded in World War I.

The Supreme Court, as in earlier conflicts, did not interfere; even in dissenting opinions, justices acknowledged the dire situation the nation faced and the general principle that the government could wield awesome powers in responding to the emergency. "War such as we now fight calls into play the full power of the government in extreme emergency," noted Justice Wiley B. Rutledge, who otherwise dissented from a 1944 decision upholding the Emergency Price Control Act. "Citizens must surrender or forego existing rights which in other times could not be impaired" (*Yakus v. United States*). Few people disagreed. The nation accepted the judgment of its elected leaders that the Constitution imposed no restraints on the effort required to defeat the total tyranny of Nazi Germany and Imperial Japan.

The Court supported Roosevelt's actions as commander-in-chief, even when doing so placed the justices in an awkward position. In 1942, for example, the FBI captured and secluded eight Nazi saboteurs, including one who claimed to be a naturalized American citizen. They had landed under cover of darkness on East Coast beaches and made their way inland, some as far as Chicago with the aim of destroying war industries and stealthily committing acts, such as blowing up department stores, to terrorize civilians. When the president and Justice Department decided that the men were enemy combatants who must be tried quickly by a military commission, and not in an open civilian court, the Germans filed a petition of habeas corpus that soon found its way to the Supreme Court. Upon learning about the petition, Roosevelt let it be known that "I want one thing clearly understood. . . . I won't give them up."[5] Within twenty-four hours the Court upheld the president's decision to try the saboteurs as unlawful combatants in a military tribunal; five days later, six of the eight Germans were executed (FDR commuted two sentences to life in prison).

Not until three months later did the Court release its unanimous opinion. The justices asserted the right of judicial review but accepted the president's actions under his broad powers as commander-in-chief and under congressional legislation authorizing military trials for persons accused of committing offenses against the laws of war. They distinguished the decision from *Ex parte Milligan* on the grounds that Milligan was not declared an enemy belligerent. Civil libertarians criticized *Ex parte Quirin* (1942), but the decision received broad public support, even though it quickly became forgotten until the attacks of September 11, 2001, resurrected the decision as a justification for the government's efforts to try unlawful combatants in military tribunals created by executive order.

Public opinion also overwhelmingly supported the effective suspension of the Bill of Rights, at least for individuals whose loyalty was in doubt. In February 1942 President Roosevelt issued Executive Order 9066, requiring the segregation and confinement of Japanese-Americans and resident Japanese aliens on the West Coast based on the fear that a misguided loyalty to Japan would compromise American security. More than 112,000 residents of Japanese ancestry, 70,000 of them native-born American citizens (Nisei) and the rest resident aliens (Issei), were forced to abandon their homes and businesses to enter so-called relocation centers for the duration of the war.

The centers were nothing less than racial detention camps. Fed by wartime hysteria, as well as by white Americans' resentment and envy of the economic success of the Japanese American Nisei, the relocation program was a patent denial of due process. There was no accusation of any crime, and no judicial review occurred, yet when it was challenged, the Supreme Court, by a vote of 6–3, upheld the exclusion. Military necessity required it, Justice Hugo Black, an erstwhile libertarian wrote for the majority, adding gratuitously that "hardships are a part of war and war is an aggregation of hardships" (*Korematsu v. United States*, 1944). A second case decided the same day held that a Japanese American girl whose loyalty was not in question had a right to habeas corpus (*Ex parte Endo*), but it was little comfort to the detainees. For most of them, the Bill of Rights did not exist.

The same conclusion was not true for civil liberties in general, which fared somewhat better than in either the Civil War or World War I. The anti-German hysteria that had supported the suppression of speech and press in 1917 was largely absent, and the Soviet Union was an important ally, muting the fear of communism so evident in the aftermath of the first war. The nature of the conflict in Europe fed the greater concern for civil liberties. Nazi tyranny made the war appear more a crusade for democracy than a battle for empire, especially given the New Deal's emphasis on civil rights during the previous decade.

The Court, too, had begun its swing toward a greater protection for individual liberty. The now-famous Footnote Four in the *Carolene Products Case* in 1938 signaled the emergence of rights claims, especially from minorities, as worthy of special attention from justices who already had nationalized much of the First Amendment. As a result, most civil liberties cases decided during World War II were much more solicitous of individual freedoms than had been the case in earlier wars. Religious liberty, for example, benefited from a revival of the clear and present danger test, as the flag-salute cases involving the Jehovah's Witnesses demonstrated. In the majority opinion in *West Virginia Board of Education v. Barnette* (1943), Justice Robert H. Jackson, in an unsubtle allusion to Germany, wrote that people who sought to force an end to dissent would "soon find themselves exterminating dissenters." It would be misleading to conclude that national security concerns did not trump the rights of speech and press—censorship was as common as it had been in other wars—but no longer were civil liberties held in suspension during a crisis.

World War II had barely ended when the United States entered the Cold War. The destruction of Hiroshima and Nagasaki by nuclear weapons, which effectively ended the American war with Japan, raised two immediate concerns: the atomic bomb would soon find its way into the hands of America's adversaries; and as a result, any future war could lead to the destruction of human existence. They were not idle fears. Within months the Soviet Union had an atomic bomb, in part because its espionage gained access to American nuclear secrets. Formerly an ally against Germany and Japan, the communist state was now a rival superpower.

The world quickly became divided between competing ideologies, democracy and communism, one characterized as free and the other as totalitarian. Two large, heavily armed alliances, the Warsaw Pact and the North American Treaty Organization (NATO), defined the new international order, with each side signaling its intention to stockpile enough weapons to deter an attack by the other. This doctrine, designed to ensure peace, no matter how uneasy, was known as mutually assured destruction, or, appropriately, MAD. Germany was the symbol of conflict in this atomic age. Split into two states, East Germany and West Germany, it was the epicenter of a dangerous new fault line in world politics; beginning in 1948, a year-long, round-the-clock American airlift to rescue a blockaded West Berlin revealed the scope of the effort that would be required to contain communism.

More was at risk than the fate of Berlin. In fact, Americans felt tremors everywhere—across Europe, in Asia and Africa, and in the Western Hemisphere. Most ominously, the menace seemed to exist in the United States itself, evidenced by spy rings and theft of military secrets. The threat was real, but the degree of danger and the consequences were unknown, which only made them more frightening. The result was another Red Scare—and a state of perpetual war, this time against an enemy armed and visible yet also secretive and surreptitious. At times, such as in Korea (1950–53) and later in Vietnam (1964–73), the Cold War became hot, with superpower alliances battling each other directly or through proxies, demonstrating to many Americans, at least initially, that their concerns were not misplaced.

This circumstance had important implications for American constitutionalism. For the first time in the nation's history, military readiness was a part of daily life, with bomb shelters, preparedness drills, and the draft serving as constant reminders of an ever-present threat. Most Americans believed that peace now rested on the presence of a large military establishment—unlike previous wars, the United States did not disarm after World War II—and a defense industry capable of supplying its needs. Both required an expansive federal bureaucracy to manage them. The Supreme Court's acceptance of congressional authority to govern the economy, fashioned first in the New Deal, and presidential power to protect the nation in an emergency, ratified in both world wars, continued to serve as constitutional touchstones. Likewise, the Court's newfound respect for the Bill of Rights as a legitimate, if limited, restraint during wartime had its parallels in the Cold War. The trumpeting of freedom and individual rights were powerful elements in the propaganda crusade against Soviet-style dictatorship, just as they were against Nazi Germany. The Court's affirmation of civil rights for African Americans, symbolized in *Brown v. Board of Education* (1954), was an element in this narrative, which explains in part its acceptance, the South notwithstanding, by a nation long accustomed to segregation.

Rights claims faced limits when they were thought to threaten national security, even if the harm was imagined or exaggerated. In the late 1940s, the House Un-American Activities Committee (HUAC) staged a series of highly controversial, dramatic hearings trying to show that communist infiltrators had pervaded American life. The committee's investigations of accusations by journalist and confessed former communist Whittaker Chambers against American diplomat Alger Hiss helped to launch the career of a young member of the House, Richard M. Nixon (R-California). Early in the next decade, on February 19, 1950, Senator Joseph R. McCarthy (R-Wisconsin) charged the State Department with harboring either 57 or 205 Communist Party members within its staff. McCarthy's list was a lie, but the hysteria it unleashed was real, coming as it did on top of the fear and alarm generated by the HUAC investigations.

The accusations and investigations spurred witch hunts in government and blacklists in defense industries, education, and even Hollywood. One consequence was the conviction of leaders of the American Communist Party for conspiring to overthrow the government because they urged workers to follow the anti-capitalist teachings of Marx and Engels. The Supreme Court upheld the conviction, resurrecting the clear and present danger rule in the process, even though no evidence existed of any action designed to harm the government (*Dennis v. United States*, 1951). The decision freed the government to prosecute almost all leaders of the Communist Party and led state and local governments to require loyalty oaths from their employees and even from students attending state colleges and universities.

The Red Scare ended in the mid-1950s, with the televised exposure of Senator McCarthy's bullying tactics in 1954 and his subsequent censure by the Senate. The ensuing turn in public opinion made it easier to argue for greater protection for individual rights against claims of national security. A new liberal majority on the Supreme Court, led by Chief Justice Earl Warren, soon limited or reversed the more conservative decisions of the previous decade, ruling that communists could not be prosecuted for merely advocating revolution unless they also took steps to overthrow the government (*Yates v. U.S.*, 1957). By the 1960s the justices banned loyalty oaths in a series of cases, and in 1968 they concluded that the First Amendment even protected advocacy of a violent overthrow except in cases that led to "imminent lawless action" (*Brandenburg v. Ohio*). Rights and security also were in play during the Vietnam War when the government sought to stop the *New York Times* from publishing the so-called Pentagon Papers, top-secret documents about the origin and conduct of the war. The Court sided with the paper, deciding that the government had not met the high standard of imminent harm required for prior restraint (*New York Times v. United States*, 1971).

What had happened, in the view of many scholars, was an implicit constitutional bargain. Beginning in the 1930s, Americans had demonstrated in numerous national elections a willingness to accept a more powerful central government in exchange for economic security and protection of their lives and their rights. This bargain rested on two premises: centralized power was necessary to promote prosperity, the apparent lesson of the New Deal; and it was required to ensure the nation's security, as the Cold War seemed to demonstrate. But would this tacit understanding hold when events raised doubts about these assumptions?

The last three decades of the twentieth century suggested not. Recessions, inflation, and a decline in productivity marked the American economy from the 1970s until the late 1980s, leading to a politically successful conservative counter-revolution against New Deal liberalism. Although the size and scope of the national government did not shrink, neither did it expand significantly. Unpopular wars and civil unrest in the late 1960s and early 1970s also challenged the use of national power to promote security, but these efforts to limit the central government were less successful. The difference in these opposite outcomes was the theory and role of presidential power.

During the 1930s and 1940s, the demands of economic revival and world war had led to a rapidly expanding administrative state, which placed a premium on organization and management of the executive branch. To accommodate rapidly changing conditions, Congress granted ever-wider discretionary authority to the president. By the Truman administration in the late 1940s, it was common for bills to include permissive language allowing the president to change priorities, defer spending, and take other actions to achieve legislative objectives.

When combined with the president's acknowledged leadership of foreign affairs, the discretionary authority led to a new conception of the office itself. A menacing world and an uncertain economy, analysts and pundits argued, required a strong, vigorous presidency. In a landmark book, *Presidential Power*, the political scientist (and former aide to President Truman) Richard E. Neustadt concluded that "what is good for the country is good for the President, and vice versa."[6] The executive was not a threat to liberty and democracy but their savior, or as another political scientist concluded: "presidential government . . . has been the single institution sustaining [democracy]—a bulwark of individual liberty, an agency of popular representation, and a magnet for real talent and leadership."[7] Not everyone agreed—conservatives, for instance, warned about an unbridled presidency—but even the adoption of the Twenty-second Amendment (1951), limiting the president to two terms in office, did not slow the shift of power to the Oval Office.

The Supreme Court generally gave a wide berth to presidential responsibility in war and foreign relations, especially when the actions were cast as an obligation under a treaty. President Truman committed troops to fight in Korea without a declaration of war, calling it a police action authorized by the United Nations treaty to which the United States was a signatory. Presidents Eisenhower, Kennedy, and Johnson sent troops and advisors to the Dominican Republic, Vietnam, and the Middle East under similar claims. But the Court balked when the president sought to assert control over domestic policies affecting national security. A classic test came in 1952 when the Court rejected President Truman's seizure of the nation's steel mills to ensure continued production during the Korean War, with a slim majority (5–4) concluding that the emergency in this instance was not dire enough to warrant the seizure unless Congress approved it (*Youngstown Sheet and Tube Co. v. Sawyer*, 1952). This limitation, although important, still left the president with significant discretion in matters of war and peace. At the height of the Cold War during the 1950s and early 1960s, most Americans, including most members of Congress, believed such power existed as a constitutional necessity.

Vietnam and Watergate changed this perception. President Lyndon B. Johnson sent large numbers of troops to Southeast Asia in 1965, citing authority granted by Congress following an alleged attack in August 1964 on American warships in the Gulf of Tonkin; he was the third consecutive president to take steps to involve the United States in the conflict between North and South Vietnam. By 1968, after a series of large anti-war rallies in major cities and on college campuses and increasingly skeptical coverage of the war in the nation's news media, public opinion turned sharply against the war, causing Johnson to withdraw his bid for reelection.

The Republican candidate, Richard M. Nixon, won the ensuing presidential election in large part by pledging to bring "peace with honor." He instead sent more troops to Vietnam and authorized a massive bombing campaign to force North Vietnam to negotiate peace terms. Two years later, on his own authority, he secretly invaded a neutral Cambodia in pursuit of the Viet Cong insurgents allied with the North Vietnamese. These actions met stiff opposition, as did Nixon's attempts to prevent newspapers from publishing the Pentagon Papers, a secret government history of decision making in the Vietnam conflict that cast growing doubt on the war's origins, effectiveness, and chances of success. Even so, Nixon's overwhelming reelection in 1972 against an anti-war Democrat, Senator George S. McGovern, persuaded Congress not to interfere with his conduct of the war.

This stance changed when Nixon became implicated in the Watergate affair, a domestic scandal growing out of the 1972 election that weakened his political support. Congressional hearings soon followed, probing not only Watergate but also the extent of unilateral executive war-making since Korea. One result was the War Powers Resolution of 1973. Passed over Nixon's veto, the act provided guidelines for reaching a "collective judgment" between Congress and the president regarding the use of armed forces. The president was required to consult Congress "in every possible instance" before committing troops and to inform both houses within forty-eight hours otherwise. If Congress withheld its consent, the president had sixty days to withdraw the military. Other measures sought to halt the executive practice of covert agreements with other nations to further American interests. These steps signaled a congressional intention to write no more blank checks for the president to carry on the Cold War, but they have had little effect. All presidents since Nixon have contended that the restrictions are an unconstitutional infringement on their authority and, absent public pressure, they generally have not allowed the guidelines to curtail their actions.

An expansive war power was only one of many claims of executive prerogatives that led to charges in the 1970s of an imperial presidency. The presidential staff under Nixon became significantly larger and more powerful, exercising authority previously assumed by the heads of the various federal departments. It was a troublesome development because few members of the White House staff were confirmed by the Senate or routinely underwent congressional oversight. This neglect raised concerns about a counter-bureaucracy that exercised great authority without any accountability to the legislative branch.

The problem became apparent to the larger public when Nixon repeatedly asserted executive privilege to prevent subordinates from responding to congressional subpoenas to compel their testimony about various policies. Nixon also claimed the authority to impound money appropriated by Congress and a broad executive immunity for his actions as president; he argued further that presidential power was unlimited except by his own judgment, especially in military and foreign affairs. By this view, he could mislead Congress and ignore rules of criminal investigations when necessary to protect national security.

It was a position he could not sustain. Faced with a demand by a federal district court that he turn over secret tapes that might establish his complicity in a crime, Nixon refused. With Justice William Rehnquist recusing himself—he had helped to devise the administration's theory of executive privilege when working at the Justice Department—the Supreme Court unanimously rejected Nixon's appeal and ordered the release of the tapes (*United States v. Nixon*, 1974). The president was entitled to great deference and even a presumption in his favor, the justices agreed, but he was subject to the law, with the courts responsible for defining the extent of his constitutional authority.

Nixon's resignation in disgrace, the first for a president in American history, checked the growth of an imperial presidency, at least temporarily, although in a widely viewed interview with the journalist David Frost, Nixon held fast to his view of executive power: "When the President does it, that means that it is not illegal." Congress became much more vigilant in its oversight of executive agencies, most notably the Federal Bureau of Investigation and the Central Intelligence Agency (both agencies had been implicated in the executive abuse of power). In 1978 Congress also established a system for appointing independent counsels, commonly known as special prosecutors, to investigate charges of criminal misconduct in the executive branch. For many liberal observers, most of them Democrats, who since Franklin D. Roosevelt had supported a vigorous executive, these actions marked a necessary rebalancing of power: what they approved in Roosevelt, they feared in Nixon. Conservatives who had long sought to restrain liberal presidents believed the pendulum of reform had swung too far, leaving the president too weak to protect the nation's interests.

For this latter group, centered in the Republican Party, Ronald Reagan became the model president, especially after what was widely perceived as the weak and ineffectual presidency of Jimmy Carter. A sunny warrior and believer in America's historic mission to advance liberty, Reagan was strong on national defense and sought to reverse the centralization of power at home. His policy of massive military buildups and a confrontational policy against the USSR—and his subsequent willingness to engage in a policy of détente and cooperation with Soviet leader Mikhail Gorbachev—were widely applauded as a catalyst for ending the Cold War. Like his predecessors, however, President Reagan acted unilaterally in foreign policy, often leading to conflict with Congress. His administration's cover-up of its illegal efforts to support anti-communist rebels in Nicaragua by using funds derived from covert sales of armaments to Iran brought public embarrassment and more congressional oversight.

Reagan's successor, George H. W. Bush, who also was implicated in the Iran-Contra scandal (the name given to the Nicaraguan fiasco), reluctantly accepted the new restraints, as did the Democrat who succeeded him as president, William J. Clinton. When Iraq invaded Kuwait in 1990, for example, and threatened the oil supply required for U.S. economic growth, President Bush carefully enlisted the support of Congress as well as that of American allies before launching the Gulf War to restore Kuwait's sovereignty and its pipelines.

Concern about the weakening of the presidency after Watergate led conservatives to propose a more muscular theory of executive power. Known as the unitary executive, it rested upon the argument that the separation-of-powers doctrine gave each branch of government an independent authority to interpret the Constitution, especially with regard to its own delegated powers. The idea was not new. In *Federalist No. 49*, James Madison argued that "the several departments being perfectly co-ordinate by the terms of their common commission, none of them, it is evident, can pretend to an exclusive or superior right of settling the boundaries between their respective powers." What this meant, proponents of a unitary executive argued, was a set of broad and unlimited powers within the president's sphere of authority, including the power to resist legislation or other constraints on his freedom to act.

Also central to the theory was the vesting clause of Article II, which simply spoke of "the executive Power," in contrast to the more restrictive language of Article I, which referred to "all legislative Powers herein granted." Did this different phrasing recognize an inherent executive power, derived from the British Crown, which the Constitution vested intact in the president, as advocates of the unitary executive argued, with the specific powers listed later in the Article serving as examples of his power and not restrictions of it? The framers were silent on this matter during the Convention, though Alexander Hamilton's *The Federalist No. 69* sought to reassure his readers in 1788 that the president had significantly less power than the king. Yet the debate in the 1790s between Hamilton and Madison over President Washington's authority to issue a proclamation of neutrality on his own authority revealed opposite opinions on the issue. Even so, most scholars have concluded that even the broad arguments advanced by Hamilton on behalf of executive power did not approach the sweeping claims made by advocates of the unitary presidency.

The unitary executive theory, combined with the president's role as commander-in-chief, became the centerpiece of the response to terrorist threats during the presidency of George W. Bush. Supported in this view by Vice President Richard Cheney and Secretary of Defense Donald Rumsfeld, who had long resisted congressional attempts to impose oversight on presidential actions in foreign affairs, Bush could point to ample precedent for his expansive view of presidential authority. Both World War II and the Cold War offered many examples of unilateral executive action, followed by congressional and public acceptance.

But in pursuing the war on terror, which administration officials described as a new kind of war, the Bush administration advanced new claims to be the sole judge of its own actions. For example, hundreds of prisoners from Afghanistan were taken to the U.S. military base at Guantanamo Bay, Cuba, where the government argued they were beyond the jurisdiction of U.S. courts yet not outside the president's power as commander-in-chief to hold them indefinitely. These detainees also were deemed "unlawful combatants," a designation that placed them outside the protections of the Third Geneva Convention, an international treaty for treating prisoners of war to which the United States was a signatory. Guantanamo Bay, in other words, appeared to be a "law-free" zone, subject only to the president's powers as commander-in-chief.

The administration also asserted its authority under the unitary executive theory in other areas as well. On eighty-two occasions in his first term alone, Bush cited the theory when issuing signing statements to accompany legislation passed by Congress and presented for his approval. Although such statements had a long history, they largely were ceremonial until President Reagan used them to signal how or whether he would enforce the law he was signing. These signing statements became even more sweeping under the second President Bush. He objected on constitutional grounds in 78 percent of his statements, frequently citing his sole authority over foreign affairs, his powers as commander-in-chief, or his inherent authority to control the executive branch, including withholding information from Congress. In sum, the president was using signing statements as effective vetoes of legislation that he otherwise was signing into law. In both international and domestic affairs, the president claimed sole power to define the lawful scope of his own actions.

In three cases from 2004 to 2006, the Supreme Court rejected the more extreme claims of presidential power made by the Bush administration. In 2001 Yaser Hamdi, an American citizen, was captured in Afghanistan and held by the U.S. military as an unlawful combatant. A federal district court ordered the Bush administration to justify his detention, but on appeal the Fourth Circuit Court blocked the order. It was an infringement on the president's authority as commander-in-chief as recognized by the Authorization for the Use of Military Force Act passed after the terrorist attacks, the circuit court concluded.

Eight justices of the U.S. Supreme Court disagreed, with Justice Clarence Thomas alone supporting the Bush administration's position completely. Although there was no opinion for the Court but only a plurality opinion and a smattering of concurrences, the result was clear: a suspected enemy combatant who also was a U.S. citizen could not be held without judicial review (*Hamdi v. Rumsfeld*, 2004). The same day, the Court by a 6–3 margin held that the federal courts, not the executive branch, had the power to decide whether foreign nationals held at Guantanamo Bay were wrongly imprisoned (*Rasul v. Bush*, 2004). This case reversed a World War II precedent, *Johnson v. Eisentrager* (1950), which held that U.S. courts had no jurisdiction over German war criminals held in a U.S.-administered camp in Germany because the United States lacked sovereignty there.

Two years later, in *Hamdan v. Rumsfeld* (2006), the justices again narrowed the president's authority to act unilaterally. The case was unusual because in 2005 Congress passed the Detainee Treatment Act giving exclusive jurisdiction to the District of Columbia Circuit Court of Appeals to hear appeals from prisoners tried by military courts. These courts, the justices concluded, again 6–3, violated due process rights under the Military Code of Justice and the Geneva Convention, both of which had received congressional approval. Although the Court did not decide whether the president had the power to establish military tribunals, any action by the president had to conform to the law.

In a fourth case, *Boumediene v. Bush* (2008), the justices decided, 5–4, that the Military Commissions Act of 2006, sought by President Bush to resolve the problems exposed by *Hamdan*, unconstitutionally denied the right of habeas corpus to prisoners held at Guantanamo Bay. The facility, the Court held, was under the de facto control of the United States. The decision relied upon the *Insular Cases* (1901–4), a series of cases stemming from the U.S. acquisition of Spanish territories (Philippines, Puerto Rico, and Guam) following the Spanish-American War of 1898. Then, the Court had ruled that the Constitution followed the flag and extended limited constitutional protections to residents of these territories.

It is easy to interpret the decisions relating to the war on terror as restricting the president's claim of authority in matters of war and peace—and they do—but it is unclear how much restraint they will impose. By the time they were issued the Bush administration had come under increasing attack for its policies. The military's mistreatment of prisoners at Abu Ghraib, the administration's mismanagement of the Iraq and Afghan conflicts, public exposure of the illegal surveillance of citizens, and the absence of any subsequent terrorist attacks caused many Americans to question justifications for the wars, as well as for claims that the president could act unilaterally and at his own discretion in the nation's defense.

The election of Barack Obama in 2008 represented a repudiation in part of the Bush administration's more extreme claims—candidate Obama opposed the wars and pledged to reverse Bush's policies on terror—but in fact the new president continued many of the practices that he had condemned. It suggests, at a minimum, the difficulty of reconciling constitutional ideals with conditions in an uncertain and dangerous world, one in which military action may not wait for the congressional approval that the founding generation believed was necessary in a republic.

More than any other circumstance, the state of continual war poses the greatest challenge to the framers' constitution. The founding generation assumed that the division and restraint of power was the greatest protection for the people's rights, and that, properly hedged, power in government could be trusted to foster liberty. War has always tested this belief, and few presidents have been content with restrictions on their power when the nation's security is at stake.

Today, the risks facing the now-powerful United States could scarcely have been imagined in the eighteenth century. Even so, it is doubtful that any of the delegates to the Federal Convention would have argued that the solution to the problems of security was unrestrained power. They, too, lived in a world of great insecurity. War was ever present and it was even more worrisome because the new republic was demonstrably so weak, at least when measured against the great powers of the day. For these revolutionaries, war created an emergency but not an excuse. Its purpose was to defend a system of government that rested always upon the people's consent, for it was popular sovereignty, the creators of 1787 recognized, that offered the only sure defense of liberty.

As he often did, Benjamin Franklin, the oldest member of the Constitutional Convention, put the issue plainly. At the end of the deliberations in Philadelphia, he noted the carved silhouette of a sun on the back of George Washington's chair. He always wondered, he told the delegates, whether it was a rising or a setting sun. Now, he was optimistic that the nation had a bright future because it had successfully addressed the issue of power. He declared the carving to depict a rising sun. A few minutes later, as he left Independence Hall, a woman called out to him, "Well, Dr. Franklin, have you given us a republic or a monarchy?" "A republic," he replied, "if you can keep it." How we interpret the Constitution during times of war makes Franklin's challenge the most important one that we as a nation will ever face.

NOTES

Introduction

1. *National Gazette*, January 19, 1972.

Chapter 1

1. The description of the Plymouth settlement comes from Nathaniel Philbrick, *Mayflower: A Story of Courage, Community and War* (New York: Viking, 2006), cited at 41 (Mayflower Compact) and 352 (Adams quote).

2. As quoted in Christopher Tomlins and Michael Grossberg, eds., *The Cambridge History of Law in America* (3 vols., Cambridge, UK: Cambridge University Press, 2008), I *Early America (1580–1815)*, 97.

3. *The Journal of John Winthrop, 1630–1649*, ed. Richard S. Dunn, James Savage, and Laetitia Yeandle (Cambridge, MA: Harvard University Press, 1996), 314.

Chapter 2

1. John Adams to Thomas Jefferson, August 24, 1815. Lester J. Cappon, ed., *The Adams-Jefferson Letters: The Complete Correspondence between Thomas Jefferson and Abigail and John Adams* (2 vols., Chapel Hill: University of North Carolina Press, 1961), II: 358, 455.

2. Quotes are from John Philip Reid, *Constitutional History of the American Revolution: The Authority of Rights* (Madison: University of Wisconsin Press, 1986), 177 (Boston), 180 (Newburyport).

3. Sir William Blackstone, *Commentaries on the Laws of England*, ed. William Draper Lewis (4 vols., Philadelphia: George Bisel, 1922), I: 161.

4. Quoted in Forrest McDonald, *States' Rights and the Union, 1776–1876: Imperium in Imperia* (Lawrence: University Press of Kansas, 2000), 3.

5. *Resolutions of the House of Representatives of Massachusetts. A Congress highly expedient and necessary, to consult upon the present state of the Colonies. Delegates on the part of the Province appointed. Discontinuance of the use of India Teas, and of the use of all Goods and Manufactures imported from the East Indies and Great Britain, recommended. Encouragement of American Manufactures, recommended* (adopted June 17, 1774). *American Archives* Series 4, Volume 1, Page 0421, accessed April 4, 2011, http://lincoln.lib.niu.edu/cgi-bin/amarch/documentidx.pl?doc_id=S4-V1-P03-sp11-D0098&;showfullrecord=on.

6. Suffolk Resolves, 1774, accessed April 4, 2011, http://www.constitution.org/primarysources/suffolk.html.

7. Cited in Pauline Maier, *America Scripture: Making the Declaration of Independence* (New York: Alfred A. Knopf, 1997), 34.

8. Eric Foner, ed., *Thomas Paine: Collected Writings* (New York: Library of America, 1995), 5.

9. Sir William Blackstone, *Commentaries on the Laws of England in Four Books* (2 vols., Philadelphia: J.B. Lippincott, 1893), I: 245, accessed April 4, 2011, http://oll.libertyfund. org/title/2140/198665/3147126.

10. Quoted in Christian G. Fritz, *American Sovereigns: The People and America's Constitutional Tradition before the Civil War* (Cambridge, UK: Cambridge University Press, 2008), 15 at note 11.

11. Foner, *Paine: Writings*, 548.

12. Quoted in Fletcher Melvin Green, *Constitutional Development in the South Atlantic States, 1776–1860: A Study in the Evolution of Democracy* (Chapel Hill: University of North Carolina Press, 1930), 106 at note 8.

13. Foner, *Paine: Writings*, 52.

14. *Chisholm v. Georgia*, 2 U.S. (2 Dall.) 419 (1793), 471–72.

15. Philip S. Foner, ed., *The Complete Writings of Thomas Paine* (2 vols., New York: Citadel Press, 1945), II, 274.

16. John Adams, *Thoughts on Government, Applicable to the Present State of the American Colonies* (1776), in *The Revolutionary Writings of John Adams* (Indianapolis: Liberty Fund, 2000), accessed April 4, 2011, http://oll.libertyfund.org/?option=com_staticxt&staticfile= show.php%3Ftitle=592&chapter=76854&layout=html&Itemid=27.

17. Washington quote from Michael Les Benedict, *The Blessings of Liberty: A Concise History of the Constitution of the United States* (Lexington, MA: D.C. Heath, 1996), 76; Greenwich quote from Woody Holton, *Unruly Americans and the Origins of the Constitution* (New York: Hill and Wang, 2007), 29.

Chapter 3

1. Washington and Knox quotes from Gordon Wood, *Revolutionary Characters: What Made the Founders Different* (New York: Penguin, 2006), 45.

2. John Adams, *The Works of John Adams, Second President of the United States* (10 vols., Boston: Little, Brown, 1856), Vol. 8, *January 24, 1787: TO SECRETARY JAY*, accessed on August 8, 2010, http://oll.libertyfund.org/title/2106/161740.

3. Quoted in Wood, *Revolutionary Characters*, 148.

4. Max Farrand, ed., *The Records of the Federal Convention of 1787* (New Haven: Yale University Press, 1911): Saturday, June 30, 1787, accessed August 30, 2010, http://oll .libertyfund.org/title/1057/95878.

5. *Papers of James Madison*, comp. Henry D. Gilpin (3 vols., Washington: Langtree & O'Sullivan, 1840), II: 906.

6. *Notes of the Debates in the Federal Convention of 1787 Reported by James Madison* (New York: W. W. Norton, 1987), 306.

7. Philip B. Kurland and Ralph Lerner, eds., *The Founders' Constitution* (Chicago: University of Chicago Press, 1987), Vol. 4, Article 7, Doc. 3, accessed February 28, 2010, http:// press-pubs.uchicago.edu/founders/documents/a7s3.html.

8. John Kaminski and Gaspare J. Saladino, eds., *The Documentary History of the Ratification of the Constitution*, Vol. 13, *Commentaries on the Constitution*, Vol. 1 (Madison: Wisconsin Historical Society, 1981), 474.

9. "The Addresses and Reasons of Dissent of the Minority of the Convention of the State of Pennsylvania to Their Constitution," in Bernard Schwartz, ed., *The Bill of Rights: A Documentary History* (2 vols., New York: Chelsea House, 1971), II: 667.

10. Quoted in Dumas Malone, *The Jeffersonian Heritage* (Boston: Beacon Press, 1953), 89.

11. All Madison quotes from "Speech on Amendments to Constitution, June 8, 1789," William Hutchinson et al., eds., *Papers of James Madison, Congressional Series* (17 vols., Charlottesville: University Press of Virginia,1962–1991), 12: 196–97.

Chapter 4

1. Quoted in Saul Cornell and Gerald Leonard, "The Consolidation of the Early Federal System, 1791–1812," in Grossberg and Tomlins, *The Cambridge History of Law in America,* Vol. 1, *Early America (1580–1815),* 519 (barkeeper), 520 (Barlow).

2. Texts of the three resolutions—the Kentucky Resolutions of 1798 and 1799 and the Virginia Resolution of 1798—may be found in Henry Steele Commager, ed., *Documents of American History* (8th ed., 2 vols., New York: Appleton-Century-Crofts, 1968), I: 178–84.

3. Quoted in Forrest McDonald, *States' Rights and the Union: Imperium in Imperio, 1776–1876* (Lawrence: University Press of Kansas, 2000), 68.

4. Quoted in Charles F. Hobson, *The Great Chief Justice: John Marshall and the Rule of Law* (Lawrence: University Press of Kansas, 1996), 21.

5. Hartford Convention, *Report,* 376, as cited by Christian G. Fritz, *American Sovereigns: The People and America's Constitutional Tradition before the Civil War* (Cambridge, UK: Cambridge University Press, 2008), 213.

6. *Proclamation to the People of South Carolina,* Dec. 10, 1832, in Commager, *Documents,* I: 266.

Chapter 5

1. Robert J. Donovan, *Tumultuous Years: The Presidency of Harry S. Truman, 1949–1953* (New York: W. W. Norton, 1982), 387.

2. Quotes from Maeva Marcus, *Truman and the Steel Seizure Case: The Limits of Presidential Power* (New York: Columbia University Press, 1977), 88 (CEO), 100 (Truman, "hooey").

3. Baron de Montesquieu, *Spirit of Laws,* Book 6, accessed September 9, 2010, http://press-pubs.uchicago.edu/founders/documents/v1ch17s9.html.

4. Quoted in "Judicial Power and Jurisdiction" in Kermit Hall et al., eds., *Oxford Companion to the Supreme Court of the United States* (New York: Oxford University Press, 1992), 456.

5. Alexis de Tocqueville, *Democracy in America,* trans. George Lawrence, ed. J. P. Mayer (New York: Harper & Row, 1969), 270.

Chapter 6

1. Quotes from Clyde W. Barrow, *More Than a Historian: The Political and Economic Thought of Charles A. Beard* (New Brunswick, NJ: Transaction, 2000), 5.

2. Charles A. Beard, *The Supreme Court and the Constitution* (New York: Macmillan, 1912), 92.

3. Rutledge and Adams quotes from James W. Ely Jr., *The Guardian of Every Other Right* (3rd ed., New York: Oxford University Press, 2008), 43.

4. "Property," in *The Founders' Constitution*, Vol. 1, Ch. 16, Document 23, accessed September 22, 2010, http://press-pubs.uchicago.edu/founders/documents/v1ch16s23.html.

5. Quoted in Michael Lienesch, *New Order of the Ages: Time, the Constitution, and the Making of Modern American Political Thought* (Princeton: Princeton University Press, 1988), 101.

6. Stephen J. Field, "The Centenary of the Supreme Court of the United States," *American Law Review*, 24 (May 1890), 365.

7. Letter to Harold J. Laski, March 4, 1920, in Mark DeWolfe Howe, ed., *The Holmes-Laski Letter: The Correspondence of Mr. Justice Holmes and Harold J. Laski* (2 vols., Cambridge: Harvard University Press, 1953), I: 249.

8. John Maynard Keynes, *The General Theory of Employment, Interest, and Money* (New York: Macmillan, 1936), 383.

9. Learned Hand, *The Bill of Rights: The Oliver Wendell Holmes Lectures of 1958* (Cambridge: Harvard University Press, 1958), 50.

Chapter 7

1. The term "women's suffrage" is a modern usage. Contemporaries usually used "woman suffrage."

2. "Speech of James Wilson before the Pennsylvania Ratifying Convention (November 24, 1787)," accessed January 19, 2010, http://www.constitution.org/rc/rat_pa.htm.

3. "Speech in the Federal Convention on Suffrage" (August 7, 1787), in James Madison, *Writings,* ed. Jack Rakove (New York: Library of America, 1999), 132–33.

4. Quoted in Christian G. Fritz, *American Sovereigns: The People and America's Constitutional Tradition before the Civil War* (Cambridge: Cambridge University Press, 2008), xx.

5. Quoted in Alexander Keyssar, *The Right to Vote: The Contested History of Democracy in the United States* (rev. ed., New York: Basic Books, 2009), 30.

6. Walter Lynwood Fleming, *Documentary History of Reconstruction* (2 vols., Cleveland: Arthur H. Clark, 1907), II: 434.

7. Quotes from Keyssar, *The Right to Vote*, 90–91 (Elizabeth Gage).

8. Francis Parkman, "The Failure of Universal Suffrage," *North American Review* 263 (July–August 1878), 7.

9. Susan B. Anthony, Matilda Joycelyn Cady Stanton, and Ida H. Harper, *The History of Woman Suffrage* (6 vols., New York: Fowler and Wells, 1881–1922), I: 59.

Chapter 8

1. Quoted in Ronald C. White Jr., *The Eloquent President: A Portrait of Lincoln through His Words* (New York: Random House, 2005), 256–57.

2. Quoted in Richard Carwardine, *Lincoln: A Life of Purpose and Power* (New York: Knopf, 2006), 41, 68, 146.

3. Roy P. Basler, *The Collected Works of Abraham Lincoln* (6 vols., Brunswick: Rutgers University Press, 1953), 6: 168–69.

4. Quoted in Gordon S. Wood, *Creation of the American Republic, 1776–1787* (Chapel Hill: University of North Carolina Press, 1969, 1998), 495.

5. Quote from Donald G. Nieman, *Promises to Keep: African Americans and the Constitutional Order, 1776 to the Present* (New York: Oxford University Press, 1991), 37.

6. James Cockcroft et al., *The American and English Encyclopedia of Law* (2nd ed., Northport, NY: Edward Thompson, 1898), 6: 64. Sir William Blackstone, *Commentaries on the Laws of England in Four Books*, ed. George Sharswood (2 vols., Philadelphia: J. B. Lippincott, 1893), Book 1, Chap. 15, Of Husband and Wife, accessed November 3, 2010, http://oll.libertyfund.org/title/2141.

7. Quotes from Mary Ryan, *Womanhood in America: From Colonial Times to the Present* (2nd ed., New York: Franklin Watts, 1979), 88 (antislavery society), 115 (Grimké).

8. Quoted in Barbara Young Welke, "Law Personhood, and Citizenship in the Late Nineteenth Century," in Michael Grossberg and Christopher Tomlins, eds., *The Cambridge History of Law in America,* Vol. 2, *The Long Nineteenth Century, 1789–1920* (Cambridge, UK: Cambridge University Press 2008), 372.

9. William Graham Sumner, *Folkways* (Boston: Athenaeum Press, 1907), 77.

10. Quoted in Nieman, *Promises to Keep*, 140.

Chapter 9

1. The full text of the proposed amendment was "The Congress shall have power to prohibit the physical desecration of the flag of the United States."

2. Quoted in Daniel Rodgers, *Contested Truths: Keywords in American Politics since Independence* (Cambridge, MA: Harvard University Press, 1986), 58.

3. Document 6, Amendment X [House of Representatives debate, August 18, 21, 1789], in Philip B. Kurland and Ralph Lerner, eds., *The Founders' Constitution* (Chicago: University of Chicago Press, 1987), accessed February 28, 2010, http://press-pubs.uchicago.edu/founders/documents/amendXs6.html.

4. Quoted in Jason Mazzone, "The Bill of Rights in Early State Courts," *Minnesota Law Review* (2007), 49.

5. Quoted in David J. Bodenhamer, *Fair Trial: Rights of the Accused in American History* (New York: Oxford University Press, 1992), 45.

6. Earl Warren, *The Memoirs of Earl Warren* (New York: Doubleday, 1977), 332–33.

7. Earl Warren, "The Law and the Future," *Fortune* (November 1955), 106, 226.

8. Letter to the Danbury Baptists, January 1, 1802, accessed November 1, 2010, in http://www.loc.gov/loc/lcib/9806/danpre.html.

Chapter 10

1. Quoted in Charles A. Lofgren, "War-Making under the Constitution: The Original Understanding," *Yale Law Journal*, 81 (1971–72), 685.

2. Letter from Thomas Jefferson to John B. Colvin, September 20, 1810, in Philip B. Kurland and Ralph Lerner, eds., *The Founders' Constitution* (Chicago: University of Chicago Press, 1987), accessed October 10, 2010, http://press-pubs.uchicago.edu/founders/documents/a2_3s8.html.

3. All quotes from Lincoln's First Inaugural Address (March 4, 1861), in Roy P. Basler, ed., *The Collected Works of Abraham Lincoln* (9 vols., New Brunswick: Rutgers University Press, 1953), 4: 262–71.

4. Message to Congress, September 7, 1942, in 88 Cong. Rec. 7044.

5. Quoted in David J. Danelski, "The Saboteur's Case," *Journal of Supreme Court History* (1996), 62.

6. Richard E. Neustadt, *Presidential Power: The Politics of Leadership from Roosevelt to Reagan* (rev. ed., New York: Free Press, 1990), 185.

7. James MacGregor Burns, *Presidential Government: The Crucible of Leadership* (New York, 1973), 346–47.

FURTHER READING

The secondary literature on the U.S. Constitution and American constitutionalism is rich and voluminous, encompassing the disciplines of history, law, and political science, among others. These necessarily selective suggestions focus primarily on books, but readers will not want to ignore the vast journal literature noted in the monographs identified below.

The best general treatments of the U.S. Constitution include the classic but now-dated work by Alfred Kelly, Winfred Harbison, and Herman Belz, *The American Constitution: Its Origins and Developments* (7th ed., New York: W. W. Norton, 1991), prized for its ability to relate public law to social and political developments. Equally masterful and more current is Melvin I. Urofsky and Paul Finkelman, *The March of Liberty: A Constitutional History of the United States* (3rd ed., New York: Oxford University Press, 2011). Good short treatments from much different perspectives are Michael Les Benedict, *The Blessings of Liberty: A Concise History of the Constitution of the United States* (Lexington, MA: D. C. Heath, 1996), and Forrest McDonald, *A Constitutional History of the United States* (Malabar, FL: Krieger, 1986), an avowedly conservative work.

William Wiecek focuses on the Supreme Court's influence on American constitutionalism in *Liberty under Law: The Supreme Court in American Life* (Baltimore: Johns Hopkins University Press, 1988). Legal history is a close cousin to constitutional history, so readers also will want to consult Kermit L. Hall and Peter Karsten, *The Magic Mirror: Law in American History* (New York: Oxford University Press, 2008), and the various essays in *The Cambridge History of Law in America*, a three-volume set edited by Michael Grossberg and Christopher Tomlins (Cambridge: Cambridge University Press, 2008). Two major reference works are Kermit L. Hall, *The Oxford Companion to the Supreme Court* (2nd ed., New York: Oxford University Press, 2005), and Kermit L. Hall et al., *The Oxford Companion to American Law* (New York: Oxford University Press, 2002). *The Oliver Wendell Devise History of the Supreme Court of the United States* (12 vols., New York: Cambridge University Press, 1973–), currently nearing completion, is the definitive history of the Court.

Chapter 1: Antecedents

Since the 1960s a series of excellent works have appeared on the legal and constitutional heritage of the American colonies, but no single-volume survey exists. A useful introduction is George Dargo, *Roots of the Republic: A New Perspective on American Constitutionalism* (New York: Praeger, 1974); it should be supplemented by Bernard Bailyn, *The Origins of American Politics* (New York: Knopf, 1968), and the essays in Christopher Tomlins and Bruce H. Mann, eds., *The Many Legalities of Colonial America* (Chapel Hill: University of North Carolina Press, 2001), which examines the legal pluralism of the early modern Atlantic world. Michael Kammen, *Deputyes and Libertyes: The Origins of Representative Government in Colonial America* (New York: Knopf, 1968), offers a good introduction to its topic; a more detailed institutional history is Charles M. Andrews, *The Colonial Period of*

American History (4 vols., New Haven: Yale University Press, 1934–39). Donald S. Lutz, *Colonial Origins of the American Constitution: A Documentary History* (Indianapolis: Liberty Fund, 2010), is an excellent collection of primary documents.

Colonial Massachusetts and Virginia have received the most attention from scholars and often stand, mistakenly, as surrogates for the colonial experience. Important works on Massachusetts include George L. Haskins, *Law and Authority in Early Massachusetts: A Study in Tradition and Design* (New York: Macmillan,1960), and David Thomas Konig, *Law and Society in Puritan Massachusetts: Essex County, 1629–1692* (Chapel Hill: University of North Carolina Press, 1979); for Virginia, see Warren M. Billings, *A Little Parliament: The Virginia General Assembly in the Seventeenth Century* (Richmond: Library of Virginia, 2004), Jack P. Greene, *The Quest for Power: The Lower Houses of the Assembly in the Southern Royal Colonies, 1680–1776* (Chapel Hill: University of North Carolina Press, 1963), and David Thomas Konig, "Virginia and the Imperial State: Law, Enlightenment, and the 'crooked cord of discretion,'" in David Lemmings, ed., *The British and Their Laws in the Eighteenth Century* (Woodbridge, UK: Boydell Press, 2005). William E. Nelson, *The Common Law of Colonial America,* Vol. 1, *The Chesapeake and New England, 1607–1660* (New York: Oxford University Press, 2008), explores how the different religious and economic imperatives guiding English colonization gradually merged into a common American legal order that differed significantly from that of Great Britain. Other important contributions on the influence of transatlantic constitutionalism are Daniel J. Hulsebosch, *Constituting Empire: New York and the Transformation of Constitutionalism in the Atlantic World, 1664–1830* (Chapel Hill: University of North Carolina Press, 2005), and Mary Sarah Bilder, *The Transatlantic Constitution: Colonial Legal Culture and the Empire* (Cambridge: Harvard University Press, 2004), which examines Rhode Island. Another work by Jack P. Greene also offers valuable perspective on the constitutional framework of the empire in theory and practice: *Peripheries and Center: Constitutional Development in the Extended Politics of the British Empire and the United States, 1607–1788* (Athens: University of Georgia Press, 1987).

The English constitutional heritage has been the subject of much noteworthy scholarship. The role of Magna Carta and the ancient constitution can be found in J. G. A. Pocock, *The Ancient Constitution and the Feudal Law: English Historical Thought in the Seventeenth Century* (2nd ed., Cambridge: Cambridge University Press, 1987), a work that traces the way English intellectuals thought about the past, especially its law, and explains how this perspective shaped the eighteenth-century constitution. Also see John Phillip Reid, *The Ancient Constitution and the Origins of Anglo-American Liberty* (DeKalb: Northern Illinois University Press, 2005), and A. E. Dick Howard, *The Road from Runnymede: Magna Carta and Constitutionalism in America* (Charlottesville: University Press of Virginia, 1968). For a good survey of constitutional ideas that emerged during the mid-seventeenth century in England, see D. E. Kennedy, *The English Revolution, 1642–1649* (London: Palgrave Macmillan, 2000). C. B. MacPherson, *The Theory of Possessive Individualism: Hobbes to Locke* (Oxford: Oxford University Press, 1962), discusses the influence of these two philosophers on the individualistic elements in English political thought in the seventeenth and eighteenth centuries. Donald Lutz, *The Origins of American Constitutionalism* (Baton Rouge: Louisiana State University Press, 1988), argues that colonial experience and the ideas of radical Protestantism were important in the emergence of an American constitutionalism that modified English theories and practice of government. The role of slavery in the development of ideas about liberty and power is examined gracefully and with insight by Edmund S. Morgan, *American Slavery, American Freedom: The Ordeal of Colonial Virginia* (New York: W. W. Norton, 1975). Lawrence Henry Gibson, *The British Empire before the American Revolution* (15 vols., New York: Harper and Row, 1936–70), is exhaustive in its coverage but students will profit more from Michael Kammen, *Empire and Interest: The American Colonies and the Politics of Mercantilism* (Philadelphia: J. B. Lippincott, 1970). On the role of religion, see Patricia Bonomi, *Under the Cope of Heaven: Religion, Society, and Politics in Colonial America* (New York: Oxford University Press, 1986), and Frank Lambert, *Inventing the Great Awakening* (Princeton: Princeton University Press, 1999). David S. Lovejoy, *The Glorious Revolution in America* (New York: Harper and Row, 1972), is a standard treatment.

Chapter 2: Revolution

Readers who wish to know more about the ideas that propelled colonial resistance to Great Britain should begin with Bernard Bailyn, *The Ideological Origins of the American Revolution* (Cambridge: Harvard University Press, 1967), and Gordon S. Wood, *The Creation of the American Republic* (Chapel Hill: University of North Carolina Press, 1968). The best treatment of how these ideas played out as a constitutional matter can be found in the magisterial work by John Phillip Reid, *Constitutional History of the American Revolution* (Madison: University of Wisconsin Press, 1986–93), in four volumes: *The Authority of Rights* (1986), *The Authority to Tax* (1987), *The Authority to Legislate* (1991), and *The Authority of Law* (1993); an abridged version of the set appeared in a single volume as *The Constitutional History of the American Revolution* (Madison: University of Wisconsin Press, 1995). Reid also explains the notion of two constitutions—one imperial and focused on power; the other local and centered on rights and representation—in *In Defiance of Law: The Standing Army Controversy, the Two Constitutions, and the Coming of the American Revolution* (Chapel Hill: University of North Carolina Press, 1981). Robert Middlekauf, *The Glorious Cause: The American Revolution, 1763–1789* (rev. and expanded ed., New York: Oxford University Press, 2007), is a good single-volume treatment of the movement toward impendence and the war with Great Britain. Useful studies of specific constitutional developments leading to independence include J. R. Pole, *Representation in England and the Origins of the American Republic* (New York: St. Martin's, 1966), Edmund S. Morgan and Helen M. Morgan, *The Stamp Act Crisis: Prologue to Revolution* (3rd ed., Chapel Hill: University of North Carolina Press, 1995), two books by Peter D. G. Thomas, *The Townshend Duties Crisis: The Second Phase of the American Revolution, 1767–1773* (New York: Oxford University Press, 1987), and *Tea Party to Independence: The Third Phase of the American Revolution, 1773–1776* (New York: Oxford University Press, 1991), and David Ammerman, *In the Common Cause: American Response to the Coercive Acts of 1774* (New York: W. W. Norton,1974).

Gary McDowell and Jonathan O'Neill, eds., *Enlightenment and American Constitutionalism* (New York: Palgrave Macmillan, 2006), contains a number of important essays on the ideas that informed the views of government and society held by the founding generation. Pauline Maier provides the best treatment of the Declaration of Independence in *American Scripture: Making of the Declaration of Independence* (New York: Knopf, 1997); it can be supplemented with the still-valuable work by Carl Becker, *The Declaration of Independence:*

A Study in the History of Ideas (New York: Harcourt, Brace, 1922), and Garry Wills, *Inventing America: Jefferson's Declaration of Independence* (New York: Simon & Schuster, 1978). Thomas Pangle, *The Spirit of Modern Republicanism: The Moral Vision of the American Founders and the Philosophy of Locke* (Chicago: University of Chicago Press, 1988), is a useful critical survey of republican ideas, as is Morton White, *The Philosophy of the American Revolution* (New York: Oxford University Press, 1978). Caroline Robbins examines the development of the philosophy embodied in Cato's Letters in *The Eighteenth Century Commonwealthman* (Cambridge: Harvard University Press, 1961). Edmund S. Morgan traces the evolution of ideas about popular sovereignty in *Inventing the People: The Rise of Popular Sovereignty in England and America* (New York: W. W. Norton, 1988). The development of republicanism in the Atlantic world, including its appeal in revolutionary America, is the subject of a masterful treatment by J. G. A. Pocock, *The Machiavellian Moment: Florentine Political Thought and the Atlantic Republican Tradition* (Princeton: Princeton University Press, 1975). Philip Pettit re-examines the seventeenth- and eighteenth-century roots of republican theory and suggests its applicability to modern government in *Republicanism: A Theory of Freedom and Government* (Oxford: Oxford University Press, 1999).

State constitutional developments are examined best in Willi Paul Adams, *The First American Constitutions: Republican Ideology and the Making of the State Constitutions in the Revolutionary Era* (Chapel Hill: University of North Carolina Press, 1980), Donald S. Lutz, *Popular Consent and Popular Control: Whig Political Theory in the Early State Constitutions* (Baton Rouge: Louisiana State University Press, 1981), and Marc W. Kruman, *Between Authority and Liberty: State Constitution Making in Revolutionary America* (Chapel Hill: University of North Carolina Press, 1997). Fletcher Melvin Green, *Constitutional Development in the South Atlantic States, 1776–1860: A Study in the Evolution of Democracy* (Chapel Hill: University of North Carolina Press, 1930), remains valuable. Forrest McDonald treats state constitutionalism and the Articles of Confederation in *E Pluribus Unum: The Formation of the American Republic, 1776–1790* (Boston: Houghton Mifflin, 1965); a view of the Articles as an expression of democratic ideas is found in Merrill Jensen, *The Articles of Confederation: An Interpretation of the Social-Constitutional History of the American Revolution, 1774–1781* (Madison: University of Wisconsin Press, 1940). Also important is Jack N. Rakove, *The Beginnings of National Politics: An Interpretive History of the Continental Congress* (New York: Knopf, 1979). Leonard Richards, *Shays' Rebellion: The American Revolution's Final Battle* (Philadelphia: University of Pennsylvania Press, 2002), explains the role of popular discontent in undermining confidence in the Articles of Confederation.

Chapter 3: Mechanics

The story of the Constitutional Convention is told well, if uncritically, in Catherine Drinker Bowen, *Miracle in Philadelphia: The Story of the Constitutional Convention, May–September 1787* (Boston: Little, Brown, 1966). A readable recent account is Carol Berkin, *A Brilliant Solution: Inventing the American Constitution* (New York: Houghton Mifflin, 2002). A provocative and unique analysis of the Constitution is made by Akhil Reed Amar, *The Constitution: A Biography* (New York: Random House, 2005). The best collection of primary documents related to the Constitution is Philip B. Kurland and Ralph Lerner, eds., *The Founders Constitution* (5 vols., Chicago: University of Chicago Press, 1986), which can now be accessed online at http://press-pubs.uchicago.edu/founders. John P. Kaminski et al., eds., *The Documentary History of the Ratification of the Constitution* (23 vols. to date, Madison: Wisconsin Historical Society, 1976–), presents a rich collection of documents from the Convention and ratification process. Herbert J. Storing, ed., *The Complete Antifederalist* (7 vols., Chicago: University of Chicago Press, 1981), is a good source for documents from opponents of the Constitution. *The Federalist Papers*, the 1787–88 essays written by Alexander Hamilton, James Madison, and John Jay in defense of the Constitution, of course, is a must-read. A reliable edition is *The Federalist Papers*, ed. Lawrence Goldman (New York: Oxford University Press, 1987); the original texts can be found at http://thomas.loc.gov/home/histdox/fedpapers.html, a site maintained by the Library of Congress. Good companion works are Garry Wills, *Explaining America: The Federalist* (Garden City: Doubleday, 1981), and Edward Millican, *One United People: The Federalist Papers and the National Idea* (Lexington: University of Kentucky Press, 1990).

The sources of constitutional ideas are discussed expertly in Forrest McDonald, *Novus Ordo Seclorum: Intellectual Origins of the Constitution* (Lawrence: University Press of Kansas, 1985). Jack N. Rakove examines these ideas in action at the Philadelphia Convention in *Original Meanings: Politics and Ideas in the Making of the Constitution* (New York: Knopf, 1996). Also useful in understanding the intellectual currents of the period is Michael Lienesch, *New Order of the Ages: Time, the Constitution, and the Making of Modern American Political Thought* (Princeton: Princeton University Press, 1988). Gordon S. Wood provides an important perspective on the continuing influence of revolutionary ideas in the *Radicalism of the American Revolution* (New York: Random House, 1993). M. J. C. Vile, *Constitutionalism and the Separation of Powers* (Oxford: Oxford University Press, 1967), places one of the Constitution's structural ideas in a historical and comparative framework. Paul K. Conkin provides a primer in some of the seminal ideas that informed revolutionary republicanism in *Self-Evident Truths: Being a Discourse on the Origins & Development of the First Principles of American Government—Popular Sovereignty, Natural Rights, and Balance & Separation of Powers* (Bloomington: Indiana University Press, 1974). Also see Bruce Ackerman, *We the People*, Vol. 1, *Foundations* (Cambridge: Harvard University Press, 1991), for a vigorous analysis of how founding ideas have played out over the course of American history. Sophisticated yet accessible discussions of James Madison's intellectual contributions can be found in Lance Banning, *The Sacred Fire of Liberty: James Madison and the Founding of the Federal Republic* (Ithaca: Cornell University Press, 1998), and Colleen A. Sheehan, *James Madison and the Spirit of Republican Self-Government* (Cambridge: Cambridge University Press, 2009).

A counter-argument that economic conflict mattered more than ideological commitments was the point of one of the most influential works in American historiography, Charles A. Beard, *An Economic Interpretation of the Constitution* (1913; reprint, New York: Free Press, 1987); Forrest McDonald re-traced Beard's work in *We the People* (Chicago: University of Chicago Press, 1958) and provided a more complex view of economic interests in the ratification of the Constitution. Joyce Appleby, *Liberalism and Republicanism in the Historical Imagination* (Cambridge: Harvard University Press, 1992), brings economic and political ideas together in the context of revolutionary America. Peter Onuf, *The Origins of the Federal Republic* (Philadelphia: University of Pennsylvania Press, 1983), traces the role played by discontent in and among the states in the movement toward a strong central government. Jackson Turner Main, *The Antifederalists: Critics of*

the Constitution, 1781–1788 (Chapel Hill: University of North Carolina Press, 1961), provides a sympathetic view of the arguments against the Constitution; Gary B. Nash, *The
Unknown American Revolution: The Unruly Birth of Democracy and the Struggle to Create
America* (New York: Viking, 2005), and Woody Holton, *Unruly Americans and the Origins
of the Constitution* (New York: Hill and Wang, 2007), emphasize the democratic impulses
that shaped the Revolution and led to the demands for a Bill of Rights to be added to the
Constitution as a condition for ratification. Pauline Maier, *Ratification: The People Debate
the Constitution, 1787–1788* (New York: Simon & Schuster, 2010), portrays the rough and
tumble politics of the state-by-state debates on adoption. Robert A. Rutland, *The Birth of
the Bill of Rights* (Chapel Hill: University of North Carolina Press, 1955), is still the standard work; it should be read with Akhil Reed Amar, *The Bill of Rights: Creation and Reconstruction* (New Haven: Yale University Press, 1998), which views the amendments as
rights empowering the majority rather than protecting the minority, a much disputed view.

Chapter 4: Federalism

Frederick D. Drake and Lynn R. Nelson, *States' Rights and American Federalism: A Documentary History* (Westport, CT: Greenwood Press, 1999), is a good source for primary
documents relating to federalism. A good survey of modern federalism may be found in
Joseph F. Zimmerman, *Contemporary Federalism: The Growth of National Power* (2nd ed.,
New York: Praeger, 2008). Alison LaCroix, *The Ideological Origins of American Federalism*
(Cambridge: Harvard University Press, 2010), offers an excellent introduction to the history of the most innovative contribution of the Constitutional Convention. Stanley Elkins
and Eric McKitrick, *The Age of Federalism* (New York: Oxford University Press, 1993),
and Gordon S. Wood, *Empire of Liberty: A History of the Early Republic, 1789–1815* (New
York: Oxford University Press, 2009), are good surveys of the politics and socioeconomic
developments of the critical first decades under the new Constitution. Richard Hofstadter,
*The Idea of a Party System: The Rise of Legitimate Opposition in the United States, 1780–
1840* (Berkeley: University of California Press, 1969), and Saul Cornell, *The Other Founders: Anti-Federalism and the Dissenting Tradition in America, 1788–1828* (Chapel Hill:
University of North Carolina Press, 1999), explore how the champions of localism continued to define the limits of legitimate dissent within the American constitutional tradition,
especially in the early republic. Joanne Freeman offers a Republican rationale for Federalist
actions in "Explaining the Unexplainable: The Cultural Logic of the Sedition Act," in
Julian Zelizer et al., *The Democratic Experiment: New Directions in American Political History* (Princeton: Princeton University Press, 2003). William J. Watkins Jr. examines early
national politics and federal-state relations through the constitutional arguments of Jefferson and Madison in *Reclaiming the American Revolution: The Virginia and Kentucky
Resolutions and Their Legacy* (New York: Palgrave Macmillan, 2004). Also see David N.
Mayer, *The Constitutional Thought of Thomas Jefferson* (Charlottesville: University Press
of Virginia, 1994), Lance Banning, *The Jeffersonian Persuasion: Evolution of a Party Ideology* (Ithaca: Cornell University Press, 1978), and Richard Buel, *Securing the Revolution:
Ideology in American Politics, 1789–1815* (Ithaca: Cornell University Press, 1972).

   Christian G. Fritz, *American Sovereigns: The People and America's Constitutional Tradition before the Civil War* (Cambridge: Cambridge University Press, 2008), illustrates how
the debates over the meaning of popular rule and state sovereignty continued unabated

from the ratification conventions to the crisis of southern secession. James M. Banner discusses the secessionist movement in New England in *To the Hartford Convention: The Federalists and the Origins of Party Politics in Massachusetts, 1789–1815* (New York: Knopf, 1970). The reform of state constitutions within the federal system is covered in Laura J. Scalia, *America's Jeffersonian Experiment: Remaking State Constitutions* (DeKalb: Northern Illinois University Press, 1999). Also see Forrest McDonald, *States Rights and the Union: Imperium in Imperio, 1776–1876* (Lawrence: University Press of Kansas, 2000), as a good single-volume introduction to the state sovereignty debates. R. Kent Newmyer provides an accessible treatment of federalism in the Marshall and Taney Courts in *The Supreme Court under Marshall and Taney* (2nd ed., Wheeling, IL: Harlan Davidson, 2006); also see his book, *John Marshall and the Heroic Age of the Supreme Court* (Baton Rouge: Louisiana State University Press, 2001). Richard E. Ellis provides a sound treatment of the Marshall Court's signal case on federalism in *Aggressive Nationalism: McCulloch v. Maryland and the Foundation of Federal Authority in the Young Republic* (New York: Oxford University Press, 2007). Two good books on the Nullification Crisis are Richard E. Ellis, *The Union at Risk: Jacksonian Democracy, States' Rights and the Nullification Crisis* (New York: Oxford University Press, 1987), and John Niven, *John C. Calhoun and the Price of Union* (Baton Rouge: Louisiana State University Press, 1988). The stress slavery put on the federal system is the subject of Paul Finkelman, *Imperfect Union: Slavery, Freedom, and Comity* (Chapel Hill: University of North Carolina Press, 1981). Don E. Fehrenbacher, *The Dred Scott Case: Its Significance in American Law and Politics* (New York: Oxford University Press, 1978), is an important study.

The best guide to the constitutional changes brought by the Civil War and Reconstruction is Harold Hyman, *A More Perfect Union: The Impact of the Civil War and Reconstruction on the Constitution* (New York: Knopf, 1973). Few scholars have written more often or with more insight on changes in American federalism than Harry N. Scheiber; see, especially, "Redesigning the Architecture of Federalism—An American Tradition," *Yale Law and Policy Review/Yale Journal of Regulation, Symposium Issue* (1996), 227–96. Bruce Ackerman, *We the People*, Vol. 2, *Transformations* (Cambridge: Harvard University Press, 2000), provides a detailed and provocative analysis of the postwar amendments. Loren Beth traces the growth in the power of the national government in the late nineteenth century in *The Development of the American Constitution, 1877–1917* (New York: Harper & Row, 1971). A defense of dual federalism may be found in Raoul Berger, *Federalism: The Founders' Design* (Norman: University of Oklahoma Press, 1987). Morton Keller, *Affairs of State: Public Life in Late Nineteenth Century America* (Cambridge: Harvard University Press, 1977), provides a masterful analysis of government during this period. Stephen Skowronek, *Building a New American State: The Expansion of National Administrative Capacities, 1877–1920* (Cambridge: Cambridge University Press, 1982), discusses the rise of a national bureaucracy; also see Richard F. Bensel, *Yankee Leviathan: The Origins of Central State Authority in America, 1859–1877* (New York: Cambridge University Press, 1990). William F. Swindler, *Court and Constitution in the Twentieth Century*, Vol. 1, *The Old Legality, 1889–1932*, and Vol. 2, *The New Legality, 1932–1968* (Indianapolis: Bobbs-Merrill, 1969–70), are comprehensive treatments of Supreme Court decisions, especially tracing the rise and fall of dual federalism. Eric N. Waltenburg and Bill Swinford, *Litigating Federalism: The States before the U.S. Supreme Court* (New York: Praeger, 1999), is a provocative quantitative analysis of the contours of modern federalism. Samuel H. Beer, *To Make a*

Nation: The Rediscovery of American Federalism (Cambridge: Harvard University Press, 1993), is a masterful survey by a political scientist. For the emergence of New Federalism in the Rehnquist Court, see Mark Tushnet, *A Court Divided: The Rehnquist Court and the Future of Constitutional Law* (New York: W. W. Norton, 2005); also see David B. Walker, *The Rebirth of Federalism: Slouching toward Washington* (2nd ed., New York: Chatham House, 2000). Jon C. Teaford, *The Rise of the States: The Evolution of American State Government*, (Baltimore: Johns Hopkins University Press, 2002), provides a valuable survey of the counter-narrative of local control in federalism.

Chapter 5: Balance

The best starting point for the doctrine of separation and balance of powers is M. J. C. Vile, *Constitutionalism and the Separation of Powers* (Oxford: Oxford University Press, 1967). The role of John Marshall in asserting national power and establishing the power of the federal judiciary is explored masterfully in Charles Hobson, *The Great Chief Justice: John Marshall and the Rule of Law* (Lawrence: University Press of Kansas, 1996). Sylvia Snowiss argues that Marshall transformed the existing practices of judicial review in radical fashion in *Judicial Review and the Law of the Constitution* (New Haven: Yale University Press, 1990); also see J. M. Sosin, *The Aristocracy of the Long Robe: The Origins of Judicial Review in America* (Westport, CT: Greenwood Press, 1989). The role of another great jurist in establishing the American judicial tradition is told in R. Kent Newmyer, *Supreme Court Justice Joseph Story: Statesman of the Old Republic* (Chapel Hill: University of North Carolina Press, 1985). Popular constitutionalism and the origins of judicial review are explored in Larry D. Kramer, *The People Themselves: Popular Constitutionalism and Judicial Review* (New York: Oxford University Press, 2004). Brian Balogh, *A Government Out of Sight: The Mystery of National Authority in Nineteenth-Century America* (New York: Cambridge University Press, 2009), reveals an active and vigorous national government in the nineteenth century, even though not in the manner we associate with it today.

The debate over how to interpret the Constitution has continued unabated from the earliest days of the republic. The role of interpretive history in constitutional interpretation is explored in David A. J. Richards, *Foundations of American Constitutionalism* (New York: Oxford University Press, 1989). A strong defense of originalism by its most vocal advocate on the Supreme Court is Antonin Scalia, *A Matter of Interpretation: Federal Courts and the Law* (Princeton: Princeton University Press, 1997). Christopher Wolfe, *The Rise of Modern Judicial Review: From Constitutional Interpretation to Judge-Made Law* (rev. ed., New York: Basic Books, 1994), describes three major periods of judicial review from an original-ist perspective. An equally forceful case for the idea of a living constitution is made by Scalia's colleague on the Court, Stephen Breyer, in *Active Liberty: Our Democratic Constitution* (New York: Knopf, 2005). David Strauss argues that originalism is incoherent and indefensible in *The Living Constitution* (New York: Oxford University Press, 2010). Daniel A. Farber and Suzanna Sherry, *Judgment Calls: Principle and Politics in Constitutional Law* (New York: Oxford University Press, 2008), strike a middle ground by suggesting that judging must be both principled and flexible. Lawrence Tribe, *The Invisible Constitution* (New York: Oxford University Press, 2008), concludes that most of our most fundamental constitutional principles are not included in the text of the Constitution or cannot reason-ably be inferred from its text. Neal Devins and Louis Fisher, *The Democratic Constitution*

(New York: Oxford University Press, 2004), use case studies to argue that constitutional interpretation historically is far more than the province of the Supreme Court. The essays in Kermit L. Hall and Kevin T. McGuire, *The Judicial Branch* (New York: Oxford University Press, 2002), explore the role of the judiciary and its relationship with the other branches of government both historically and in contemporary America.

The essays in Kenneth Bowling, ed., *Neither Separate nor Equal: Congress and the Executive Branch in the 1790s* (Athens: Ohio University Press, 2000), provide perspective on the early understanding of separation of powers. Keith E. Whittington, *Constitutional Construction: Divided Powers and Constitutional Meaning* (Cambridge: Harvard University Press, 1999), explores how the Constitution shapes politics in the Congress and presidency even as politics shapes the Constitution in turn. Nelson W. Polsby, *How Congress Evolves: Social Bases of Institutional Change* (New York: Oxford University Press, 2004), and James L. Sundquist, *The Development of Congress* (Washington: Congressional Quarterly, 1981), are useful guides to the institutional history and workings of the people's branch of the federal government. Louis Fisher, *Constitutional Conflicts between Congress and the President* (4th rev. ed., Lawrence: University Press of Kansas, 1997), can be supplemented with Charles Gardner Geyh, *When Courts and Congress Collide: The Struggle for Control of America's Judicial System* (Ann Arbor: University of Michigan Press, 2006). James L. Sundquist discusses the post-Watergate efforts to revive congressional authority in *The Decline and Resurgence of Congress* (Washington: Brookings Institution, 1981); also see Charles O. Jones, *Separate but Equal Branches: Congress and the Presidency* (Washington: Congressional Quarterly, 1999). Jessica Korn, *The Power of Separation: American Constitutionalism and the Myth of the Legislative Veto* (Princeton: Princeton University Press, 1996), argues that the framers designed the structure of government, notably separation of powers, not as a restraint as much as a way of increasing government's capacity through a division of labors.

The classic study of the presidency is Edwin S. Corwin, *The President: Office and Powers* (5th ed., New York: New York University Press, 1984). It should be supplemented with Forrest McDonald, *The American Presidency: An Intellectual History* (Lawrence: University Press of Kansas, 1994). Glenn A. Phelps, *George Washington and American Constitutionalism* (Lawrence: University Press of Kansas, 1993), discusses the first president's role in establishing important precedents for the office. Charles C. Thach, *The Creation of the Presidency, 1775–1789: A Constitutional History* (Baltimore: Johns Hopkins University Press,1923, 1970), is an early but still useful work; the essays in Thomas E. Cronin, ed., *Inventing the American Presidency* (Lawrence: University Press of Kansas, 1989), offer useful introductions to the early development of the office. Joseph M. Bessette and Jeffrey K. Tulis, eds., *The Constitutional Presidency* (Baltimore: Johns Hopkins University Press, 2009), provide insights from a variety of scholars on the ever-changing nature of the office and its relationship to Congress, the courts, and public opinion. James MacGregor Burns, *Presidential Government: The Crucible of Leadership* (New York: Houghton Mifflin, 1973), is a political scientist's take on how presidents exercise their authority. The best account of the *Steel Seizure Case* is Maeva Marcus, *Truman and the Steel Seizure Case: The Limits of Presidential Power* (New York: Columbia University Press, 1977). Stanley I. Kutler, *The Wars of Watergate: The Last Crisis of Richard Nixon* (New York: Knopf, 1990), and Arthur M. Schlesinger Jr., *The Imperial Presidency* (rev. ed., New York: Mariner, 2004), are important for understanding the growth and crises of presidential authority in the last half of the twentieth century. Other titles on the presidency may be found in the selected readings for Chapter 10, below.

A good introduction to the Court and its nineteenth-century development is found in Robert G. McCloskey and Sanford Levinson, *The American Supreme Court* (5th ed., Chicago: University of Chicago Press, 2010). Stephen B. Presser, *The Original Misunderstanding: The English, the Americans, and the Dialectic of Federalist Jurisprudence* (Durham: Carolina Academic Press, 1991), and William E. Nelson, *Marbury v. Madison: The Origins and Legacy of Judicial Review* (Lawrence: University Press of Kansas, 2000), are important studies of the emergence of judicial review. David P. Currie, *The Constitution and the Supreme Court: The First Hundred Years, 1789–1888* (Chicago: University of Chicago Press, 1985), is valuable on the Court's emergence as a separate and equal branch of government. Peter Karstens, *Heart versus Head: Judge-Made Law in Nineteenth-Century America* (Chapel Hill: University of North Carolina Press, 1996), and Leonard W. Levy, *The Law of the Commonwealth and Chief Justice Shaw* (Cambridge: Harvard University Press, 1957), offer good guides to how judges made law in the nation's first century. Robert Kaczorowski, *The Politics of Judicial Interpretation* (New York: Oceana, 1985), and Stanley I. Kutler, *Judicial Power and Reconstruction Politics* (Chicago: University of Chicago Press, 1968), are important studies on the role of the judiciary in the decades after the Civil War. The politics of the court-packing plan and the emergence of the New Deal Court are the subject of William E. Leuchtenberg, *The Supreme Court Reborn: The Constitutional Revolution in the Age of Roosevelt* (New York: Oxford University Press, 1995). Noah Feldman, *Scorpions: The Battles and Triumphs of FDR's Great Supreme Court Justices* (New York: Twelve, 2010), is a lively account of how four liberal justices on the post–New Deal Court addressed the judicial role in American democracy. Paul L. Murphy, *The Constitution in Crisis Times, 1918–1969* (New York: Harper & Row, 1972), is valuable on the twentieth-century Court, as is William M. Wiecek, *The Birth of the Modern Constitution: The United States Supreme Court, 1941–53* (Cambridge: Cambridge University Press, 2006), and Morton J. Horwitz, *The Warren Court and the Pursuit of Justice* (New York: Hill & Wang, 1998). Also see John E. Semonche, *Keeping the Faith: A Cultural History of the Supreme Court* (Lanham, MD: Rowman and Littlefield, 1998). Barry Friedman, *The Will of the People: How Public Opinion Has Influenced the Supreme Court and Shaped the Meaning of the Constitution* (New York: Farrar, Straus and Giroux, 2009), argues that the U.S. Supreme Court is engaged in a continuing dialogue with political leadership and public opinion. An engaging introduction to the more influential justices is G. Edward White, *The American Judicial Tradition: Profiles of Leading American Judges* (3rd rev. ed., New York: Oxford University Press, 2007).

Chapter 6: Property

The best brief survey of the Constitution and property is James W. Ely Jr., *The Guardian of Every Other Right: A Constitutional History of Property Rights* (3rd rev. ed., New York: Oxford University Press, 2008). Joyce Appleby, *The Relentless Revolution* (New York: W. W. Norton, 2010), insists that capitalism, like revolutionary republicanism, required a radical reconception of human nature. Jennifer Nedelsky stresses the central role of private property in the framers' conception of limited government in *Private Property and the Limits of American Constitutionalism: The Madisonian Framework and Its Legacy* (Chicago: University of

Chicago Press, 1994), and Charles Sellers examines the emergence of free-market ideology in *The Market Revolution: Jacksonian America, 1815–1876* (New York: Oxford University Press, 1991). Harry L. Watson traces the conflict between republican ideology and free market forces in *Liberty and Power: The Politics of Jacksonian America* (2nd ed., New York: Hill & Wang, 2006). William J. Novak, *The People's Welfare: Law and Regulation in Nineteenth Century America* (Chapel Hill: University of North Carolina Press, 1996), argues that the United States was not a laissez-faire, free-market nation but rather a highly regulated state profoundly concerned with public welfare and market involvement. Harry N. Scheiber outlines the development of public purpose in "The Road to Munn: Eminent Domain and the Concept of Public Purpose in the State Courts," *Perspectives in American History*, 5 (Cambridge: Harvard University Press, 1971), 327–402; also "Federalism and the American Economic Order, 1789–1910," *Law and Society Review*, 10 (1975–76), 57–118. Lawrence M. Friedman, *American Law in the Twentieth Century* (New Haven: Yale University Press, 2002), is a readable guide to the relationship of economic and cultural change to the shifting judicial role during a tumultuous century. Shifts in legal thought that accompanied the new economic order are the subject of Stephen M. Feldman, *American Legal Thought from Premodernism to Postmodernism: An Intellectual Voyage* (New York: Oxford University Press, 2000).

The classic study by Benjamin F. Wright, *The contract clause of the Constitution* (Cambridge: Harvard University Press, 1938), is still useful, but it should be read with the essays in James W. Ely Jr., ed., *The contract clause in American History* (New York: Routledge, 1997). Francis Stites, *Private Interest and Public Gain* (Amherst: University of Massachusetts Press, 1972), discusses *Dartmouth College v. Woodward*, the key Marshall Court contract clause case. Felix Frankfurter, *The Commerce Clause under Marshall, Taney, and Waite* (Chapel Hill: University of North Carolina Press, 1937), traces interpretation of the commerce power. Studies of landmark cases abound, including Maurice G. Baxter, *The Steamboat Monopoly: Gibbons v. Ogden, 1824* (New York: Knopf, 1972); Herbert Alan Johnson, *Gibbons v. Ogden: John Marshall, Steamboats, and the Commerce Clause* (Lawrence: University Press of Kansas, 2010); C. Peter Magrath, *Yazoo: Law and Politics in the New Republic: The Case of Fletcher v. Peck* (Providence: Brown University Press, 1966); Mark Robert Killenbeck, *M'Culloch v. Maryland: Securing a Nation* (Lawrence: University Press of Kansas, 2006); Stanley I. Cutler, *Privilege and Creative Destruction: The Charles River Bridge Case* (Philadelphia: Lippincott, 1971); and Elizabeth B. Monroe, *The Wheeling Bridge Case: Its Significance in Law and Technology* (Boston: Northeastern University Press, 1992). Tony Freyer has produced a veritable bookshelf of valuable works on constitutional issues related to property; see especially *Forums of Order: The Federal Courts and Business in American History* (New York: JAI Press, 1979); *Harmony & Dissonance: The Swift & Erie Cases in American Federalism* (New York: New York University Press, 1981); *Producers versus Capitalists: Constitutional Conflict in Antebellum America* (Charlottesville: University Press of Virginia, 1994).

James Willard Hurst, *Law and the Conditions of Freedom in the Nineteenth-Century United States* (Madison: University of Wisconsin Press, 1956), is a pioneering work on the legal history of political economy by the dean of American legal historians. An essential study of courts and economic development is Morton J. Horwitz, *The Transformation of American Law, 1780–1860* (Cambridge: Harvard University Press, 1977), and *The Transformation of American Law, 1870–1960: The Crisis of Legal Orthodoxy* (Cambridge: Harvard

University Press, 1992). Michael Les Benedict, "Laissez Faire and Liberty: A Re-Evaluation of the Origins of Laissez-Faire Constitutionalism," *Law and History Review*, 3 (1985), 293–331, is important in understanding the emergence of laissez-faire economic theory in the judiciary. The role of locally exercised police powers and urban change in late nineteenth-century America may be found in Ronald M. Labbé and Jonathan Lurie, *The Slaughterhouse Cases: Regulation, Reconstruction, and the Fourteenth Amendment* (Lawrence: University Press of Kansas, 2003). See Howard Gillman, *The Constitution Besieged: The Rise and Demise of Lochner Era Police Powers Jurisprudence* (Durham, NC: Duke University Press, 1993), for the attack on formalism. John E. Semonche discusses Supreme Court decisions during the Progressive Era in *Charting the Future: The Supreme Court Responds to a Changing Society, 1890–1920* (Westport: Greenwood Publishers, 1978). "The Debate over the Constitutional Revolution of 1937," *American Historical Review*, 110:4 (2005), 1046–115, provides a useful introduction to the impact of the New Deal on constitutional law affecting the economy. Also see Barry Cushman, *Rethinking the New Deal Court: The Structure of a Constitutional Revolution* (New York: Oxford University Press, 1998), and Edward G. White, *The Constitution and the New Deal* (Cambridge: Harvard University Press, 2000). Paul R. Benson assesses the broadened sweep of the post–New Deal commerce power in *The Supreme Court and the Commerce Clause, 1937–1970* (New York: Dunellen, 1970). For a critique of post–New Deal contract clause jurisprudence from a conservative perspective, see David N. Mayer, *Liberty of Contract: Rediscovery of a Lost Constitutional Right* (Washington, DC: Cato Institute, 2011). Herbert Hovenkamp, *Enterprise and American Law, 1836–1937* (Cambridge: Harvard University Press, 1991), is valuable on the rise of the corporation, as well as the antitrust and regulation movements. For a comparative view, see Tony Freyer, *Regulating Big Business: Antitrust in Great Britain and America, 1880–1990* (Cambridge: Cambridge University Press, 1992). Richard A. Epstein has written extensively on constitutional provisions that bear on property rights, including the takings clause; see, for example, *Takings: Private Property and the Power of Eminent Domain* (Cambridge: Harvard University Press, 1985) and *Supreme Neglect: How to Revive Constitutional Protection for Private Property* (New York: Oxford University Press, 2008). Bernard Schwartz challenges this renewed interest in property rights in *The New Right and the Constitution: Turning Back the Legal Clock* (Boston: Northeastern University Press, 1990).

Chapter 7: Representation

Alexander Keyssar, *The Right to Vote: The Contested History of Democracy in the United States* (rev. ed., New York: Basic Books, 2009), is the best survey of the struggle to extend the franchise throughout American history. An earlier and still valuable study, although more limited chronologically, is Chilton Williamson, *American Suffrage: From Property to Democracy, 1760–1860* (Princeton: Princeton University Press, 1960). Robert Wiebe, *Self-Rule, A Cultural History of American Democracy* (Chicago: University of Chicago Press, 1995), is a good overview, as is Eric Foner, *The Story of American Freedom* (New York: W. W. Norton, 1998).

The early emergence of democracy as a political and constitutional value is surveyed in Sean Wilentz, *The Rise of Democracy: From Jefferson to Lincoln* (New York: W. W. Norton, 2005). Gerald Leonard, *The Invention of Party Politics: Federalism, Popular Sovereignty, and Constitutional Development in Jacksonian Illinois* (Chapel Hill: University of North Carolina Press, 2002), examines the constitutional arguments for parties and an expanded suffrage in a midwestern state. George M. Dennison; *The Dorr War: Republicanism on Trial, 1831–1861* (Lexington: University Press of Kentucky, 1976), is the best study of the struggle for democracy in Rhode Island.

George T. Fletcher, *Our Secret Constitution: How Lincoln Redefined American Democracy* (New York: Oxford University Press, 2001), argues that the Civil War, and especially Lincoln's interpretation of its meaning, set in motion democracy and equality as core constitutional values. Mary N. Ryan discusses the role of urbanization in extending suffrage in *Civic Wars: Democracy and Public Life in the American City of the Nineteenth Century* (Berkeley: University of California Press, 1997). David E. Kyvig, *Explicit and Authentic Acts: Amending the U.S. Constitution, 1776–1995* (Lawrence: University Press of Kansas, 1996), examines the amending impulse, which appeared even before the Constitution was adopted and has continued ever since to reflect revolutionary ideas of popular sovereignty and equality. The history of the Fifteenth Amendment is the subject of William Gillette, *The Right to Vote: Politics and the Passage of the Fifteenth Amendment* (Baltimore: Johns Hopkins University Press, 1965).

James Kettner, *Development of American Citizenship, 1608–1870* (Chapel Hill: University of North Carolina Press, 1978), is the best work on the meaning of citizenship during the nation's early development and demonstrates how slavery and racism affected American understanding of citizenship. Rogers Smith, *Civic Ideals: Conflicting Visions of Citizenship in U.S. History* (New Haven: Yale University Press, 1997), argues that Americans drew on multiple traditions to justify gender inequality; also see Kenneth Karst, *Belonging to America: Equal Citizenship and the Constitution* (New Haven: Yale University Press, 1989), and Judith Shklar, *Citizenship: The Quest for Inclusion* (Cambridge: Harvard University Press, 1991).

Ellen Carol DuBois, *Feminism and Suffrage: The Emergence of an Independent Women's Movement in America, 1848–1869* (Ithaca: Cornell University Press, 1978), is essential on the early history of woman suffrage. Aileen Kraditor's *Ideas of the Women's Suffrage Movement, 1890–1920* (New York: Columbia University Press, 1965), remains valuable; also see Christine Lunardini, *From Equal Suffrage to Equal Rights: Alice Paul and the National Women's Party, 1910–1928* (New York: New York University Press, 1986), and the collected essays in Ellen Carol DuBois, ed., *Woman Suffrage and Women's Rights* (New York: New York University Press, 1998), Marjorie Spruill Wheeler, ed., *One Woman, One Vote: Rediscovering the Woman Suffrage Movement* (Troutdale: NewSage Press, 1995), and Jean H. Baker, *Votes for Women: The Struggle for Suffrage Revisited* (New York: Oxford University Press, 2002). Mary P. Ryan, *Women in Public: Between Banners and Ballots, 1825–1880* (Baltimore: Johns Hopkins University Press, 1990), and Kristi Andersen, *After Suffrage: Women in Partisan and Electoral Politics before the New Deal* (Chicago: University of Chicago Press, 1996), trace women's efforts to enter public life. Christine Bolt, *The Women's Movements in the United States and Britain from the 1790s to the 1920s* (Amherst: University of Massachusetts Press, 1993), is quite strong on suffragism in a helpful comparative perspective.

A vast literature exists on the struggles of African Americans to practice their right to vote. The best treatment of the constitutional issues of the Civil War and Reconstruction are Harold M. Hyman, *A More Perfect Union: The Impact of the Civil War and Reconstruction on the Constitution* (New York: Knopf, 1973); also see Robert J. Kaczorowski, *The Politics of Federal Judicial Interpretation: The Federal Courts, the Department of Justice and Civil Rights, 1866–1876* (New York: Oceana, 1985). J. Morgan Kousser demonstrated the continuing efforts of African Americans to protect their right to vote in *The Shaping of Southern Politics: Suffrage Restriction and the Establishment of the One-Party South, 1880–1910* (New Haven: Yale University Press, 1974), and *Colorblind Injustice: Minority Voting Rights and the Undoing of the Second Reconstruction* (Chapel Hill: University of North Carolina Press, 1999). C. Vann Woodward, *The Strange Career of Jim Crow* (4th rev. ed., New York: Oxford University Press, 2002), is the classic study of the rise of segregation in the post-bellum South. Darlene Clark Hine discusses the white-only Texas primary and its challengers in *Black Victory: The Rise and Fall of the White Primary in Texas* (Millwood: KTO Press, 1979). Stephen Lawson offers a good survey of the campaign for voting rights for African Americans in *Black Ballots: Voting Rights in the South, 1944–1969* (New York: Columbia University Press, 1976).

The history and aftermath of the "one man, one vote" decisions are explored in Robert G. Dixon, *Democratic Representation: Reapportionment in Law and Politics* (New York: Oxford University Press, 1968). Robert A. Dahl, *How Democratic Is the American Constitution?* (New Haven: Yale University Press, 2001), compares the Constitution to other national charters as a democratic instrument. Kenneth P. Miller, *Direct Democracy and the Courts* (Cambridge: Cambridge University Press, 2009), examines how the judiciary has served as a countervailing force to direct democracy. The impact of the presidential election of 2000 is explored in Charles L. Zelden, *Bush v. Gore: Exposing the Hidden Crisis in American Democracy* (rev. and abridged, Lawrence: University Press of Kansas, 2010).

Chapter 8: Equality

J. R. Pole, *The Pursuit of Equality in American History* (2nd ed., Berkeley: University of California Press, 1993), is a superb introduction to the subject. An excellent, readable survey of the struggles of African Americans to enjoy the promise of equality is Donald G. Nieman, *Promises to Keep: African-Americans and the Constitutional Order, 1776 to the Present* (New York: Oxford University Press, 1991). John Phillip Reid, *The Concept of Liberty in the Age of American Revolution* (Madison: University of Wisconsin Press, 1988), contains a brilliant analysis of the conflict between liberty and racial subordination during the Revolutionary era. The problem of slavery is discussed also in Paul Finkelman, *Slavery and the Founders: Race and Liberty in the Age of Jefferson* (Armonk, NY: M.E. Sharpe, 2001). Mary Frances Berry, *Black Resistance/White Law: A History of Constitutional Racism in America* (rev. ed., New York: Penguin, 1994), is a sharp indictment of how the state and federal governments have used the Constitution to support racial discrimination. William Wiecek, *The Sources of Antislavery Constitutionalism in America, 1760–1848* (Ithaca: Cornell University Press, 1977), makes a strong case for viewing the Constitution as proslavery.

Readers interested in the law of gender equality will want to begin with Sandra F. Van-Burkleo, *Belonging to the World: Women's Rights and American Constitutional Culture* (New York: Oxford University Press, 2001). Joan Hoff's *Law, Gender, and Injustice: A Legal History of U.S. Women* (New York: New York University Press, 1991), is a comprehensive guide to the role of sex in American law. Useful essays may be found in Kermit Hall, ed.,

Women, the Law, and the Constitution: Major Historical Interpretations (New York: Garland, 1987). Norma Basch, *In the Eyes of the Law: Women, Marriage, and Property in Nineteenth-Century New York* (Ithaca: Cornell University Press, 1982), is helpful on the legal status of women in an important state; also see Elizabeth Bowles Warbasse, *The Changing Legal Rights of Women, 1800–1861* (New York: Garland, 1987). Donald Nieman, ed., *The Constitution, Law, and American Life: Critical Aspects of the Nineteenth Century Experience* (Athens: University of Georgia Press, 1992), contains good essays on the role of the Civil War in altering women's roles in law and society. Suzanne Mettler, *Dividing Citizens: Gender and Federalism in New Deal Public Policy* (Ithaca: Cornell University Press, 1998), argues that structures of federalism more than gender bias were more significant in defining women's citizenship. Linda Kerber takes a different view in *Constitutional Right to Be Ladies: Women and the Obligations of Citizenship* (New York: Hill and Wang, 1998). William Chafe, *Women and Equality: Changing Patterns in American Culture* (New York: Oxford University Press, 1978), places the movement toward gender equality in its cultural context. The history of the failed Equal Rights Amendment is examined in Donald Mathews and Jane Sharron De Hart, *Sex, Gender, and the Politics of ERA* (New York: Oxford University Press, 1990).

Herman Belz, *Emancipation and Equal Rights* (New York: W. W. Norton, 1978), explores the Radical Republicans' role in securing the Reconstruction amendments; it should be supplemented with David A. J. Richards, *Conscience and the Constitution: History, Theory, and Law of the Reconstruction Amendments* (Princeton: Princeton University Press, 1993). The Thirteenth Amendment's history is recounted in Michael Vorenberg, *Final Freedom: The Civil War, the Abolition of Slavery, and the Thirteenth Amendment* (Cambridge: Cambridge University Press, 2001). William E. Nelson, *The Fourteenth Amendment: From Political Principle to Judicial Doctrine* (Cambridge: Harvard University Press, 1988), is the best account of the amendment's adoption and early history. The "separate but equal" case, *Plessy v. Ferguson*, is treated expertly in Charles A. Lofgren, *The Plessy Case: A Legal-Historical Interpretation* (New York: Oxford University Press, 1987). Paul Moreno traces the history of affirmative action in *From Direct Action to Affirmative Action: Fair Employment Law and Policy in America, 1933–1972* (Baton Rouge: Louisiana State University Press, 1997). Jerold Auerbach argues that the national bar adopted an insincere stance toward representing underprivileged clients in *Unequal Justice: Lawyers and Social Change in Modern America* (New York: Oxford University Press, 1976).

The best and most accessible book on the history of civil rights litigation before the Supreme Court is Richard Kluger, *Simple Justice: The History of Brown v. Board of Education and Black America's Struggle for Equality* (rev. and expanded ed., New York: Knopf, 2004). Michael J. Klarman, *From Jim Crow to Civil Rights: The Supreme Court and the Struggle for Racial Equality* (New York: Oxford University Press, 2004), is a masterful treatment of the long civil rights revolution in law. The post-*Brown* history of school desegregation and the rise of affirmative action is the focus of James T. Patterson, *Brown v. Board of Education: A Civil Rights Milestone and Its Troubled Legacy* (New York: Oxford University Press, 2001), and J. Harvie Wilkerson, *From Brown to Bakke: The Supreme Court and School Integration, 1954–1978* (New York: Oxford University Press, 1981). Michael R. Belknap, *Federal Law and Southern Order: Racial Violence and Constitutional Conflict in the Post-Brown South* (Athens: University of Georgia Press, 1987), is useful in understanding the context and impact of Supreme Court decisions on racial equality. Herman Belz, *Equality*

Transformed: A Quarter Century of Affirmative Rights (Piscataway: Transaction, 1991), examines the courts' role in transforming the principles of equal opportunity. Also helpful are two books by Mark V. Tushnet, *The NAACP's Legal Strategy against Segregated Education, 1925–1964* (2nd ed., Chapel Hill: University of North Carolina Press, 2005), and *Making Civil Rights Law: Thurgood Marshall and the Supreme Court, 1936–1961* (New York: Oxford University Press, 1994). A case study of school busing is Joyce A. Baugh, *The Detroit School Busing Case: Milliken v. Bradley and the Controversy over School Desegregation* (Lawrence: University Press of Kansas, 2011). An optimistic appraisal of the role of law and lawyers in bringing about social change is Jack Greenberg, *Crusaders in the Courts: How a Dedicated Band of Lawyers Fought for the Civil Rights Revolution* (New York: Basic Books, 1994); more pessimistic is Gerald N. Rosenberg, *The Hollow Hope: Can Courts Bring about Social Change?* (2nd ed., Chicago: University of Chicago Press, 2008). On the role of the Cold War in bringing about racial change, see Mary Dudziak, *Cold War Civil Rights: Race and the Image of American Democracy* (Princeton: Princeton University Press, 2000).

Chapter 9: Rights

Akhil Reed Amar, *The Bill of Rights: Creation and Reconstruction* (New Haven: Yale University Press, 1998), offers a provocative interpretation of the nation's constitutional protection of rights, which Amar argues was designed originally to empower majorities against government, with the notion of individual rights arising only with the Reconstruction amendments. Frank Lambert, *The Founding Fathers and the Place of Religion in America* (Princeton: Princeton University Press, 2003), is useful for understanding the framers' perspectives. Richard C. Cortner discussed the nationalization of the first ten amendments to the Constitution in *The Supreme Court and the Second Bill of Rights: The Fourteenth Amendment and the Nationalization of Civil Liberties* (Madison: University of Wisconsin Press, 1981). Also see Michael Kent Curtis, *No State Shall Abridge: The Fourteenth Amendment and the Bill of Rights* (Durham, NC: Duke University Press, 1986). The essays in David J. Bodenhamer and James W. Ely Jr., *The Bill of Rights in Modern America* (rev. ed., Bloomington: Indiana University Press, 2008), explore the contemporary meaning of many of the rights guaranteed by the first ten amendments.

John Dinan, *Keeping the People's Liberties: Legislators, Citizens, and Judges as Guardians of Rights* (Lawrence: University Press of Kansas, 1998), explores the transition from citizen and legislatively protected rights in the eighteenth and nineteenth centuries to the twentieth-century emergence of judicial guardianship of rights; also see John Dinan, *The American State Constitutional Tradition* (Lawrence: University Press of Kansas, 2006). James Morton Smith, *Freedom's Fetters: The Alien and Sedition Acts and American Civil Liberties* (Ithaca: Cornell University Press, 1956), is a standard treatment; it should be supplemented by Peter Charles Hoffer, *Free Press Crisis of 1800: Thomas Cooper's Trial for Seditious Libel* (Lawrence: University Press of Kansas, 2011). Michael Kent Curtis, *Free Speech, "The People's Darling Privilege": Struggles for Freedom of Expression in American History* (Durham, NC: Duke University Press, 2000), traces the controversies over free speech in the nineteenth century. The subject of civil liberties from the Reconstruction until the Warren Court is treated in John Braeman, *Before the Civil Rights Revolution: The Old Court and Individual Rights* (Westport, CT: Greenwood Press, 1988); David M. Rabban,

Free Speech in the Forgotten Years (Cambridge: Cambridge University Press, 1997); Paul Murphy, *World War I and the Origins of Civil Liberties in the United States* (New York: W. W. Norton, 1979); Alpheus T. Mason, *The Supreme Court from Taft to Burger* (Baton Rouge: Louisiana State University Press, 1979); and Michael R. Belknap, *Cold War Political Justice: The Smith Act, the Communist Party, and American Civil Liberties* (Westport: Greenwood Press, 1977).

The First Amendment has been the proving ground for an expansive interpretation and nationalization of individual rights, as an extensive scholarly literature reveals. Melvin I. Urofsky, *The Continuity of Change: The Supreme Court and Individual Liberties, 1953–1986* (Belmont: Wadsworth, 1989), offers a solid overview. Among the vast array of titles, readers may wish to consult Daniel A. Farber, *The First Amendment* (3rd ed., New York: Foundation Press, 2010); Zechariah Chafee, *Free Speech in the United States* (6th ed., Cambridge: Harvard University Press, 1967); the essays in Lee Bollinger and Geoffrey R. Stone, eds., *Eternally Vigilant: Free Speech in the Modern Era* (Chicago: University of Chicago Press, 2002); Leonard Levy, *The Establishment Clause: Religion and the First Amendment* (2nd ed., Chapel Hill: University of North Carolina Press, 1994); Melvin I. Urofsky, *Religious Freedom: Rights and Liberties under the Law* (Santa Barbara: ABC-CLIO, 2002); Lucas A. Powe Jr., *The Fourth Estate and the Constitution: Freedom of the Press in America* (Berkeley: University of California Press, 1991); and Anthony Lewis, *Freedom for the Thought That We Hate: A Biography of the First Amendment* (New York: Basic Books, 2010).

David J. Bodenhamer traces the history and modern application of twenty-three individual rights in *Our Rights* (New York: Oxford University Press, 2007); he also surveys the origins and development of criminal due process in *Fair Trial: Rights of the Accused in American History* (New York: Oxford University Press, 1993). Dan T. Carter, *Scottsboro: A Tragedy of the American South* (Baton Rouge: Louisiana State University Press, 1979), provides the history of *Powell v. Alabama*, an important due process case in the 1930s. Anthony Lewis, a veteran observer of the Supreme Court, tells the story of the Warren Court's major right to counsel case, *Gideon v. Wainwright*, in *Gideon's Trumpet* (New York: Random House, 1964). David Garrow's exhaustive *Liberty and Sexuality: The Right to Privacy and the Making of Roe v. Wade* (Berkeley: University of California Press, 1994), is essential on the Supreme Court's privacy and abortion decisions; also see N. E. H. Hull and Peter Charles Hoffer, *Roe v. Wade: The Abortion Rights Controversy in American History* (2nd ed., Lawrence: University Press of Kansas, 2010). John W. Johnson discusses the right to privacy in *Griswold v. Connecticut: Birth Control and the Constitutional Right to Privacy* (Lawrence: University Press of Kansas, 2005).

Conflicting views of the Warren Court are found in Morton J. Horwitz, *The Warren Court and the Pursuit of Justice* (New York: Hill & Wang, 1998), which argues that the justices held an expansive view of democracy, and Lucas A. Powe Jr., *The Warren Court and American Politics* (Cambridge: Harvard University Press, 2000), which sees the Court as a political institution as well as a judicial one. The Rehnquist Court is addressed ably in Tinsley Yarbrough, *The Rehnquist Court and the Constitution* (New York: Oxford University Press, 2000), and in the essays in Craig Bradley, ed., *The Rehnquist Legacy* (Cambridge: Cambridge University Press, 2005). Good judicial biographies of figures include Edward G. White, *Earl Warren: A Public Life* (New York: Oxford University Press, 1982); Melvin I. Urofsky, *Felix Frankfurter: Judicial Restraint and Individual Liberties* (New York: Twayne, 1991), and *Louis D. Brandeis: A Life* (New York: Pantheon, 2009); Roger K. Newman,

Hugo Black: A Biography (New York: Pantheon, 1994); Bruce Allen Murphy, *Wild Bill: The Legend and Life of William O. Douglas* (New York: Random House, 2003); and James F. Simon, *The Antagonists: Hugo Black, Felix Frankfurter and Civil Liberties in Modern America* (New York: Simon & Schuster, 1989).

Important critiques of the rights revolution may be found in Amitai Etzioni, *The New Golden Rule: Community and Morality in a Democratic Society* (New York: Basic Books, 1996), and Mary Ann Glendon, *Rights Talk: The Impoverishment of Political Discourse* (New York: Free Press, 1991). Samuel Walker acknowledges the tensions present in civil rights constitutionalism but rebuts communitarian attacks on the rights revolution in *The Rights Revolution: Rights and Community in Modern America* (New York: Oxford University Press, 1998).

Chapter 10: Security

Charles A. Lofgren, "War-Making under the Constitution: The Original Understanding," *Yale Law Journal*, 81 (1971–72), 672–702, is a good introduction to the thinking of the framers. An older but still valuable study is Edward S. Corwin, *Total War and the Constitution* (New York: Knopf, 1947). On the act of initiating war, useful essays can be found in Gary M. Stern and Morton H. Halperin, *The U.S. Constitution and the Power to Go to War: Historical and Current Perspectives* (Westport, CT: Greenwood Press, 1993). The standard work on presidential war power is Louis Fisher, *Presidential War Power* (2nd rev. ed., Lawrence: University Press of Kansas, 2004); a more critical survey is Peter Irons, *War Power: How the Imperial Presidency Hijacked the Constitution* (New York: Henry Holt, 2003). For a good collection of essays that treat the subject historically, see Demetrios Caraley, ed., *The President's War Powers: From the Federalists to Reagan* (New York: Academy of Political Science, 1984). Congressional war powers are examined in Francis D. Wormuth and Edwin B. Firmage, *To Chain the Dog of War: The War Powers of Congress in History and Law* (Dallas: Southern Methodist University Press, 1986). Christopher N. May, *In the Name of War: Judicial Review and the War Powers after 1918* (Cambridge: Harvard University Press, 1989), examines the role of the judiciary in wartime and traces the lingering impact of World War I on American constitutionalism.

The history of military tribunals is the subject of Louis Fisher, *Military Tribunals and Presidential Power: American Revolution to the War on Terrorism* (Lawrence: University Press of Kansas, 2005); Fisher also has a good treatment of the Nazi saboteurs in *Nazi Saboteurs on Trial: A Military Tribunal and American Law* (Lawrence: University Press of Kansas, 2005). A work by Chief Justice William H. Rehnquist, *All the Laws but One: Civil Liberties in Wartime* (New York: Knopf, 1998), traces the history of individual rights during wartime, with a principal focus on the Civil War. Lincoln's use of executive power in war is best examined in Phillip S. Paludan, *The Presidency of Abraham Lincoln* (Lawrence: University Press of Kansas, 1994); its impact on civil liberties is expertly discussed in Mark E. Neely Jr., *The Fate of Liberty: Abraham Lincoln and Civil Liberties* (New York: Oxford University Press, 1991). Also see Daniel Farber, *Lincoln's Constitution* (Chicago: University of Chicago Press, 2003). Peter Irons, *Justice at War: The Story of the Japanese Internment Cases* (Berkeley: University of California Press, 1983), traces the history of litigation that led to the decisions in *Korematsu* and related cases. Valuable treatments of the impact of World War II on constitutional law include Daniel R. Ernst and Victor Jew, *Total War and the Law: The American Home Front in World War II* (Westport, CT: Praeger, 2002); Melvin I. Urofsky, *Division and Discord: The Supreme Courts under Stone and Vincent, 1941–1953* (Columbia: University of South Carolina Press, 1997); and Greg Robinson, *By Order of the President: FDR and the Internment of Japanese Americans* (Cambridge: Harvard University Press, 2001).

Robert Higgs, *Crisis and Leviathan: Episodes in the Growth of American Government* (New York: Oxford University Press, 1987), examines how war and economic crises have led to the expansion of national government. Fred Anderson and Andrew Cayton, *The Dominion of War: Empire and Liberty in North America, 1500–2000* (New York: Viking Penguin, 2002), offer a useful perspective on the role of war in shaping American culture. Michael Sherry, *In the Shadow of War: The United States since the 1930s* (New Haven: Yale University Press, 1995), argues that war and militarism have been central features in American society since World War II. The essays in Mark Tushnet, ed., *The Constitution in Wartime: Beyond Alarmism and Complacency* (Durham, NC: Duke University Press, 2005), examine the trade-off between security and rights during periods of national threat. John Yoo, an advisor to President George W. Bush, argues for expansive executive power in times of threats to national security in *The Powers of War and Peace: The Constitution and Foreign Affairs after 9/11* (Chicago: University of Chicago Press, 2005). Andrew Rudalevige, *The New Imperial Presidency: Renewing Presidential Power after Watergate* (Ann Arbor: University of Michigan Press, 2005), takes a much more skeptical view. A critical look at Bush-era policies is found in David Cole, *Enemy Aliens: Double Standards and Constitutional Freedoms in the War on Terrorism* (New York: Free Press, 2003).

INDEX